ELIZABETHAN AND JACOBEAN STUDIES

Gilbert Spencer 1958

ELIZABETHAN AND JACOBEAN STUDIES

Presented to
FRANK PERCY WILSON
in honour of
his seventieth birthday

OXFORD
AT THE CLARENDON PRESS
1959

Oxford University Press, Amen House, London E.C.4

GLASGOW NEW YORK TORONTO MELBOURNE WELLINGTON
BOMBAY CALCUTTA MADRAS KARACHI KUALA LUMPUR
CAPE TOWN IBADAN NAIROBI ACCRA

PRINTED IN GREAT BRITAIN

Preface

THE authors of the studies collected in this volume are only too well aware that they represent a far larger group of pupils, friends, and colleagues all over the world who would wish to show their affection and gratitude to F. P. Wilson on his seventieth birthday. The editors believed, however, that the fittest tribute to him would be a volume of substantial essays, all concerned with one period, and on topics within that period which would represent the range of his interests. They were thus able to invite only a limited number of contributors, and many who would have wished to be included were debarred by the fact that their interests lay outside the period, or that they had no work in hand which would fit the general plan. This is then only a token volume in honour of a great Elizabethan scholar who, in the course of his years as first tutor and then Reader at Oxford, as Professor at Leeds, London, and Oxford, and in his frequent and extensive pilgrimages to seats and shrines of learning in the North American continent, has signally advanced our knowledge of Elizabethan and Jacobean literature. He has done this not only by his own published work but most notably also by the generous encouragement and help which he has given to others.

It is our hope that the author of *Elizabethan and Jacobean*, the General Editor of the Malone Society, the late President of the Bibliographical Society, and the Collector of Proverbs will find some pleasure in reading these essays, and will accept them with our grateful thanks and admiration. They are offered with all best wishes that his retirement from teaching duties will give him the leisure to crown a life devoted to literary scholarship with the book which only he can write on Shakespeare and the Elizabethan Drama.

Herbert Davis
Helen Gardner

Contents

A MIRROR FOR MAGISTRATES REVISITED   I
E. M. W. TILLYARD, *Jesus College, Cambridge*

MARLOWE'S LIGHT READING   17
ETHEL SEATON, *St. Hugh's College, Oxford*

THE COMPLAINT OF THOMAS DIGGES   36
FRANCIS R. JOHNSON, *Stanford University*

HARINGTON'S *FOLLY*   42
KATHLEEN M. LEA, *Lady Margaret Hall, Oxford*

TWO NOTES: (i) When was Twelfth Night? (ii) Copyright in
Unauthorized Texts   59
W. W. GREG

CLASSICAL MYTH IN SHAKESPEARE'S PLAYS   65
DOUGLAS BUSH, *Harvard University*

SHAKESPEARE'S READING IN CHAUCER   86
NEVILL COGHILL, *Merton College, Oxford*

ON *VENUS AND ADONIS*   100
DON CAMERON ALLEN, *Johns Hopkins University*

VARIATIONS ON A THEME IN SHAKESPEARE'S
SONNETS   112
J. B. LEISHMAN, *Oxford University*

SHAKESPEARE'S USE OF POPULAR SONG   150
FREDERICK W. STERNFELD, *Oxford University*

'UNDER WHICH KING, BEZONIAN?'   167
PETER ALEXANDER, *Glasgow University*

THE RIDER ON THE WINGED HORSE   173
MARY LASCELLES, *Somerville College, Oxford*

SIR WALTER RALEGH'S *INSTRUCTIONS TO HIS SON*   199
AGNES M. C. LATHAM, *Bedford College, London*

ELIZABETH, ESSEX, AND JAMES 219
JAMES McMANAWAY, *Folger Shakespeare Library, Washington*

HUME'S HISTORY OF THE REIGN OF JAMES I 231
GODFREY DAVIES

SOME JACOBEAN CATCH-PHRASES AND SOME LIGHT
ON THOMAS BRETNOR 250
JOHN CROW, *King's College, London*

THE ARGUMENT ABOUT 'THE ECSTASY' 279
HELEN GARDNER, *St. Hilda's College, Oxford*

DONNE'S POETRY IN THE NINETEENTH CENTURY 307
KATHLEEN TILLOTSON, *Bedford College, London*

MEMORIES OF HARLEY GRANVILLE-BARKER AND
TWO OF HIS FRIENDS 327
J. DOVER WILSON

A SELECT LIST OF THE WRITINGS OF F. P. WILSON 339
Compiled by H. S. BENNETT, *Emmanuel College, Cambridge*

INDEX 349

List of Plates

F. P. WILSON. *From a Drawing by* Gilbert Spencer *Frontispiece*

MS. Rawl. Poet. 125, p. 250. Orlando Furioso XV, showing
the final Stanza written in from the verso *facing page* 44

MS. Rawl. Poet. 125, p. 216. Orlando Furioso XIV ⎱

British Museum MS. Add. 18920, p. 3. Orlando Furioso ⎰ *between pages* 46–47
XVI, showing the stanza omitted from the Bodley MS.
and consequent renumbering

MS. Rawl. B. 162. 'A Short View of the State of Ireland', p. 13 *facing page* 48

A *Mirror for Magistrates* Revisited

E. M. W. TILLYARD

I DO not intend to plead that, as poetry, the *Mirror* has been seriously misjudged, my main business being with its interest and not with its beauty. Nevertheless, thinking that it is rather better as poetry than the average of modern criticism allows, I will by way of preface point to a few places, usually, if not inveterately, ignored, which can give pleasure to the reader.

Miss Lily Campbell, whose editions I, of course, use and to whom every student of the *Mirror* is immeasurably indebted, calls John Dolman's solitary contribution (one of the 1563 additions) 'probably the worst poetry in the *Mirror*'.[1] C. S. Lewis, on the other hand, while calling Dolman's *Lord Hastings* unsatisfactory and immature, finds it the most promising part of the collection. Dolman

understands better than any of his collaborators, better even than Sackville, what a poem ought to be. The other ghosts are mere mouthpieces of moral and political doctrine: but Dolman really tries by changes of mood and human inconsistencies to dramatize his Hastings. . . . The poem is confused, crowded, and uncomfortable. But it anticipates, in however dim a form, nearly every one of the excellences which were soon to be knocking at the door.[2]

In their ways both are right. Dolman can write very bad verse, crude and halting. But he has infused life into parts of his story. And I would go beyond Lewis in holding that he can achieve not only memorable lines but memorable passages. The most memorable is the passage describing Hastings's flight with his master, Edward IV, from Lynn and the sea voyage: the embarkation, the isolation on the ship at sea, the flight from enemy ships. Dolman is close to the real happening. This is his account of the passengers' plight at sea:

> As banished wightes, such ioyes we mought have made,
> Easd of aye thretnyng death, that late we dradde.

---

[1] *The Mirror for Magistrates*, edited by Lily B. Campbell, 1938, p. 45.
[2] *English Literature in the Sixteenth Century*, 1954, pp. 243–4. Maurice Evans, *English Poetry in the Sixteenth Century*, 1955, p. 123, also praises Dolman's contribution.

But once our countreyes syght (not care) exempt,
No harboure shewyng, that mought our feare relent,
No covert cave, no shrubbe to shroud our lyves,
No hollow wodde, no flyght, that oft depryves
The myghty his pray, no Sanctuary left
For exyled prynce, that shroudes eche slave from theft:

In pryson pent, whose woddye walles to passe
Of no lesse peryll than the dying was:
With the Oceane moated, battered with the waves,
(As chaynd at Oares the wretched Galley slaves,
At mercy sit of Sea and enmyes shott,
And shonne with death what they with flyght may not)
But greenysh waves, and desert lowrying Skyes
All comfort ells forclosed oure exyled eyes.

The two stanzas are not very coherent but they force our attention, they force us to consider the fugitives' plight and the contrasted perils of being hunted on land and drowned at sea. We have escaped from the abstract moralizings that are the norm of the *Mirror* to an imagined piece of real life.

There is another section that merits the kind of praise that Lewis gave Dolman's. It is the one immediately before, the story of Anthony Woodville, Lord Rivers and Scales, of unknown authorship. Coming as the first story in the additions of 1563, it marks the improved quality of some of these over the short and thin stories that composed the first issue of 1559. In the 1559 volume by far the longest section is that of the Duke of Clarence with 399 lines, but many of the sections run to less than a hundred. The average length of the 1563 stories is about 500 lines. This discrepancy between the 1559 volume and the 1563 additions is the stranger since there is evidence that several of the additions existed at the time when the first lot were collected. The reason may be that Baldwin, who edited both collections, did not wish to have his own thin substance put to shame by the more weighty. In his revised dedication to the nobility in the 1563 volume[1] he stated that the additions contained 'as little of myne owne, as the fyrst part doth of other mens'. He knew the merit of Sackville's *Induction* and *Complaint of Buckingham* and the probable popularity of Churchyard's *Jane Shore*; and in order to have it both ways he held back these and others so that both his own work would make the greatest impact

[1] Ed. cit., p. 66.

possible and the fame of the total collection be enhanced by including ultimately the best work he had been able to procure. This
about Baldwin's motives is conjecture; but, whatever his motives,
the story of Lord Rivers is altogether ampler and more lively than
anything printed in 1559. The narrator's account of how Gloucester
and Buckingham trapped him at his inn at Northampton, where he
had remained because there was no room in the small town of Stony
Stratford, where the king lay, is not less vivid than Hastings's
account of being a fugitive at sea. Lord Rivers and Scales recounts
how his treacherous brother and his accomplices come to his inn
and congratulate him on his good work in Wales, where he had
suppressed some bandits.

> Fyrst to myne Inne, cummeth in my brother false
> Embraceth me: wel met good brother Skales,
> And wepes withall: the other me enhalse
> With welcum coosyn, now welcum out of Wales,
> O happy day, for now all stormy gales
> Of stryfe and rancor vtterly are swaged,
> And we your owne to lyve or dye vnwaged.

This verse captures the accent of true speech as nothing in the 1559
volume had done. After a little homily on dissimulation the
narrator returns to real life with:

> They supped with me, propoundyng frendly talke
> Of our affayres, still gevyng me the prayse.
> And ever among the cups to mewarde walke:
> I drynk to you good Cuz ech traytor sayes:
> Our banquet doen whan they should go theyr wayes
> They tooke theyr leave, oft wyshyng me good nyght
> As hartily as any creature myght.

The traitors inform the two dukes where Lord Rivers is lodging
and during the night his servants tell him he has been betrayed.

> When I had opened the wyndow to looke out
> There myght I see the streetes eche where beset,
> My inne on ech syde compassed about
> With armed watchmen, all escapes to let.

Easy in conscience, Lord Rivers cannot believe in the betrayal. He
thinks that his house has been surrounded so that he shall not be
the first to ride to Stratford to greet the king next morning.

> By thys the Dukes were cum into myne inne
> For they were lodged in an other by.
> I gote me to them, thinkyng it a synne
> Within my chamber cowardly to lye.
> And meryly I asked my brother why
> He vsed me so? he sterne in evyll sadnes
> Cryed out: I arrest the traytor for thy badnes.
>
> How so (quoth I) whence ryseth your suspicion?
> Thou art a traytor (quoth he) I thee arrest.
> Arrest (quoth I) why where is your commission?
> He drew hys weapon, so dyd all the rest
> Crying: yeld the traytor. I so sore distrest
> Made no resystaunce: but was sent to ward
> None save theyr seruauntes assygned to my gard.

Not only does the dialogue suggest real people talking but the author is genuinely possessed by his mental picture of the whole episode. He sees the inn and its surroundings; he has entered the mind of the victim. Sackville may write better poetry but he is farther from what he describes than is the anonymous author of Lord Rivers's complaint.

There are good things too in the complaint of the poet Colling-bourne, executed by Richard III because of an indiscreet distich: namely the opening that bids poets beware tyrants and the passage describing the poet's office by likening him to Pegasus. In the opening the writer first complains that whatever the poet does is wrong:

> Be rough in ryme, and then they say you rayle,
> Though Iuvenal so be, that makes no matter.
>
> Touche covertly in termes, and then you taunt,
> Though praysed Poetes, alway dyd the lyke.

And then he suddenly personates the overbearing ruler, who declares that he knows all about his own sins and fortune's wheel—in fact about the main doctrine and object of the *Mirror*—and that he needs no poet to inform him. Moreover, he holds the rudder and means to keep hold and has a good chance of escaping the punishment of his crimes. There is a humorous touch about the whole passage that looks forward to Harington's translation of Ariosto. The passage about the poet beginning, 'The Greekes do paynt a Poetes office whole | In Pegasus', achieves a sustained eloquence culminating in these last two stanzas: a culmination which does not exclude the humorous lowering of tone in the final couplet and which is all the better for it:

> Like Pegasus a Poet must have wynges,
> To flye to heaven, thereto to feede and rest:
> He must have knoweledge of eternal thynges,
> Almighty Iove must harber in his brest.
> With worldly cares he may not be opprest,
> The wynges of skyll and hope must heave him hyer,
> Than al the ioyes which worldly wyts desyre.

> He must be also nymble, free, and swyft
> To trauayle farre to viewe the trades of men,
> Great knowledge oft is gotten by the shyft:
> Thynges notable he must be quicke to pen,
> Reprouyng vyces sharpely now and then.
> He must be swyft when touched tyrants chafe,
> To gallop thence to kepe his carkas safe.

The complaint of Shore's Wife by Churchyard was throughout the sixteenth century one of the most admired sections of the *Mirror*. Modern opinion has been more hostile. Courthope,[1] for instance, contrasts the weight of Sackville with the emptiness of Churchyard. Possibly less than justice has been done to Churchyard's smooth vacuity. After all, to be smooth and elegant in the reign of Edward VI was not a negligible achievement; and if you condemn all the poetry that says the same things in different ways you condemn a great deal. Here is a stanza, enlarging on Jane Shore's submission to the advances of Edward IV, which illustrates both the smoothness and the repetition.

> The Egles force, subdues eche byrd that flyes,
> What mettal may resist the flaming fyre?
> Doth not the sonne, dasill the clearest eyes,
> And melt the ise, and make the frost retire?
> Who can withstand a puissant kynges desyre?
> The stiffest stones are perced through with tooles,
> The wisest are with princes made but fooles.

This is perfect commonplace: the king-eagle-sun equation, the succession of well-worn sentiments. Yet it runs agreeably as did little contemporary verse. Churchyard can even convey feeling:

---

[1] W. J. Courthope, *A History of English Poetry*, 1897, ii. 126.

the stanzas near the end describing Jane Shore's ultimate beggary remind one of Henryson's *Testament of Cresseid* in point of feeling as well as in point of substance:

> Where I was wont the golden chaynes to weare,
> A payre of beades about my necke was wound,
> A lynnen clothe was lapt about my heare,
> A ragged gowne that trayled on the ground,
> A dishe that clapt and gave a heavie sound,
> A stayeng staffe and wallet therewithal,
> I bare about as witnesse of my fal.
>
> I had no house wherein to hyde my head,
> The open strete my lodging was perforce,
> Ful ofte I went al hungry to my bed,
> My flesh consumed, I looked like a corse,
> Yet in that plyght who had on me remorse?
> O God thou knowest my frendes forsooke me than,
> Not one holpe me that suckered many a man.

Churchyard's *Cardinal Wolsey*, included in the final additions to the original *Mirror* in 1587 but almost certainly written much earlier (Wolsey's reference to Jane Shore as resembling himself for kindness in forwarding poor men's suits suggests that the two poems make a pair), has just the same qualities: the same smooth commonplace, the same capacity once in a way to feel a little and to lend a touch of distinction to his verse. In *Cardinal Wolsey* it is the account of Wolsey's state (ll. 134 ff.) that corresponds in quality to that of Jane Shore in her distress.

I cannot extend my plea for a kinder opinion of the poetry of the *Mirror* to the additions made by Higgins in 1574, 1575, and 1587 and by Blenerhasset in 1578. There are occasional pieces of crude vigour as in the account of Morindus in the belly of the monster that emerged from the Irish sea to afflict the north-west of Britain:

> The way was large, and downe he drew me in:
> A monstrous paunche for rowmthe and wondrous wide,
> But for I felte more softer there the skinne,
> At once I drewe, a dagger by my side:
> I knew my life, no longer could abide:
> For rammishe stenche, bloud, poyson, slymy glere:
> That in his body, so aboundant were.

But that is about all that can be said on their behalf as literature.

Turning from the aesthetic to the interesting I find the subject dividing itself naturally into two. First, there is the strange fact of the *Mirror*'s persistent popularity, a fact rich in psychological interest. Second, there is the engaging sight of a group of men trying to work out literary problems among themselves and creating something which, whatever its deficiencies by modern standards, had the virtues of novelty and absolute integrity. I will enlarge on these two topics in turn.

There are many testimonies to the popularity of *A Mirror for Magistrates*, from the number and nature of the editions to Sidney's inclusion of it ('meetely furnished of beautiful parts') in his most select list of commendable English poems. But I know of no testimony so striking as that of Thomas Blenerhasset, whose additions to the *Mirror* the printer, Richard Webster, published in 1578 while the author, absent on garrison duty, was ignorant of the publication. After his own preface the printer placed a letter from Blenerhasset to the friend who had encouraged him in his presumptuous venture.[1] Blenerhasset, while aware of a gap in the series of laments that compose the *Mirror*, namely 'from the conquest of Caesar unto the coming of Duke William the Conqueror', has no confidence about his own fitness to fill it. However, two of the Muses comfort him and he sees himself galloping (presumably in the form of Pegasus) through his possible rivals into the company of Sackville, Gascoigne,[2] and Churchyard, whose contributions he begs his friend to forget while reading his own. Blenerhasset then apologizes for his deficiencies on the ground that in Guernsey, where he is serving, he has with him none of the chronicles which could serve as originals for the span of history he is concerned with and has to rely on his memory alone. Nor has he literary companions, 'I sittyng on a Rocke in the Sea, not in *Spaine*, *Italie*, *Fraunce*, *Scotlande*, or *Englande*, but in *Garnzie* Castle, where although there be learned men, yet none which spende their tyme so vainely as in Poetrie.' Not only does he lack copies of the chronicles but he has only four books with him: 'the thirde *Decade* of *Titus Liuye*, with *Boswelles Concordes of Armorie*, with *Monsignor de Lange*, that notable Warriour,[3] and with the vnperfect *Mirrour for Magistrates*'. What

---

[1] *Parts added to 'The Mirror for Magistrates' by John Higgins and Thomas Blenerhasset*, ed. Lily B. Campbell, 1946, pp. 379–83.

[2] The passage seems to me clearly to indicate that Blenerhasset looked on Gascoigne (or 'Gascon' as he calls him) as a contributor to the *Mirror*. I know of no attempt to identify such a contribution.

[3] Miss Campbell (ed. cit., p. 368) identifies this as Guillaume du Bellay's *Instructions sur le faict de la Guerre*, published in 1548 and frequently reissued.

better testimony to the popularity of the *Mirror* than that a young officer going on lonely garrison duty should choose it as the one volume of poetry he allowed himself for his delectation?

And this popularity was long-lived as well as great. Only great popular support, well sustained, could have induced Baldwin, the *Mirror*'s original editor, to continue to reissue and expand up to the year 1587 a volume ready for publication, though not actually published, in 1555. And though the *Mirror* ceased to grow after 1587 (whether through Baldwin or Higgins or Blenerhasset), the literary mode it represented persisted well past the end of the century,[1] the latest example perhaps being Patrick Hannay's *Shere-tine and Mariana*. This was published in 1622 and has been reprinted in the first volume of Saintsbury's *Caroline Poets*. It is unlike the *Mirror* in recounting a Hungarian not a British tragedy, but it is essentially like the *Mirror* in that the story is recounted in the first person by the ghost of Mariana.

Granted the popularity of the *Mirror*, what were the reasons for it? First, the political doctrines contained in it were, to the epoch its successive publications span, persistently living and present; and in two ways. The political theory is the perfect orthodoxy of the time. It is abundant and it covers most of the current, conventional, yet heart-felt opinions on kingship, obedience to authority, on the dividing-line between kingship and tyranny, on the sin of rebellion and the individual's ultimate responsibility, whatever the influence of the stars. Having written fairly fully on these matters[2] I will not pursue them here and I will go on to the second condition that made the political doctrine of the *Mirror* so living and hence so likely to be popular. And it is that the pattern of politics from 1555, when the *Mirror* should have seen its first publication (or even from a date in the reign of Edward VI, when at least one of the *Mirror*'s sections was written), to 1587 was near enough to the pattern of politics from the reign of Richard II to that of Henry VIII to lend to the political misfortunes that are the subject of Baldwin's part of the *Mirror* a sense of actuality that it is most difficult for a modern reader to grasp. Students of history may grasp and give due weight to the changes that took place during Elizabeth's long reign; but by far the majority of readers or even students of literature allow

---

[1] For this continuation see W. F. Trench, *A Mirror for Magistrates, its Origin and Influence*, 1898, pp. 81–83, 126 ff.

[2] In my *Shakespeare's History Plays*, 1945, pp. 71–90.

the late years, between the Armada and the Essex rebellion, to stand for the whole of it. There was, of course, a very great deal more shedding of blood in the epoch in which the tragedies of the *Mirror* are set; yet the general political causes of danger and unrest are the same in both epochs. The succession was disputed, there were treason and revolt throughout all the years from the reign of Richard II to the accession of James I; and to think of the few, more settled, years after the Armada as representative is an error.

The first edition of the *Mirror* came out during the great hazards of Elizabeth's first year of rule. The second edition was contemporary with the momentous struggle between the Protestant and Catholic parties in Scotland. A little before the third edition (1571) came the actual Catholic rebellion in the north led by the Earls of Northumberland and Westmorland. A rebellious Percy had already provided a section of the *Mirror*, and the modern representative of the family would have provided a section with equal propriety. Thomas Percy, seventh Earl of Northumberland, was a main leader of the rebellions of 1569 and 1570. On their collapse he found asylum in Scotland and remained there two years. After much negotiation he was handed over to Elizabeth in 1572 and lost his head at York in August of that year. About two months before, there was executed in London a still more prominent nobleman after a career ideally suited to the norm of the *Mirror for Magistrates*. This was Thomas Howard, fourth Duke of Norfolk, the most eminent and the richest nobleman in England. He was not a declared Catholic but he was not at all averse to becoming one if this should profit him. He was greatly ambitious, for he aspired to marrying Mary of Scotland. When he found that Elizabeth disapproved and blocked his way, he drifted into treason and covertly supported the Spaniard, Ridolfi, who was fostering a possible invasion of England. The Duke's treason was discovered and he was beheaded on Tower Hill. With such apt repetitions of the subject-matter of the *Mirror* how could its substance fail to live?

In the year of the second rebellion Elizabeth was excommunicated and the Jesuits began their infiltration. The next year a new homily, 'Against Disobedience and Wilful Rebellion', was added to the existing collection. Its sentiments were in perfect harmony with those of *A Mirror for Magistrates*. In the year when the two earls were executed occurred the St. Bartholomew Massacre, the Dutch revolt against Spain, and the first of the Commons' petitions for the

death of Mary. Uncertainty of the future, fear, and suspicion prevailed in England between the beginning of Queen Mary's captivity
and her death in 1587. During that span there were three reissues of
the *Mirror*; and in the year of Mary's execution, after the discovery
of Babington's plot, the last additions (two of them, strangely
enough, dealing with Scotland) were made to Baldwin's section of
the *Mirror*. In fact, throughout the years when Baldwin's *Mirror* was
being created, history re-enacted the main themes of its political
morality.

A second reason for the *Mirror*'s popularity was that it provided
through the trappings of the poetical rhetoric of the day a portion
of those matters of history and legend with which many Elizabethans wished to be familiar. It is a reason that applies equally to
Baldwin's *Mirror* and to the additions of Higgins and Blenerhasset.
These additions lack the political earnestness of the original *Mirror*
but they are highly informative on the legends and history which,
deriving from Geoffrey of Monmouth as well as from more trust-
worthy sources, were part of the living commonplaces of the age of
Elizabeth.

The modern reader is apt to ask: why, when the Elizabethans
could get these commonplaces through the tolerable prose of the
chronicles, did they insist on getting it also through the execrable
verse of Warner or Higgins or Blenerhasset?; how came it that
Meres could have 'heard him [Warner] termd of the best wits of
both our Universities our English Homer' when those best wits
could have got the substance of *Albion's England* in harmless prose
elsewhere? The answer is that certain poems, however alien to
modern taste and however poor as poetry by enduring standards,
mediated their information through a rhetoric which the Elizabethans found highly entertaining. I will give two types of illustration.

First, the very form of the soliloquy, in which the tragedies of the
Mirror were cast, was for the Elizabethans more live and dramatic
than for us. Characters in the medieval drama were often informative
about themselves and their doings; and this habit left its legacy to
the succeeding age. Readers of the *Mirror* would have enjoyed
picturing the ghosts of the characters returning from the dead and
addressing Baldwin and his fellows. Their enjoyment was increased
by the help Baldwin himself on many occasions (and Sackville on
a single occasion) gave to the process of dramatizing. Constantly in

the end-links Baldwin introduces a new story by asking us to picture the teller. Before the complaint of James IV of Scotland he wrote: 'Thinke then (quoth I) that you see him standing all wounded, with a shafte in his body, and emongst other woundes, one geuen by a byll, both deadly, to say in his rude and faithlesse manner as followeth.' The author of the complaint of Richard II is made to say in the preceding end-link: 'And therefore imagine *Baldwin* that you see him al to be mangled, with blew woundes, lying pale and wanne al naked upon the cold stones in Paules church, the people standing round, about him, and making his mone in this sort.' More elaborate is the introduction of the poet Collingbourne:

I haue his Tragedie here (quoth I) For the better perceyuing whereof, you must ymagin that you se him a meruaylous wel fauoured man, holdinge in his hand his owne hart, newely ripped out of his brest, and smoaking forth the lively spirit: and with his other hand, beckening to and fro, as it were to warne vs to auoyde: and with his faynte tounge and voyce, sayeng as coragiously as he may, these wordes that follow.

There is no prose end-link before Sackville's tragedy of Buckingham, there being the same author's induction in verse. But he is careful to heighten the drama by devoting the last three stanzas of his induction to a melodramatic description of Buckingham's appearance as he tells his tale. Most elaborate of all is Baldwin's preface to the tragedy of Richard Duke of York, killed at the Battle of Wakefield. Here, exceptionally, Baldwin adopts the dream technique and has this vision:

Me thought there stode before vs, a tall mans body full of fresshe woundes, but lackyng a head, holdyng by the hande a goodlye childe, whose brest was so wounded that his hearte myght be seen, his louely face and eyes disfigured with dropping teares, his heare through horrour standyng vpryght, his mercy cravyng handes all to bemangled, and all his body embrued with his own bloud. And whan through the gastfulnes of this pyteous spectacle, I waxed afeard, and turned awaye my face, me thought there came a shrekyng voyce out of the weasande pipe of the headles bodye, saying as foloweth.

I have to admit that in reading the *Mirror* I simply cannot induce my imagination to take such pictures seriously or use them to animate the stories that follow; and I doubt if others today have succeeded better. But I am sure that the case was different in the sixteenth century and that this dramatic staging of the tragedies was one reason why *A Mirror for Magistrates* was so widely read.

My second type of illustration has to do with the way some of the tragedies in the *Mirror* amplify and embellish the stories found in the chronicles. I will give examples from Higgins's portion of the *Mirror*.

Among the tragedies in Higgins's first issue, in 1574, is that of Bladud, one of the earliest kings of Britain. His legend goes back to Geoffrey of Monmouth, who briefly informs us that he built Kaerbadus or Bath and made hot baths for the benefit of the public. Later he turned to magic, tried to fly, and suffered the fate of Icarus. Fabyan and Holinshed are brief on Bladud, adding little to Geoffrey. But Grafton has the further story of Bladud's going to the University of Athens to be educated, of his bringing back philosophers to Britain, and of his founding a university at Stamford. Higgins turned Grafton's fuller account into 316 lines of crude but speedy ballad-metre. Repenting of this metre, he told the same story in abbreviated form in his second edition, 1587, using rime royal. It is the first version that should make us see why narrative in poor verse could compete with narrative in tolerable prose. Though Higgins writes crudely, he infuses some kind of life into his story by the wealth of detail he adds. He gives Prince Bladud a thoroughly traditional education at Athens in the Trivium and Quadrivium, going into precise details; and anticipates his later disasters by having him taught the rudiments of magic at the same place. A further embellishment is that Bladud had a great reception when he returned to Britain:

> I was receaude with triumphes great,
> With pageauntes in eache towne I paste:
> And at the courte my princly seate,
> Was by my fathers ioyned faste.
>
> The nobles then desirde to haue
> On me their children wayte and tende:
> And royall giftes with them me gaue,
> As might their powres therto extende.

The four philosophers he brought from Greece were at great pains to find the right site; and in the end find Stamford

> With water streames, and springes for welles:
> And medowes sweete, and valeyes grene:
> And woodes, groaues, quaries, all thinge else
> For studentes weale, or pleasure bene.

The chroniclers had not troubled to remind us that there is Ketton and Barnack stone near Stamford. Higgins is even ampler in his mustering all the diseases which the waters of Bladud's newly founded spa could cure; and after the list he makes Bladud break out into rhetoric:

> Shall I renege I made them then?
> Shall I denye my cunning founde,
> By helpe I had of learned men,
> Those worthy welles in gratefull grounde?

If, as I do, I find Higgins's account of Bladud more diverting than the account in the chronicles, an Elizabethan is likely to have found it so in a still higher degree.

Or take the next story in Higgins's first series, that of Cordila. It runs to 371 lines and in its account of Cordila's suicide in prison is far more detailed and embroidered than anything in the chronicles. She laments her lot in strict accord with what contemporary notions of rhetoric demanded:

> Was euer lady in such wofull wreckfull wo:
> Depriude of princely powre, berefte of libertie,
> Depriud in all these worldly pompes, hir pleasures fro,
> And brought from welthe, to nede distresse, and misery?
> From palace proude, in prison poore to lye:
> From kingdomes twayne, to dungion one no more:
> From Ladies wayting, vnto vermine store.

And so on, with a lot more *from*'s and *to*'s. Nor does she merely take her life. Instead, she is persuaded to do so by a 'gryzely ghost' called 'Despayre', who tells her she will never regain her kingdom and offers her a fine selection of the means of destruction: 'knyves, sharpe swordes, poynadoes all bedyde with bloud, and poysons'. In view of all this rhetoric and melodrama, so perfectly in the prevailing fashion, we need not now be shocked, as most of our fathers would have been, at the strong evidence in favour of Shakespeare's familiarity with the Cordelia story in the *Mirror* and indeed with the whole book, its worst parts included.[1] Born in 1564, Shakespeare was just of an age to be subject to the popularity of the enlarged issues of the *Mirror* in 1574 and 1587. Despair

---

[1] See Kenneth Muir, *Shakespeare's Sources*, vol. i, 1957, especially p. 143, and Harold F. Brooks, Appendix A, pp. 212–16, of J. M. Nosworthy's (Arden) edition of *Cymbeline*, 1955.

offering her instruments of self-destruction to Cordila was the perfect aliment for the digestion of the adolescent reader of the day. Nothing in the chronicles was so nicely suited. In sum, there are pretty good reasons for the *Mirror's* popularity in its own day.

I said that the dramatic stage-directions of the end-links made little impression on me but I did not mean thereby to imply that these end-links are negligible. On the contrary I believe that for modern readers they supply the best means of bringing *A Mirror for Magistrates* to life. Indeed they gain from a distant view and are worth more to us than to the readers at whom they were aimed. They make a piece of history more living than the literature to which they are appended. Their great virtues are of being intimate and authentic. And through those virtues they give a fascinating glimpse of a group of rising young men working out their problems of literary creation.

Of the intimacy there is no doubt. Baldwin's end-links tell of the thoughts and aims of a group of friends. The authenticity is different. The accounts given of the genesis of the poem cannot be literally true: for too much is crowded into a single session of friends to admit the reality of actual life. For instance, in the opening account contained in 'William Baldwin to the Reader' everything happens at once. The seven men who have assembled discuss how to continue Lydgate's translation of Boccaccio. They will personate 'wretched princes' and make their moan to Baldwin, the editor. They consult the chronicles for finding fit subjects, and Ferrers proposes that they should concentrate on English unfortunates who lived after the date of Boccaccio's most recent characters. So the stories of Richard I and King John, though excellent material, must be excluded, because the printer wants the time-sequence preserved, and these kings come too early. Ferrers then passes from theory to practice and recounts the story of Chief Justice Tresilian, who came to an evil end in the reign of Richard II. Now, though things cannot have happened just like that, there is not the least doubt that one time or another they did happen. What we have is a number of true events which occurred at several different times telescoped into a single session. This telescoping is a trivial distortion of the truth; and the authenticity remains paramount.

Exactly the same mixture of authenticity and telescoping marks Baldwin's address to the reader in his second, 1563, edition. He recounts how he and the printer and all his helpers except Ferrers met together. After a little Ferrers enters, is blamed for his lateness, and apologizes for it on the plea that he has been collecting tragedies from his friends and that all but a few have let him down because they are so slow:

for sum wyttes are readye, and dispatch many matters spedilye, lyke the Conye which lyttereth every moneth: sum other are slowe lyke the Olyfaunt, skarce delyueryng any matter in .x. yeares. I disprayse ney-ther of these byrthes, For both be naturall: But I commende most the meane, which is neyther to slowe nor to swyft, for that is Lion lyke, and therefore most noble. For the ryght poet doth neyther through haste bring furth swift feble Rabettes, neither doth he weary men in lookyng for hys strong ioyntles Olyphantes: But in reasonable tyme he bryngeth furth a perfect and liuely Lion, Not a Bearwhelp that must be longar in lyckyng than in breedynge.

Ferrers goes on to say what tragedies he has procured; the printer and Baldwin do the same; and the company settle to hear them read aloud. Plainly, the scene is largely fictitious. It is unthinkable that Ferrers waited till the day appointed for meeting and reading the new material before collecting his friends' contributions. Nor is it the least conceivable that all the new matter was read during a single session. Again, several visits, several meetings and readings, have been telescoped. And again this telescoping counts for nothing, while the authenticity counts for a great deal. We are given a glimpse of real meetings to discuss the composition of the volume and to hear the contributions read aloud. I do not doubt that the talk about rabbits and elephants is genuine talk, especially because the rabbits crop up again in a later end-link, making one surmise that they were a stock joke in the company.

Apart from this general authenticity there is the pleasure of see-ing the group interested in the details of their craft; and here the end-links join with the great amount of metrical experiment that occurs throughout the whole length of the *Mirror*. This reinforces very powerfully the impression that in the *Mirror* we have the spectacle of a group of men feeling their way towards the right literary procedure. Alwin Thaler[1] has written on the literary criticism of the *Mirror*; but in truth it amounts in itself to little. The company discuss, for instance, the principle of decorum, but

[1] See *J.E.G.P.*, 1950, xlix. 1–13.

they do not carry the topic farther than the need to make the kind of metre suit the kind of speaker. For instance, the end-link after the story of the Blacksmith begins:

It is pitie (quoth one) that the meter is no better seing the matter is so good: you maye doo verye well to helpe it, and a littell fylyng would make it formall. The Author him selfe (quoth I) could haue doen that, but he woulde not, and hath desyred me that it maye passe in suche rude sort as you haue heard it: for he obserueth therein a double *decorum* both of the Smith, and of him selfe: for he thinketh it not mete for the Smyth to speke, nor for himselfe to write in any exacte kynde of meter.

That is all very well, but no one of the company observes that the tale itself is full of high sentiments perfectly inappropriate to the character of the speaker and to the intentional roughness of the metre, including an eloquent plea that the nobility should be properly educated. Actually the same observation had been made after Jack Cade told his story:

By saint mary (quoth one) yf Iacke wer as well learned, as you haue made his oracion, What so ever he was by byrth, I warraunt hym a gentylman by his learnyng. Howe notably and Philosopher like hath he discrybed Fortune and the causes of worldly cumbraunce? howe vp-ryghtly also and howe like a deuine hath he determined the states both of officers and Rebelles.

But no one takes up this satirical comment. No, it is not the criticism in itself that matters but the fresh and genuine picture that the *Mirror* provides of real people airing their opinions. They are genuinely concerned with the questions of why the chronicles are so often at variance with one another, whether the fat prior of Tiptree, who was squeezed to death in the throng on London Bridge, could furnish an edifying tale, whether good Protestants may introduce the Popish creation of Purgatory into their verses, what freedom the poet may be allowed, whether women may be learned. We may be absolutely assured that this eager group of people discussed these topics; and it is this assurance that gives to *A Mirror for Magistrates* its main attraction for the reader of today.

Marlowe's Light Reading

ETHEL SEATON

THE student has been well served for the solid reading of Marlowe. Dr. F. S. Boas helped us to see him as a sound classical scholar, using to advantage his classical reading, both Greek and Latin, as source and poetic inspiration, especially Virgil, Ovid, Lucan, Seneca, and Musaeus. The reading that he must have done for *Tamburlaine* and *The Jew of Malta*, as Professor Ellis-Fermor and others have traced it, shows him to have been a close student of fifteenth- and sixteenth-century chronicles and cosmographies, of the Near and the Far East; and close reading they are. As a politically minded man of the Renaissance and an uninhibited thinker, he was acquainted with Macchiavelli, and was in touch with free scientific and philosophic inquiry.

Few, however, seem to have asked themselves, What did Marlowe read in his off-time?—few except perhaps Professor Douglas Bush, and that mostly in footnotes. As a boy, a lad, what more popular stuff did Marlowe get hold of and devour? We know something of the reading, the possibly acquired tastes of his later adolescence and young manhood; but there remains the question of his earlier, his more uncritical tastes. We are so much accustomed to think of Marlowe as a representative of Elizabethan intellectualism, as the iconoclast of the eighties and the nineties, that we forget the boy of the seventies. Yet youthful impressions shape and deeply colour the mind's apprehension. This fiery young dramatist must have been an ardent, imaginative boy, a voracious reader, feeding his curiosity with whatever literature he could lay hands on, whether penny plain or twopence coloured, much of it romantic and adventurous. Many of the romances dear to the fourteenth and fifteenth centuries were still to hand, in comparatively cheap reprints, more easy to find than the chronicles only accessible in a college library, or in a great man's collection. Young Master Robert Ashley, a year Marlowe's junior, confessed that whenever he got hold of *Bevis of Hampton*, *Guy of Warwick*, *Valentine and Orson*, or *Arthur and the Round Table*, he surreptitiously devoured them, at

C

the expense of time meant for sleep, food, and even play.[1] In confessing this in later life, he makes the derogatory disavowals of a sober and legal middle age; Marlowe was saved from that by never growing old. But we may assume that Master Kit was just such another boy as Master Robert, and such another reader as Thomas Quiney, Shakespeare's son-in-law, who thought fit to adorn the cover of a new account-book, now at Stratford, with a gnomic couplet from a medieval French romance,[2] *St. Galais*.

Reading Marlowe's chronicle sources had led me to trust him in points of detail; but I was long puzzled by an elusive bird in *Tamburlaine*. The conqueror, encamped before Damascus, cries to his generals:

> Now may we see *Damascus* lofty towers. . . .
> The golden stature of their feathered bird
> That spreads her wings vpon the citie wals,
> Shall not defend it. (*I Tamb.*, IV. ii. 102–6)

No chronicle, no description of the Holy Land that I could find, said anything about that potent bird; it seemed to have taken wing. But I shot an arrow of curiosity after it; and long afterward, as in the old song, I found that arrow sticking in the heart of a popular romance, *Bevis of Hampton*. Bevis, coming to Damascus to defy its Saracen king, observes its moat, its bridge:[3]

> At the Bryge stode a toure,
> Peynted with gold and asure.
> Riche it was to be-hold.
> There on stode an egull of gold;
> His eyn were of precious stones
> Of gret vertue for the nones.
> [The stones were so riche and bright
> That al the place shone of lyght.]

That description is not found in all versions of *Bevis of Hampton*, but it is in Pynson's edition of about 1503, and in East's of about 1582.

The question then arose, how much more did Marlowe get from such romances? And gradually I began to suspect the presence of a third and as yet untapped layer in Marlowe's references, allusions,

---

[1] See R. S. Crane, *M.P.*, 1913, xi. 271.
[2] Birthplace Exhibits, Item 66, Catalogue 1925.
[3] Ed. Kölbing, E.E.T.S., E.S. 46, Part I, p. 67.

and similes, below the classical, below the chronicle reading, the layer of medieval romance, probably the layer first formed and the one of which he was the least conscious.

Here in this stratum of romance we can distinguish two veins of value. First, the chapbooks, such as could be bought for sixpence or tenpence, the popular romances, especially the native stories, such as *Richard Cœur de Lyon*, or the noble pair, *Bevis of Hampton* and *Guy of Warwick*, the English Castor and Pollux of the fourteenth century as Havelock and Horn had been of the thirteenth: the kind of popular reading that Robert Laneham's *Letter* describes as forming the library of Captain Cox of Coventry. Secondly, there is the more reputable medieval matter, Lord Berner's *Froissart*, and his *Huon of Bordeaux* and *Arthur of Little Britain*, Malory's *Morte Darthur*, the great poetic redactions of Lydgate, and finally the substantial romances that Caxton printed, and often translated first, the *Eneydos*, the *Recueil of the Hystoryes of Troye*: more reputable now as literature, but not more acceptable to the Tudor moralist such as Ascham, and incurring the scorn of Marlowe's associate Nashe, and later the ridicule of Beaumont.

Three springs of medieval influence can be seen welling up in Marlowe's plays: first, general reminiscences of the romances, especially the popular or English ones, and the Alexander saga; secondly, the Troy Legend; and thirdly, the more historical material, such as *Godfrey of Boulogne*.

I

First in importance are the general reminiscences. They are of many kinds, and sometimes of much poetic attractiveness. Marlowe makes great play dramatically with the three symbolic colours of Tamburlaine's tents or flags; his white flags of mercy, his red flags of menace, and his black flags of general doom appear in the Western, though curiously not in the Eastern, versions of his life. Marlowe alone extends the idea, and makes Tamburlaine appear fully accoutred in the colour:

> Black are his collours, blacke Pauilion,
> His speare, his shield, his horse, his armour, plumes,
> And Ietty Feathers menace death and hell.
>
> (*I Tamb.*, IV. i. 60–62)

It was long ago pointed out[1] that this brings the idea into line with the motif of the three days' tournament common in romances of chivalry: as in Malory,[2] with the knights of the black, the green, the red, and the blue launds; with Richard Cœur de Lion's three days' jousting at Salisbury (ll. 273–555); and with Ipomedon's exploits. The last bears quoting, in the stanza parallel to the above; the young knight has

> a blake stede . . .
> A blake sheld aboute his halsse,
> Blake was all his armur alse . . .
> Cole-blake sadull and conysance;
> The chyld bare on his launse
> A pensell all off blake.
>
> (*Ipomedon* C, st. 204)

The significance attached to the changes is found fully only in the story of Tamburlaine; but the colours were already in Marlowe's mental vision.

We might agree with Mr. Bakeless[3] that this was mere coincidence, if there were no more; but there is much more. For example, there are the descriptions of battle, violence, and bloodshed. Surprise is sometimes felt that Marlowe, for all his adult Renaissance questioning, should yet seem not to have become fully adult in his feeling and taste. He is, it is argued, like a small boy indulging in a ghoulish fascination for gore, and for scenes of bloodshed and rapine which can be *enjoyed* only by a mentally arrested or a perverted personality. It is even insinuated that Marlowe does exhibit perversion, delight in cruelty, or at best a superficial unthinking pleasure in describing such scenes. This to the reflective and idealistic reader spoils the value of his ideas, and brands him as coarse-fibred and callous.

If there is anything in all this, it is in the idea of the undeveloped personality, or perhaps the one-sidedly developed personality. In *Tamburlaine* one discerns, I think, the outward-thrusting growth of Marlowe, like the rings in a tree-trunk. These romances which he must have read avidly as a boy, as a youth, amaze the modern reader with their mixture of simplicity and shrewdness, of obtuseness and penetration, of individual vision and 'common form'. Here the medieval fighting man could read—or hear recited—vivid

[1] J. D. Bruce, *M.L.N.*, Dec. 1909, xxiv. 257–8.
[2] *Morte Darthur*, VII. 6–11.
[3] *The Tragical History of Marlowe*, Cambridge, Mass., 1942, i. 233, note.

descriptions of the bloodiest of hand-to-hand combats. Even Chaucer's maidenly-meek knight shows, by lapsing into the alliterative verse-rhythms, that he knew the traditional battle descriptions, as well as the elegant heroic formalities. Presumably it was only the clerk, like Gower,[1] who dared to suggest that the crusading slaughter of the Saracens was a needless and even an unchristian business.

These descriptions are more or less stylized, and have an effect of recurrent pattern, which by its very repetition first impresses itself upon the memory, and finally blunts the reader's susceptibilities. We are apt to smile at Malory's knights when they 'ride a great wallop', and fight 'racing, tracing and foyning'; nevertheless the casual reader remembers these phrases as he does few others in the book; so too Marlowe's memory of the romances was probably an unconscious assimilation, but used with great dramatic effect. When, then, we read in Marlowe of horses besmeared with blood (as in the wine-press of the Apocalypse), of the battlefield covered as with a liquid purple veil, of frightful wounds and mangled bodies, we should remember that all these things abound in the romances, where they are described with unimaginative precision. To give but one example, from that same *Bevis of Hampton*: Bevis's famous steed Arundel, at the battle in London streets, stood 'Vp to þe fytlokkes in mannys blood'; it is a stock phrase, and recurs in Malory, in *Richard Cœur de Lyon* (l. 5858), and where not? As for the mangling of bodies, the starkly realistic lines are there in horrible profusion.

There too are more imaginative descriptions, as of the advance of a great host. Marlowe has three main images to convey this effect: its earth-quaking strength; its sky-darkening density; or its numbers like the stars, the leaves, the drops of rain:

> So great an host,
> As with their waight shall make the mountains quake;
> (*I Tamb.*, I. ii. 48)

> The spring is hindred by your smoothering host,
> For neither rain can fall vpon the earth,
> Nor Sun reflexe his vertuous beames thereon.
> The ground is mantled with such multitudes . . .
> And all the trees are blasted with our breathes.
> (*I Tamb.*, III. i. 50–55)

---

[1] *Confessio Amantis*, IV. 1659 ff.

In *Richard Cœur de Lyon*[1] the Saracen army advances, 'and al þe erþe Vndyr þe hors-feet it quook', and Richard is warned, 'The ground ne may vnneth them bere, | The folke that cometh the to dere' (ll. 6917–18). In *Huon of Bordeaux*[2] this kind of statement is repeated again and again:

With rynnyng of theyr horses yᵉ erth trymbled, & the sonne lost his lyght by reason of the pouder that rose vp in to the ayre (chap. 93);

the sonne . . . waxed darke, and the shote . . . flew so faste and as thicke as thoughe it had snowed (chap. 130).

In the *Prose Life of Alexander*, at the battle of Granicus, 'þare was so thikke schott of arowes, þat the ayer was couerde, as it had bene wit a clowde'.[3] Once Tamburlaine, combining the idea of a great host and of terrible bloodshed, describes the effect on the sun in almost Miltonic terms:

> Such lauish will I make of Turkish blood, . . .
> The Sun vnable to sustaine the sight,
> Shall hide his head in *Thetis* watery lap.
>
> (*II Tamb.*, I. vi. 38–42)

So when Amorca fights Alexander, 'þare was so mekill folke dede in þat bataile, þat þe sone wexe eclipte, and wit-drewe his lighte, vggande for to see so mekill scheddynge of blude'.[4]

It is there, too, in the life of this great conqueror whom Marlowe so often admires, that there comes one of the finest of many descriptions of another effect which excites Marlowe. Alexander's host on the march 'schane rigte as it had been sternes, for sum of thaire armoures ware of golde, sum of siluer, and sum of precious stanes. And when Alexander saw þe araye of his Oste, and þaire baners bifore þam Schynande so faire, he was rigte gladde.'[5] Tamburlaine cries:

> . . . with our Sun-bright armour as we march,
> Weel chase the Stars from heauen, and dim their eies
> That stand and muse at our admyred armes.
>
> (*I Tamb.*, II. iii. 22–24)

This pomp and glory of an army terrible with banners always arouses the medieval poet and chronicler, dazzled by the heraldic

---

[1] Ed. K. Brunner, 1913, Wiener Beiträge 42.
[2] Ed. S. L. Lee, E.E.T.S., E.S. 41, pp. 297, 474.
[3] Ed. J. S. Westlake, E.E.T.S., O.S. 143, p. 49.
[4] Ibid., p. 27.   [5] Ibid., p. 67.

brilliance of personal ensigns; Froissart cries more than once: 'It was a great beauty to behold the banners and standards wavyng in the wind.' The author of *Generydes* transfers it to the Saracen army, and tells how the Sultan rides out on a summer's day to view his embattled host:[1]

> Anon with all ther Baneres were displayed
> A riall sight it was to behold . . .
> Ther cote Armers of siluer and of gold . . .
> The trompettys blewe; it was A Ioye to here.

Lydgate[2] will write of the wind roaring in the broad banners and rich standards of the Greek host, and again of

> Baners vnrollid, & longe fresche penouns
> Of rede and whyte, grene, blew & blake.

Marlowe will give it an imaginative touch for the army of the King of Jerusalem:

> That on mount *Sinay* with their ensignes spread,
> Looke like the parti-coloured cloudes of heauen,
> That shew faire weather to the neighbor morne.
> (*II Tamb.*, III. i. 47)

There are still to come in *Macbeth* the Norweyan banners that 'flout the sky, And fan our people cold'. Classical myth is by no means the only stimulus to Marlowe's sense of beauty; when he desires descriptions of romance or fantasy, he is as likely as not to find them in the romances. It may be the gorgeous (and most unseaworthy) ship that Dido offers to Aeneas:

> Ile giue thee tackling made of riueld gold,
> Wound on the barkes of odoriferous trees,
> Oares of massie Iuorie full of holes,
> Through which the water shall delight to play:
> Thy Anchors shall be hewed from Christall Rockes,
> Which if thou lose shall shine aboue the waues:
> The Masts whereon thy swelling sailes shall hang,
> Hollow Pyramides of siluer plate:
> The sailes of foulded Lawne, where shall be wrought
> The warres of *Troy*.   (*Dido*, III. i. 115–24)

The ship that brought to England the princess of Antioch who was

---

[1] Ed. W. Aldis Wright, E.E.T.S., O.S. 55, p. 68.
[2] *Troy Book*, III. 716 ff., 500–1.

to become (*pace* the historians) the mother of Richard Cœur de Lion, must have been built on the same slips:

> Al it was whyt of ruel-bon
> And euery nayl wiþ gold begraue;
>   Off pure gold was the staue the [rudder],
> Here mast was of yuory,
> Of samyte þe sayl wytterly.
> Here ropes were off tuely sylk,
> Also whyte as ony mylk.
> Þat noble schyp was al wiþ oute
> Wiþ cloþis off gold spred aboute;
> And here looff and here wyndas
>   Off asure forsoþe it was.   (ll. 60–70)

Or Huon of Bordeaux near the Fountain of Youth is provided by the angel with a magic ship, likewise of ivory and gold, with a fore-castle of white crystal and rich chalcedony.[1] It is Marlowe, I think, and not Peele who adds the touch of unpractical fantasy of the holes in the oars that will fret the surface of the water.

In *Huon of Bordeaux* we find too another poetic ornament that pleased Marlowe. In the marble hall of the Castle of the Adamant, the emerald lintel is 'traylyd with a wyng [*sic*] of fyne golde, and the Grapys of fine Saphers'.[2] That bejewelled vine flaunts its glittering tendrils through the more richly and orientally romantic of the world's stories, from the Latin *Epistola Alexandri ad Aristotelem* down to Mandeville. In that unique blackletter fragment which is the only proof that the Romance of Alexander was printed in the mid-sixteenth century, the vine forms a trellis in the great hall of Porus, king of Inde:[3]

> Betwene the pelouris hyng a vyne
> All sad gold and seluer fyne.
> Of pured gold eych lef was als.
> This story is not holdon fals.
> This was no vyne made of iape
> Of fyne cristall was euery grape,
> And of emeraunde the riche stonys
> Fayre be set for the nonys

Alexander found another before the doors of the temple of the Sun,

---

[1] Ed. cit., p. 440: chap. 123.   [2] Ed. cit., p. 383: chap. 111.
[3] *Kyng Alisaunder*, ed. G.V. Smithers, E.E.T.S. 227, p. 290.

a golden vine bearing grapes of carbuncles, rubies, diamonds. The vine winds its way into the Troy legend, and is added in three manuscripts of the *Roman d'Enéas* to the description of Dido's palace, a trellised vine behind the throne.[1] Mandeville (chap. 67) depicts one in the palace of the Khan of Tartary in Xanadu: a vine of gold about the tables at great feasts with grapes of crystal, topaz, emeralds, and beryls. Finally, Marlowe trains it round the temple of Venus in *Hero and Leander*, but condenses it into one line: 'A liuelie vine of greene sea-agget spread.'

In *Hero and Leander* too there is yet another circumstance of favour and of prettiness, only a hundred lines earlier. Many readers must have smiled at the absurd buskins worn by Hero, made of silver shells and pink coral, and ornamented with sparrows of pearl and gold artificially made to 'cherupe through the bils' as Hero walks; 'She shall have music wherever she goes'. Magical or artificial singing-birds are one of the most charming treasures of the medieval romances. They even inhabit the vine, as they do in Dido's Palace; when she sits on her throne, ten thousand great and little birds made of fine gold (the least is worth a city) sing and fly as the wind blows, each singing after its guise, so that the palace rings. The plane trees growing in the hall of Porus (where was the golden vine) were full of painted birds, with beaks and claws of gold: 'And ay, when Porus liste, thir fowles thurgh crafte of music walde synge after þaire kynde askede.' Mandeville's rich man in Prester John's land had in his chambers birds 'yt song and turned by engin and orbage, as they had been quick' (chap. 90). Marlowe, like Mandeville, prefers mechanism to magic; but it is Marlowe who gives the touch of heightened, and rococo fancy, by turning them into personal adornments.

All this is very general, but it is the general taking-off ground for Marlowe's more particular flights of fancy. One instance, an actual borrowing, is of a very different nature. The Jew of Malta comes to his dreadful end through double-crossing both the Christian defenders and also the Turkish besiegers of the island. He feigns death, and the Christians throw his body over the walls. Found by the Turks, he offers himself to the Turkish leader as a spy. 'Didst thou breake prison?' asks Calymath. He tells them of a secret entry into the city, and promises to open the gates. The plan succeeds, and the Turks as a reward make Barabas governor of the city. Then he

---

[1] Ed. J. S. de Grave, La Haye, 1888, p. 389.

offers to the captured Christians to restore the town to them by slaughtering the Turks at a feast in the citadel. He next contrives a gallery which by cranes and pulleys will fall into a deep pit provided with a boiling caldron. Rather ingenuously, he displays it to the Christian ex-governor, who promptly cuts the cable and dispatches Barabas to destruction.

A similar episode occurs in *Richard Cœur de Lyon*,[1] though with reversed positions. Sir Thomas Multoun is besieging the Saracens in Castle Orgylous in the Holy Land. The Saracens send out a renegade as a spy; as prearranged, he offers his services to Sir Thomas to betray the town to him:

> Sere, I am a Crystene man:
> I brak prisoun and out I wan.

Sir Thomas disbelieves him and threatens to string him up. The renegade then confesses, and makes amends by warning him of the mechanism of the town's bridge, a trap with a hasp and pin, and with a pit sixty fathoms deep beneath. The renegade, under instructions, returns to the town, and persuades the Saracens to surrender; Sir Thomas makes them break the trap-bridge and fill up the pit. The town is entered, but the captured Saracen admiral plots to murder the Christians asleep after a banquet. Fortunately the renegade (now completely reconciled) overhears, foils their entry, warns the Christians, and departs in the odour of sanctity as a pilgrim. It is obvious that the two episodes do not run exactly parallel; but the *points d'appui* of the story are the same: besiegers and besieged; Christians *versus* Saracens; a *tertium quid*, the spy, a renegade Christian in the romance, a Jew in Marlowe; a mechanical trap with a pit; and a false invitation to a banquet. True, there is no caldron in *Richard Cœur de Lyon*; but this is the punishment that Sir Bevis prepared for his ancient enemy Sir Murdour:[2]

> Syr Beuys wythout any let,
> Made a caudron on the fyre be set
> Ful of pytche and of brymstone:
> A wors deth was neuer none.
> Whan the caudron boyled harde,
> Murdour was cast in the mydwarde.

I had often felt uncertain whether Marlowe really had a hand in the

---

[1] Lines 4075 ff. [2] Ed. Kölbing, E.E.T.S., E.S. 48, p. 162.

end of *The Jew*, but these parallels seem to suggest that he may have had.

II

So much for Marlowe's stray correspondences with descriptions and episodes in the romances. A more limited, yet more important, subject concerns Marlowe's medieval matter and manner in his only play on a classical theme. Obviously *The Tragedy of Dido* is mainly derived from Virgil; equally obviously it treats Virgil very freely; and the following is offered as a medieval footnote to the work of Dr. Boas and of Professor Tucker Brooke on the subject.

There is clear proof that Marlowe knew the medieval view of Aeneas; indeed he could hardly help knowing it, for the writers in the main stream of the medieval Troy legend agreed in covering Aeneas in the waters of infamy. He is a vile traitor, only less vile than his co-traitor Antenor because of occasional visitings of compassion. Dictys, Dares, the so-called Cornelius Nepos, Benoît de Sainte Maure, Guido delle Colonne and therefore Lydgate, Raoul Lefevre and therefore Caxton in his *Recueil*, all assert Aeneas's treachery. But on the other side the *Roman d'Enéas*, the *Eneydos* of Raoul Lefevre and therefore Caxton's translation, and above all Gavin Douglas and Surrey, the translators of Virgil, follow the *Aeneid* in its picture of *pius Aeneas*, loyal defender of Troy, founder of Rome, and ancestor of the British race. Already in some of the later romances, such as *Partonope of Blois*, attempts were made to whitewash this dubious hero; Anchises was a traitor, but this Aeneas was no kin to him, but a worthy man.[1] After the Renaissance, because of Western Europe's admiration for Virgil, and because of England's pride in her Trojan-Roman descent, Aeneas lost his parti-coloured medieval cloak, and shone forth in Virgilian rectitude. And Marlowe's fusion of the two accounts, the Virgilian and the medieval, results in some anomalies; for if Aeneas knew in such dire detail how Priam died, it was because he and Antenor had led Pyrrhus to the king's place of refuge, and had even stood by and consented to the murder.

The proof that Marlowe knew the medieval charges lies in the carefully tactful question of his Dido to Aeneas:

> Some say *Antenor* did betray the towne,
> Others report twas *Sinon's* periurie.
> (*Dido*, II. i. 108)

[1] Ed. A. T. Bödtker, E.E.T.S., E.S. 109, ll. 268-75.

If Marlowe knew of Antenor's treachery, he also knew of Aeneas's. Which then was Marlowe's chief medieval authority for his non-Virgilian, non-Ovidian additions? It seems to be generally assumed that any Elizabethan went to Caxton's *Recueil of the Hystoryes of Troye* for his Trojan stories. But for Marlowe I believe the answer is, the fullest, most poetic, and most deservedly respected of the English versions, Lydgate's *Troy Book,* translated and versified from Guido delle Colonne's prose version at the request of Prince Hal, never printed by Caxton, but twice printed in the sixteenth century, the later issue in 1555.

Every poet who has handled the Troy legend has treated it with fresh and free invention; and Marlowe is no exception. He has added another love interest: Anna's hopeless love for Iarbas, Iarbas's equally hopeless love for Dido, and the self-slaughter of both before Dido's pyre. Just so did the poet of the *Roman d'Enéas* expand romantically the relation of Aeneas with Lavinia.

One scene in especial, Aeneas's account to Dido of the destruction of Troy (II. i) comes from Virgil in its main outlines, but in only 200 lines contrasted with Virgil's 800. Yet even in that small compass there are very obvious divergences; and they are medieval. Aeneas starts fairly close to his Virgilian prototype, though he omits the story of the Palladium; he describes the making of the wooden horse, the planned capture of Sinon (another story of the 'planting' of a spy), the Trojans' fatal acceptance of the horse, and the dragging of it into the city. But when Aeneas comes to the Greek warriors issuing forth from the horse, Marlowe begins to turn to Lydgate. It is a fine passage:

> Then he vnlockt the Horse, and suddenly
> From out his entrailes, *Neoptolemus*
> Setting his speare vpon the ground, leapt forth,
> And after him a thousand Grecians more,
> In whose sterne faces shin'd the quenchles fire
> That after burnt the pride of Asia.   (II. i. 182–7)

Virgil does not here call Pyrrhus by his other name of Neoptolemus; nor does Lydgate here, but earlier he had explained how Pyrrhus came by the name. Marlowe can, I believe, take credit for that vividly natural description of an athletic action,

> Setting his speare vpon the ground, leapt forth.

In Virgil, the warriors lower a rope and slide down it (*demissum lapsi*

per funem, Aen. II. 262), and the focusing of interest on the leader is
blurred by a list of names. The last lines of the quotation have the
very stamp of Marlowe at his highest. Yet if the reader casts back
and forth in Lydgate he will find words and ideas which have gone
to aid the inspiration. The phrase 'stern face' is almost a signature
tune of Lydgate; it is his significant label for the heroic fighting
man. Thus Jason 'With sterne face to-fore the kyng in cam' (I.
3116); Hector is 'Lyk a lyoun, with a sterne face' (III. 1539); and
especially to be noted in view of the murder of Priam is the description of the statue of Apollo 'with his power and his sterne face' (IV.
6413). The words 'quenchles fire' stayed in Marlowe's mind, and
he echoed himself in *Tamburlaine* and in *Edward II.* Is Marlowe here
remembering an episode elaborated by Lydgate more than by most,
that of the ill-omened Trojan sacrifice? Cassandra explains how to
avert the omen by lighting sacred fire at Achilles' tomb:

> Þe whiche fire be noon occasioun
> Shal nat quenche, but his flawmys holde
> Þoruȝ noon assaut of stormy wyndes colde.
>   (IV. 5982–4)

When the Greeks get into Troy, Marlowe thrice deviates from,
and elaborates, the comparatively plain Virgilian narrative. He adds,
first, the detail of the massacre in Troy; secondly, the detail of
Priam's murder by Pyrrhus, and the divine wrath seen in the face
of the statue; and thirdly, the detail of Hecuba's ravings, and the
account of Polyxena's and Cassandra's fate.

First, almost all the later medieval versions of the Sack of Troy
expand in some way the brief statement of Dictys (bk. v) that
children were slain before the eyes of their parents, parents before
their children; or of Guido delle Colonne that the slayers made no
distinction of sex or age. Lydgate combines the two:

> Al for-baþed in her owne blood,
> Both man & childe, with-oute excepcioun,
> Þe Grekis sparinge no condicioun
> Of old nor ȝong, womman, wif, nor maide.
>   (IV. 6308–11)

The minstrel of *The Seege or Bataile of Troy*[1] expands thus:

> Doughter and sone, moder and fader,
> And þe yong chyld in the Cradell,

[1] Ed. Barnicle, E.E.T.S. 172, p. 213.

Olde blynde men and all soche,
And Crepullis þat yeden with her croche.

Marlowe's lines are more like this in their violence of style:

Yong infants swimming in their parents bloud,
Headles carkasses piled vp in heapes,
Virgins halfe dead dragged by their golden haire,
And with maine force flung on a ring of pikes,
Old men with swords thrust through their aged sides,
Kneeling for mercie to a Greekish lad
Who with steele Pol-axes dasht out their braines.

(II. i. 193–9)

With the word 'poleaxes' Marlowe returns to Lydgate, for this is Lydgate's favourite weapon; just so with the 'balls of wild-fire' thrown by the Myrmidons, he is back in the medieval atmosphere:

For now allas! þe wilde fire is seyn
In touris hiȝe with þe wynde y-blasid,

writes Lydgate. Wild fire, the *feu Grégois* of the Crusaders, is an anachronism in the Trojan story, but the name was suggestive, and Lydgate uses it as freely as do all the romance-writers.

The second deviation concerns the death of Priam. In Virgil, Pyrrhus pursues Polites, son of Priam, through the deserted palace to the inner sanctuary, and kills him before the eyes of his father. Priam, though facing his own death, cannot refrain from bitterly rebuking Pyrrhus, and reminding him of his father Achilles' clemency. He casts a spear at the slayer, but weakly and to no avail. Pyrrhus brutally tells him to go seek Achilles among the dead. He drags the trembling king, slipping in his son's blood, to the altars, and seizing him by the hair, strikes off his head. Lydgate renders Guido delle Colonne's account thus:

And Pirrus after to þe temple goth
Of Apollo by gret cruelte,
And fil on Priam knelynge on his kne,
And wiþ his swerd, furious and wood,
To-fore þe autere shadde þere his blood
Þat þe stremys of his woundys rede
So hiȝe rauȝt, boþe in lengþe and brede,
Þat þe statue of gold bornyd briȝt
Of þis Appollo, for al his grete myȝt,
For al his power and his sterne face,

Defouled was, and pollut al þe place . . .
While Anthenor and Enee stod be-side.
(IV. 6404–18)

In Marlowe, Pyrrhus has already killed Priam's youngest son, and
appears carrying the boy's head on his spear. He finds Priam and
Hecuba at Jove's altar. Priam speaks, but only to beg for his life;
for answer Pyrrhus strikes off his supplicating hands. Hecuba
springs to his rescue, but is dragged away by the soldiers. The king
falls before the sword, and Pyrrhus rips him up:

> at whose latter gaspe
> *Ioue's* marble statue gan to bend the brow,
> As lothing *Pirrhus* for this wicked act:
> Yet he vndaunted tooke his fathers flagge,
> And dipt it in the old Kings chill cold bloud,
> And then in triumph ran into the streetes,
> Through which he could not passe for slaughtred men:
> So leaning on his sword he stood stone still,
> Viewing the fire wherewith rich *Ilion* burnt.
>
> (*Dido*, II. i. 256–64)

The presence of the god's statue, and the suggestion of sacrilege in
Lydgate, are deepened by Marlowe to a supernatural expression of
divine wrath and horror. Rather surprisingly Marlowe omits the
statue being spattered with blood; he substitutes the dipping of
Pyrrhus's flag in the blood—'a medieval touch' as Professor Tucker   X
Brooke comments; and indeed the last lines could be paralleled point
by point out of the romances.

The third deviation from Virgil lies in the violent opposition
offered by Hecuba, and her maltreatment. In Virgil, and in Lydgate,
she is present, but inactive. Marlowe alone, I believe, transfers to
this scene her frenzied behaviour at the ritual murder of her
daughter Polyxena before the tomb of Achilles, as more moderately
described by Guido and Lydgate (IV. 6896–6903). As Professor
Tucker Brooke shows, it is also like Ovid's description (in Gould-
ing's translation) of her violence at the death of Polymnestor.
Marlowe's crudest touch,

> At last the souldiers puld her by the heeles,
> And swong her howling in the emptie ayre
>
> (II. i. 247–8)

is not in the more restrained Lydgate, but it may be a memory of

X the hankerchief in "Troue Contention" also dipped in blood.

the minstrel of the *Seege or Bataile of Troy*, who tells how Achilles unarmed, defended himself by main strength against his assassins:

> Wiþ þe schuldres to heom he reches
> And slang heom abowte and lette heom gon
> Þat heo to-barsten aȝeyn þeo ston;
> And anoþir he slang aȝeyn a wal.

Lydgate then would seem to be the chief, though not the only source for the differences from Virgil in this account. I believe yet another author may also intrude, but one who would hardly come within the limits of 'light reading'.

Just as we found Marlowe touched to horror or beauty by his other romance sources, so again in this play; and here Caxton's *Eneydos* also comes in, and another work of Lydgate's. The crudity of Venus's threat to Juno gives the reader a shock of horror:

> I will teare thy eyes fro forth thy head,
> And feast the birds with their bloud-shotten balles.
>
> (*Dido*, III. ii. 34–35)

It is parallel, though not exactly, to Seneca's description of Oedipus's self-blinding, which Lydgate seems to follow in his *Seege of Thebes* (l. 105), and which Shakespeare too may have remembered in Cornwall's vicious threat, 'Upon these eyes of thine I'll set my foot'.

Fortunately the beauty outweighs the horror. One of Marlowe's most attractive seemingly classical similes has been passed to him by medieval hands: that of the 'fair-tressed sun', not just 'golden-haired Apollo', *flavus Apollo*, but with the rays of light like tresses. In the first scene of *Dido*, Phoebus 'refraines To taint his tresses in the Tyrrhen maine', i.e. to soil his beams in the storm-tossed Mediterranean (I. i. 111–12). Some fifty lines farther, and 'the aged Sunne shed forth his haire' to comfort the shipwrecked Trojans (l. 159). My classical friends cannot adduce a parallel. But Lydgate's two finest nature-descriptions in this same Fourth Book on the sack of Troy are on this theme. Polyxena's hair unbound is

> like vn-to þe siȝt
> [Of] Phebus bemys in his spere briȝt,
> When he to vs doth his liȝt avale. (ll. 591–3)

Or the new-risen sun shines on painted shields,

> Firy Titan, gold-tressed in his spere,
> At his vprist with his bemys clere. (ll. 2645–6)

So too in his *Seege of Thebes*, the afternoon sun

> fro the south westward gan hym drawe
> His gylte tressys to bathen in the wawe.   (ll. 4257-8)

In Caxton's *Eneydos* (chap. 15) there is a passage, more like a lyric by Charles d'Orléans than its brief original in Virgil, on the life-giving power of Apollo: 'his grete beaulte whan he, comynge, casteth his bemes vpon costes and mountaynes of the countrey in manere of golden heres descendynge from his hed, . . . wherby alle thynges renewen them at his commynge'; and the earth's renewal is ecstatically described. So too in the next chapter of the *Eneydos*, the strong shoulders of Atlas, covered with snow, whereon Mercury rests on his way down to earth, are made the symbol of his massive strength; and Professor Tucker Brooke has shown how often Marlowe remembers that myth, and 'aged *Atlas* shoulder' (*Dido*, IV. i. 12).

On these notes of beauty I would leave the Troy legend, for to Marlowe it was, I believe, a constant source of inspiration; later he will epitomize its effect on him in his greatest lines;

> Was this the face that lancht a thousand shippes.
> And burnt the toplesse Towres of *Ilium*?

III

Space does not serve to explore in detail Marlowe's knowledge of the Matter of Britain and the Matter of France. In the Arthur story he shows least interest; *amour courtois* is not for him, nor the usages of chivalry that delight Spenser. Yet Tamburlaine does once express the fundamental idea of chivalry in warfare:

> We will not steale vpon him cowardly,
> But giue him warning and more warriours.
> (*I Tamb.*, II. v. 102-3)

In the Matter of France Marlowe might well have more interest; yet he never mentions Charlemagne or the *douze pairs*. But wars which involve the Saracen or the Turk have relevance for him. The more historical accounts of the First Crusade, such as William of Tyre's *Godffrey of Boloyne* (printed by Caxton), would give him confirmation of the ways of Eastern conquerors. For instance, he would find there yet another example of a victor treating an emperor of Constantinople as a footstool; in chapter 10, Belphet the Eastern Prince (i.e. Abulfath, Sultan of Persia, 1059–72) humiliates in this way the Byzantine Emperor Romanus Diogenes:[1] 'He sette his foote vpon the necke of themperour, & this dyde he ofte, & whan he shold mounte vpon horsback or descende, in shame and despite of the fayth . . . of the cristen peple.'

It is amusing to see how warily in geography Marlowe, though constantly crossing the Crusaders' tracks, avoids their castles and the great names of their campaigns, Antioch, Gaza, and St. Jean d'Acre. But his seven-league-booted strides are well in the tradition of the traversings of seas and countries in the romances, where time and distance are annihilated. Thus Huon of Bordeaux, refusing proffered help, airily says that if need be, he will send for it—send, from France to Persia![2]

All these things, the movement of marching armies, the methods of assault or siege warfare against walled towns, the lists of names of heroes and of places, the rivers of blood in the streets of conquered cities, the compulsory conversions from one faith to another, the insults hurled at the other deity, all these were to be found in the romances, more picturesquely told than in the prose chronicles or annals, and written so vividly as to appeal to a young reader. Can one begin to trace certain tastes in Marlowe, certain selections and rejections? His reading in medieval romance seems to disregard the most high-strained of chivalric *devoirs*—the patience of Grissel, the excessive self-sacrifice to friendship of Amis and Amilon, the delicacies of the more sophisticated forms of Courtly Love, as of a Sir Degrevant. These are not to his taste. What he likes are the cut and thrust of fighting knight against Saracen, and the splendours of the gorgeous East. But he interprets with the mind of a Renaissance man, and suffuses it with a Renaissance glow, which is another glory than that of the Middle Ages. Marlowe is the child of the English high Renaissance, but also a great-grandchild of the later Middle Ages, and he turns, often perhaps unconsciously, to what were by then the discredited but still popular romances. His sceptical temper shows in his disregard in *Tamburlaine* of all marvels other than those of human endeavour; magnetic isles, enchanted armour and weapons, griffins, 'the dragon's wing, the magic ring' are not admitted by him. But much remains. One might suggest

---

[1] Ed. M. N. Colvin, E.E.T.S., E.S. 64, p. 34.
[2] Ed. cit., p. 526: chap. 141.

one reason for the immediate popular success of *Tamburlaine*: that for all the new wine of Renaissance thought poured into it, yet the shape is recognizably that of an old bottle. Just so Mozart's hearers immediately felt at ease with his music, because its ratio was two parts traditional to one part unexpected.

Tamburlaine is to Marlowe as *The Conquest of Granada* is to Dryden, a sudden efflorescence of half-hidden memories and new ideas, bursting into glory like a multi-coloured rocket. No wonder that the Elizabethan audience acclaimed it; for these had been their childhood's dreams too. In that tangled wood of half-remembered images which is the poet's subconscious, images of horror and images of beauty from Marlowe's youthful reading lay dormant. In *Dido* his judgement deliberately used and fused them. In *Faustus*, though so medieval a tale, another spirit, a spirit stabbed broad awake, took control. (Yet even there the acme of his magic is to conjure up simulacra of Alexander, and of Helen as she was 'when *Sir* Paris crost the seas with her'.) In *Tamburlaine* these dormant images found soil fit for their germens, and there they burst into the light. In this oriental subject they found their associations; and the crimson-stained field, the splendour and terror of victorious armies on the march, and the smoke of burning cities, recur and punctuate the drama, as trumpet-calls punctuate the soldier's day. There is not complete artistic fusion, as there is, for example, in Shakespeare's Chorus on the eve of Agincourt. One can analyse the elements, and they prove to be two parts the stuff of boyhood's dreams, the long thoughts of youth—the golden bird on Damascus walls, the frozen pools of Mandeville's Tartary; and one part the story of a conqueror, who, like Alexander, 'spreads his conquests farther'; who living, robed and crowned, is drawn by princes 'with thaire brestes'—as was Alexander dead from Babylon.[1] The romances are the culture-bed in which the seeds of Marlowe's young imagination germinated. It is no wonder that, crossed with classical and oriental stocks, the full flowering is exotic, flamboyant, brilliant in colour and light.

[1] Prose *Life*, E.E.T.S. 143, p. 114.

The Complaint of Thomas Digges

FRANCIS R. JOHNSON

MUCH of our knowledge of the costs of publishing certain types of books during the reign of Queen Elizabeth I comes from the court records resulting from transactions that later became the subjects of legal controversy; hence, the relevant documents happen still to be preserved in the Public Record Office or are extant in some collection of sixteenth-century manuscripts.[1]

This essay is concerned with the story of the 'privately published' second editions of two mathematical and scientific treatises by extremely popular writers, Leonard Digges and his son Thomas—the *Pantometria* (first published in 1571 by Thomas Digges and printed by Henry Bynneman; second edition printed in 1591 by Abel Jeffes) and the *Stratioticos* (first published by Thomas Digges in 1579 and printed by Henry Bynneman; second edition printed by Richard Field in 1590).

The story is one which involves speculation for a profitable rise in price of a greatly sought-after technical publication, and a clever attempt to defraud the author of his just profits—an attempt that counted upon political favouritism and intrigue to enable the perpetrators to escape punishment.

The principal facts are most succinctly and comprehensively set forth in the letter Thomas Digges sent to Lord Burghley, entitled: 'Plaine praesumptions or rather proofs that Leonard Keare scrivener or his confederates meant not only to cozen and deceive Thomas Digges esquire of 2 or 3 hundred pounds debt, but also to have drawn him by device into treble forfeitures by penal statutes. And now seek to draw in Mr. Astelie the pensioner and his friends to countenance their wicked cozening plot: And fully to defame the said Digges.'[2] Further confirmation appears in another letter to Lord Burghley: 'The true state of my proceedings in the matter

---

[1] See, for example, Margaret Dowling, 'The Printing of John Dowland's *Second Booke of Songs or Ayres*', *The Library*, 1932, xii. 365–80; and Charles Sisson, *The Judicious Marriage of Mr. Hooker and the Birth of 'The Lawes of Ecclesiastical Polity'*, 1940.

[2] MS. Lansdowne 69, ff. 133 and 134. For the reader's convenience, I have modernized spelling and punctuation in quotations from sixteenth-century documents.

between me and Mr. Ashley the Pensioner. And also concerning my brother James and him, so far as is in my knowledge truly, as on my credit or discredit with your honour shall be proved.'[1] The letters to Burghley were preliminary to the filing of a complaint in the Court of the Star Chamber[2] in which the same facts are again recited. In the deposition taken from the defendant in answer to Digges's complaint, Keare, on the advice of his counsel, skilfully avoids any unequivocal denial of the principal allegations in the complaint but maintains that, even if true, they are not 'determinable or punishable in this honourable court'.[3]

Therefore, in the absence of other evidence, we will take Digges's story as the basis of our account of the incident. First a word concerning the participants. Thomas Digges (1546–95), the son of Leonard Digges, was the foremost scientific and mathematical writer of Elizabethan England. He had been on the staff of the Earl of Leicester in the wars in the Netherlands, as Leicester's Mustermaster-General. After Robert Dudley's death in 1588, Thomas Digges returned to England and was succeeded as Mustermaster-General in the Netherlands by his younger brother, James Digges. Sir Thomas Shirley (1542–1612) was treasurer-at-war for the English army in the Netherlands and had no love for Digges because of the latter's insistence that every soldier for whom pay was drawn from the Crown must be present at the musters. No doubt his animosity toward Digges prompted him to use his influence adversely when Digges brought suit against Keare in the Court of the Queen's Bench on 31 May 1593.[4] Failure to receive satisfaction there forced Digges to appeal to the still higher Court of the Star Chamber as the only court powerful enough to cope with his political adversaries now that his patron the Earl of Leicester was dead. Since Digges died on 29 August 1595 there is no record of a decision in this case. It was probably dropped, although his widow spent some years trying to recover from the possession of Sir Thomas Shirley the chest containing his papers and accounts as Mustermaster-General in the Netherlands.

Now to summarize the story recounted in the various documents already mentioned.

Shortly before Christmas of 1590 Thomas Digges was living in

---

[1] Ibid., f. 17.   [2] Sta. Cha. 5/D22 (1).
[3] Sta. Cha. 5/D22 (5). The date of this deposition is 19 January 1595.
[4] KB 27/1324/440 d.

London in the section known as the Old Bailey. One of his neighbours there was Leonard Keare, a scrivener, who had managed to insinuate himself into his good graces so that Digges trusted him and used Keare's services frequently in his business transactions. Thus it came about that Digges told Keare that he had made arrangements with a printer for a new impression of 1,000 copies of his book, *Pantometria*. Printing and paper would cost him over 100 marks (1,333 shillings); the manuscript and the woodcuts for the diagrams would cost an equal amount, making his total investment approximately 2,700 shillings. Therefore in order to 'break even' he would have to sell the copies for three shillings apiece. Inasmuch as the booksellers were then selling copies of the *Pantometria* for more than seven shillings, Digges had every expectation that his investment would net him a handsome profit. At the same time he informed Keare that he had completed arrangements for a new impression of the *Stratioticos* at a price that would enable him to sell that book at two shillings a copy.[1]

Digges also confided in Keare that on occasion he had large sums to pay and on other occasions received large sums and that when he had large sums on hand he would be willing to lend money *gratis* for six months on an agreement to have the same amount lent to him *gratis* for the same length of time in order to be sure of the money when his payments came due. He emphasized that he was relying upon Keare to ascertain that any prospective borrowers that he brought to him were 'very good and sufficient men'. Keare had assured him that they should, and that he would 'bring him none but able and honest men for his security'.[2] But when Digges least suspected any treachery in him, Keare brought unto him such 'unthrifts, bankrupts, and notorious cozeners as in the whole city the like or worse could not be found'. More important, he brought him one George Burnell, whom he represented to be a gentleman of Staple Inn and one who by the death of his brother had just inherited 200 pounds in land and gone down to Yorkshire to take possession of it. Furthermore, he claimed that he could give Digges 'very sufficient' bond to pay his price for his books (3 shillings per copy for the *Pantometria*).

Digges then told Keare that he had already promised the new

---

[1] The detailed cost figures for the *Pantometria* are present in MS. Lansdowne 69, f. 17 only.
[2] Ibid., f. 133ᵛ.

books at that price to his brother James Digges for 150 pounds that he owed him for his service under him in the Netherlands and other matters and thought that James might make in time 100 pounds profit by them because the books might well be sold for at least five shillings a copy inasmuch as the booksellers were then selling them for more.[1]

With George Burnell, Keare brought John Astley the pensioner who offered to sign the bond with his purported friend Burnell. Thomas Digges then carried out his promise to his brother James and made out a bill of sale to James for the 1,000 copies of the book *Pantometria* then still at the printers. Thereupon James immediately sold them to Burnell and Astley, taking their bond for 150 pounds in payment.[1] Keare's next move in his swindling game was to tell Digges that Burnell was presently to marry a rich widow and offer Digges his own books as security for a loan of sixty pounds to furnish Burnell until his marriage was past. Digges refused, saying he had no more money to spare, but suggested that Mr. Ballet in Cheapside might be able to lend the money on such good collateral. Later, in passing by Cheapside, he spoke to Ballet, assuring him that the value of the collateral was more than the amount of the loan; consequently Ballet lent the sixty pounds on the books and was content to allow the books to remain at the bookbinders, to be delivered to Mr. Burnell or to Mr. Astley when they were redeemed, or to Mr. Ballet if they should be forfeited.

By this time Digges suspected that the scrivener Keare, George Burnell, and others were parties to a conspiracy to defraud him and his brother of a considerable sum of money. His suspicions increased when reports came to him that Burnell was a notorious cozener along with accounts of other successful swindles perpetrated by Burnell. Moreover, Keare at this point came to him with reports that Burnell was planning to default on the loan Digges had made to him and Astley, and the collateral (the copies of the second edition of the *Pantometria*) would then be sold at a sacrifice and so debase their value; hence it would be better for Digges to protect his investment by himself buying back from Ballet the copies of his own book.

Digges was, of course, distressed because John Astley, son and heir of John Astley, the master of Queen Elizabeth's jewel-house, an old friend and Kentish neighbour of Digges, was involved as

[1] Ibid., f. 17.

co-signer with George Burnell of the bond for 150 pounds to James Digges and for sixty pounds to Thomas himself. In fact, his confidence in the reliability of John Astley, the younger, Queen Elizabeth's pensioner,[1] had been the chief reason that Digges, after verifying that young John Astley was already of legal age, had been willing to accept Astley's and his purported friend Burnell's bond. In his letter to Burghley,[2] he mentions that he had already asked Mr. Woolley (Sir John Woolley, Latin secretary to Queen Elizabeth at the time) to communicate the circumstances of his son's involvement with George Burnell to old Mr. Astley and that Woolley had done so.

Thomas Digges was already involved in the devious dealings of a clever Elizabethan swindler. He offered to cancel the bonds if his money was returned to him. But Keare and his confederates had another trick up their sleeve. To counteract Digges's threat to bring suit, Keare, having had the copying out of many writings of Digges and his brother having to do with their service in the Netherlands, and among others

finding some that concerned her Majesty's service in the Low Countries and Sir Thomas Shirley, Treasurer at Wars, there presently he carried him the copy of one, for the which he hath confessed he had a very liberal reward (*many pieces of gold*), and so of like continued to carry to him still, whom he found so full of gold, and most bountiful, as he hath boasted, and presuming of his liberality and friendship this Keare hath vaunted he cared not for the Digges, Let them do their worst, he had as good and could have better and greater friends than the said Digges had any, so far he presumed on the golden purse of his new patron as it appeareth to be borne out in this his damnable practise.[3]

Digges in his contest with Keare and his friends had reason to discover 'his patrons or maintainors were indeed great as he vaunted'.[4] He complained that he found it strange how Keare or his friends could win Mr. Astley of the Jewel House to favour him that had associated his son with George Burnell 'by the accusation of many a notorious Cozenour'. 'And the omnipotency of Sir Thomas

---

[1] In 1584 Elizabeth had granted him the manor of Maidstone to hold by knight's service; this manor had formerly been held by Sir Thomas Wyatt, the younger, but had become confiscate to the Crown at the time of Wyatt's rebellion under Queen Mary (Hasted, *History of Kent*, iv. 287–8).

[2] MS. Lansdowne 69, f. 18.

[3] Ibid., ff. 133–4. Shirley, it must be remembered, was accused, largely on Digges's evidence, of debts to the Crown.

[4] Ibid., f. 134.

Shirley (since he had her Majesty's purse) I have to my grief and damage many ways already tried: but truth shall not with slanders always be oppressed. *Non semper inter Latrones pendebit Christus.*'

With this devout maxim we must take our leave of Thomas Digges, who did not live to verify it. His case in the Court of the Star Chamber dragged on until his death in 1595. The documents in the case give us a lively glimpse of the circumstances surrounding the publication of two of the most influential of the scientific textbooks of Elizabethan England.

Harington's *Folly*

KATHLEEN M. LEA

IN April 1605 Sir John Harington made out a claim for himself as well suited to be Ireland's Chancellor as well in 'his sperytuall office as his temporall'. He sees no reason why his reputation as a poet should stand in the way and in an old metaphor sums up his career and qualifications.

> I conclude (as one pretily argued last day in the Schools,) that the world ys a stage and wee that lyve in yt are all stage players, some are good for many parts, some only for dumme shows, some deserve a *plaudite* some a *plorate*.
>
> I playd my chyldes part happily, the schollar and students part to neglygently, the sowldyer and cowrtyer faythfully, the husband lovingly, the contryman not basely nor corruptly. Once I played the foole to frendly, in breaking the wyse Solomons Cownsell had not a Just Solomon gevn the condemnd chyld to the parent that had most ryght. Now I desyre to act a Chawncellors part hollyly, that my last act may equall my fyrst, and that I may not *in extremo actu deficere*.

He addresses himself to 'my Lords' as Saints and to the King as 'Sanctus Sanctorum' and beyond all to Providence.

A copy of this letter directed to 'my Lo: of Devonshyre and my Lo. of Cramborne' is in a Bodley manuscript (Rawlinson B. 162). It is certainly corrected by Harington's hand, but not signed, and it may well be a holograph as I shall argue later. It was published in 1879 by Macray, under the title *A Short View of the State of Ireland*. Harington's cheerful confidence is attractive and completely in character; he had a sharp eye for what might turn up. That this suggestion was turned down is hardly surprising though he was likely to have been quite sincere and had had considerable experience of Irish affairs. He urges as qualifications that his genius leads him to that Island, he has crossed four times without being seasick; that he was friendly with Irish people of all ranks; that he had tested himself for spiritual qualities (since he was aspiring to the See of Dublin) by the chapter in *Timothy* and found, that like a true bishop, he was ἀφιλάργυρος and had only one wife.

I am to concern myself here with the 'fool's part' of his life though not perhaps precisely in the sense he had in mind. Possibly he was referring to the scandal he caused in 1596 over the *Metamorphosis of Ajax*, but that has had as much attention as it deserves and according to John Chamberlayne it earned him, at the time when Essex knighted him in July 1599, the mocking title of Sir Ajax Harington. He had another folly of more lasting literary value. There seems no good reason to doubt the substantial truth of the story that being well versed in the Italian language, he translated a tale out of Ariosto's *Orlando Furioso*, which was highly pleasing to the ladies; but the Queen, who was not unacquainted with what passed around her, soon got a sight of her god-son's poetry, and, thinking it proper to affect indignation at some indelicate passages, forbade our author the Court till he had translated the entire work.

This anecdote is given in the *Nugae Antiquae* as 'imparted to Mr. Walker by the late Earl of Charlemont', but there is a confirmatory hint in *An Apologie* incorporated in *An Anatomie of the Metamorpho-sed Ajax* in 1596.[1] The references to *Orlando Furioso* in this passage, which later I shall need to examine more closely, are to Books XXII, XXVII, and XXVIII, treated rather freely, but there is little doubt that the pilot piece was the story of Giocondo in Book XXVIII. The legend is so well in keeping with what we know of Harington as a courtier, and particularly as a royal god-son, that if it is not factually precise it must be representatively true.

Whatever the motive and occasion may have been there is no doubt that the translation of the huge Italian poem, perhaps initially a penance, became his task, his ploy, his hobby, and that in the book itself, in another sense, we may see his 'folly' building for some years. It was no small undertaking. Others before him, Gascoyne, Whetstone, Watson, Daniel, and Byrd,[2] not to mention some of the contributors to Tottel's *Miscellany*, had been content to render a few stray stanzas. Peter Beverley had made a loose but lively version of a single tale in his *Historie of Ariodanto and Ieneura* (1565/6);[3] John Stewart of Baldynneis had given the Scottish Court

---

[1] Sig. Cc 7ʳ: 'The whole worke being enioyned me as a pennance by that Saint, nay rather goddesse, whose service I am onely devoted unto.'
[2] See J. Schoembs, *Ariosts 'Orlando Furioso'* in *der Eng. Litt. des Zeitalters der Eliz.* 1898.
[3] Reprinted by C. T. Prouty in *Sources of 'Much Ado'*, 1950.

a vernacular selection in his *Abbregement of Roland furious*;[1] Greene's travesty Harington scornfully entered in his play-list as 'Orlando Foolioso'.[2] Some contemporaries, notably Florio,[3] Lodge,[4] and Buc,[5] dabbled a little but not in serious competition; others paid compliments, with the exception of Jonson who told Drummond roundly that 'John Harington's Ariosto under all translations, was the worst'.[6] But Harington carried the load of the forty-six books and acknowledged what help he had from the family: the first stanza of Book XIX from his father, and the first fifty stanzas of XXXII from his brother Francis. He bestowed much care on his book and composed a preface, or rather a *Brief Apologie of Poetrie* in three parts; supplied marginal notes with cross-references, and elaborate additional notes after each book elucidating the 'Morall, the History, and the Allusion', which are incidentally full of personal interest; he gave an appendix on the Allegory; a Short Life of Ariosto; an alphabetical table of characters usefully tracing each through the intricacies of the poem; and a list of twenty-four tales which may be read by themselves. For each book he had an engraving 'cut in brasse' by 'the best workmen in that kind', among them Thomas Coxon, following the fine perspective illustrations by Porro for the 1584 edition of *Orlando*, and supplementing once from Valgrisi's edition of 1565.[7] As Miss B. E. Burton has shown[8] he freely used critical matter from the 1584 edition provided by Ruscelli, Pigna, Eugenio, Lavezuola, Garofalo, and Bononome: he himself often refers to Fornari and knew of Castelvetro. The long notes are his own and they came under fire from his contemporaries so that he grumbles in the Preface: 'Sure they were a worke (as I may so call it) of supererogation, and I would wish sometimes they had bin left out, and the rather, if I be in such faire possibilitie to be thought a foole, or fantasticall for my labour.' Posterity is more grateful, the notes give the book an intimate character none too common in that age. Harington is a singularly friendly Elizabethan and confiding to the point of indiscretion. He was designing a book to be enjoyed and

[1] Ed. T. Crockett in Scottish Text Society, ii, 1913: see also J. Purves, *Italian Studies*, iii, 1946, and M. P. McDiarmid, *R.E.S.*, xxiv, 1948.
[2] B.M. MS. Add. 27632, f. 43. See E. K. Chambers, *Elizabethan Stage*, iii. 183.
[3] *Firste Fruites*, 1578, cap. 25.
[4] *Catharos*, 1591, p. 25ᵛ.
[5] *The Third Universitie of England*, 1615, cap. 13, published as an appendix to Stow's *Annales*.
[6] *Conversations*, ed. R. F. Patterson, 1923, p. 4.
[7] T. Rich, *Harington and Ariosto*, 1940.
[8] In an unpublished thesis: Bodley MS. B.Litt., d. 323.

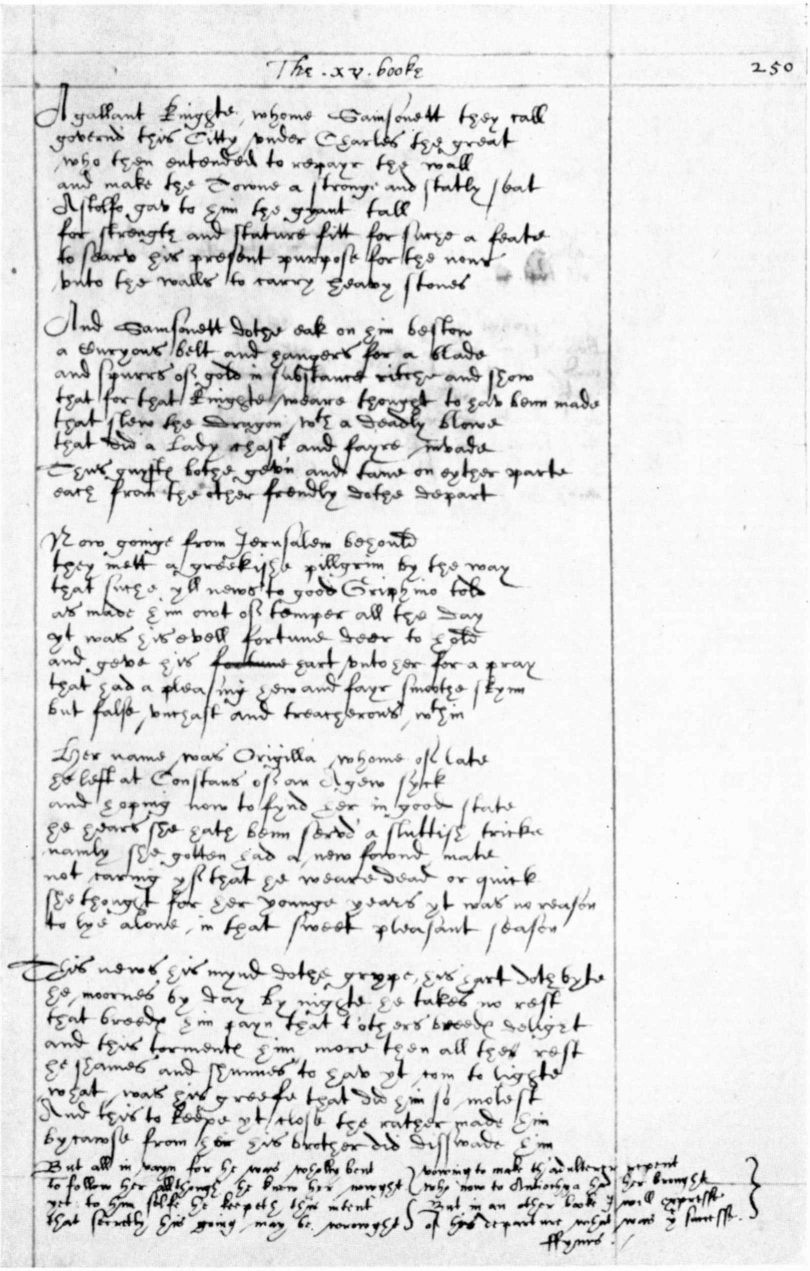
The .xv. booke 250

A gallant knight, whome Sainsonett they call
govern'd this Citty under Charles the great
who then entended to repayre the wall
and make the Towne a stronge and stately seat
Astolfo gave to him the giant tall
for strength and stature fitt for such a feate
to serve his present purpose for the nonce
unto the walls to carry heavy stones

And Sainsonett dothe eak on him bestow
a curious belt and hangers for a blade
and spurres of gold in substance riche and shew
that for that knight were thought to have been made
that slew the Dragon with a deadly blowe
that did a Lady reskew and fayre made
Then gyfts bothe given and taken on eyther parte
each from the other frendly dothe depart

Now goinge from Jerusalem beyonde
they mett a greekishe pillgrim by the way
that such ill newes to good Griphino told
as made him out of temper all the day
yt was his evell fortune dear to hold
and gave his ~~fortune~~ hart unto her for a pray
that had a pleasing hew and fayre smoothe skyn
but false, unchast and treacherous within

Her name was Origilla whome of late
he left at Constans of an ague sick
and hoping now to fynd her in good state
he heares she hath been served a sluttish tricke
namely she gotten had a new found mate
not caring yf that he weare dead or quick
she thought for her younge years yt was no reason
to lye alone, in that sweet pleasant season

This newes his mynd dothe grype, his hart dothe byte
he moornes by day by night he takes no rest
that breeds him payn that others breeds delight
and this tormente him more then all the rest
he shames and shunnes to have yt com to lighte
what was his greefe that did him so molest
And this to keepe yt close the rather made him
bycause from her his brother did dissuade him

But all in vayn for he was wholly bent / vowing to make th'adulterer repent
to follow her although he knew her nought / who now to Antiochia had her brought
yet to him selfe he keepeth this intent / But in an other booke I will expresse
that secretly his going may be wrought / of his departure what was the successe.

ffynis.

MS. Rawl. Poet. 125, p. 250. *Orlando Furioso*. XV. Showing the final stanza written in from the verso

he moves alongside his reader pointing things out as he goes, turning aside from his author to explain, interpolate, and comment, eager to help over hard places, occasionally bold to improve on a moral, intent on savouring all thoroughly. His accessibility is well known. It is in full evidence in the Letters and Epigrams; it has been admirably popularized by Raleigh and more recently touched on by Grimble who uses a few salient passages from the *Orlando* notes to supplement the more directly autobiographical material available.[1] But this has been done chiefly in search of Harington without Ariosto, just as other readers profess to prefer to take their Ariosto without Harington. There is also a yield from the pursuit of Harington in Ariosto's company, and it may be worth while staying a little upon Harington, his book.

In 1923 Raleigh remarked in passing that 'an examination of this forgotten work, which anticipates, in places, the cadences of Shakespeare's twin poems, would ask a chapter'.[2] It merits more than a chapter and it has since received careful treatment in two theses already mentioned, one unpublished by the late Barbara Burton, and the other by Townsend Rich printed in 1940. I have often been indebted to the careful comparisons and countings of both to check my own findings, but I shall concentrate upon a line of approach that was not wholly pertinent to the first or apparently possible for the second, and attend to Harington licking his work into shape.

It so happens that this is a book which we can see in the making a little more clearly than is usual in its period. We have it also in manuscript. The unique interest of the British Museum MS. Add. 18920 has been shown by Sir Walter Greg in 'An Elizabethan Printer and his Copy'[3] and by Dr. Percy Simpson in his *Proof-Reading in the Sixteenth, Seventeenth and Eighteenth Centuries* (1935).[4] This manuscript gives us Books XIV–XLVI in the actual form that was used by Field. A manuscript in the Bodleian is earlier than the one in the British Museum but it has not the distinction of being printer's copy. It contains the first twenty-four books and therefore overlaps with MS. Add. 18920 for eleven books and provides a manuscript version for the first thirteen which is otherwise lacking. It was examined by Miss Burton who made an observation about

---

[1] *The Harington Family*, 1957.
[2] Walter Raleigh, *Some Authors*, 1923, p. 148.
[3] *Library*, 4th ser., iv, 1923, pp. 102–18.
[4] See pp. 71–75.

one set of its illustrations and remarked some of its readings in her section on Harington's alterations, otherwise it has not, I believe, been scrutinized. This manuscript (Rawlinson poet. 125, formerly 14618) is described as 'written shortly before 1591 partly by Sir J. Harington . . . with autograph corrections . . . with inserted engravings from both English and Italian printed editions, some coloured'. It is a small paper book measuring 9 by 6½ inches. The binding, which has been repaired, is solid brown leather heavily tooled in the style of the early seventeenth century. The collation is noted as 'vi+512 pages for 98/9 are one and 495 is double', but this statement fails to remark that there is an accidental jump from p. 276 to p. 377 which reduces the pages to 412. The second of the two front end-papers is of a thick texture with a watermark of a hand and star resembling Briquet No. 11381 with the substitution of H H for the L.P. of his example (Metz, 1552). The single end-paper at the back has the Briquet watermark No. 14048 (Angoulême, 1589, and Quimperlé, 1592). The manuscript itself is of a much thinner, smoother paper. The pages are pricked for ruling into a box frame with faint red lines, and one unpaged blank sheet is also ruled up. The lines occasionally run over the writing and the illustrations, as on p. 436, and stop short of the pasted slip on p. 198, and are broken for a rewritten stanza on p. 250, so that the ruling would seem to have been the last process in tidying up the sheets into a little book. Red ink is used once on p. 19 for a heading. The illustrations are of three kinds. The frontispiece consists of a poor specimen of the engraving prepared for Book I of the first edition. It has been trimmed down and is defective across the top. The word 'Bataglia' is missing from the middle and 'the battel' has been supplied in ink. Two stanzas before the end of Book IV another spare engraving is inserted as p. 61/62 and labelled 'the v booke'. It corresponds to the illustration for Book V: the stub after p. 70 is conjugate with the illustration which has been neatly coloured, chiefly in purple, red, and gold. As pp. 168/9, with the stub between pp. 155/6, there is an amusingly ingenious adaptation. A picture of Perseus and Andromeda is pasted in and headed 'The xth booke'. Below the figures the descriptive lines have been heavily scored out but they can be deciphered as

> Andromede fuerat monstris devota marinis
> Haec eadem Persei nobilis uxor erat.

Andromeda has been made over into Angelica and so labelled in

Withe those of Esperia cam Corydano
and Dorybon did come wth those of Sot
wth those of Nasomany + Onlyano
Emige Agrycalt Amonyos thardy dw goll
mealabufero came wth them of Afiano
the rest dotze ffynadwre in order soll
Ballastro those that follond orst Cardotio
Wose of Canarya and of Morotto

ffrom Mulga and Arsilla otgers came
the frtste theire formor Captayn still dotze holde
vnto the next the Emige a nero dotze name
on Corynows a trusty man and bold
then Balyvosse a man of obell fame
Clarindo next of vohome great dovde ar told
Sobryno next a man of older age
In all the Campe was none more voyse & sage

Wose of Getulya came wth Tymedont
wth Marytaldo those of Bolga went
and those of Costa came wth Ballmy front
theire formor Lord Eis byfe in battell spont
then came the Emige of Algier Rodomont
that Lathe into Turky had been sont
to bringe some nero supplyes of Egrfe & men
and back agayne was nero returnd as then

In all the Campe was not a man more stout
In all the Campe's was not a man more stronge
nor one of vohome the front the stood more in dout
was their the Turkishe army all amonge
In Agramant nor in Marsilios wont
nor all the followers dw to them bolonge
Besyde he was wth made them dread hym twere
the greatest enemy to one boleose

Now all their bande woone mustord saving two
those of Noryfia and of Tromyson
Emige Agramant dotze mandoll what they do
he knores not whear to hear of them nor when
now as he was dispatchyng hedu vnto
some messengor before one of the men
that sawbote the Emige of Tromyson in East
came and dishorderd all that East been past

from Mulga and Arsilla others came,
the first they former capten still dose hold,
vnto the next the king a new doth name,
on Corineus a trusty man and bold,
then Babylesse a man of evell fame,
Clarindo next of whome great deeds are told,
Sobryno next a man of their age,
In all the campe none more wyse and sage.

22

Those of Getulya came with Rymedonte
with marybaldo, those of Bolga wernt,
and those of Cosra came with Balinfronte,
theyr former Lord his lyfe in battell spent,
then came the king of Algier Rodomonte,
that lately into Emry had been sent,
to bring some new supplyes of horse and men,
and back agayn were new returnd to then.

23

In all the campe was not a man more stowt,
In all the campe, was not a man more stronger,
nor on of whom the frennche stood more in dowbt
were then the turkesse army, all amonge.
In Agramantes now in Mauselrick court,
nor all the followers did to them belonge,
besyde, he was, who made them dred him there
the greatest enemy to over beleefe.

24

Now all theyr bandes wear mustred saving two,
those of Roristia, and of Tremysen,
Seing Agramant dose, marvell what they doo,
he knowes not where, to heer of them nor when,
Now as he was dispatching heer sonto
som messenger, behold on of the men
that sawd the king of Tremysen, in hast
came, and dyscovered all that had been past.

26

Of king quoth by fortune and ylhaprove,
the noble king of Alfyrd and Manyland,
hapned to meet a stewtt king of Aframonte,
wohyle wt theyr bandes, they travelld hither ward
he overthrew them both, (oh hard mysshappmt)
and kild and spoyld and drave away theyr gard,
And syr quoth he, I think his force ys such,
to all your campe he wowld have done as moche.

Sobrino.

f. 11
105
b Rodomonte, a
notable turke of
whome moche en=
sewth in the booke.
he was kinge of
Algyre and ys called
sometyme Algyre, or
the Sarzan king.

The 2 Rubiano and, a gallant king,
and Agramantes cosin dardinell,
whether some owld dd at theyr window sing,
or other hableff byrd, I cannot tell,
wt off wee see, yt ys an vsuall thing,
& some presage ones mischeeff shall befall
but have yt were appoyntd in heaven on hye
what tyme and howr next dye they both

Cant xig°. in hys
latter end.

British Museum, MS. Add. 18920, p. 3. *Orlando Furioso.* XIV. Showing
the stanza omitted from the Bodley MS. and consequent renumbering

ink; Perseus is dubbed Rogero; the monster is now Orco and the horse fitted up with claws is Hippogriffo. The page is tinted. The engraver, Phls Gall., was perhaps the Philipp Galle (1537–1612) of Haarlem and Antwerp noted by A. D. Hind in his *Short History of Engraving and Etching* (1911). I have not been able to identify the book from which the page was cut. Simpler illustrations are supplied by pasting in at any point in a page, to serve as canto headings, small cuts (88 mm. × 48 mm.) which in design are identical with those found in Giolito's 1548 edition of *Orlando*. The side ornaments are either of fishes or swags. Miss Burton detected that there is not a perfect correspondence with the Bodley copy and noted that between 1542 and 1559 Giolito published fifteen editions. I find that ten out of the twenty-three match exactly. All except the one for Book XXII are coloured, often very clumsily. At the foot of p. 460 there are signs of something once pasted in, now lost. It would appear that the manuscript was made up into a little book and decorated at once, for on p. 250 Harington has rewritten the last stanza of XV into a tiny space presumably because the illustration stuck in to head XVI was obscuring the last three lines at the top of p. 251. One is reminded of a project for 'an Ariosto in Englishe in coulours' referred to in the Stationers Register for 23 April 1593.[1] Rich records the sale on 11 June 1923 at Sotheby's of a 1591 edition hand-coloured.

The text begins formally 'Orlando furioso. Canto primo. the .1. booke', and each book is clearly headed. There are no verse arguments as yet and the stanzas are not numbered: XIV. 24 is omitted. The marginal notes to twenty-three stanzas in the first book correspond in substance but not in phrasing to those worked up for the printer. Only two notes are provided in what remains: 'Phenix' against XV. 28 and 'Heliogabalus was surnamed Varyus' for XVII. 1.

The catch-words are frequent but not quite regular, for many seem to have been added possibly by another hand, certainly by someone using a crisper quill such as is used for an occasional addition (pp. 19 and 48), for some running titles and a few paragraph marks (pp. 100 and 148).

The Bodley Catalogue claims only the corrections as in Harington's autograph but it is tempting to make a case for much more. The first two books are almost certainly in the same hand as the

[1] Greg and Boswell, *Records of the Court of the Stationers Company, 1576–1602*.

rewritten stanza on p. 250 which is undoubtedly his writing. The transition to a slightly more current hand than is found in this passage is made almost imperceptibly and may be no more than the modification which is any individual's habit. The general impression when this book is confronted with MS. Add. 18920 is that the hands are so similar that allowing for changes of ink, quill, and paper they could be one and the same. It is almost impossible to tell from which manuscript a facsimile page is taken.

On close analysis, however, there are some differences to be reckoned with. The capitals A, C, D, and H are found in two forms in both manuscripts but each has a favourite use. The same is true of e, g, and h; while d, l, and r tend to be more sharply defined in the British Museum manuscript and i, m, and n are led up to by firmer strokes. These differences are very slight and not exclusive; all other letters are identical. It can be seen from specimen XLV (d) in Greg's *Literary Autographs* that Harington commonly made an italic capital M with a distinctive loop. This I cannot parallel in the Bodley manuscript where the letter is rare because of the paucity of marginal notes. When it occurs in the verses (III. 38, 43, 55, and 56) it is not made in this way. On the strength of this looped M, however, in conjunction with other features in the italic and secretary hands, MS. Rawl. B. 162 (the copy of the letter about the Chancellorship) might well be claimed as an addition to this autograph. Umfreville wrote to Rawlinson that ''tis only a copy', but it has been corrected and annotated in exactly Harington's style and may be his throughout.

Comparing the text with the first edition I have noticed some 456 differences. Of these, thirty-nine should be regarded as mere slips; the remainder may be roughly classified as alterations to smooth the metre; to bring tense and number into accord; to make trivial adjustments as between other / tother, ne / nor, ar / be, his / the, takes / takst, and so forth. More interesting are a few instances of recasting, very occasionally for accuracy, often for euphony, or more telling expression. I have noted five cases where the manuscript might be preferred to the first edition and in the first four of these the choice is confirmed by the readings of the second (III. 59 thinn / fall; VI. 60 beaten / better; X. 38 more / mo; XIX. 22 prowd / poore; XXIV. 67 sowles / sole). At XV. 11 and XVI. 42 there are rephrasings of some importance and at XXIV. 88 a blank is left, presumably in embarrassment at the clumsy rhyming of

X Ch. M. of Amor Constans also wrote
M M.

Si quid adhuc ego sum muneris omne sui est.

And therfore in hope to his Maᵗⁱᵉ seruyce ther I am
bett content to leaue my Cowntry and sweetest home, In wᶜʰ
thowgh I possesse not all that magnificall sollace, yᵗ
yᵒ Loᵖ and soch great states are owners of, yet I enioy
some of those proyvat contentments that greater men wysh
for and want, and least yowr Loᵖ showld ymagin that
this conceyt for Ireland ys a new sprung desyre in mee
yt was my hap to wryte (now more then trro yeares past)
a kynde of farewell to all poetry and hygst studyes, e
as yt were a tender of my devoted seruyce to his Maᵗⁱᵉ
in what kynde so ever of studyes hee wold employ mee, e
~~that~~, wᶜʰ being not onplea-
sing to his Maᵗⁱᵉ then, I presume shall not be tedyowse to
yᵉ Loᵖ now. In hæc verba.

Musa Jocosa, meos solari assueta dolores
    Et mecum medijs ludere docta malis,
Me peregrinantem comitata, et castra sequentem,
    Ausa mihi in tumidis et comes ire fretis,
Quæ me ruricolam, tractantem et aratra sequuta es
    Nec poteras thalamis abstinuisse meis
Te nunc Ætonæ (namq̃ hinc es nata) relinquo,
    Filius hic hæres te colat vsq̃ meus.
Nunc iuvat oblitis meditari seria ludis,
    Hos annos, animum hunc Musa severa decet
Jam pro fictijs solatia vera relucent,
    Cum Dominum, Regem cum resaluto meum.
Jam dabitur veras audire ac reddere voces   Jam.
    Nostra sat est pietas dissimulata diu.

MS. Rawl. B. 162. 'A Short View of the State of Ireland', p. 13

'backe' with 'backe' which is never improved. A major change at
x. 58 I will deal with later.

An examination of the eleven books common to the two manuscripts shows that Bodley is likely to have been the original (or a
fair copy of that original) from which Harington worked as he
prepared MS. Add. 18920 for the printer. Spelling, capitalization,
and punctuation do not conform exactly, but wherever there is a
verbal discrepancy between Bodley and the first edition the B.M.
manuscript shows the intermediate stages of correction. Where the
process is more elaborate than the substitution of a word or two
and requires a pasted slip discernible traces sometimes remain of
the first draft to tell the same tale (e.g. xv. 11). The most convincing
instance is the omission of stanza xiv. 24 in both: it is added in the
margin of the B.M. and all the subsequent stanzas are renumbered.
In xv. 13 even the underlining and star marking the reference to a
North-West passage correspond exactly. Only one marking, that
against xiv. 53, is not reproduced in the copy for the printer.

Out of the 220-odd instances noted some forty show a correspondence between B.M. and 1591 against Bodley, but they are very
trivial variants such as, other / tother, he / so, both / do, one / ton.
There are also a few cases when the translator may well have
substituted a synonym as he went along; three times in xvii (11,
56, and 68) and again in xviii. 34 and xxiv. 61 and 62 a word so
ventured has been retracted. In xiv. 108 'greyhound' becomes
'grewnd' but reverts in 1634. I have noted a few cases where the
manuscripts agree against the first edition, and two where Bodley
and 1591 stand against B.M. (xxii. 33 and xxiv. 67). Harington's hesi-
tations over a word in xix. 53 (Ariosto xix. 77) are amusing. Marfisa's
mount is described as

un destrier leardo
Tutto sparso di macchie, e di rottelle.

In Bodley there is a gap

his cullor   was wth many a spott.

In Add. 18920 there is a strange word 'powesse' for which I can
find no parallel. Harington has gone over some fainter letters and
left the 'w' and the 'sse' in darker ink such as is used on the same
page for other correcting touches. In 1591 it reads

His coullor pyd and deckt with many a spot

and this in 1607 is modified to 'pide powderd with'.

Sir Walter Greg drew attention to the engaging intrusion of a reference to Hillyard in the B.M. version which was then relegated to the Notes. As a parallel to this in the Bodley manuscript there is a little speculation on Drake. A parenthesis concluding x. 58 runs

> (Contrary to the course of woorthie *Drake*
> Who in the space of twelv monthes as men saye
> followd the sonne untill he gaynd a daye).

But the patriotic anachronism was too much for the translator's conscience and is sobered in 1591 to

> And though the thing were much to undertake,
> Yet hope of praise makes men no travell shunne,
> To say another day, this we have donne.

The reference to Drake is drafted as a note to xv. 14.

The literary interest of the manuscripts is in displaying how Harington worked at his craft, and his polishing can be compared with the changes for the second edition. There, to judge from the sampling of seven cantos chosen at random, the proportion of corrections is slighter—an average of seventeen to the canto—but the changes are the same in kind. They hardly ever affect the sense but attend to the niceties of versification. They match what he has to say of the technique of rhyming in the third section of the *Apologie*. Plainly, he was prepared to take much trouble; it amused him to fiddle and file. If Elizabeth bade the fool take himself away, he served his 'sweet madonna' well behind the scenes.

The impression we get from the manuscripts might seem contradictory to what is commonly said about Harington's liberties, not to say licences, as a translator, but the contrast is not inexplicable. His purpose was to make a readable version, not a crib, for young Elizabethans. He is dealing with a book he has enjoyed and he wants to spread the pleasure. He is quite frank and commends the first six books to anyone who cares to test him. This is what we find. In Books I, II, V, and VI no stanzas are lost, the rendering is close and often neat; there are even a few extra details as in the description of Bradamante's hair and dress (V. 26, 38, and 47) to offset the feebler phrasing in V. 12, 57, and 63. In VI. 19 he slightly adapts an allusion. Book III is fourteen stanzas short and Book IV, thirteen. Bradamante's genealogy is contracted and some details of her journey with Brunello are skipped, the conversation between Bradamante and Atlante is condensed.

The total loss of 728 stanzas which shocked Huggins into a vicious comment may certainly make us suspicious. How much have Englishmen got? Some 4,114 stanzas, of which two of pious musing represent additions to the Italian (X. 74, 75 cp. Ariosto 94 and XXIV. 71–73 cp. Ariosto 88, 89).

An instance of free translation more revealing than countings, and with interest of another kind, occurs at the end of Book XXVII. Here Harington simplifies a subtle passage and revises a detail which seems to have caught the eye of a greater contemporary. I cannot now read the second verse of Donne's *Song* without raising a ghost from *Orlando Furioso* XXVII. 123, 124.

If thou beest borne to strange sights,
Things invisible to see,
Ride ten thousand daies and nights,
Till age snow white haires on thee,
Thou, when thou retorn'st, wilt tell mee
All strange wonders that befell thee,
And sweare,
No where
Lives a woman true, and faire.

See
The arguments on
the return from Cadiz
in New Meta.

The echo may be accidental; I would not advance the *Orlando* as a source but rather as a possible, fertilizing association. The detail of whitening hair in Ariosto would be too commonplace to startle if it stood alone, but it comes at a crucial point where one story is grafted into another and both are charged with the cynicism from which the lyric essence is distilled. It needs a substantial context to make my point.

Discord has been at work in the pagan camp and Agramante, unable to choose between the claims of Mandricardo and Rodomonte for the possession of Doralice, has left the choice to her. She takes Mandricardo, to the astonishment of Rodomonte who rides off in a rage with a couple of servants, roaring to himself like an afflicted bull. He rails against the fickleness of women. Why did an angry god fashion the sex in addition to other vexations of Nature? Why may men not propagate like trees? If women are necessary, then they are necessary evils; he curses them roundly:

Importune, superbe, e dispettose,
Prive d'amor, di fede, e di consiglio;
Temerarie, crudeli, inique, ingrate;
Per pestilentia eterna al mondo nate. (121)

So far Harington is reasonably close, and then, for some reason, he contracts violently and so foregoes a passage of Ariosto's inexhaustible irony. The poet intervenes upon his hero's vituperation and remarks demurely, first, that Rodomonte must be exaggerating, for his one or two bad women, a hundred good ones may be found; and then, slyly undercutting his ostentatious fairness, he admits that, all the same, these faithful ones have never come *his* way. Still, he will not give up hope and before he dies, before more white hairs come, he will go on seeking so that there may chance to come a day in which he can say that one woman has kept her word. Such an event he will celebrate by tongue and pen, and in verse and prose.

> Se ben di quante io n'habbia fin qui amate,
> Non n'habbia mai trovata una fedele;
> Perfide tutte io non vo dir, nè ingrate,
> Ma darne colpa al mio destin crudele,
> Molte or ne sono, e più già ne son state,
> Che non dan causa ad huom che si querele;
> Ma mia fortuna vuol, che s'una ria
> Ne sia tra cento, io di lei preda sia.
>
> Pur vo tanto cercar prima ch'io mora,
> Anzi prima che' l crin più mi s'imbianchi,
> Che forse dirò un dì, che per me ancora
> Alcuna sia, che di sua fè non manchi.
> Se questo avien (che di disperanza fuora
> Io non ne son) non fia mai ch'io mi stanchi
> Di farla a mia possanza gloriosa
> Con lingua, con inchiostro, e in verso e in prosa.
>
> (123, 124)

None of this is in the English version. Resuming the tale the translator keeps even with his original. Rodomonte makes for Provence and reaches an inn. For a while he sits moodily apart and then inquires of all present how many are married, and of those how many believe their wives faithful. Only the host doubts and he claims that the rest are deceived. The man who has a chaste wife is a phoenix, there is only one of his kind at a time. He had thought himself to be that lucky one, but since he has talked with a Venetian, one Valerio, he has been persuaded that his peace of mind was illusory. He offers to tell one of Valerio's stories to convince the rest. They agree, Rodomonte eagerly, and the indecorous tale of Giocondo is what they get in Book XXVIII.

Rodomonte's invective had attracted other readers before Harington published, for in the same year T. L.(odge) in *Catharos* quotes
three stanzas against women from Canto XXVII. 119–121, adding
smugly, 'I had rather some other should take the paynes to translate these verses into our mother tongue than myselfe'. Harington's
omission seems odd at first, he was not squeamish and Ariosto's
wit would not be lost on him. But his evasion was perhaps deliberate
and he is not without irony on his own account. In the *Apologie* in
the *Anatomie of the Metamorpho-sed Ajax* there is a defensive passage
to which I referred earlier. This, taken whole, may throw some
light on the way in which Rodomonte has been handled. Harington
takes up the charge that he had wronged not only ladies of the
Court but the whole sex on the evidence of 'a stanse in *Hary Osto*
beginning thus

> *Yee Courtly Dames that are both kinde and true,*
> *Unto your Lordes, if kinde and true be any,*
> *As sure I am in all your lovely crue,*
> *Of so chast minde, there be not over many:*

These four lines are from the opening of Canto XXII. He then quotes
four from XXVIII. 36 with one trifling inaccuracy. These are followed
by six lines curiously compounded of a couplet from Rodomonte's
curse (XXVII. 98) stuck on to four lines from Giocondo's accusation
to the same effect (XXVIII. 36). In the verse, says Harington, 'I did
but followe my author', and since these verses were 'so flat against
my conscience' . . . 'inserted somewhat <u>more</u> than once, to qualifie
the rigor of those hard speeches. For example, against rai<u>ling</u>
Rodomont, I said thus:

> *I tremble to set downe in my poore verse,*
> *The blasphemies that he to speake presumes:*
> *And writing this, I do know this that I,*
> *Oft in my hart do give my pen the lye.'*

This is the second half of XXVII. 99 where the translation had
begun to contract.

And in another place, to free mee from all suspition of pretended
malice, and to shewe a manifest evidence of intended love, where my
author very sparingly had praised some wives, I added of mine own
(   ) so much more I thinke was never saide for them, which I will
heere set downe *ad perpetuam rei memoriam*, and that al posteritie may
knowe howe good a husband I would bee thought.

The empty bracket refers to a sly marginal note 'Mine owne subauditur verse or wife which you will'.

The stanza which follows as evidence of his good will towards women looks well enough, but it happens to be an improvisation for the purpose, consisting of two lines freshly devised to lead into a quotation from the reply by the contented but deceived guests in answer to Rodomonte's question whether they were happily wedded.

> *Loe here a verse in laud of loving wives*
> *Extolling still our happie married state,*
> *I say they are the comfort of our lives,*
> *Drawing a happie yoke, without debate.*
> *A plai-fellow, that far off all griefe drives,*
> *A Steward, early that provides and late;*
> *Faithfull, and kind, sober, and sweet, and trustie.*
> *Nurse to weake age, and pleasure to the lustie.*

This is Harington's elaboration (tongue in cheek, one must suppose) for the simple reply in XXVII. 135.

> fer tuti risposta,
> Che si credeano haverle e caste e buone.

The English wit is far coarser but it is not negligible and it is no more perhaps than such a joke as Petruchio might have thrown for his Kate to catch, especially when we consider it alongside the pleasant anecdote in one of his letters:

The Queene did once aske my wife in merrie sorte, how she kepte my goode wyll and love. . . . My *Mall*, in wise and discreete manner, tolde her Highnesse, she had confidence in her husbandes understandinge and courage, well founded on her own stedfastness not to offend or thwart, but to cherishe and obey, hereby did persuade her husbande of her own affectione, and in so doinge did commande his. Go to, go to, mistresse, saithe the Queene, you are wisely bente I finde; after suche sorte do I keepe the good wyll of all my husbandes, my good people. . . .[1]

The remarks on matrimony in the notes to Book V are consistent with this kindly shrewdness and pointed by the comment on Book XLIV.

In dame *Beatrice* we may note the notable ambicious humor of women, specially in matching their children above their calling, . . . neither are the wiser sort of men free from this folly, for if they may match their

---

[1] *Nugae Antiquae,* 1779, ii. 223.

daughters, so as they may say my Lord my sonne, they thinke they have God almightie by the toe (as the proverbe saith) whereas many times they have the divell by the claw.

One would expect Donne to read his Ariosto in the original but would not so readily guess that Shakespeare might do so. Yet the editors of the New Cambridge edition of *Othello* (p. xiv) pick up an older suggestion and argue a connexion from an echo in the description (XLVI. 80) of the pavilion embroidered over 2,000 years ago by 'Una donzella della Terra d'Ilia' (or according to Boiardo, by a sybil) working with 'furor profetico' and Othello's

> There's magic in the web of it
> A sibyl in her prophetic fury sewed the silk.

The remarkable expression is lost in Harington's

> By faire *Cassandra*, that same Prophetesse.   (XLVI. 64)

Spenser had no chance, or need, to have an *Orlando* in English, and indeed it is to Spenser's story of the Squire of Dames that Harington pays a compliment in the notes to Book XLIII.

Younger contemporaries, however, used the translation freely and two great ones can be tracked in its snow. Bacon remembered the fable of the swans in Book XXXIV.[1] Milton quoted and slightly adapted eight lines from the same book (st. 72 and 79) in 'Of Reformation in England'[2] and annotated his own copy of the 1591 edition and wrote at the end of Book XLVI

> Questo libro due volte Io letto
> Sept. 21. 1642.[3]

Lesser folk gratified Harington by their appreciation.

'My "Ariosto" has been entertained into Gallway before I came. When I got thither, a great lady, a young lady, and a fair lady, read herself asleep, nay dead, with a tale of it; the verse, I think, so lively figured her fortune.'[4] In 1599 he found the Earl of Tyrone's sons, lads of between thirteen and fifteen,

of a good chearful aspect, freckle-faced, not tall of stature, but strong, and well-set; both of them [learning] the English tongue; I gave them (not without the advice of Sir William Warren) my English translation

---

[1] *Works*, ed. Spedding, i. 510.   [2] Columbia edition, iii. 27.
[3] J. M. French, *Life Records of Milton*, ii. 78, and E. A. Haug, *M.L.Q.*, 1943, iv. 291.
[4] *Nugae Antiquae*, ed. Park, i. 260.

of "Ariosto", which I got at Dublin; which their teachers took very thankfully, and soon after shewed it the earl, who call'd to see it openly, and would needs hear some part of it read. I turn'd (as it had been by chance) to the beginning of the 45th canto, and some other passages of the book, which he seemed to like so well, that he solemnly swore his boys should read all the book over to him.[1]

It entertained Lady Arabella Stuart, Robert Sidney, and Prince Henry, too.

What did such readers lose by the version? Not the world of fine fabling, that is whole; but some of the exquisite detail and splendid rhetoric. There is a coarsening and an impression of too facile a wit, a loss of the blandest irony. Their going would be on a stanza that wheeled along smoothly but without the spring of the Italian octave. They would be tickled, or vexed, by a way of rhyming which brings Byron, and even Browning, to a modern reader's ear. They would get an easy-going book where the substance is safe but the style muted. They would get the speed and intertexture of the narrative: the splendid tales of Orlando's frenzy and recovery, of Rodomonte's passionate energy, of the vicissitudes of the loves of Bradamante and Ruggiero; all these are there, and so is Astolfo's charm. It is a pretty coincidence that Ariosto's most attractive character should be this English duke. When Orlando's madness is storming itself out and may seem overpowering, when the intricacies are almost beyond our following (thought not beyond Spenser's), there come the episodes of Astolfo's independence, better than the stories inset, though not more popular than some of these. Astolfo is fancy free; we learn later that he fell in love—Harington picks this up from the *Cinque Canti* and works it into a marginal note (XXXIV. 85)—but for the most part he is untrammelled by ladies and happily glides about on his borrowed hippogriff. It is notoriously hard to choose, but perhaps the canto which shows both author and translator to most even advantage, if not at their best, for it would be rash to choose for Ariosto, is XXXIV in which Astolfo recovers Orlando's wits from St. John and Harington rises to the demands of the satirical reflective touches. His version is close and reads remarkably well.

> He saw some of his own lost time and deeds,
> But yet he knew them not to be his own,
> They seemd to him disguisd in so straunge weeds,

[1] *Nugae Antiquae*, ed. Park, i. 249.

Till his instructer made them better known:
Lastlie, the thing which no man thinks he needs,
Yet each man needeth most, to him was shown,
Namely mans wit, which here we leese so fast,
As that one substance, all the other past.

It seemd to be a body moyst and soft,
Apt to ascend by ev'ry exhalation,
And when it hither mounted was aloft,
It there was kept in potts of such a fashion,
As we calle Iarrs, where oyle is kept in oft:
The Duke beheld with no small admiration,
The Iarrs of wit, amongst which one had writ,
Upon the side thereof *Orlandos wit.*

This vessell bigger was then all the rest,
And ev'ry vessell had ingrav'n with art,
His name, that earst the wit therein possest:
There of his own, the Duke did finde a part,
And much he musd, and much him selfe he blest,
To see some names of men of great desart,
That thinke they have great store of wit, and bost it,
When it playne appeard they quite had lost it.   (81–83)

This was not turned by a man without a gift (and he believed in gift), or without the careful artistry which we can test for ourselves in the manuscripts. He claimed that he would rather men should see and know that 'I borrow all, then that I steale any: and I would wish to be called rather one of the not worst translators, then one of the meaner makers'.[1] His estimation is not far out. He was never afraid of making mistakes nor, in another sense, was he ever mean. His life in the country had its troubles too and shows up the same qualities of realism and good humour.

I hear muche (by pryvate means) of strange plottes by Cobham, Grey, Raleighe, and others. I have no concerns of this sorte, save that my man Ralphe hathe stolen two cheeses from my dairy-house;—I wish he were chokede herewyth! and yet the fellow hathe five childerne; I wyll not sue hym if he repentethe and amendethe.[2]

When things went badly at Court there was always a retreat into the life of a 'private country knight, that lives among clouted shoes, in his frize jacket and galloshes'.[3] Within this country dull-

---

[1] *Apologie*, pt. 3, sig. ¶ viii.   [2] *Nugae Antiquae*, ed. Park, i. 180.
[3] Ibid., p. 311.

ness he knew how to keep himself alive. In April 1603 he wrote to Lord Howard

I am now settynge forthe for the countrie, where I will read Petrarch, Ariosto, Horace, and suche wise ones. I will make verses on the maidens, and give my wine to the maisters; but it shall be such as I do love, and do love me. I do muche delight to meete my good freindes, and dis-course of getting rid of our foes. Each nighte do I spende, or much better parte thereof, in counceil with the aunciente examples of lerninge; I con over their histories, their poetrie, their instructions, and thence glean my own proper conducte in matters bothe of merrimente or discretion; otherwyse, my goode Lorde, I ne'er had overcome the rugged pathes of Ariosto, nor wonne the highe palme of glorie, which you broughte unto me, (I venture to saie it) namely, our late Queenes approbation, esteeme, and rewarde. How my poetrie may be relishde in tyme to come, I will not hazard to saie.[1]

Here we catch sight of his 'folly' in its foundations. He enjoyed a good book and he has added one to our own store.

[1] *Nugae Antiquae,* ed. Park, i. 338.

Lady Elizabeth stayed at Haringtons nov. 1605 when Gun Powder plot failed. She was to have been kidnapped and made queen.

Two Notes

W. W. GREG

(i) *When was Twelfth Night?*

THERE is, of course, no question what and when Twelfth Day was and is; it is the last of the twelve days of Christmas, the feast of the Epiphany on 6 January.[1] And I imagine that anyone asked when Twelfth Night was would reply offhand that it was the night of Twelfth Day. I fancy he would be right.

There is, however, no less an authority than the *Oxford English Dictionary* to the contrary. It gives, 'Twelfth-night. . . . The evening before Twelfth-day, formerly observed as a time of merry-making', and 'Twelfth-even', the meaning of which is not in doubt, it defines as 'The eve of Twelfth-day; Twelfth-night'.[2] This authority, however, I have the temerity to question.[3] Of the eight quotations given not one suggests that Twelfth Night is distinct from Twelfth Day, and one medieval example definitely identifies them.[4]

What evidence is there respecting actual usage in Elizabethan and Jacobean times? Evidently it was in connexion with the masques that Ben Jonson wrote for the entertainment of the Court that one was most likely to find what one wanted, and a rapid search at once satisfied me that not only had editors from Malone onward generally

---

[1] But from Christmas on 25 Dec. to Epiphany on 6 Jan. inclusive there are thirteen days not twelve. The explanation is presumably that Christmas Day is a festival of the Church, and that the popular Christmas festivities—the pagan Saturnalia—did not begin till the feast of Stephen on 26 Dec. Christmas Day was not one of the days of Christmas.

[2] The letter T appears to have been edited by Sir James Murray in 1916. There is no entry concerning Twelfth Night in the *Supplement* of 1933, and the latest (fourth) edition of the *Concise Oxford Dictionary* (1951) repeats the same information. Dr. C. T. Onions, however, revising the third edition of the *Shorter Oxford Dictionary* in 1955, took the generally accepted view, writing: 'Twelfth-night. The night of the twelfth day after Christmas (6 January) marked by merrymaking.'

[3] Dr. Leslie Hotson, who always knows his own mind and is never afraid to speak it, stigmatizes the *Dictionary*'s definition bluntly as 'unhappy' and 'misleading' and adds: 'In Queen Elizabeth's Household Accounts, the crowning festival night appears indifferently as "Twelfth day at night" and "Twelfth night".' (*The First Night of* 'Twelfth Night', 1954, p. 12, note.)

[4] '13 .. *K. Alis.* (Laud MS.) 6388 Of þat cite comen .. þe kyngis thre, þat foloweden goddis sterre .. In cristemasse, on þe twelueþ niȝth.' Here the Epiphany is on Twelfth Night.

believed that Twelfth Night was the evening of Twelfth Day, but that contemporary evidence appeared to point in the same direction. It occurred to me, however, that if there was one man who must have gone into the matter, and be in a position to give an authoritative ruling, it was Professor G. E. Bentley, whose exhaustive study of *The Jacobean and Caroline Stage* (vols. I–V) was at my elbow. How tempting to write straight away to Princeton and ask to be told the truth!

To my surprise Professor Bentley wrote in return: 'The truth is that I, too, was shocked to find that there was any doubt that Twelfth Night celebrations always occurred on the night of January 6th. As soon as I got your letter I referred to several places where I was sure that the identification of the two dates was obvious and found to my amazement that the original record said only Twelfth Night, and the date of the 6th of January, which had been attached to it, was in nearly every instance the work of some 19th or 20th century editor. In deep chagrin I set out to assemble all the evidence I could on the subject', and this, with characteristic generosity, he placed at my disposal. It is with his kind permission that I summarize it here.

1605/6. The 1606 quarto of Jonson's *Hymenaei* describes, according to the title-page, 'The Solemnities of Masque, and Barriers, magnificently performed on the eleventh, and twelfth Nights, from Christmas'. That this means 5 and 6 January we know from a letter written by John Pory to Sir Robert Cotton on the 7th, in which he says, 'I haue seen both the mask on Sunday and the barriers on Munday night', for Sunday and Monday were the 5th and 6th (Cotton MSS. *apud* Chambers, *Eliz. St.*, iii. 379, and Herford and Simpson, *Jonson*, x. 466). To Jonson, therefore, the eleventh night of Christmas meant 5 January, and Twelfth Night 6 January.

1613/14. In 1614 appeared a quarto of 'The Maske of Flowers. Presented by the Gentlemen of Graies-Inne, at the Court of Whitehall . . . vpon Twelfe night, 1613'. John Finett records that on 23 December 1613 he was sent to invite the Venetian ambassador to 'the Maske of Gentlemen of the Inns of Court to be performed on Twelfe night' (*Finetti Philoxenis*, 1656, p. 12), and on 5 January 1613/14 Chamberlain wrote to Sir Dudley Carleton, 'Master Atturneyes maske is for to morrow' (*Letters of John Chamberlain*, ed. N. E. McClure, i. 499). This 'Twelfe night' masque was, therefore, performed on 6 January.

1614/15. Finett records that on 5 January he was directed to invite the Spanish and Venetian ambassadors 'to a Maske of Gentlemen set forth at the charge of his Majesty', and that they 'came the next day' (*ut sup.*, p. 19), and the same day Chamberlain wrote, 'To morow night there is a maske at court'; and again on the 12th he reported 'the successe of the maske on Twelfe Night' (*Letters*, i. 567, 569–70). This unknown masque was therefore on 6 January, but Chamberlain calls it a 'Twelfe Night' masque.

1617/18. The 1640 folio does not give the date of Jonson's *Pleasure Reconciled to Virtue* except for the year '1619', which is wrong, for it belongs to 1618. Sir Edward Harwood writing to Sir Dudley Carleton on 7 January says, 'the last night beinge twelfthnight was the masque' (S.P.D., *apud* Bentley, iv. 670), and Chamberlain writing to the same on the 10th also calls it a 'Twelfth Night' masque (*Letters*, ii. 128), as also do others (Bentley, iv. 670–1).

1622/3. The undated quarto of Jonson's *Time Vindicated* describes it as 'In the presentation at Court on Twelfth Night. 1622'. Sir Henry Herbert, however, noted in his Office Book, 'Upon Twelfe night, the Masque being put off . . .', and later 'Upon Sonday, being the 19th of January, the *Princes Masque* appointed for Twelfe daye, was performed'.

1633/4. Herbert noted, 'On Monday night, the sixth of January and the Twelfe Night, was presented . . . *The Faithfull Shepheardesse*' (*Dramatic Records of Sir H. Herbert*, ed. J. Q. Adams, pp. 50, 53).

These two examples leave no doubt that to Herbert Twelfth Day and Twelfth Night were interchangeable terms, and if the Master of the Revels did not know, who did?

There appears to be only one piece of contradictory evidence.

1621/2. The undated quarto of Jonson's *Masque of Augurs* gives it as 'Presented on Twelfe night, 1621'. Now in a letter dated 'From London this 4ᵗʰ of January 1621' Chamberlain told Carleton that 'To morow shalbe the Princes maske at court' (*Letters*, ii. 420), which would make the performance on the 5th. But we have already seen that by Twelfth Night Chamberlain habitually meant the night of the 6th, and there can be little doubt that in the present instance he made a mistake. Since the letter is, as usual, dated at the end, there can be no question of Chamberlain having begun it on the 4th and finished it on the following day; we must assume either that by a slip he wrote '4th' for '5th', or else that when he wrote 'To morow' he meant the day after.

I cannot but regard the evidence collected by Professor Bentley as conclusive. In the sixteenth and seventeenth centuries at least Twelfth Night was taken to mean Twelfth Day at night (6 January) and not the eve of Twelfth Day (5 January). Whether it ever meant anything else I cannot tell, but there seems not the slightest reason to suppose so.

(ii) *Copyright in Unauthorized Texts*

THE obstacle that copyright might put in the way of replacing a bad and surreptitious by a superior and authorized text of a literary work has been long known to bibliographers from the case of *The Spanish Tragedy* in 1592,[1] and it may well have played a part in the bibliographical history of the Shakespeare Folio thirty years later. The theme crops up again in a curious little story told in the domestic state papers of 1631.

Michael Sparke, who, incidentally, was the chosen publisher of William Prynne's habitually controversial works, was no doubt a rather unruly member of the society of Stationers, and often proved a thorn in the side of authority. We know that he spent part of 1629 in the Fleet for publishing an offensive book without licence or warrant,[2] and his persistence in procuring the printing of un-licensed works and the unauthorized reprinting of works licensed to other men led the Wardens to forbid London printers to work for him, and so drove him into association with William Turner, an accredited but, according to the Vice-Chancellor, not very creditable printer to the University of Oxford.[3] There resulted a series of articles objected against the pair of them by the commissioners for causes ecclesiastical (otherwise the High Commission) on 2 April 1631: Turner's answers, which do not concern us, were returned on the 6th of the following month, Sparke's on the 10th.[4] One of the many misdeeds with which Sparke was charged was that he caused to be printed what is described as 'the booke of Promises', which belonged, by right of entrance in the Hall Book, to another man;

---

[1] See *The Library*, June 1925, vi. 47.
[2] The warrant for his committal is S.P.16, vol. 140, art. 15.
[3] Richard Baylie to Archbishop Laud, 16 Jan. 1636/7. S.P. 16, vol. 344, art. 20.
[4] S.P. 16, vol. 188, art. 13; vol. 190, arts. 40 and 64.

and in fact Turner did print an edition of this work for Sparke at Oxford in 1631 under the title of *The Saints' Legacies* (*S.T.C.* 10635).

The story Sparke tells in his answer is this. The copy, he admits, had belonged to one Robert Swaine, and Swaine had died owing him money. By way of recouping himself for his loss, Sparke proposed, with the widow's consent, to possess himself of the copy. But on inquiry he found that this had been unlawfully obtained, and, although duly licensed and registered, had been printed against the wishes of the author. Thereupon Sparke got in touch with the author, whom we know only by his initials A. F. appended to Sparke's edition, and bargained with him for the authentic manuscript. Meanwhile, however, Mrs. Swaine, instigated, Sparke believed, by the Under-Warden, John Harrison IV, who had already shown ill will towards him, altered her mind and sought to recover the copy from him, alleging it to be included in a deed of gift of all Swaine's effects executed in favour of a third party unnamed. This, Sparke argued, was of no force, and added that in fact the party in question made no claim to the copy.

This story can in part be confirmed. Though no edition by Swaine is now known, it is true that on 6 February 1631/2 a Martha Swaine, whom it is natural to suppose the widow of Robert Swaine the elder, assigned to Richard Royston, 'by consent of a full Court', his right in 'the Promises or Saintes Legacy', which was doubtless the copy registered by Swaine on 21 June 1629 under the hand of a Dr. Jefferay and the title of 'A Collection of Certaine Promisis out of the Word of God'.

We have, therefore, reasonable grounds for believing that it was Sparke's action in providing an authorized text to replace a surreptitious edition previously entered and printed that was in part the cause of his being cited before the Court of High Commission.

There is one other point of interest, namely Sparke's allegation that the copy 'was unlawfully gotten from the author, and printed against the authors will'. These words may mean that Swaine had obtained the author's manuscript by actual fraud and published it contrary to his express directions. But Sparke was evidently concerned to put the transaction in the worst light, and it is perhaps more likely that Swaine, as a picker-up of unconsidered trifles, did no more than print a manuscript that had come his way without by-your-leave of the author, of whose identity he may even have been ignorant. If that is what happened, then Sparke's use of the

term 'unlawful', though losing most of its point, may still imply
that at this time such practice was thought not quite the thing.[1]

[1] It may be well, for the sake of authentication, to quote the passage as it stands
in the original. I expand contractions, normalize capitals and punctuation, and disregard the rather haphazard use of Italian script.

'And otherwise [this examinate] doth not beleive this Article to be trewe in any
parte thereof, saveing, he saith, that the booke of Promises articulate was formerly
entred in the Stacioners hall booke of London in the name and for the benefitt of one
Robert Swayne, nowe deceased, whoe dyeing indebted to this examinat, and his
relict renounceing, he this examinat, willinge to haue some satisfaction for his debte,
enquired and found that the sayde booke of Promises was vnlawfully gotten from the
author, and printed against the authors will, although lawfully licenced and entred
in the hall booke, as afores[a]yde, wherevpon this examinat dealt with the sayde
author for the perfect copie of the foresayde booke and printed the same at Oxford,
as before is declared; after which the widowe of the sayde Swayne, being, as this
examinat beleiveth, instigated by the foresayde Wardens, challengeth the sayde
copie from this examinat as their gifte to her [? *read* to another], which this examinat
conceiveth and knoweth they haue noe power to doe, and the rather for that the
partie to whome a deed of gifte of the bookes, goodes, and chattelles of the foresayde
Swayne deceased was made hath and doth renounce the sayde copie as not belonginge
to him.'

Michael Sparke was still selling books in 165-
at the Blew Bible in Green Arber for
his name and address was printed
at the bottom of the title page of
"Truth Brought to light and discovered
by Time or A discourse and Historiall
narration of the first XIIII years of
King James Reigne". Printed by
Richard Cotes

Classical Myth in Shakespeare's Plays

DOUGLAS BUSH

D ISCUSSIONS, long or short, of Shakespeare's allusions to classical myth have as a rule been focused on sources, and that is not our concern here—though I have an old, thick, and growing pile of notes. Nor can we take account of problems of disputed authorship, though mythological and classical allusions have figured as evidence. This paper is an attempt, obviously quite inadequate, to suggest the distribution, the functions, and the changing quality of the allusions; and even the most sketchy outline must try to hold a balance between historical relativity and a dubious modern absolute, in other words, between Elizabethan taste and ours.

It might as well be admitted, or asserted, that not very many of Shakespeare's mythological allusions are fixed in our memories because of their poetic and dramatic quality. In him, as in other Renaissance authors, a high proportion of such allusions are, or seem to us, mere counters, smooth coins from the universal exchequer, the natural product of the grammar school, of the familiarity with at least Ovid and Virgil that was a bond between writer and reader. As we should expect, and as Virgil Whitaker has lately emphasized in his *Shakespeare's Use of Learning*, allusions of this kind are most abundant in the earlier plays, which also, no less logically, include a number of the less commonplace and more elaborate items. But flat and almost inert references to Phœbus and Titan (the sun), Neptune, Mars, the Furies, the Hydra, and the like can appear up through the late plays too. Such tags are so familiar and colourless that we hardly notice them. We may remember what Coleridge said, in partly deprecating Wordsworth's censure of Gray's 'reddening Phœbus',[1] of the natural eagerness with which Renaissance poets, 'cut off by Christianity from all *accredited* machinery', adopted, 'as a *poetic* language, those fabulous personages, those forms of the supernatural in nature, which had given them such dear delight in the poems of their great masters'. We may remember, too, that so rich and independently sceptical a moralist as Montaigne appealed

---

[1] *Biographia Literaria*, ed. Shawcross, 1907, ii. 58-59.

constantly to classical examples, and that such a likewise independent (if not over-rich) mind as Bacon continually invoked classical myths and compiled a book of them, allegorized in scientific and 'civil' terms. It was inevitable that imaginative writers good and bad should allude to myths with automatic spontaneity. The characters and incidents they themselves created were, so to speak, new, naked, and homeless in the great world; linked, however baldly, with figures and tales that possessed a timeless reality, they gained authenticity and glamour. Mythological beings, if often great in evil as well as good, were in a sense the huge shadows cast by man, the embodiments of power, passion, or beauty beyond human limitations (witness Faustus's vision of Helen). Very commonly, too, the classical deities represented the elements of nature beyond human control. Such feelings, even if half-unconscious, were shared by poet and audience, and if, in Shakespeare as well as lesser writers, practice in general fell below theory, it did not always do so.

In mythology as in larger matters Shakespeare carried on from his immediate predecessors and early contemporaries, Marlowe, Kyd, Greene, Peele, and Lyly; and the terms 'Ovidian' and 'Senecan', when applied to Shakespeare, embrace established Elizabethan as much as ancient styles. We may look first at the history plays, since this series—to leave out *Henry VIII*—came to an end by or before 1600, when most of the great comedies and tragedies were still unwritten. In the histories many allusions, because of their context as well as of their own character, tend to stand out as at once conventional and adventitious. Perhaps some statistics, if not pursued far, may be forgiven. The third part of *Henry VI* has some twenty-two references,[1] more than either of the other two parts (the second and third parts have tags of Latin also). To lump all three parts, repeated allusions come out thus: heroes and events of the Trojan war (13), Amazons (3), Jove (3), Hercules (3), Daedalus and Icarus (3), Elysium (2), Phaethon (2). The implied or explicit parallels between the Trojan war and the Wars of the Roses have their obvious heroic significance. Some allusions (e.g. Medea and Absyrtus, *2 Henry VI*, v. ii. 58–60; Ulysses' and

---

[1] All references (except *The Tempest*, II. i. 168) are to the Globe text. Here and later, statistics are only approximate, since some passages include several related or diverse names that might be counted in different ways. Among the many studies of Shakespeare's classical and mythological lore are: Robert K. Root, *Classical Mythology in Shakespeare*, 1903; Thomas W. Baldwin, *William Shakspere's Small Latine and Lesse Greeke*, 2 vols., 1944; J. A. K. Thomson, *Shakespeare and the Classics*, 1952; and J. Dover Wilson, 'Shakespeare's "Small Latin"—How Much?', *Shakespeare Survey*, 1957, x. 12–26.

Diomede's raid on Rhesus's tents, *3 Henry VI*, IV. ii. 19–21) are, relatively, a bit more recondite than those in later plays commonly are; one suspects a display of grammar-school learning. (By the way, as commentators long ago noted, the reference to Althaea's firebrand in *2 Henry VI*, I. i. 234–5 is accurate, while that of Falstaff's page in *2 Henry IV*, II. ii. 96–97 is not, and the error does not seem to be conscious and comic.) Examples of what is, to our taste, both forced and over-elaborate are the three allusions to Daedalus and Icarus. The first two come, in the midst of battle, from the valiant Talbot, addressing his valiant son alive and dead (*1 Henry VI*, IV. vi. 54–55, IV. vii. 14–16); in *3 Henry VI*, V. vi. 18–25, Richard, a little while before he stabs King Henry, speaks in characteristic—and dramatic —terms of the 'peevish fool' of Crete 'That taught his son the office of a fowl', and Henry, less dramatically, works out the details of the application to himself, Richard, and three other persons.

The three parts of *Henry VI* have some fifty allusions. There is a diminution in the six later history plays, which have about sixty-six: eight in *Richard III*, six in *Richard II*, four (three of them satirical) in *King John*, eleven (four comic) in *1 Henry IV*, some twenty-two (more than half of them Pistol's or otherwise comic) in *2 Henry IV*, and fifteen (mainly serious) in *Henry V*. In these six plays the order of frequency is: Mars (9), Troy (8), Mercury (5), Phœbus (5), Pegasus (4), Hydra (4), the Furies, Fates, Lethe, Jove, Neptune, Hercules (3 each), and so on. Apart from Pistol's Senecan fustian (which indicates Shakespeare's critical awareness of an outmoded style) and other comic items, such as Falstaff's, there are as usual serious references not always remote from Pistol's vein; and, also as usual, there are the conventional counters. In general, allusions in these later plays do not go beyond the familiar and the names by themselves are enough, with less descriptive or identifying detail than a number of allusions in *Henry VI*. Along with Trojan parallels and miscellaneous items, some allusions have a touch of the idealism that inspired Renaissance mythologizing as a whole: for example, Vernon's report to Hotspur of Prince Hal, whom he saw 'Rise from the ground like feather'd Mercury' and vault

> with such ease into his seat
> As if an angel dropp'd down from the clouds,
> To turn and wind a fiery Pegasus
> And witch the world with noble horsemanship.
> (*1 Henry IV*, IV. i. 106–10)

In the six early comedies of almost the same period (*c.* 1591-7), though the number of allusions varies greatly from play to play, the total is almost exactly that of the histories. The *Comedy of Errors* has only half a dozen allusions, all in serious speeches, to the gods, the Fates, the mermaid and the siren, and Love; and the bemused Duke's 'I think you all have drunk of Circe's cup' (v. i. 270). Love or Cupid (III. ii. 52), who seems to appear only once in the histories (in Henry's wooing of Katharine, *Henry V*, v. ii. 324-5), in the comedies soon inspires an infinity of references, under many sobriquets. The two large groups of miscellaneous allusions are naturally the romantic and the comic, and the former are much less likely to be dramatic than the latter.

The label 'romantic' bears both its broad and its amatory sense, and examples of the first may acquire an amatory tinge from their context. In *Two Gentlemen of Verona* the Duke, in exposing Valentine's plan for elopement, denounces him in Marlovian rhetoric:

> Why, Phaethon,—for thou art Merops' son—
> Wilt thou aspire to guide the heavenly car
> And with thy daring folly burn the world?   (III. i. 153-5)

Julia's reference to the part she had played in a pageant—'Ariadne passioning / For Theseus' perjury and unjust flight' (ibid., IV. iv. 171-3)—is Ovidian in theme though shorn of Ovid's pictorial detail. But Proteus, giving advice to the inarticulate lover, Thurio, turns Ovid, freely, into undramatic poetizing, the 'copiousness' of rhetorical manuals:

> For Orpheus' lute was strung with poets' sinews,
> Whose golden touch could soften steel and stones,
> Make tigers tame and huge leviathans
> Forsake unsounded deeps to dance on sands.
> (Ibid., III. ii. 78-81)

Even in such a boisterous farce as the *Shrew* (which has much less, and less detailed, allusion than *A Shrew*) the sophisticated Lucentio can speak to his man-servant with stilted irrelevance—'That art to me as secret and as dear / As Anna to the queen of Carthage was' (I. i. 158-9)—or with the undramatic elaboration of the allusion to Europa in I. i. 173-5. Though the subplot of the *Shrew* has been commonly assigned to another hand, the mythological allusions give no support to the notion; they are quite in Shakespeare's early manner. The same kind of rhetoric appears in *A Midsummer-Night's*

Dream in the serious asseverations of the lovers—'And by that fire which burn'd the Carthage queen' (I. i. 169 f.)—and in random phrases like 'drooping fog as black as Acheron' (III. ii. 357). So too in *The Merchant of Venice* Antonio's business friends talk of Janus and Nestor and Venus's pigeons (I. i. 50, 56, II. vi. 5), and lovers indulge in the usual rhetorical elaboration. The Prince of Morocco considers, in four lines, that Lichas, at dice, may conquer Hercules (II. i. 32–35). We do not complain when Bassanio sees Portia's hair as a golden fleece and 'her seat of Belmont Colchos' strand', visited by many Jasons, but we may when the normally human heroine, in her anxiety over his choice, spouts eight lines on Hercules' rescue of Hesione from the sea-monster (III. ii. 53–60).

Now and then Ovidianism is less high-flown and more dramatic. The luscious pictures offered to the drunken Sly in the Induction to the *Shrew* have their point, even if there is a confusion of myths in this one (I. ii. 52 f.):

> Adonis painted by a running brook,
> And Cytherea all in sedges hid,
> Which seem to move and wanton with her breath.

In *Love's Labour's Lost* Biron jokes about Cupid and Ajax, but also sees in women's eyes the true Promethean fire (IV. iii. 304, 351), and can let himself go with the eloquence of a convert:

> Love's tongue proves dainty Bacchus gross in taste:
> For valour, is not Love a Hercules,
> Still climbing trees in the Hesperides?
> Subtle as Sphinx; as sweet and musical
> As bright Apollo's lute, strung with his hair:
> And when Love speaks, the voice of all the gods
> Make heaven drowsy with the harmony.   (IV. iii. 339 f.)

Here romantic and self-conscious fancy blend in fresh and charming extravagance. And in the *Dream* serious rhetoric becomes, perhaps for the first time, poetry. The transmutation may be only partial in the lines that Milton apparently remembered in *L'Allegro*:

> Even till the eastern gate, all fiery-red,
> Opening on Neptune with fair blessed beams,
> Turns into yellow gold his salt green streams.

> (III. ii. 391 f.)

But it may be called complete, at least in terms of Shakespeare's early maturity, in the passage about the mermaid on the dolphin's back (II. i. 150 f.), and in the speeches of Hippolyta and Theseus (IV. i. 117 f.) in which the actuality of the hounds makes us think more of Warwickshire than of Crete and Hercules and Cadmus. The *Dream* has, moreover, two new elements, both large and obvious: the setting, the court of Theseus, which derives its atmosphere from Chaucer, North's Plutarch, and Shakespeare's own world and his own idealizing imagination; and the highly original 'antimasque' of Pyramus and Thisbe. Finally, although, as we observed, undramatic rhetoric appears in *The Merchant of Venice*, one of the first mythological things in Shakespeare that we call to mind is the moonlight dialogue between Lorenzo and Jessica. If two items, Thisbe fearfully o'ertripping the dew and Medea gathering enchanted herbs, are not in themselves notable, they share in the lyrical romanticism that suffuses the whole scene and is distilled in the picture of Chaucer's Troilus sighing his soul toward the Grecian tents and above all in the lines based on Chaucer's account of Ariadne:

> In such a night
> Stood Dido with a willow in her hand
> Upon the wild sea banks and waft her love
> To come again to Carthage. (v. i. 9 f.)

This quite un-Virgilian scene is unlike most of Shakespeare's actual reminiscences of Virgil, which are rather in the hard, high epic or Senecan style. In these four allusions—three of them Ovidian—Shakespeare evidently relied wholly or mainly, as Dover Wilson has re-emphasized, on native sources, Chaucer (including the 'yle amyd the wilde se' of *Ariadne*, line 2163) and Golding; and one magical agent in the romantic transmutation is the poet's sense of nature (there was no moonlight in *Troilus*). So too in the returning Portia's

> Peace, ho! the moon sleeps with Endymion
> And would not be awaked,[1] (v. i. 109–10)

myth is vivified by being humanized and re-created with imaginative 'primitivism'. In Portia's lines on Hesione, and in the many other patches classified as early rhetoric, the myth is not re-created but remains an impersonal entity, related to the speaker by logic rather than feeling, so that it is only an external importation wrapped in a declamatory style.

[1] L. C. Martin (*Marlowe's Poems*, p. 17) suggests an echo of Marlowe's 'The moon sleeps with Endymion every day' (*Elegies*, I. xiii. 43); Shakespeare might have seen the unpublished translation.

Doesn't another possibility occur?

As for the comic use of mythology, there is a gulf between, say, the burlesque of pedantry (mostly tedious to us) in *Love's Labour's Lost* and the burlesque of Seneca's and King Cambyses' vein in the play of Pyramus and Thisbe. In *The Merchant of Venice,* along with the serious rhetoric we have Launcelot Gobbo's talk of the 'Fates and Destinies and such odd sayings, the Sisters Three and such branches of learning' (II. ii. 65) and of Scylla and Charybdis (III. v. 19). In general, characters like Hercules and Ajax can do both serious and comic service; the mad Ajax's killing of sheep is invoked by York at the head of his Irish army (*2 Henry VI,* v. i. 26–27) and by Biron in love (*L.L.L.,* IV. iii. 6–8). Unconsciously, on the lips of pedants and half-wits, or consciously—and more commonly—on the lips of wits, the heroic and ideal figures of myth can become ridiculous. It may be observed, however, that such burlesque leaves a mythological character quite unscathed for heroic use again. Shakespeare (apart from *Troilus*) and most other poets and dramatists of his time do not, like some modern writers, have a darkly and consistently anti-heroic attitude. They are, to use a favourite term of our day, ambivalent, and quite happily so; they can be wholly irreverent about a body of fable they hold in high reverence.

In the mature comedies, *Much Ado, As You Like It,* and *Twelfth Night,* there is a marked change. Vestiges of serious Ovidian rhetoric are few and are almost all confined to the poetizing lovers, Claudio and Orsino. The sentimental Orsino, by the way, in his second speech employs the common allegorization of Actaeon's hounds as his own pursuing thoughts; allegorized myth, though cherished by Shakespeare's contemporaries as it had been for centuries, rarely appealed to him, perhaps because it tended to turn the concrete into the abstract. The great bulk of allusions in these plays are comic and are in prose; to pass by Malvolio's grateful ejaculations to Jove, they are heard chiefly from the consciously sportive Benedick, Pedro, Rosalind, and Feste. Rosalind, for instance, debunks the notion that Troilus and Leander died for love (*A.Y.L.,* IV. i. 97 f.), and Benedick is facetious about the same canonical pair (*M.A.,* v. ii. 30–31). Allusions in *As You Like It,* we may observe, are not taken over from the abundance in Lodge's *Rosalynde.*

To turn to the tragedies, the earliest, *Titus Andronicus,* carries as heavy a weight of mythology as of horrors. Allusions (not to mention tags of Latin) are in substance and tone predominantly of the grim kind we have in the early histories, though more numerous.

Most of them are brief (a line or two) and may be classed as Ovidian or Senecan in manner; by the time allusions have been caught up in the strong, crude, high-flown tragic style of the early 1590's, it is usually hard to distinguish. Among the dozens of miscellaneous and mainly commonplace items, some—such as Prometheus tied to Caucasus (II. i. 17), Cocytus (II. iii. 236), and Enceladus (IV. ii. 93) —are unique in Shakespeare, yet such relatively unusual references are characteristic of his earliest plays, and commentators nowadays are less disposed than they once were to the circular argument that anything 'un-Shakespearian' is from another hand. Nine allusions are Trojan, and these include the two most detailed ones—the union of Dido and Aeneas in the cave (II. iii. 21 f.) and the fall of Troy (V. iii. 80–87). The only other group of course comprises those that have to do with the Ovidian myth of Tereus and Progne (II. iv. 26 f., IV. i. 42 f.), 'the central symbol of disorder, both moral and political', the 'rape and mutilation of Lavinia'.[1]

In *Romeo and Juliet* mythology is much more sparingly used than the date and theme might lead us to expect, and even counters like 'Titan's fiery wheels' are few. Mercutio supplies, in prose as well as verse, a number of anti-romantic notes, such as 'my gossip Venus', 'Young Adam Cupid' (II. i. 11 f.), 'the blind bow-boy's butt-shaft' (II. iv. 16), and 'Dido a dowdy; Cleopatra a gipsy; Helen and Hero hildings and harlots; Thisbe a grey eye or so' (II. iv. 43 f.). On the romantic level, Romeo's praise of Rosaline (I. i. 214–20), with its allusions to Cupid, Dian, and Danae, is appropriate enough, and, though thin in texture and tone, is more dramatically personal than the first lines of Juliet's famous speech (III. ii. 1 f.), in which Shakespeare is more palpably and youthfully Ovidian (and Marlovian: editors cite *Edward II*, IV. iii. 45):

> Gallop apace, you fiery-footed steeds,
> Towards Phœbus' lodging: such a waggoner
> As Phaethon would whip you to the west,
> And bring in cloudy night immediately.

Whatever the theatrical power of the speech as a whole, this is not the voice of the Juliet the world has loved; if we want a poetical— though undramatic—criterion for these lines, we may think of Spenser's *Epithalamion*:

---

[1] Eugene M. Waith, 'The Metamorphosis of Violence in *Titus Andronicus*,' *Shakespeare Survey*, 1957, X. 44.

> Ah when will this long weary day have end,
> And lende me leave to come unto my love?
> How slowly do the houres theyr numbers spend?
> How slowly does sad Time his feathers move?
> Hast thee O fayrest Planet to thy home
> Within the Westerne fome:
> Thy tyred steeds long since have need of rest.

To move up to *Hamlet* (and to stick to concrete data and avoid such matters as Hamlet's affinities with Orestes), we have one big chunk, the speech on the fall of Troy delivered by Hamlet and the Player (II. ii. 472 f.):

> The rugged Pyrrhus, he whose sable arms,
> Black as his purpose, did the night resemble
> When he lay couched in the ominous horse. . . .

Here, with many conceits but less extravagance than in Pistol's tags, Shakespeare reproduces seriously the Senecan-epic vein of an earlier day. How richly dramatic the Trojan parallels become Professor Levin has demonstrated.[1] Thus the Player, in the role of Aeneas, weeping as he recites the woes of 'the mobled' Hecuba, offers Hamlet the same kind of challenge and reproach as the active Fortinbras:

> What's Hecuba to him, or he to Hecuba,
> That he should weep for her?

Incidental mythology in *Hamlet* is mainly of the usual kinds. In the graveyard scene, replying to Laertes' Pelion and Olympus, Hamlet bursts into the speech that ends:

> Make Ossa like a wart! Nay, an thou'lt mouth,
> I'll rant as well as thou.   (v. i. 276–7, 306–7)

Yet here, and in still later plays, Shakespeare, while generally stopping short of rant, gives Hamlet as well as others small bits of rhetorical mythology old-fashioned less in violence than in their grammar-school adventitiousness. Along with Horatio's scraps about Neptune's empire and the god of day (I. i. 118–20, 152), Hamlet speaks of his mother's following his father's body 'Like Niobe, all tears' (I. ii. 148–9); and after he has talked with the ghost, his fate cries out

> And makes each petty artery in this body
> As hardy as the Nemean lion's nerve.   (I. iv. 82–83)

[1] *Kenyon Review*, 1950.

In *Hamlet*, and in the other plays of Shakespeare's middle and later period, a high proportion of allusions fall into the two main categories we have observed from the beginning, the heroic or ideal and the anti-heroic. The ideal quality that the gods had for the Renaissance imagination supplies ample warrant for Hamlet's contrasts between his father and Claudius:

> So excellent a king: that was, to this,
> Hyperion to a satyr.   (I. ii. 139–40)

> My father's brother, but no more like my father
> Than I to Hercules.   (I. ii. 152–3)

> Hyperion's curls; the front of Jove himself;
> An eye like Mars, to threaten and command;
> A station like the herald Mercury
> New-lighted on a heaven-kissing hill.   (III. iv. 56 f.)

These last images are particularized and visual in comparison, say, with the unsophisticated similes of Kyd's *Soliman and Perseda*, IV. i. 77–78:

> Faire lockes, resembling Phœbus radiant beames;
> Smooth forhead, like the table of high Jove.

But more fully effective, because more fully and instinctively assimilated into Shakespeare's imagination and style, are expressions of disgust and revulsion, such as the ghost's re-creation of a reference ordinarily perfunctory:

> And duller shouldst thou be than the fat weed
> That roots itself in ease on Lethe wharf,
> Wouldst thou not stir in this,[1]   (I. v. 32–34)

or Hamlet's

> And my imaginations are as foul
> As Vulcan's stithy.   (III. ii. 88–89)

---

[1] On this allusion Root (pp. 67–68) cited Ovid, *Met.* XI. 602–5 and VII. 152 and Virgil, *Georg.* I. 78 and IV. 545. Baldwin (ii. 469–70) adds *Aen.* VI. 713–15. J. E. Hankins (*Shakespeare's Derived Imagery*, 1953, pp. 119–20) sees the source, especially because of the word 'fat', in Googe's translation, *The Zodiake of Life* (ed. R. Tuve, New York, 1947, p. 39): 'His name is Sleepe, his nourse is Leth, his foode is poppy fat.' At any rate this drab line is a measure of comparison. I have not observed that anyone has quoted a bit of North's Plutarch ('Coriolanus', Temple Classics, iii. 2) which has three of Shakespeare's words close together and a partial similarity of idea: 'That a rare and excellent wit untaught, doth bring forth many good and evil things together, as a *fat* soil that lieth unmanured bringeth forth herbs and *weeds*. For this Marcius' natural wit and great heart did marvellously *stir* up his courage to do and attempt notable acts.'

Hamlet's last allusion, the last of his several allusions to Hercules, follows directly upon his conscious rant about Ossa, and is a quietly ironic acceptance of his inability to set the world right:

> Let Hercules himself do what he may,
> The cat will mew and dog will have his day. (v. i. 314–15)

A degree of affinity as well as chronology links *Hamlet* with the problem comedies, and in these the ideal element of mythology is largely wanting; indeed in the later two mythology of any kind is scanty. *Measure for Measure* has less than any other play—only one allusion each from Isabella (II. ii. 110–11) and Lucio (III. ii. 47–48), the latter of course a joke. The only things in *All's Well* that call attention to themselves are two decidedly old-fashioned items. The Countess refers to Helena's tears in as strained a conceit as Shakespeare was ever guilty of:

> That this distemper'd messenger of wet,
> The many-colour'd Iris, rounds thine eye. (I. iii. 157–8)

And we are reminded of the opening lines of the Player-King in *Hamlet* (III. ii. 165 f.) by Helena's rhymed, oracular assurance to the King:

> Ere twice the horses of the sun shall bring
> Their fiery torcher his diurnal ring,
> Ere twice in murk and occidental damp,
> Moist Hesperus hath quench'd his sleepy lamp. . . .
> (II. i. 164 f.)

The earliest of these plays, the medieval-mythological *Troilus and Cressida*, is, of course, *sui generis*, and we can look only at incidental references. Some are of the old-fashioned literary kind, like Nestor's 'the ruffian Boreas once enrage / The gentle Thetis' (I. iii. 38–39). The anti-heroic is supplied in part by Thersites. The chief 'romantic' allusions come from Troilus the idealist, but he, in his intense, complex self-consciousness, is far from the sighing lover recalled by Lorenzo:

> I stalk about her door,
> Like a strange soul upon the Stygian banks
> Staying for waftage. O, be thou my Charon,
> And give me swift transportance to those fields
> Where I may wallow in the lily-beds
> Proposed for the deserver! O gentle Pandarus,
> From Cupid's shoulder pluck his painted wings,
> And fly with me to Cressid! (III. ii. 9 f.)

Here the sensual fever suddenly revealed in 'wallow' is merged—though not wholly lost—in the high romantic passion evoked by the mythological allusions. And when Troilus witnesses Cressida's betrayal of their love (v. ii.), mythology—which had been almost wholly lacking in his 'political' speeches—returns to intensify and enlarge his personal anguish.

To come back to the tragedies, mythology is sparse in both *Othello* and *Macbeth*, but it is richly representative of the two protagonists. Othello's few and high-pitched allusions are in keeping with his military prowess and simple magnanimity. He scorns the 'light-wing'd toys / Of feather'd Cupid' (I. iii. 269), and apostrophizes his artillery and profession in the terms of a mortal Jove dethroned:

> And, O you mortal engines, whose rude throats
> The immortal Jove's dread clamours counterfeit,
> Farewell! Othello's occupation's gone!   (III. iii. 355 f.)

And myth provides the measure for his other tragic loss:

> Her name, that was as fresh
> As Dian's visage, is now begrimed and black
> As mine own face.   (III. iii. 386–8)

The last phrase, from any other man than Othello, might have been 'As Vulcan's stithy'. A later allusion takes us far from Biron's:

> I know not where is that Promethean heat
> That can thy light relume.   (v. ii. 12–13)

The ideal and the twisted ideal have brief expression in Cassio's 'Great Jove, Othello guard' (II. i. 77) and Iago's 'she is sport for Jove' (II. iii. 17).

The first allusion we meet in *Macbeth* is

> Till that Bellona's bridegroom, lapp'd in proof,
> Confronted him with self-comparisons,   (I. ii. 54–55)

which Matthew Arnold pronounced 'detestable' and unhappily not untypical. To be less blunt, we might have expected such lines in the early histories; perhaps Ross's narrative, carrying on from the Sergeant's, fell into the old style of the Senecan messenger. The probably spurious Hecate passages may be disregarded, but, since Macbeth has leagued himself with the powers of darkness, his own allusions to Hecate (II. i. 51–52, III. ii. 41) are not fustian. It is

Macbeth's fevered imagination that strikes out the most pictorially sinister of Shakespeare's allusions to one 'historical' tale which is here, like the Tereus-Progne myth in *Titus*, a symbol of moral and political disorder:[1]

> thus with his stealthy pace,
> With Tarquin's ravishing strides, towards his design
> Moves like a ghost. (II. i. 54-56)

While Neptune commonly gets a flat or turgid phrase, there would be a notable loss of force if the name were absent from Macbeth's agonized cry: 'Will all great Neptune's ocean wash this blood / Clean from my hand?'[2] (II. ii. 60).

In *King Lear* mythology in the ordinary sense is of small account, but, because of Shakespeare's re-creation of the whole theme in a pre-Christian setting, references to 'the gods' are of the first importance. They are, however, so rich and complex in significance that a brief comment cannot even begin to indicate their individual value or total effect. Appeals to the gods, collectively or by name, are made chiefly by the good, Kent, Gloucester, Edgar, Albany, and, of course, most powerfully, by Lear. For him, as R. B. Heilman says in discussing this matter,[3] 'the supernatural is a reality of every moment', though his attitude changes as his experience becomes more cruel, his insight deeper. He may be said, roughly, to move from the assured pagan creed of his first invocation of the sun and Hecate and night (I. i. 111-14) to prayers in the form of curses, and from these to prayers for patience and to that confidence in divine justice which at times is or seems misplaced. But even Lear's appeals to the gods cannot be so simply schematized, and there are many others that contribute to diversity and unity of orchestration. In the history plays, even if human wickedness is at work, God's providence is at work too; but in *King Lear* 'the gods' carry a less valid assurance of ultimate rightness and good, a purer and more profound good, seems more helpless in the face of evil. (There is some mitigation in references to 'heaven', such as those in I. i. 50, II. iv. 192-5, II. iv. 274, IV. ii. 46-48, IV. vi. 228.) Lear is 'bound / Upon a

---

[1] E. M. Waith, p. 72, n. above. Kenneth Muir (Arden ed., p. 195) discusses affinities between *Macbeth* and *Lucrece*: see also his *Shakespeare's Sources*, 1957, pp. 184-6.
[2] For this commentators (though Baldwin, ii. 559, is sceptical) cite Seneca, *Hippolytus*, 717-18 (and *Hercules Furens*, 1327-9): 'non ipse toto magnus Oceano pater/ tantum expiarit sceleris.' Studley (Tudor Translations, i. 162) renders 'Neptune graundsire grave'. See K. Muir, Arden ed., pp. 57-58, 195.
[3] *This Great Stage*, Louisiana State University Press, 1948, pp. 255 f.

wheel of fire' (IV. vii. 46–47)—if Shakespeare was recalling Ixion, fire is not in the familiar sources—and Gloucester, who calls the gods 'kind' twice (III. vii. 35, 92) and 'ever-gentle' (IV. vi. 221), is also the speaker of 'As flies to wanton boys, are we to the gods, / They kill us for their sport' (IV. i. 38–39). Edgar at the end can partly answer that, but with reference rather to Gloucester's fate and Edmund's than to Lear's and Cordelia's: 'The gods are just, and of our pleasant vices / Make instruments to plague us' (V. iii. 170–1). The mythological 'ideal' is largely submerged in the anti-ideal:

> Down from the waist they are Centaurs,
> Though women all above:
> But to the girdle do the gods inherit,
> Beneath is all the fiends'.   (IV. vi. 126 f.)

Though Cordelia can say 'O you kind gods' (IV. vii. 14) and Lear 'Upon such sacrifices, my Cordelia, / The gods themselves throw incense' (V. iii. 20–21), the last reference in the play is the irony of Albany's 'The gods defend her!' (V. iii. 256), uttered when Cordelia is already dead. If in the end the gods can be said to have destroyed the wicked, and Cordelia, they can hardly be given credit for the growth out of suffering of humility, love, and gentleness; there is no clear suggestion of divine grace.

In the Roman and 'Greek' plays allusions to the gods, though they have their value, are too natural to be noticed. In *Julius Caesar*, the earliest (to leave out *Titus*) of the group and Shakespeare's first mature tragedy, other allusions are scanty and offer little or nothing remarkable. We may be somewhat surprised by some lines—spoken, too, by the practical Cassius—which, despite their irregular rhythm, recall the old rhetoric:

> I, as Æneas, our great ancestor,
> Did from the flames of Troy upon his shoulder
> The old Anchises bear, so from the waves of Tiber
> Did I the tired Caesar.   (I. ii. 112 f.)

That is not so far as we might expect from *2 Henry VI*, V. ii. 62 f.:

> As did Æneas old Anchises bear,
> So bear I thee upon my manly shoulders;
> But then Æneas bare a living load,
> Nothing so heavy as these woes of mine.

Coriolanus has a larger sprinkling of miscellaneous allusions and a

number of these are linked together by the central theme, the god-
like prowess and pride of the hero:

> the nobles bended,
> As to Jove's statue   (II. i. 281)

> He would not flatter Neptune for his trident,
> Or Jove for's power to thunder.
> > (III. i. 256; cf. V. iv. 24–26)

> He is their god.   (IV. vi. 90)

The idea is not absent from Coriolanus's own mind (III. ii. 38, V. iii.
11), though filial devotion drives it out. Whereas Caesar, just
before the conspirators stabbed him, exclaimed 'Hence! wilt thou
lift up Olympus?', Coriolanus says:

> My mother bows;
> As if Olympus to a molehill should
> In supplication nod.   (V. iii. 29–31)

And, among the hundred allusions to 'the gods', the most dramatic
and moving, outside of *Lear*, is embodied in his surrender:

> O mother, mother!
> What have you done? Behold, the heavens do ope,
> The gods look down, and this unnatural scene
> They laugh at. O my mother, mother!   (V. iii. 182–5)

In combined quantity and quality of allusion, *Antony and Cleopatra*
is perhaps the richest of the plays. As in others, many references to
the just or the injurious gods and to Mars and Jupiter—and here to
Isis—have their atmospheric value. The ideal is strongly established
in our minds—Cleopatra sees Antony as 'the demi-Atlas of this
earth' (I. v. 23), and Enobarbus sees her on her barge, surrounded
by Cupids and Nereids, as 'O'er-picturing . . . Venus' (II. ii. 205)—
but it begins to be shaken even before it is set up. In the very first
speech (by Philo) the general's eyes, which in the field 'Have glow'd
like plated Mars', now bend 'Upon a tawny front'. Antony declares
that Cleopatra knows her 'full supremacy' over his spirit: 'Thy beck
might from the bidding of the gods / Command me' (III. xi. 60–61).
Hercules, the subject of countless insignificant allusions, is a significant leitmotiv here, because—as in Plutarch—he is the ancestor
and patron saint of Antony, 'this Herculean Roman' (I. iii. 84).

Strange music (IV. iii. 17–18) means that, not Bacchus (as Plutarch says) but

> 'Tis the god Hercules, whom Antony lov'd,
> Now leaves him—

an allusion Mr. Eliot turned to memorable account. Hercules appears again in Antony's despairing cry, an allusion made intensely personal and dramatic (and very far from the Prince of Morocco's reasoning):

> The shirt of Nessus is upon me: teach me,
> Alcides, thou mine ancestor, thy rage:
> Let me lodge Lichas on the horns o' the moon;
> And with those hands, that grasp'd the heaviest club,
> Subdue my worthiest self.[1]   (IV. xii. 43 f.)

One allusion, which even in late plays can be external and commonplace—such as 'the wanton spoil / Of Phœbus' burning kisses' (*Cor.* II. i. 234) and 'the greedy touch / Of common-kissing Titan' (*Cymb.* III. iv. 165)—undergoes a quintessential transmutation and makes the dusky Cleopatra the ageless mistress of the sun:

> Think on me,
> That am with Phœbus' amorous pinches black,
> And wrinkled deep in time?   (I. v. 27–29)

In this play the ideal in a measure survives defeat and ruin and even life, in Antony's 'romantic' and un-Virgilian vision of a prolonging of earthly love:

> Eros!—I come, my queen:—Eros!—Stay for me:
> Where souls do couch on flowers, we'll hand in hand,
> And with our sprightly port make the ghosts gaze:
> Dido and her Æneas shall want troops,
> And all the haunt be ours.   (IV. xiv. 50 f.)

But no such vision inspires Charmian's last tribute to her mistress, in which the commonest of allusions again receives new life, this time from the conjunction of regality and death, of bright day and the dark:

> Downy windows, close;
> And golden Phœbus never be beheld
> Of eyes again so royal!

---

[1] For Shakespeare's possible use of Seneca's Latin (*Hercules Oetaeus*, 817–22), see Root, p. 62; and F. R. Johnson, 'Shakespearian Imagery and Senecan Imitation', *Joseph Quincy Adams: Memorial Studies*, 1948, pp. 42–43.

From the beginning, as we have partly seen, Shakespeare's allusions might carry that radiantly ideal quality which the gods and goddesses possessed in his and other poets' imaginations, and in the last group of plays, the romances or tragi-comedies, we may say that that quality is predominant, though now, along with the old idea of the superhuman individual, the likewise old idea of beneficent power becomes more conspicuous, more suggestive of a world in which things are finally set right.

In *The Winter's Tale* the business of Apollo's oracle comes from Greene, who furnished suggestions for some other mythological bits. While Dorastus merely gave a Euphuistic catalogue of gods who took an earthly form to win an earthly woman, Shakespeare (IV. iv. 25–35) created a contrast between the gods' sensuality and Florizel's ideal love.[1] Where Greene says that the shepherdess wore a garland of boughs and flowers, 'which attire became her so gallantly as she seemed to be the goddess Flora herself for beauty', this naïve and pallid picture is quickened into dramatic life: 'no shepherdess, but Flora / Peering in April's front' (IV. iv. 2–3). And Greene supplies no hint for the loveliest of all Shakespeare's pastoral visions, where his myth-making imagination—using the homely, authentic 'waggon'—turns Proserpine and the goddesses into elements of the English spring, almost as real and fragrant as the flowers:

> O Proserpina,
> For the flowers now, that frighted thou let'st fall
> From Dis's waggon! daffodils,
> That come before the swallow dares, and take
> The winds of March with beauty; violets dim,
> But sweeter than the lids of Juno's eyes
> Or Cytherea's breath; pale primroses,
> That die unmarried, ere they can behold
> Bright Phœbus in his strength.   (IV. iv. 116 f.)

Nature has eliminated, or transformed, bookish classicism. Ovidian allusion is at once assimilated by English senses into the English scene and invests with 'mythic' glamour the idea of fertility and renewal. The young Perdita's mention of Phœbus, by the way, recalls, with a difference, Charmian's last speech to the dead Cleopatra.

In these final plays, while many heterogeneous and insignificant

---

[1] D. Traversi, *Shakespeare: the Last Phase*, 1954, p. 142.

allusions occur, some have a degree of oblique complexity or are
consciously focused on a theme. Imogen (*Cymb.* IV. ii. 310–12) uses
the conventional 'ideal' terms of eulogy— 'His foot Mercurial: his
Martial thigh; / The brawns of Hercules: but his Jovial face . . .'—
but she is mourning over Cloten's headless body, which she takes
to be her husband's. Imogen herself is enveloped in partly ideal
allusions uttered by Iachimo and partly refracted through his
sensual imagination—Diana (I. vi. 133, II. iv. 81–82, V. v. 180),
Tarquin and Cytherea (II. ii. 12 f.), Tereus and Philomel (II. ii.
44 f.), 'you dragons of the night' (II. ii. 48), Venus and Minerva
(V. v. 164). *Pericles* has two main clusters, so handled that they
develop a mythic atmosphere. One comprises the allusions to
Diana that begin with Thaisa's vow (II. v. 10–12) and attend her
restoration to life (III. ii. 105) and her becoming a priestess; then
Diana's appearance to Pericles 'as in a vision' leads to the reunion
in her temple of husband and wife. Diana is associated also with
their daughter Marina, the incarnation of purity in the midst of
corruption (IV. ii. 161–2). Allusions to Neptune are reminders of
Pericles' voyages and vicissitudes and of the loss at sea of his wife
and new-born daughter; and it is on Neptune's annual feast that he
is reunited with Marina. One must mention—though one cannot
discuss—a mainly novel feature which, in various forms, links these
last plays together, that is, the mythological theophany or masque.
In *Pericles*, V. i. 241–50, there is Pericles' vision of Diana, a *dea ex
machina*; in *Cymbeline*, V. iv. 30–122, Posthumus' vision of his relations and of Jupiter; in *The Tempest*, IV. i. 60–138, the masque of Iris,
Ceres, and Juno set forth by Prospero in honour of Miranda's and
Ferdinand's betrothal (and *The Winter's Tale* has a sort of equivalent in the coming to life, in Paulina's chapel, of the supposed
statue of Hermione). Though the authenticity of some of these
scenes has been questioned, they are in accord with the mythic and
miraculous character of the plays; they partake of 'the artifice of
eternity'.[1]

Another noteworthy and pervasive element in these four plays
is the mixed pagan and Christian atmosphere, which differs in some
ways from the ordinary kind of mixture that began with the *Comedy
of Errors*. In his classical and pseudo-classical plays Shakespeare

---

[1] The chief expounder and defender of these scenes has been G. Wilson Knight, in
The Crown of Life, 1947. See also, among others, J. M. Nosworthy, *Cymbeline* (Arden
ed.), pp. xxxiii–xxxvii, and, for comments on the 'myth', Northrop Frye, *Anatomy
of Criticism*, 1957, pp. 138, 183, &c.

varied between a loose and a less loose decorum. *Julius Caesar* and *Timon* have many references to the gods and none to God (Brutus does address Caesar's ghost as 'some god, some angel, or some devil'). But other classical plays, along with dozens of appeals to the gods, have phrases that invoke God, in the main homely formulas of greeting or farewell (*T.A.*, IV. iii. 76, 90, 120; *M.N.D.*, I. i. 180, &c.; *T.C.*, III. iii. 294; *Cor.*, II. i. 159, II. iii. 144; *A.C.*, III. xiii. 124); such phrases might be called equivalents of classical formulas, but that would probably be to exaggerate Shakespeare's scholarly concern. In *Lear* also, among the two dozen appeals to the gods there is one apparent exception—'As if we were God's spies' (V. iii. 17)— though some commentators try to explain it away.[1] *Pericles* has over forty references to the gods (mainly prayerful and grateful) and a 'God give you joy' and 'God save you' (II. v. 87, III. i. 38). In *Cymbeline* 'the gods' occur some thirty-six times, in *The Winter's Tale* ten times, in *The Tempest* once (V. i. 201), and only this last play has a reference to God, a veiled and jocular one ("Save his Majesty!', II. i. 168). But these four plays, like others, have allusions, many or few, to 'heaven' and 'the heavens' which, if often susceptible of a pagan sense, may sometimes, even when mere ejaculations, be taken more naturally as Christian; and the same instinctive breaches of decorum can appear, more noticeably, in such pagan contexts as *Titus*, *Troilus*, *Timon*, *Coriolanus*, and *Antony and Cleopatra*. In the latest group of plays the pagan-Christian mixture does not seem to detract from what much modern criticism has been disposed to emphasize, their Christian and miraculous quality.

In *The Tempest* incidental mythology, though somewhat meagre,

---

[1] Muir (Arden ed., p. 200) follows Wilfrid Perrett, *The Story of King Lear* (*Palaestra*, 1904, xxxv. 250–1) and prints 'gods' spies' on the grounds that 'There is no apostrophe in F or Q' and that 'Shakespeare intended the plural since he was writing of a pagan world'. This reading was independently and elaborately defended by T. M. Parrott, *Shakespeare Quarterly*, 1953, iv. 427–32. I am not convinced. The lack of an apostrophe in early seventeenth-century printing is surely without significance. Shakespeare—as examples above partly indicate—is decidedly not a purist in avoiding mixtures of pagan and Christian but quite the contrary. The plural without the definite article would be a very odd, indeed unidiomatic, phrase for which there seems to be no parallel in Shakespeare; 'that dwells with gods above' (*T.C.*, III. ii. 164) is not the same kind of idiom. Nor do I recall mythological warrant for the idea of 'the gods' spies' in the Shakespearian context; Professor Parrott's sole example, from *Iliad* i, of Achilles begging Thetis to inform Zeus of Agamemnon's insult, hardly fits the case. Finally, along with the references to heaven cited in the text, which seem to bear a Christian rather than a pagan sense, there are such Christian phrases as 'a faith that reason without miracle / Could never plant in me' (I. i. 225) and 'Thou art a soul in bliss' (IV. vii. 46).

is not insignificant.[1] Ariel wields 'Jove's lightnings' and creates a storm in which Neptune, so often a colourless name for the ocean (as in v. i. 35), is something like a real deity (I. ii. 201–5); Ariel takes, too, the form of 'a nymph o' th' sea' (I. ii. 301) and of a harpy (III. iii. 52, 83). Sebastian thinks of Amphion's or Apollo's music raising a city (II. i. 86–87), Ferdinand of music attending 'Some god o' the island', of Miranda as a goddess, and of Phœbus' steeds and Night (I. ii. 389, 421, IV. i. 30). Such items belong to the world of myth as well as mythology. So, more potently, does Prospero's 'Ye elves of hills, brooks, standing lakes and groves' (v. i. 33 f.), which includes echoes of Golding (*Met.* vii. 265 f.) but owes its far greater vividness to its richer particularity, partly drawn from Ovid's Latin,[2] and to the combination of Medea's spells with English folk-lore.

The mixture of pagan and Christian may allow a word more beyond our brief. Whatever religious themes or overtones the fable may have, this play obviously differs from the other 'miracles' in that Prospero's controlling magic makes him almost a providential deity and also, in spite of realistic evil and realistic comedy, creates a unique unearthly atmosphere. While there is, as we observed, only one veiled and humorous reference to God, there are the good Gonzalo's earnest ejaculations, 'Now, good angels / Preserve the king' and 'Look down, you gods' (II. i. 306, v. i. 201). Of the references to heaven, prayers, 'a cherubin', providence, grace, hell, devils, the damned, a number—to which must be added the lines in Prospero's Epilogue—are seriously Christian. On the other hand, even if mythological allusions are universally common in Christian settings, there is Prospero's address to the tutelary divinities of nature, and, above all, the most famous lines in the play are not very markedly Christian:[3]

> We are such stuff
> As dreams are made on, and our little life
> Is rounded with a sleep. (IV. i. 156–8)

Perhaps, since our humble topic is classical myth, we can say of *The*

---

[1] J. M. Nosworthy (*R.E.S.*, 1948, xxiv. 281–94) sees the *Aeneid* 'as a narrative source and a pervasive influence'.

[2] Baldwin, ii. 443 f.; Muir, *Shakespeare's Sources*, pp. 3–4.

[3] Baldwin (i. 673–7), discussing possible sources of this whole speech in Palingenius, Virgil, Chrysostom, Job xiv. 10–12, and Isaiah xxxiv. 14, observes that Shakespeare's theology in the quoted lines has been blamed, and that objectors should read the note on Job in the Geneva (or Bishops') Bible. But Prospero is not speaking 'as a man in extreme peine, when reason is ouercom by affections & torments'.

Tempest only that it is a mythic dream-world in which all things are reconciled.

As for Shakespeare's allusions in general, a summary and self-evident conclusion might be that they range from Renaissance mythologizing to 'myth'; that, while bookish, rhetorical, and perfunctory items never vanish altogether, they give place increasingly to inspired felicities born of an instinctive and imaginative response to nature and human experience, and that elaborate patches gratuitously stuck on give place to allusions of integral and dramatic significance for character and the total theme.

Shakespeare's Reading in Chaucer

NEVILL COGHILL

A CORAL growth of scholarship, resulting from a long search for sources, has gradually spread itself out towards the later Middle Ages, to link a part of Shakespeare's thought and matter with its origins in Chaucer, Gower, and Lydgate. That he had a kind of acquaintance with their works is hardly to be doubted; *Troilus and Cressida* and *The Two Noble Kinsmen* are, ultimately, as firmly anchored to Chaucer as *Pericles* is to Gower, however far they have dragged their moorings.

Yet the evidence that Shakespeare actually read Chaucer, or, if he did, what parts of Chaucer and how deeply, is very tenuous; there is an accumulation of little scattered touches, hardly one of which would be considerable by itself; some of them indeed have a snow-flake quality of melting away under further criticism, only to re-appear in some later snowfall of suggested parallels, references, and clues. Under this snow, the frontiers of the objective and the sub-jective have sometimes seemed to change.

It is, of course, extremely likely that Shakespeare was read in Chaucer, for Chaucer was common Tudor reading; during the first thirty years and more of Shakespeare's life, his might even be con-sidered to have been what we have learnt to call 'an O.K. name'. We hear of him 'seated in a chaire of gold', and Barnaby Googe, writing in 1569, described him as 'that gem of poetrie who passed the reach of any English braine'. Yet there came a change in taste; a generation later, Chaucer seemed a figure looming uncertainly out of a misty past: 'Chaucer is harde even to our understanding' wrote Marston in 1598.[1] He was going out of fashion as the century turned.

Yet if, like other people, Shakespeare read his Chaucer, that is not

---

[1] For these and other sixteenth- and seventeenth-century references to Chaucer see Caroline Spurgeon, *Five Hundred Years of Chaucer Criticisms and Allusion*, 1925; Hyder E. Rollins, 'The Troilus-Cressida Story', *P.M.L.A.*, 1917, xxxii. 383; Franklin B. Williams, 'Unnoticed Chaucer Allusions, 1550–1650', *P.Q.*, 1937, xvi. 67; Brice Harris, 'Some Seventeenth-Century Chaucer Allusions', *P.Q.*, 1939, xviii. 395; Helen Sanderson, 'An Elizabethan Economist's Method of Literary Composition', *H.L.Q.*, 1942–3, vi. 205.

to say that he ever came under his influence, that he felt his imagination touched or tuned or kindled by his poetry, that he took delight in him. He may simply have quarried in him, a little unsuccessfully, for stories to dramatize; he may have read him as a man reads when he is consulting one work in order to write another, when he is reading to rob.

That Shakespeare really knew and loved Chaucer would be a far more important affirmation to us—were we in a position to make it—than that he merely used him. But where is the evidence for it? Not in *Troilus and Cressida*, not in *The Two Noble Kinsmen*; the Prologue to the latter, it is true, makes handsome acknowledgement to Chaucer; but the play itself seems only to recollect him at a great distance, and misses many of his finest things—the wisdom of Theseus, for instance, and Arcite's dying speech; as for Troilus and Cressida and Pandarus, these have suffered ignoble changes under Shakespeare's hand and, under it, are part of an immeasurably larger intention than ever Chaucer had in writing of them. None of this suggests any great love or deep influence felt by Shakespeare; there is scarcely a verbal echo caught from Chaucer in the entire play, unless it be in the line

Hector is dead; there is no more to say,

where the Chaucerian tag is given a sudden, tragic force by a Shakespearian twist.

Yet from some other plays, less inevitably derived from Chaucer, there is some accumulation of evidence that Shakespeare read him with a rich appreciation, at one time in his life; and I think the evidence will stretch so far as to tell us when that time was.

It is evidence that varies in solidity and weight; and what at first seems solid can sometimes prove less so; the evidence, for instance, from nomenclature seems sharp and firm: the name *Titania* is nowhere found but in the Third Book of Ovid's *Metamorphoses*, for it is not in Golding's translation. That seems strong proof that Shakespeare raided Ovid, or his memories of Ovid, for it, unless the name was bandied to him by some fluke of conversation. The names *Philostrate* and *Duke Theseus* seem to be as firm evidence for Chaucer as *Titania* is for Ovid, for Plutarch has no *Philostrate* and his *Theseus* is no Duke; but, as we shall see, both the names and the title can be found in another likely but less obvious source; taken by themselves they prove no indebtedness to *The Knight's Tale*.

In the newe meta

Invented to fit
Theseus twin brother of Perseus, Princes in the historie
The Nature of a Woman

It is only by assembling the minute, individually disputable items of evidence that their whole force and validity can be judged; so far as I know, only one such general assemblage has as yet been attempted. It appeared in an unsigned article,[1] contributed by J. W. Hales to the *Quarterly Review* in 1873—a review of certain publications of the Chaucer Society. As I have never seen this article referred to in subsequent discussions of the subject we are considering, it is necessary briefly to restate Hales's position and the evidence he offered for having taken it up; he wrote:

The two works of Chaucer which evidently attracted Shakespeare most were 'The Knight's Tale' and 'Troilus and Criseyde'; and the tokens of this attraction are to be seen in the 'Midsummer Night's Dream' and in 'The Two Noble Kinsmen', in 'Venus and Adonis', 'Tarquin and Lucrece', 'Troilus and Cressida', and 'Romeo and Juliet'. . . . Besides these connections, there are scattered throughout Shakespeare's plays and poems various other indications that the writings of Chaucer were anything but a sealed or an unopened book to him.

In considering this claim let us first return to *A Midsummer Night's Dream* and *The Knight's Tale* which have always been the happiest hunting-grounds in this particular quest for sources. Hales notes, like others, the names Theseus, Hippolyta, and Philostrate; he draws attention to Athens and its nearby woods, to the hunting scenes and to the great wedding celebrations. All these, he points out, are in *The Knight's Tale* too; Chaucer's line

With muchel glorie and gret solempnitee

is matched with Shakespeare's

With pomp, with triumph and with revelling.

(He might have cast his eye a line or two higher to find an echo of *solempnitee* in Theseus's phrase 'the night of our solemnities'; but the detail escaped him.)

When Furness's variorum of *M.N.D.* appeared in 1895, no direct reference was made in it to Hales's article, but the notion that there was any important connexion between the play and Chaucer's poem was scouted; the names of Theseus and Philostrate and the allusions to May Day ceremonies were admitted, but grudgingly. A

---

[1] *Quarterly Review*, cxxxiv, Jan.–April 1873; reprinted by the author, J. W. Hales, in *Notes and Essays on Shakespeare*, 1884, pp. 91–92.

weightier consideration of the problem, however, followed on Furness in 1903, when H. R. D. Anders published his *Shakespeare's Books*. He, too, began his discussion of the sources of *M.N.D.* by pointing out the presence of the name *Philostrate* and added what was then a fresh point, that both Chaucer and Shakespeare had made a *Duke* of Theseus.

This, however, was only to raise and then dash the hopes of Chaucerists, for he at once went on to produce an entirely different source for both details, till then unsuspected, in Richard Edwards's play *Palæmon and Arcyte*. Anders dryly stated that it contained both these details and that the play was known to Shakespeare.

The play had indeed been performed with memorable *éclat* in the great hall of Christ Church, on the occasion of the Queen's visit to Oxford in 1566. A lavish contemporary account of it and of this famous occasion (on which three spectators were crushed to death by the collapse of a stone wall) has survived. It gives a detailed synopsis of the play which was closely modelled, with minor additions, on *The Knight's Tale*, and contains the tell-tale names and the ducal title:

> Regius itaque adolescens capitale supplicium non curat, habitu indecentiori revertitur, ex Arcito, mutato nomine, Philostrates fit. . . .
>
> . . . Dux, illarum prece commotus . . . jubet pugnam in quadragesimum diem parent, præmium victori virginem pollicetur. . . .[1]

There remained Hales's argument from the hunting scenes; but another account[2] of the same Christ Church occasion disposed of that too:

> In the play was acted a cry of hounds in the Quadrant, upon the train of a fox in the hunting of Theseus, with which the young scholars, who stood in the windows, were so much taken (supposing it was real), that they cried out 'Now, now!—there, there!—he's caught, he's caught!' All which the Queen merrily beholding, said 'O, excellent! those boys, in very troth, are ready to leap out of the windows, to follow the hounds.'

This story supplied Anders with a reason for thinking that the play was known to Shakespeare; he even believed it to have been performed in London. The 'cry of hounds' that had made such a stir

---

[1] Charles Plummer, *Elizabethan Oxford* (Oxford Hist. Soc.), 1887, for 1886, pp. 128–9. See also W. Y. Durand, *P.M.L.A.*, xx, 1905, pp. 502–28.
[2] John Nichols, *Progresses and Public Processions of Queen Elizabeth*, 1823, i. 212.

at Oxford was too good an effect to lose, and became a stage tradition (he thought) underlying the stage-direction in *Titus Andronicus*:

Heere a cry of houndes, and winde hornes in a peale.

Although Anders seemed to have silenced Chaucer's claims to *Philostrate* and *Duke Theseus* for ever, it was not long before they were revived. Frank Sidgwick's *Sources and Analogues of A Midsummer-Night's Dream* appeared in 1908, in which all the evidence from nomenclature so far considered was repeated, but no mention was made of *Palæmon and Arcyte*; two more names were added to the score; *Lygurge* and *Emetreus*, the splendid foreign kings that tourney for Palamon and Arcite in *The Knight's Tale*, now lent their names to *Lysander* and *Demetrius*; an unlikely guess, it may well be thought. But Sidgwick also pointed to a firm, albeit infinitesimal, fact that in both Chaucer and Shakespeare there is mention of Theseus as the conqueror of *Thebes*.

A Midsummer-Night's Dream rested in this not wholly certain relationship to *The Knight's Tale* until Miss Bethurum[1] took up and advanced the argument in 1945. She found new affinities between them, till then unsuspected, of a more notional kind. Slight but undeniable finger-prints, like the mention of Thebes, she passes over in favour of airier similarities; it is not Theseus's name that is important to her, but his character. His golden magnanimity, she rightly claims, is equally displayed in both play and poem; both poets see him as 'a benevolent ruler, aware of the duties of kingship, aware also of the follies of love and sympathetic to them . . . the common norm in a world of amorous aberration'. Her wide sweep of vision discerns other large, imaginative parallels, not all quite so convincing; the pursuit of the same girl by two stormy young men; and the supernatural help they receive—from the planets in Chaucer, from the fairies in Shakespeare—is cited as a striking similarity only a little obscured by the presence of a second girl; she, it is suggested, was added by the dramatist for symmetry, so that both Jacks should, in the end, have their Jills. Another parallel is seen between the jangles of Oberon and Titania, and those of Pluto and Proserpine in *The Merchant's Tale*; and here there is also to be found a suggestion for Peter Quince's play:

> By Piramus and Tesbee may men leere;
> Thogh they were kept ful longe streite overal,

---

[1] Dorothy Bethurum, 'Shakespeare's Comment on Medieval Romance in *A Midsummer-Night's Dream*', *M.L.N.*, 1945, lx. 85.

> They been accorded, rownynge thurgh a wal,
> Ther no wight koude han founde out swich a sleighte.
>
> (E. 2128–31)

Finally, by an even bolder leap of intuition, Miss Bethurum suggests that Chaucer himself, in his *Rhyme of Sir Thopas*, had given Shakespeare a hint for Bottom's dream and Titania's infatuation:

> Me dremed al this nyght, pardee,
> An elf-queene shal my lemman be
> And slepe under my goore.   (B. 787–9)

It must be owned that these suggestions, however illuminating, are highly speculative; they do not declare the discovery of a source, but persuade us to perceive affinities, perhaps even an imaginative impulse, an influence. And that, no doubt, is what we should rather wish to find than the small change of a name or two. Yet it seems romantic to admit any such influence as a certainty, if it cannot be demonstrated beyond doubt that Shakespeare was in fact well read in Chaucer; not till then can the fancies be accepted. But to achieve this calls for much more evidence than we have seen, and especially for evidence that does not melt away before our eyes, like that of *Philostrate*.

We must return to Hales's neglected article. After his discussion of *The Knight's Tale* and *A Midsummer Night's Dream*, he turns to other plays and poems, pointing out a number of similarities of thought and image. I reassemble the most striking of his parallels.

1. From *The Parliament of Fowls*

> But brekers of the lawe, soth to seyne,
> And likerous folk, after that they ben dede,
> Shal whirle aboute th'erthe alwey in peyne . . .   (78–80)

From *Measure for Measure*

> To be imprisoned in the viewless winds
> And blown with restless violence about
> The pendent world. . . .   (III. i. 125–7)

2. From *The Parliament of Fowls*

> The wery huntere, slepynge in his bed,
> To wode ayeyn his mynde goth anon:
> The juge dremeth how his plees been sped:
> The cartere dremeth how his cartes gon:

> The riche, of gold: the knyght fyght with his fon:
> The syke met he drynketh of the tonne;
> The lovere met he hath his lady wonne.　(99–105)

From *Romeo and Juliet*

> And in this state she gallops night by night
> Through lovers' brains, and then they dream of love:
> . . . O'er lawyers' fingers, who straight dream on fees;
> . . . Sometimes she driveth o'er a soldier's neck,
> And then he dreams of cutting foreign throats. . . .
> (I. iv. 70–83)

3. From *Troilus and Criseyde*

> For though thise men for love hem first torende,
> Ful sharp bygynning breketh ofte at ende.　(II. 790–1)

From *Romeo and Juliet*

> These violent delights have violent ends.　(II. vi. 9)

4. From *Troilus and Criseyde*, at the point where Troilus, standing on the walls of Troy, feels a sudden beatitude that he is sure must be a sign that Criseyde will soon return to him:

> But, hardily, it is naught al for nought
> That in myn herte I now rejoysse thus.
> It is ayeyns som good I have a thought.
> Not I nat how, but syn that I was wrought,
> Ne felte I swich a comfort, dar I seye.　(V. 1164–8)

From *Romeo and Juliet*, at the point where Romeo, in banishment at Mantua, believes himself about to receive some happy news, though an instant afterwards his servant Balthasar brings him the news that Juliet lies in her tomb:

> If I may trust the flattering truth of sleep,
> My dreams presage some joyful news at hand.
> My bosom's lord sits lightly in his throne,
> And all this day an unaccustomed spirit
> Lifts me above the ground with cheerful thoughts.
> (V. i. 1–5)

From *The Merchant of Venice*

> The moon shines bright. In such a night as this
> . . . Troilus, methinks, mounted the Troyan walls,
> And sighed his soul towards the Grecian tents,
> Where Cressid lay that night . . .　(V. i. 1–6)

R. K. Root,[1] independently hitting upon this parallel, makes the further remark that Shakespeare had *mis*read Chaucer. In the poem, Troilus stands on the city walls in the dark of the moon:

> I saugh thyn hornes olde ek by the morwe,
> Whan hennes rood my righte lady dere.   (v. 652)

Root comments: 'The moon which to Shakespeare is but part of the romantic setting of a stage picture, is to the more sober art of Chaucer a means of measuring the passing days.' In addition to these salient parallels adduced by Hales, Anders and others have adduced the following:

5. From *The House of Fame*

(*describing Fame*)   For as feele eyen hadde she
        As fetheres upon foules be. . . .   (III. 291–2)

        . . . Had also fele up-stonding eres
        And tonges, as on bestes heres.   (III. 299–300)

From *Titus Andronicus*

> The Emperor's court is like the house of Fame,
> The palace full of tongues, of ears and eyes.   (II. i. 126)

A like image figures as *Rumour* for Prologue to *2 Henry IV*.

6. Feste briefly tells us 'Cressida was a beggar', which seems to show Shakespeare had read Henryson's *Testament of Criseyde*, then thought to be by Chaucer; and Lear's Fool at the end of Act III, scene ii, utters a crazy prophecy much resembling one that Caxton[2] printed, though without direct attribution to Chaucer:

> Than shal the land of Albyon
> Be brought to grete confusioun.

These last parallels or echoes (5 and 6) are fragments that could, perhaps, have come to Shakespeare by chance or by hearsay, like his reference to Pertelote in *The Winters Tale*, or to 'Dun's in the mire' and to 'medlar-fruit' in *Romeo and Juliet* (I. iv. 41 and I. i. 35–38).

To these similarities between Chaucer and Shakespeare claimed by Hales and others, I would now add a few more I have noticed and which, I think, have so far escaped the record.

---

[1] R. K. Root, 'Shakespeare Misreads Chaucer', *M.L.N.*, 1923, xxxviii. 346.
[2] W. W. Skeat, *The Works of Chaucer*, 1897, vii. 450.

7. Among the most famous images in *Richard II* is the image of the buckets in a well (IV. i. 184–7):

> Now is this golden crown like a deep well
> That owes two buckets, filling one another,
> That emptier ever dancing in the air,
> That other down, unseen and full of water.

In commenting upon this, Dover Wilson[1] quotes an excellent passage from Machaut:

> Pren moy deus sëaus en un puis,
> Qu'assez bien comparer li puis:
> Li uns est pleins, li autres vuis:
> Et se l'un monte,
> L'autre descent . . .

and he then remarks that Dr. Johnson, who thought Shakespeare's image not accommodated to the subject, knew nothing of Machaut. But, it must be objected, neither did Shakespeare. On the other hand, he had only to read *The Knight's Tale* to find it said of Arcite that

> Into a studie he fil sodeynly,
> As doon thise loveres in hir queynte geres,
> Now in the crope, now doun in the breres,
> Now up, now down, as boket in a welle. (1530–3)

Chaucer knew Machaut, of course, and must surely have been an intermediary in this instance, for the vivid image.

8. In *Richard II* (I. iii. 294–5) there is another famous phrase that has led to speculation among those who seek sources:

> O who can hold a fire in his hand
> By thinking on the frosty Caucasus?

On these lines J. A. K. Thomson[2] comments that the Caucasus was only known to Elizabethan poets out of books; yes, but what books? He refers us to Ovid, but all we will find there is this:

> est locus extremis Scythiæ glacialis in oris,
> triste solum, sterilis, sine fruge, sine arbore tellus:
> Frigus iners illic habitant Pallorque Tremorque
> et ieiuna Fames . . .

---

[1] *Richard II* (New Cambridge), 1939, p. 208.
[2] Quoted in *Richard II* (New Variorum), 1955, p. 85.

> rigidique cacumine montis
> (Caucason appellant) serpentum colla levavit.
>   (*Metamorphoses*, VIII. 788–98)

Peter Ure[1] makes no mention of Ovid, but quotes Malone's note that it was suggested by this passage from Lyly's *Euphues*:

hee that is colde doth not couer himselfe wyth care, but wyth clothes, he that is washed in ye rayne dryeth himselfe by the fire not by his fancie, and thou which art bannished oughtest not with teares to bewaile thy hap, but with wisedome to heale thy hurt.

The commonplace for a banished man is here, but where is the Caucasus? In Ovid we have the Caucasus (did Shakespeare suddenly combine Ovid and Lyly in his mind?), but where is the fire? They are both in Chaucer:

> Taak fyr, and ber it to the derkeste hous
> Bitwix this and the mount of Kaukasous. . . .
>   (*Wife of Bath's Tale*. D. 1139–40)

9. The Wife of Bath has other ideas that find an echo in Shakespeare. In the same speech from which I have quoted the image of bearing fire to the Caucasus, comes a passage on the nature of *gentillesse* that deserves to be put beside a passage on the same subject, and in the same serious tone, from *All's Well that Ends Well*.

From *The Wife of Bath's Tale*:

> Looke who that is moost vertuous alway,
> Pryvee and apert, and moost entendeth ay
> To do the gentil dedes that he kan;
> Taak hym for the grettest gentil man.   (D. 1113–16)

> . . . For, God it woot, men may wel often fynde
> A lorde's sone do shame and vileynye:
> And he that wole han pris of his gentrye,
> For he was boren of a gentil hous,
> And hadde his eldres noble and vertuous,
> And nel hymselven do no gentil dedis,
> He nys nat gentil, be he duc or erl. . . .   (D. 1150–7)

From *All's Well that Ends Well*:

> If she be
> All that is virtuous—save that thou dislikest,
> A poor physician's daughter, thou dislikest
> Of virtue for the name . . .

[1] *Richard II* (New Arden ed.), 1956, note to I. iii. 294–5.

> ... That is honour's scorn
> Which challenges itself as honour's born
> And is not like the sire. Honours thrive
> When rather from our acts we them derive
> Than our fore-goers. ....   (II. iii. 120–35)

10. These are notional, not verbal, similarities, but they point to a deep affinity of opinion at the least, and, taken with other similarities in the same tale—or rather the Preamble to it—and the same play, they seem more than can be accounted for by coincidence of temperament. Parolles has a striking and cynical thing to say about virginity: 'Loss of virginity is rational increase: and there was never virgin got till virginity was first lost' (I. i. 119). The same thought had occurred, two centuries before, to Dame Alison:

> For hadde God comanded maydenhede,
> Thanne hadde he dampned weddyng with the dede.
> And certes, if ther were no seed ysowe,
> Virginitee, thanne wherof sholde it growe?
> (*Prol. Wife of Bath's Tale*, D. 69–72)

11. Another notional parallel may be found between a stanza in the tale of the Man of Law and the whole metaphysical scheme of *Romeo and Juliet*.

From *The Man of Law's Tale*:

> Paraventure in thilke large book
> Which that men clepe the hevene ywriten was
> With sterres, whan that he his birthe took,
> That he for love sholde han his deeth, allas!
> (B. 190–3)

The frequent references in *Romeo and Juliet* to the consequences hanging in the stars, first adumbrated in the opening Prologue, may well be Shakespeare's application of this Chaucerian theme. It could be argued that it is a commonplace, and so it is; yet it is not one which appears in Brooke's *Tragical Historye of Romeus and Juliet*; for although the poem echoes with Fortune, Fates, and Destinies, the Sisters Three and such branches of learning, there is only one mention of the stars in any fatal connexion, and that the most perfunctory, when Romeo is bewailing his newly announced banishment:

He cryed out (with open mouth) against the sterres above.
(l. 1328)

But that is all; at the expected place, when all Shakespeare's re-iterated star-imagery touches its climax with

> Is it e'en so? Then I defy you, stars!   (v. i. 24)

Brooke has no more notion of invoking them than he has of creating that tragic irony of situation which, it has been suggested, came to Shakespeare from the walls of Chaucer's Troy. To the lines beginning

> If I may trust the flattering truth of sleep

there is no counterpart in Brooke. The concept of tragic irony was as far beyond him as that of star-crossed love.

12. There is another, isolated parallel in *Romeo and Juliet* to a passage in Chaucer. When the Nurse brings to Juliet the news that Romeo has killed Tybalt, Juliet cries out against him

> O serpent heart, hid with a flowering face!   (III. ii. 73)

This is an image, some will say, as old as Eve. It is certainly of some antiquity for it appears in *The Squire's Tale*:

> Right as a serpent hit hym under floures
> Til he may seen his tyme for to byte. . . .   (F. 512–13)

It seems to have struck Shakespeare with great imaginative force, for he repeats it in an even more famous scene, in *Macbeth*:

> look like the innocent flower
> But be the serpent under't.   (I. v. 62–63)

This, I think, completes our tale of identifiable finger-prints and upon these, for the moment, the case must rest. What emerges most noticeably from them is the sudden concentration of Chaucer-isms in *Romeo and Juliet* and *A Midsummer Night's Dream*. Since these plays come close together in accepted Shakespearian chronologies, it is tempting to rearrange the evidence we have considered chrono-logically, and see how the scattered parallels fit in with the course of Shakespeare's life as a writer. In doing this, it seems best to follow Chambers's chronological table,[1] which, in respect of most of the plays involved, has not been seriously questioned.[2] There is one, however, which offers complications. *All's Well that Ends Well* he assigns to 1602/3; but Dover Wilson[3] believes it to be the revised

---

[1] E. K. Chambers, *William Shakespeare*, 1930, i. 270–1.
[2] See James G. McManaway, 'Recent Studies in Shakespeare's Chronology', *Shakespeare Survey*, 1950, iii. 22.
[3] *All's Well that Ends Well* (New Cambridge), 1929, pp. 103–6.

form of an earlier play, and Hardin Craig[1] goes further, by a tentative identification of this earlier play with that famous ghost, *Love's Labour's Won*.

It may be that we have in *All's Well* a version, with a new title, of Shakespeare's lost *Love's Labour's Won*, a play which would conceivably be written early to serve as a companion piece to *Love's Labour's Lost*.

The case for this view has recently found some support in T. W. Baldwin's[2] discovery of the play-title *Love's Labour's Won*, in a bookseller's catalogue of 1603. This discovery rules out all the other rival candidates that have been suggested as the possible bearers of this ghost-title, and therefore makes the identification with *All's Well* less unlikely, one may even say likelier. Following this line of conjecture, it would not be unreasonable provisionally to accept Hardin Craig's suggestion and suppose that the Chaucerian echoes in *All's Well* may be dated back to the days of *Love's Labour's Lost*. The pattern that would then emerge would be as follows:

SHAKESPEARE	CHAUCER	IMAGE, IDEA
1593/4		
Titus	H. of F.	House of Fame, ears, eyes, tongues
1594/5		
R. & J.	M. of L.'s Tale	Death for love, written in stars.
	P. of F.	Mercutio's theory of dreams.
	T. & C. II	Violent delights have violent ends.
	T. & C. V	Tragic irony, joy before doom: Troilus on walls of Troy, Romeo at Mantua.
	Sq.'s Tale	Serpent under flower.
	? Prol. Reve's Tale	Medlar fruit—'open-ers'.
	? Prol. Manciple's Tale	'Dun's in the Mire.'
1595/6		
R. II	Kt.'s Tale	Buckets in a well.
	W. of B.'s Tale	Fire to the Caucasus.
? Love's Labour's	W. of B.'s Tale	Ideas of gentilesse.
Won	W. of B.'s Prol.	Ideas on loss of virginity.
M.N.D.	Kt.'s Tale	Theseus, Hippolyta, Philostrate, Lysander, Demetrius.
		Wedding 'solemnities' of Duke Theseus.
		May observances.
		Hunting scenes.
		Conquest of Thebes.
		Character of Theseus.

---

[1] Hardin Craig, *An Interpretation of Shakespeare*, 1948, p. 223.
[2] T. W. Baldwin, *Shakespeare's Love's Labour's Won*, 1958.

SHAKESPEARE	CHAUCER	IMAGE, IDEA
	Tale of Sir Thopas	Elf-queen love.
	Merch. Tale	Pluto/Proserpine and Oberon/ Titania quarrels.
		Mention of Pyramus and Thisbe.
	(? L. G. W Legend of Thisbe)	
1596/7		
M. of V.	*T. & C.* V	On such a night as this, Troilus, &c. (again).
1597/8		
2 *H. IV*	*H. of F.*	Rumour full of tongues (again).
1599/1600 ? 1601		
T.N.	*Testament of Criseyde*	Cressida a beggar.
1604/5		
M. for M.	*P. of F.*	Blown with restless violence about the pendant earth.
1605/6		
Lear	*(Caxton)*	The realm of Albion rhyme.
Macbeth	*Sq.'s Tale*	Serpent under flower (again).

Chaucer loved to parade his authorities; not so Shakespeare, upon whose sources we only come by a kind of stealth. Yet in view of this chronological table of echoes, it is hard to escape the conclusion that suddenly, towards his thirtieth year, Shakespeare came upon a copy of Chaucer, about whom he must so often have heard, and devoured it. For a year or two this new and heady reading flared and flowered in his imagination; then he passed on into regions where Chaucer could no longer touch or help him in the same way, for Chaucer had no vision of evil and it was at evil that Shakespeare had begun, steadily, to look.

But in this brief, happy, and compassionate meantime, all the affinities between him and Chaucer seem to have taken hold, and image after image imprinted itself on his thought from the older poet. They were the years of his first trinity of masterpieces—in tragedy, comedy, and history, the years of *Romeo and Juliet*, *A Midsummer Night's Dream*, and *Richard II*. In these excitements Chaucer had his part, if no more than to teach a torch, already burning, to burn brighter.

I have recently noted two more parallels: (1) *L.L.L.* IV. iii. 62, *My vow was earthly, thou a heavenly love* echoes *Kt.'s T.* 1158–9, *Thyn is affeccioun of hoolynesse, | And myn is love, as to a creature.* (2) At the end of *L.L.L.*, the lovers are dismissed, like the Tercels at the end of *P. of F.*, for a year of service in the cause of love.

On *Venus and Adonis*

DON CAMERON ALLEN

I T is possibly an error to think of Shakespeare's *Venus and Adonis* as a legitimate child of the tenth book of the *Metamorphoses* even though some of its elaborate wit is plainly fathered by twists and turns in the Latin text. When the poem is broadly regarded, it is rather certain that in tone, purpose, and structure the two poems have little to share. To begin with, the true poet of the Latin poem is by artistic pretence not Ovid at all but widower Orpheus, whose personal tragedy quietly informs each one of the songs that he sings on his Thracian hill to an assembly of wild beasts and birds. We can also be sure that the literate Roman was perfectly aware of the alternate myth of Adonis in which Pluto's queen contended with Venus for the love of the young hunter;[1] for this knowledge must certainly have been assumed by Ovid to be in the possession of his readers and to make plainer than plain the connexion between the short life of Orpheus's bride and that of Venus's minion. The wind-flower which fragilely makes the lesson sets this forth: 'brevis est tamen usus in illo.'

In Shakespeare's version none of this pathos comes through, and the Ovidian music that the annotators have heard is ghost music. True enough, the Latin poet's description of Venus in the role of a rustic Diana is the germ of Shakespeare's finished caricature of the frustrate lady, flushed and sweating. Her advice on hunting to the rumpled Adonis, tersely expressed in Latin, becomes a sportsman's lecture in English. But, in the main, the two poets saw the myth differently. Shakespeare's Adonis, contrary to the whole tradition, scorns love. In the sonnets of *The Passionate Pilgrim*, if these be Shakespeare's, the boy is mocked for missing his chance, but the longer poem takes, I think, a different position. The legend of Atalanta and Hippomenes, which Ovid relates as a harmonious part of the central legend, is also omitted by Shakespeare and replaced by an animal diversion between Adonis's stallion and an eager mare. Actually Shakespeare's intent and plan is as different from that of

---

[1] Apollodorus, *Bibliotheca*, III. 14. 3–4.

Ovid as his Venus—a forty-year-old countess with a taste for
Chapel Royal altos—is from the eternal girl of the Velia.

Venus and Adonis is clearly the work of a young and unfinished
artist, but there is no question about his independence. When we
read previous poems based on the myth, we see at once that something very new is being ventured. Parabosco has the goddess come
down from a cloudy reach and exhibit herself naked to the little
hunter. Unused to the sensation of passion, he falls at her feet, and
the text is then Italianly expanded as a warm prelude to the cold
Roman conclusion.[1] Ronsard's 'L'Adonis'[2] is a virtuoso conflation
of Ovid's narrative and Bion's lament. The French poet, who was
as curiously fearful of women as Shakespeare's Adonis, writes in
warning terms. Venus may mourn passionately for Adonis, but
almost at once she will find consolation in the young Anchises.
For Ronsard the scattering anemone is a symbol of the faith of
women. Now no one knew more about the thinness of certain
kinds of love-sorrow than Shakespeare; but in this poem, he
stresses vagaries of ladies that are beyond the intellectual reach of
the French poet; in fact, his goddess is far more seductive—at
least to men of the north—than even those conjured up by his
Italian predecessors. We must read Shakespeare's poem for its
differences from its predecessors to learn what it is about.

Orthodox commentaries have regularly observed that *Venus and
Adonis* is an epyllion like *Hero and Leander,* and, consequently, it is
possible to point to a few similar poems before it and a good many
after.[3] This measurement tells us very little about the poem, under
the surface of which one hears the faint murmur of an inverted
pastourelle,[4] of a mythological satire,[5] and of a poetic discourse on the
nature of the decent Venus. Rising above these mutes are the silver

[1] *Delle Lettere Amorose*, Venice 1568, pp. 306–21.

[2] *Œuvres*, ed. Vaganay, Paris 1924, v. 43–52.

[3] R. Putney, 'Venus and Adonis: Amour with Humour', *P.Q.*, 1941, xx. 533–48;
'Venus Agonistes', *University of Colorado Studies, Language and Literature*, 1953, iv.
52–66.

[4] The usual manner of these seduction poems is to present the effects of knightly
or scholarly blandishments on a simple shepherdess. The one pastourelle that is a
kind of ancestor of *Venus and Adonis* is 'L'autre jour en un jardin' (K. Bartsch,
Altfranzösische Romanzen und Pastourellen, Leipzig 1870, ii. 75), which describes the
assault on a knight of a strong and vigorous young girl who reverses the usual
technique.

[5] In Venus, Shakespeare satirizes women who pursue young lovers and who are
fairly scatter-brained—Erasmus gets the same ladies in his *Laus Stultitiae*—but he is
also mindful perhaps of the anti-Venus literature of the Renaissance, which begins
with Bebel's five-book hexameter poem, *Triumphus Veneris*, Tübingen 1501, a treasure
of motifs that are enhanced by the learned annotations of Joannes Altenstaig.

horn calls of an English *cynegeticon,* for *Venus and Adonis* can be partially explained in terms of a timeless hunt. Venus, the amorous Amazon (both Plautus[1] and Shakespeare say that she manhandled Adonis) hunts with her strong passions; the hunted Adonis lives to hunt the boar; and the boar is death, the eternal hunter. The text, if one is needed, hangs on a common theme, succinctly expressed by an Italian of Shakespeare's generation:

> Questo mondo è una caccia, e cacciatrice
> La Morte vincitrice.[2]

The metaphors and epithets that adorn the Shakespearian text come, if I may be permitted a metaphoric pun, from the lexicon of venery. The great goddess is an 'emptie eagle', given to 'vulture' thoughts; whereas the young hunter is a bird 'tangled in a net', a dabchick hiding in the waves, a 'wild bird being tamed', a protected deer in Venus's 'parke', a 'yeelding pray', a roe 'ty'rd with chasing', and an escaped quarry that 'runs apace' homeward 'through the dark lawnd'. The omitted Ovidian parenthesis of Atalanta and Hippomenes reminds us that in the other half of her legend the runner was a huntress and that her lover-conqueror dissolved his first disappointments in love by hunting.[3]

So it is the larger literary scheme of the hunt that controls the first four scenes of this poem, from the sunshine morning of the first day to the dismal grey of the second, and the whole notion was passed on to Shakespeare through the means of a long symbolic tradition. The Middle Ages, for instance, had laid it down that Venus, in her pursuit of Adonis, had proved herself the mistress of the chase. 'Apri dentibus extinctum Adonidem deflet Venus, habens semper cum venatione vel robusta commercium.'[4] Men who could subscribe to this conclusion naturally agreed that Ovid, archpriest of Venus, was also a mighty hunter of both beasts of venery and of the chase.[5] The Middle Ages, which stood so close to antiquity as to think of its goods as its own in a way that the Renaissance never could, knew its uncles of Greece and Rome and rightly bestowed

---

[1] *Menaechmi,* I. ii. 35.
[2] V. Belli, *Madrigali,* Venice 1599, p. 43: 'This world is a hunt, and Death the inexorable hunter.'
[3] Propertius, I. I. 11–12.
[4] John of Salisbury, *Policraticus,* ed. Webb, 1909, i. 21–22; 'Venus, herself a business-like huntress, wept Adonis killed by the boar's tusks.'
[5] Richard de Fournival, *La Vielle ou les derniers amours d'Ovide,* ed. Cocheris, Paris 1861, pp. 45–52.

this title on him who told Cupid that a good hunter pursued only *fugaces*,[1] who put hunting terms in the mouth of amorous Apollo,[2] and who describes women as fit to be hunted, likening the lover to the skilful *retiarius* spreading his nets.[3] He who knew Ovid, knew that love was a hunt.

But Ovid did not invent this simile to which he gave so much currency. Plato, who discovered most of what we know, was the first to call Eros 'the mighty hunter',[4] and to classify the 'lovers' chase' (ἡ τῶν ἐρώντων θήρα) as a subdivision of the great hunt.[5] In addition to this philosophical metaphor, the lover in antiquity is often a hunter and the hunter often a lover. We remember in this connexion the poetess Eriphanis, who fell in love with the hunter Menalcas, and, as the old phrase goes, 'hunted him in turn'.[6] The god Dionysius, tamer of animals, pleads in another Greek text with the famous huntress Nicaia that she make him companion of her hunt.[7] The deserted Oenone reminds Paris that in the days of their love she showed him where to place his nets and send his dogs.[8] The Roman elegiac poets transformed these myths into rhetorical figures and combined them into charming song. Tibullus, in his elegant last book, shows us Sulpicia begging the boar to spare Cerinthus, whose days in the forest and rocky wastes might more properly be spent in her bed.[9] And, finally, Propertius, forsaken again by Cynthia and made effeminate by love, turns for comfort to the soft hunt, the hunt that Shakespeare's Venus praises to the boy Adonis:

> ipse ego venabor: iam nunc me sacra Dianae
>   suscipere et Veneri ponere vota iuvat.
> incipiam captare feras et reddere pinu
>   cornua et audaces ipse monere canes;
> non tamen ut vastos ausim temptare leones
>   aut celer agrestes comminus ire sues.
> haec igitur mihi sit lepores audacia molles
>   excipere et stricto figere avem calamo.[10]

---

[1] *Amores*, II. 9. 9.   [2] *Met.*, I. 505–7.   [3] *Ars*, I. 45–46.   [4] *Symposium*, 203 D.
[5] *Sophist*, 222 D; see Musaeus, 146–56.
[6] Athenaeus, XIV. 619 c.
[7] Nonnos, *Dionysiaca*, xvi. 75–87: see Virgil, *Eclogues*, III. 74–75.
[8] *Heroides*, V. 17–20.   [9] IV. 3.
[10] II. 19, 17–24: 'I myself shall go out to hunt; my vows to Venus put aside, I shall do the rites of Diana. I shall begin to take wild beasts and fasten their horns to the pine and to urge on the brave dogs. I should not dare to attack the great lions or go quickly to face the boars of the field. It is daring enough for me to snare a tender hare or shoot a bird with an arrow.'

The continued imagination of the Greeks and Romans is found again when Nicolette sends messengers to Aucassin. 'Tell him', she says, 'that there is a beast in the forest (greater in worth than deer, lion, or boar) that he should come to hunt.'[1] What the Middle Ages knew so well did not pass unknown in the generations that came afterward. Like Shakespeare's Adonis, the hero of Poliziano's *La Giostra* scorns love, 'the soft insanity', and plunges into the woodland gloom after a wild deer because he does not know, as the hero of Marie de France's 'Guigemar' learns, that white deer are uncertain beasts. So Julio, thanks to his ignorance, hunts the deer to the gate of the palace of Venus, misled by the nymph who masqueraded as a creature of the chase.[2] The theme of the love-hunt undoubtedly lies behind the flight of Lorenzo de' Medici's *Ambra* through the dark forest of the world;[3] it inspires Valvasone's praise of the hunting Cupid[4] and Francisco Berni's amusing 'Caccia di Amore'.[5] For the benefit of French lovers, Marot describes the companions of Cupid hunting rabbits, hare, and deer, blowing horns and trumpets, gaining and losing trophies of the chase.[6] Baif takes up the theme in 'L'amoureux est chasseur, l'Amour est une chasse';[7] and Ronsard uses the love-hunt as the main scheme of his political allegory, 'Eurymedon et Callirée'.[8] Across the Channel, a poet of

---

[1] *C'est d'Aucassin et de Nicolete*, ed. Bourdillon, 1887, p. 42. In the Middle Ages the theme of the hunt was sometimes used religiously as the hunting of the human soul by demons, or, in the case of the *Minnejäger*, one of whom has the lead in the twelfth-century *Jagd* of Hadamar von Laber, in the chase of the beloved. Von Laber's hunter is aided by his familiar dogs: Gelück, Lust, Liebe, Genade, Fröude, Wille, Wunne, Trost, Staete, Triuwe, and Harre. After difficulties with the wolves, Auflauren and Angeben, the pack finds the hunter's beloved. Schmeller, the editor of this tedious poem (Stuttgart 1850), has found a number of similar poems in German manuscript collections (p. xx). The three-day hunt in *Gawain and the Green Knight* has certainly something to do with the greater and lesser hunts. It is also interesting to discover that the medieval hunting lover, like his classical prototypes, begins with a reluctance to love. Sir Degrevant hunts by night and day, but 'Certus, wyff wold he non, / Wench ne leman'. This attitude changes when he meets Mayd Melidor: 'Now hym lykeys no pley, / To honte ne to revey (hawk)' (ed. Casson, 1949, pp. 5, 35). The hero of *Ipomedon*, ed. Kolbing and Koschwitz, Breslau 1889, is another mighty hunter with an initial antipathy to women (p. 19); and so is Robert de Blois of *Flores et Liriope* (ed. Von Zingerle, Leipzig 1891), p. 42. The medieval lover, like his predecessors in Tibullus and Propertius, hunts for consolation and to ease his troubled soul: see *Guy of Warwick* (ed. Zupitza, 1888), E.E.T.S., xlix. 399, and *Metrical Romances* (ed. Weber, 1810), iii. 124.

[2] Op. cit., ed. Carducci, Bologna 1921, pp. 259, 274 ff. In Chretien de Troyes's *Erec*, there is some connexion between love and the Easter hunt of a white deer.

[3] *Poesie Volgari*, ed. Ross and Hutton, 1912, ii. 81.

[4] *La Caccia*, Milan 1808, p. 148.

[5] *Le Rime*, ed. Palazzi, Genoa 1915, pp. 165-9.

[6] *Œuvres*, ed. Grenier, Paris n.d., i. 17. In his 'Epigrammes' he describes Love as the hunter of virtuous men as well as of beasts.

[7] *Œuvres en rime*, ed. Marty-Laveaux, Paris 1881, i. 312.

[8] Op. cit., ii. 176-91; see also i. 132, 177; iii. 121. A parody of the love-hunt appears

the court of Henry VIII was writing, 'Who list to hount, I know
where is an hynde', a line that must have eventually pleased the
poet whose Duke Orsino could 'hunt the hart' and whose Rosalind
could sharply remark: 'Her love is not the hare I do hunt.'

But the love-hunt, dangerous and valiant as it may be, does not
on the lower venerian level ennoble the soul; hence, the classical
pedagogues did not recommend it to young men for whom life had
a grander course. Plato much prefers the hunting of the 'sacred
hunters' (ἱεροὺς θηρευτάς),[1] an assembly of brave youths, similar
to those described by Philostratus,[2] who take the great land animals
with little aid beyond that of their own physical and mental powers.
In the same section, Plato condemns 'the hunters of men', but for
many Greeks hunting was the hero's preliminary education. To the
grave end of testing and training heroes, Apollo and his sister Diana,
the legend runs, taught hunting to Chiron, who, in turn, imparted
this wisdom to a great register of demigods and noble men.[3] Both
the Middle Ages and the Renaissance had this myth by heart, and
so hunting became first the proper preparation for knighthood and,
later, for the forming of a gentleman.

At the age of twelve the great King Alfred had yet to learn to
read, but he was, none the less, of 'incomparable skill and success in
his incessant hunting'.[4] Child Horn, according to his poem, was
especially tutored in the art,[5] and King Alisaundre of romance was
likewise a mighty boy hunter.[6] It is plenteously clear, too, that
Tristram knew more at fifteen about hunting than about good
manners.[7] But while most knights were skilled hunters and the
hunt was widely commended by men of the Middle Ages, it was
not for everyone nor for every hunter were all kinds of hunting.[8]
'God', according to the precepts of the *Livre de Chasse du Roy Modus*,
'has given each man different tastes and desires, and so he authorized

in the next century in the 'Advice to the Young Hunter Lysidor', *Variétés historiques
et littéraires*, ed. Fournier, Paris 1855, i. 66.

[1] *Laws*, 823 D.   [2] *Imagines*, I. 28.
[3] Xenophon, *Cynegeticon*, I. 1–2. This list of Chiron's alumni was later revised and
increased: see Ronsard's 'La Chasse' (IV. 191–7) and Bargaeus, *Cynegeticon*, Rome
1585, pp. 27–28. The latter author says that hunting began when Venus, lamenting
Adonis's death, went to Diana for help. See also Xenophon, *Cyrop.*, I. 6, 28–29;
Aristotle, *Pol.*, 1256 B; Cicero, *De Nat. Deor.*, II. 161; and Silius Italicus, *Punica*,
VIII. 515–16.
[4] Asser, *De rebus gestis Aelfredi*, ed. Stevenson, 1904, p. 20.
[5] *King Horn*, ed. Hall, 1901, p. 75.   [6] *Metrical Romances*, I. 32.
[7] *Sir Tristram*, ed. McNeill, 1886, p. 9.
[8] *L'Escoufle*, ed. Michelant and Meyer, Paris 1884, p. 96.

several hunts accommodated to the nature of one's virtues and station.'[1]

Thanks to poetical texts from antiquity, from the Middle Ages, and from the Renaissance itself, we can now sit before Shakespeare's *Venus and Adonis* with something better than a blank understanding. We know that Love is a hunter, that the seduction of the beloved is a kind of chase, and that it is all the soft hunt, which is essentially improper. On the other hand, the hard hunt, the work of the sacred hunters, is the honest training of those who would be heroes. But there are hunts available to some and not to others, and the best that one can do is to see, as Bruno suggests, that all of life is a hunt and to hope that one has the implements helpful in its conduct.[2] The poem fits this doctrine as well as any poem fits any doctrine. Venus hunts Adonis; Adonis hunts the boar. The first hunt is the soft hunt of love; the second is the hard hunt of life. But in this simple exposition, there are some interesting implications that I should attend to before I return to the nature of the two hunts.

The myth of Atalanta and Hippomenes, which is the centre of Ovid's poem and explains the goddess's hatred and fear of the bitter beasts, is replaced in *Venus and Adonis* by the episode of the horses, which is a love chase on a bottom level. Shakespeare's Venus produces this event as a burning incitement to the adolescent Adonis and as a living text for her sermon on lust to the more mature readers. Actually, it can be interpreted as an animal allegory springing from the race described by Ovid and setting the tone for Venus's wooing. It is at once love among the beasts and a satire on courtly love, for the stallion is a noble earl and the jennet a maid-in-waiting. But before we understand the moral meaning of the episode, we should ponder the reason for Shakespeare's substitution of it for the older legend. Without doubt Shakespeare felt that the lengthy tale of Atalanta and Hippomenes was a dramatic distraction that threw the central story out of focus, and for this reason should be omitted. I also suspect that an associative process led him to add the mating of the horses.

Shakespeare's Adonis is, after all, a remaking of the notoriously chaste Hippolytus. The son of Theseus is on every list of heroic hunters, but his similarity to Shakespeare's Adonis does not end here. His chaste resistance, his death through Venus's agents, his

---

[1] Op. cit., ed. Tilander, Paris 1931, p. 4.
[2] *De gli Heroici Furori* in *Opera*, ed. Lagarde, Göttingen 1888, pp. 722–3.

connexion with horses make him a member of Adonis's set.[1] The
ancient poets and mythographers sometimes said that a jealous
Mars or an avenger Apollo sent the boar that killed Adonis, but
Passerat, a French contemporary of Shakespeare's, invented a new
and, perhaps, more congenial legend. Diana sent the boar to revenge
the killing of Hippolytus. 'Soeur de Phaebus, tu le voulus ainsi / De
longue main courrouces et despite / Contre Venus, pour la mort
d'Hippolyte.'[2] In addition to this, there is a hint in the names.
Hippomenes (ἱππο-+μένος: passion or strength of a horse) has a
connexion with Hippolytus and with Adonis's stallion that one with
'small Greek' would notice. So the episode of the stallion and the
jennet slides into the poem by normal associations. But why is it
there?

With the exception of Robert Miller,[3] no critic has seen much in
the episode of the horses beyond a splendid testimony to Shakespeare's knowledge of livestock. It is always pleasant to discover
that Shakespeare knew about as much as the average man, but it is
possible that on this occasion he knew more. Perhaps the poet who
would shortly write

> But you are more intemperate in your blood
> Than Venus, or these pamp'red animals
> That rage in savage sensuality,

had something else in mind. If one could read with Venus and
Shakespeare the book of creatures from which both of them took
this animal *exemplum*, one would find some very interesting classical footnotes about the love madness of stallions and the libidinous-
ness of jennets.[4] Of course, any pasture would hold suggestion; but,
as Miller observed, this stallion breaks his reins and crushes his bit
with his teeth, 'Controlling what he was controlled with'. He is a
creature of virtue, but he lacks 'a proud rider on so proud a back'.
It is Shakespeare who makes this complaint. When it is the turn of
Venus to speak, the horse's rebellion is praised:

> How like a iade he stood tied to the tree,
> Servilly maistred with a leatherne raine,

---

[1] The commentaries on Shakespeare's poem usually mention the story of Herma-
phroditus and Salmacis, but I expect that the more familiar one of Hippolytus is the
real basis.

[2] *Les Poésies françaises*, ed. Blanchemain, Paris 1880, i. 24.

[3] 'Venus, Adonis, and the Horses', E.L.H., 1952, xix. 249–64.

[4] Oppian, *Cynegetica*, I. 158–65; Virgil, *Georgics*, III. 250–4; Horace, *Satires*, II. 7.
47–50; Lucretius, *De Rerum Natura*, V. 1073–7.

> But when he saw his love, his youths faire fee,
> He held such pettie bondage in disdaine:
> Throwing the base thong from his bending crest,
> Enfranchising his mouth, his backe, his brest.

For Venus lust equals freedom, but when we, tutored by a longer tradition than she knew, view the chase and hear these words, we recognize the horse.

Plato, who first supplied us with the doctrine of the hunt, returns to give us the correct annotation on the horse.

Now when the charioteer sees the vision of Love and his whole soul is warmed throughout by the sight and he is filled with the itchings and prickings of desire, the obedient horse, giving in then as always to the bridle of shame, restrains himself from springing on the loved one; but the other horse pays no attention to the driver's goad or whip, but struggles with uncontrolled leaps, and doing violence to his master and team-mate, forces them to approach the beautiful and speak of carnal love.[1]

Yes, here he is;

> Imperiously he leaps, he neighs, he bounds,
> And now his woven girthes he breaks asunder,
> The bearing earth with his hard hoofe he wounds,
> Whose hollow wombe resounds like heavens thunder,
> The yron bit he crusheth tweene his teeth,
> Controlling what he was controlled with.

Adonis's stallion is certainly Plato's horse, but Venus's little lesson is sadly blunted by Shakespeare who describes the mare as a 'breeding jennet'. Venus had used her animal parable to argue that Adonis should reproduce himself (a curious obsession of Shakespeare's at this time), but Adonis, a youth learning the hard hunt, spoils her moral.

> You do it for increase, o straunge excuse!
> When reason is the bawd to lusts abuse.

It is clear that Venus's strategy was first to get Adonis dismounted so that she could demonstrate her powers. Her second task is to make the soft hunt with its meaningful ease so attractive that he will abandon the hard hunt, the preparation for the heroic life. Venus knows that Adonis is not yet ready for her kind of love: 'The tender spring upon thy tempting lip, / Shewes thee unripe.'

[1] *Phaedrus,* 254 A.

In spite of this knowledge, Venus, who is rich with experience, tries her blandishments on Adonis; she even translates him into a deer and accords him the luscious grange of her body. But Adonis knows allegory when he hears it, and so he rushes to remount his horse at the exact moment that it smells the jennet, 'sees the vision of Love'. The adolescent hunter, the sullen morning boy of 'lazie sprite', 'heavie, darke, disliking eye' loses his temper; he is angry with the older woman who has cost him his horse, who has hindered his natural duties. From this anger grows a partial kind of love, but it is not the sort Venus would have. Adonis is a child with her. When she swoons, he fusses over her as a boy might fuss over his mother. He will readily kiss her good-night when it is time for bed. The goddess takes advantage of this filial-maternal relationship which is really all Adonis wants. Then the horse-metaphor returns: 'Now is she in the verie lists of love.' But Adonis will not manage her; he will only hunt the boar. Venus equates the boar with Death, and, as becomes an otiose goddess, returns to the problem in hand and praises the soft hunt.

In Venus's venery, the soft hunt is the pursuit of the *fugaces*, of those timid animals that never turn and stand—the hare, the cony, the fox, and the deer, but especially the hare. This is the hunt for which, we will remember, Propertius was bold enough. Ovid, himself, describes the god Apollo bounding after the flying Daphne like a French hound pursuing a hare in an open meadow.[1] It is, of course, by no artistic accident that Venus who could describe the grazing of the deer so sensuously, now paints the hunting of wet 'wat' so well. The whole section, like that on the horses, has been vastly admired by the Shakespearian lovers of nature, and I do not doubt that Shakespeare like any country lad sent his dog after rabbits. But the landscape over which 'poore wat' tours, the 'farre off' hill upon which he stands erect with 'listning eare', is not too different from Venus's 'parke'; moreover, the creatures among which he seeks to lose himself—'deare', 'sheepe', 'conies'—were not without female counterparts among the Elizabethans. There is no doubt that little Will Shakespeare watched the hare run, but this 'wat' is probably more than a 'deaw-bedabbled wretch'.

It was not unusual for artists to show Venus accompanied by the hare; its unbelievable fecundity, for it was said to conceive while

[1] *Met.*, I. 533–4.

it was gestating,[1] made it a symbolic companion for the generative mother. The ancients thought that hares could exchange sex,[2] and an aggressive masculinity was attributed to the females[3] that suits Shakespeare's impression of Venus. The lubricity of the hare was also long the subject of human comment,[4] but the symbolism of the Shakespearian hare probably goes beyond this. In the *Satiricon* of Petronius, the witch who has undertaken to heal the impotence of the hero, turns at the proper moment and remarks to her assistant: 'You see, my Chrysis, you see; I have raised a hare for others.'[5] The hunting of the hare can probably have only one meaning; but Shakespeare, as only Titian[6] before him, alters Adonis from the soft hunter of hares, who meets death when he turns to the harder hunt, to a youth whose whole intent is on the hunting of the boar.

If the boar meant something to Shakespeare's generation besides the hard hunt, the proper education of the sacred hunter, and, as Venus herself names him, Death, I have not been able to find it. In the legend Adonis always dies at the tusk of the boar, and in the more orthodox accounts of the story, the commentators had no trouble with the meaning. In the medieval annotations, the boar was lechery.[7] Horologgi who explained an Italian translation of the *Metamorphoses* puts the boar down as jealousy,[8] and, interestingly enough, in Shakespeare's account Venus is strangely jealous of the boar. For the more sophisticated Sandys, the ancient weather myth holds valid, so his Adonis is destroyed as the summer is when

[1] Pliny, *Nat. Hist.*, 38. 248; Athenaeus, IX. 400; Pollux, *Onomast.*, v. 12.
[2] Varro, *De Re Rust.*, III. 12.
[3] Vincent of Beauvais, *Speculum Naturale*, Douay, 1624, p. 1360.
[4] Oppian, op. cit., III. 514–25.
[5] Op. cit., p. 131. This passage probably explains Ovid's *Ars*, III. 662: 'Et lepus hic aliis exagitatus erit.'
[6] Borghini reproves Titian for changing the myth, and making Adonis reject the advances of Venus, observing that this is beyond his rights as an artist: *Il Riposo*, Milan 1807, i. 72–73.
[7] *Ovide Moralisé*, ed. De Boer, Amsterdam 1936, p. 100.
[8] Andrea dell'Anguillara, *Le Metamorfosi di Ovidio*, Venice 1584, p. 388. The notion that the boar is death is supported by scores of literary texts. Lucretius describes the struggles of primitive men against boars, and the exploits of Hercules and Meleager make the boar the beast against which heroes test their might. The great boar hunt is an important moment in many medieval romances of chivalry, and the heroes of these pieces are sometimes likened to boars. In *Brut*, ed. Madden, 1847, Edwin urges his men to have 'boars' hearts' (III. 220) and Merlin predicts that Arthur will become a wasting boar (II. 250). The vision of danger that Venus has in the poem is reminiscent of the boar dreams that warned the heroes of romance of either their impending deaths or an almost fatal disaster; see *Nibelungen Lied*, ed. Bartsch and De Boor, Weisbaden 1956, pp. 155–65; *Horn et Rimenhild*, ed. Brede and Stengel, Marburg 1883, p. 225; *Ogier de Danemarche*, ed. Barrois, Paris, 1842, pp. 333–4; and *Gaydon*, ed. Guessard, Paris 1862, p. 11.

X The tusk of the boar and the curved knife
of the executioner —

boarish winter comes.[1] At this time in his poetic life, Shakespeare,
one should observe, may have had boars in his head because he had
only recently been looking through the life records of Richard III,
'the wretched, bloody, and usurping boar', and he was also fasci-
nated, as young men often are, by innocent and unmerited death in
youth. He needed, I imagine, no goddess to expound any of this to
him, but, none the less, he brings Venus back in the later part of the
poem to discourse foolishly on love like a fluttery and apprehensive
Doll Tearsheet of forty. As for his Adonis—since all Adonises must
die—this one, the invention of Shakespeare, gets off with a cleaner
biography than any.

[1] *Metamorphosis Englished*, 1632, p. 367.

X The deaths of the young preists in Yorkshire
in 1592/3

Variations on a Theme in Shakespeare's Sonnets

J. B. LEISHMAN

I

IT is a commonplace of criticism that there are certain obvious differences between Shakespeare's Sonnets and those of all his predecessors and contemporaries: that for no single one of them has it been possible to produce a recognizable 'source', that most of them are addressed to a man, not to a woman, and that behind the collection as a whole we are aware of situations and relationships which cannot have been invented, if for no other reason than that they have been left so tantalizingly obscure. Unfortunately, the fact of these undeniable differences seems to have been accepted by most writers on the sonnets as something like a dispensation from the task of literary criticism, and they have either devoted their whole energies to unprofitable speculations about the identity of 'Mr. W. H.', the friend, the rival poet, and the Dark Lady, or else, assuming, apparently, that because no recognizable 'sources' have been produced, Shakespeare's sonnets are in the most literal sense incomparable, they have omitted from their attempts at stylistic analysis many possible and illuminating comparisons. And yet nowhere else is comparison so possible and so profitable; in no other portion of his work can Shakespeare be so appropriately 'committed with his peers' as in the sonnets. For very many of them—perhaps, indeed, nearly all the most memorable—are concerned with a few large general topics, of which Shakespeare's treatment, both in its resemblances and in its characteristic differences, may be illuminatingly compared with that of various poets throughout the whole course of European literature. In the present study I propose to consider only one of these topics. I shall compare Shakespeare's treatment of Poetry as Immortalization with that of various poets from Pindar to Daniel.

II

In the poetry of Augustan Rome it is possible to distinguish between passages in which the poet speaks of the immortality he will achieve for himself and those in which he speaks of the immortality he will confer upon others, but in the great public Odes of Pindar, celebrating victors in the Panhellenic Games, these two themes are really inseparable. Passages on the immortalizing power of poetry are very frequent in Pindar's odes and often very splendid:[1] here it must suffice to quote (in Sandys's translation) two representative examples. From the tenth Olympian (ll. 91–96):

Whensoever a man, who hath done noble deeds, descendeth to the abode of Hâdês, without the meed of song, he hath spent his strength and his breath in vain, and winneth but a little pleasure by his toil; whereas thou hast glory shed upon thee by the soft-tongued lyre and by the sweet flute, and thy fame waxeth widely by favour of the Pierid daughters of Zeus.

From the Sixth Pythian, for Xenocrates of Acragas, where Pindar declares (ll. 1–18) that he is once more approaching the Delphic temple, where a treasure-house of song has been built up for Acragas, for Xenocrates and for his ancestors, 'which neither wintry rain with its invading onset, the pitiless host launched from deep-thundering clouds, nor the storm-wind with its swirl of shingle, shall buffet and sweep away into the recesses of the sea'. There are similar passages among the surviving fragments of Bacchylides and Simonides, and, to descend to the Alexandrian period, there is a very notable *locus* (magnificently improved upon by Horace in the Lollius Ode) in the Sixteenth Idyll of Theocritus, addressed to Hieron of Syracuse, where the poet mentions the names of many who would have been forgotten had they not been celebrated by Homer and Simonides. So far as we know, the first Roman poet to make really memorable use of this familiar Greek *topos* was Horace. He was certainly the first Roman poet to declare that lyrical, as distinct from epic, poetry could secure lasting fame both for its author and for those he deigned to celebrate, and Professor Fraenkel has noticed[2] that although, in the magnificent epilogue to the Third and last book of his first published odes, beginning 'Exegi monumentum aere perennius', he confidently prophesied his own immortality, it was only, in those odes, upon the Bandusian Spring (III. xiii) that he had actually ventured to confer it, and it was not until the later Fourth Book, after he had been selected to compose the *Carmen*

---

[1] I think the following list contains most of the really significant ones: Olympian Odes, X. 91–96, XI. 1–10; Pythian Odes, III. 110–15, VI. 1–18; Nemean Odes, IV. 81–86, VII. 11–21, VIII. 44–48, IX. 6–8; Isthmian Odes, IV. 35–42, VII. 16–19.
[2] Eduard Fraenkel, *Horace*, 1957, p. 423.

Saeculare and been publicly recognized as the Roman laureate, that
he seems to have felt entitled to follow the example of his Greek
lyric masters and to promise immortality to some of his contemporaries. In the Censorinus Ode (IV. viii), *Donarem pateras*, Horace
begins, with a kind of safeguarding modesty, by declaring that,
were he a wealthy man, he would give bronzes and tripods, statues
and paintings to his friends, but that, being what he is, all he can
offer them are poems—the superior value of which he proceeds to
imply by declaring that the fame of Scipio Africanus owes more to
the poetry of Ennius than to all the public records of his achievements, and that Romulus and Aeacus would have been forgotten
had they not been celebrated in verse (by, respectively, Ennius and
Pindar). Here the only poet to whom (or rather to whose Muses,
his *Calabrae Pierides*) Horace specifically refers is Ennius, author of
the *Annales*, and even in Rome there was nothing presumptuous or
unusual in the notion that an epic poet could confer immortality;
but in the immediately following ode to Lollius (IV. ix), *Ne forte
credas*, after proclaiming, in the very first stanza and in verse even
more resonantly impressive than that of the epilogue to the Third
Book (*Exegi monumentum*) the imperishability of his lyric achievement, Horace proceeds to justify this conviction by reminding his
friend that, although Homer is supreme, the great Greek lyric
poets (*Pindarus novemque lyrici*), whom he either names or alludes
to, are no less remembered. Then come three stanzas (doubtless
suggested by Theocritus, whom Horace immeasurably surpasses)
declaring that the deeds both of Helen and of many who fought on
either side at Troy were far from unexampled, leading to the superb
climax:

> Vixere fortes ante Agamemnona
> multi; sed omnes inlacrimabiles
>   urgentur ignotique longa
>   nocte, carent quia vate sacro.

Without pausing to insist upon the now sufficiently obvious implication that, since lyric poetry can be as enduring as Homer's, it can
confer a no less enduring fame upon those it celebrates, Horace now
reaches what one is almost tempted to regard as his ostensible
rather than his real subject, and declares that he will not allow the
great public virtues of Lollius to fall into oblivion. Thus concludes
the most impressive single treatment of the theme of poetic immortality in the whole of European poetry.

A few parenthetical remarks on certain of Shakespeare's sonnets seem relevant here. The two odes we have been considering are immediately preceded by what Housman regarded as the most beautiful of all Latin poems, *Diffugere nives* (IV. vii), that ode to Torquatus on the return of Spring and on the sad contrast between the returning seasons and the unreturning lives of men; and Professor Fraenkel has expressed the (so far as I am aware) original conviction[1] that these three odes were deliberately intended to form a kind of central triad, and that between *Diffugere nives*, declaring that we shall all end as no more than *pulvis et umbra*, and the two following odes there is, as it were, an implied, but thereby all the more impressive, 'nevertheless': upon what would else be but *pulvis et umbra* poetry, and poetry alone, can confer immortality. Professor Fraenkel has noticed a similar transition of thought, more explicitly though far more faintly expressed, in an epinikion of Bacchylides: 'Deep Aether is undefilable, water of the sea does not dry up, gold is a gladness; but to man it is not permitted, once grey age has come, to regain flourishing youth. Nevertheless the brightness of virtue does not fade, but the Muse nourishes it.' Professor Fraenkel's contention seems to me to be supported by the very interesting fact that a relationship very similar to that between *Diffugere nives* and the Censorinus and Lollius odes exists between two pairs (64 and 65, 73 and 74) of Shakespeare's finest sonnets, although in each case the transition is far more explicit than with Horace and the four sonnets in question form two almost inseparable pairs. Sonnet 64 begins

> When I have seen by Time's fell hand defaced
> The rich proud cost of outworn buried age

and leads to the conclusion:

> When I have seen such interchange of state,
> Or state itself confounded to decay,
> Ruin hath taught me thus to ruminate,
> That Time will come and take my love away.
> This thought is as a death, which cannot choose
> But weep to have that which it fears to lose.

Sonnet 65, where Shakespeare explicitly asks and explicitly answers the questions which Horace (even if Professor Fraenkel is right) only implicitly raises and implicitly replies to, must, familiar though

[1] *Horace*, 1957, pp. 419, 421, 426.

it is, be quoted in full, partly because it is impossible to summarize and partly because it contains some of the very finest of those metaphorical personifications with which, as it seems to me, the only real parallels are those in some of Horace's odes:

> Since brass, nor stone, nor earth, nor boundless sea,
> But sad mortality o'er-sways their power,
> How with this rage shall beauty hold a plea,
> Whose action is no stronger than a flower?
> O, how shall summer's honey breath hold out
> Against the wreckful siege of battering days,
> When rocks impregnable are not so stout,
> Nor gates of steel so strong, but Time decays?
> O fearful meditation! Where, alack,
> Shall Time's best jewel from Time's chest lie hid?
> Or what strong hand can hold his swift foot back?
> Or who his spoil of beauty can forbid?
>   O, none, unless this miracle have might,
>   That in black ink my love may still shine bright.

Sonnets 73 and 74 contain profoundly beautiful and original variations on this ancient topic, for in 73, beginning

> That time of year thou mayst in me behold
> When yellow leaves, or none, or few do hang
> Upon those boughs which shake against the cold,
> Bare ruin'd choirs where late the sweet birds sang,

Echoe of Bodlein
1st 16 and

and concluding

> This thou perceiv'st, which makes thy love more strong
> To love that well which thou must leave ere long,

Shakespeare is contemplating, not human transience in general, nor even, as in so many of his other sonnets, the time-threatened loveliness of his friend, but his own transience; and in 74, perhaps the most beautiful of all his sonnets, he is content to regard his own poetry as no more (and so less) than that in which his friend, should he survive the poet, will continue to possess the 'better part' of him:

> But be contented: when that fell arrest
> Without all bail shall carry me away,
> My life hath in this line some interest,
> Which for memorial still with thee shall stay.
> When thou reviewest this, thou dost review
> The very part was consecrate to thee:

The earth can have but earth, which is his due;
My spirit is thine, the better part of me:
So then thou hast but lost the dregs of life,
The prey of worms, my body being dead,
The coward conquest of a wretch's knife,
Too base of thee to be remembered.
 The worth of that is that which it contains,
 And that is this, and this with thee remains.

I find it hard not to believe that not only the phrase 'the better part of me' but the whole thought (or, since he thought in metaphors, all the metaphors) of this sonnet were suggested to Shakespeare by the proud boast of his favourite Ovid, at the end of the *Metamorphoses*, that he is ready for that day which can claim only his body to end when it will the uncertain course of his life, since by the better part of him he will be carried up in immortality above the stars on high and his name shall be indestructible and his fame as lasting as the power of Rome:

> Cum volet, illa dies, quae nil nisi corporis huius
> ius habet, incerti spatium mihi finiat aevi:
> parte tamen meliore mei super alta perennis
> astra ferar nomenque erit indelebile nostrum;
> quaque patet domitis Romana potentia terris,
> ore legar populi, perque omnia saecula fama,
> siquid habent veri vatum praesagia, vivam.

Among the many notable examples of imitation and transformation in Renaissance poetry I can think of nothing quite comparable with Shakespeare's appropriation and transformation of Ovid's proud and public boast into this so humble and private and personal reassurance.[1]

 I will conclude these parenthetical remarks upon the affinity between these four sonnets and the great Horatian triad by quoting two stanzas from *Diffugere nives*, where that affinity in metaphor to which I have already referred is especially striking:

> Frigora mitescunt zephyris, ver proterit aestas
> interitura simul
> pomifer Autumnus fruges effuderit, et mox
> bruma recurrit iners.

---

[1] It seems possible that, together with this recollection of Ovid there may also be a recollection of the Book of Job (xix. 26): 'And though . . . worms destroy this body, yet in my flesh shall I see God.'

> Damna tamen celeres reparant caelestia lunae:
>   nos, ubi decidimus
> quo pius Aeneas, quo Tullus dives et Ancus,
>   pulvis et umbra sumus.[1]

Perhaps the passage which, in mere content, the first of these stanzas most obviously resembles, a passage, though, where Shakespeare is somewhat below his best, is one in Sonnet 5 (ll. 5–8):

> For never-resting Time leads summer on
> To hideous winter, and confounds him there;
> Sap check'd with frost and lusty leaves quite gone,
> Beauty o'ersnow'd and bareness every where.

But for something more like an equivalent of the compressed and dynamic image in *ver proterit aestas*, the image of Summer, like a pursuing horseman, riding down and trampling upon fugitive Spring, one would have to turn to such things as the 'fell arrest without all bail', or the 'coward conquest of a wretch's knife'.

The contrast between what I can best describe as the *publicness* of Horace, whose eye, in *Diffugere nives*, is not so much upon his friend Torquatus as upon that spectacle of human transience from which he exhorts him to draw the appropriate moral, and who, after, as it were, preparing the ground in the Censorinus Ode, almost openly appears in its companion as the publicly acknowledged successor of the great public celebrators of public virtues and public deeds—the contrast between this and the privateness of Shakespeare, for whom the humanity threatened by Time seems to exist only in the person of his nameless and unidentifiable friend, and who, though he elsewhere speaks at times with an Horatian resonance of his poetry

> (Not marble, nor the gilded monuments
> Of princes, shall outlive this powerful rhyme. 55

---

[1] Partly because of a problem of interpretation in the second of these stanzas (it concerns the exact meaning of *caelestia damna*) which, after much badgering of more learned friends, I have settled to my own satisfaction, I append a very inadequate but perhaps useful translation:

> Chillness yields to the western wind, Spring's victim of Summer,
>   destined to perish as well
> soon as Autumn unloads her ripe-grown fruits, and, with sudden
>   numbingness, Winter returns.

> While, though, swiftly the moons upbuild those seasonal ruins,
>   we, when we've fallen to where
> pious Aeneas and richest Tullus and Ancus have fallen,
>   linger as shadow and dust.

> So long as men can breathe, or eyes can see,
> So long lives this, and this gives life to thee. 18),

mentions it in 65 only with a kind of tremulous questioning ('unless this miracle have might') and who in 74, the most beautiful of all his sayings about it, professes to regard it as no more than a 'memorial' of him which his friend can never lose—this contrast, to which I shall have to return, is sufficiently great and sufficiently obvious. Nevertheless, Horace and Shakespeare 'have shook hands as over a vast and embraced as from the ends of opposed winds'. On this topic of poetry as the Defier of Time each of them has written more great and more memorable poetry than any other European poet. Pindar is the only other ancient poet who has written something approaching as many *lines* on this topic as Horace, but the merely incidental treatments of it in Pindar's odes, magnificent as they often are, cannot, in weight and total impressiveness, compare with the epilogue to the Third Book of the Odes and the great triad (as Professor Fraenkel would have us regard it) in the Fourth. The only modern poet who has written as much as (perhaps even more than) Shakespeare on this topic is the youthful Ronsard, but those many passages in his odes where Ronsard has imitated almost everything on this topic in the ancient poets (above all in Pindar and Horace) and applied it to himself and to his own (shall we say?) not yet quite comparable achievements, these, when weighed on even the most primitive of critical balances against Shakespeare's sonnets, fly up and kick the beam. On this topic Horace is only really comparable with Shakespeare and Shakespeare only really comparable with Horace.

The various brief and incidental treatments of this topic by those whom Milton called 'the smooth Elegiac Poets' of Augustan Rome were probably both suggested and justified by the example and authority of Horace. They are worth recalling, because, although few of them would be likely to arrest the attention and remain in the memory of a modern reader, they were nearly all frequently imitated by the vernacular poets of modern Europe from Petrarch onwards. By far the most splendid and memorable of them are the concluding lines of the last book of the *Metamorphoses*, which I have already quoted as the possible 'source' of Shakespeare's 74th Sonnet. It is an epilogue which, as its opening lines reveal, was almost certainly suggested by Horace's epilogue to the Third Book of his

Odes, and in which Ovid seems to be almost deliberately placing his own *opus* beside Horace's *monumentum*:

> Iamque opus exegi quod nec Iovis ira nec ignis
> nec poterit ferrum nec edax abolere vetustas.

The phrase *edax vetustas* recalls, and was perhaps intended to recall, the phrase *tempus edax rerum* (which almost certainly gave Shakespeare his 'Devouring Time' in Sonnet 19) in the apostrophe to Time earlier in this last book (ll. 234–6):

> Tempus edax rerum, tuque, invidiosa vetustas,
> omnia destruitis vitiataque dentibus aevi
> paulatim lenta consumitis omnia morte.

In the latter part of the fourteenth, and in the fifteenth and last books of the *Metamorphoses* Ovid relates legends connected with various Roman heroes from Aeneas to Augustus. The fifteenth book begins with Numa, and Ovid accepts the tradition that he visited Croton and there became a pupil of Pythagoras. This provides an opportunity to introduce Pythagoras and make him give something like a summary of his philosophy: how, although the eternal substance of things persists and nothing utterly perishes, the appearance of things is being perpetually altered by *tempus edax rerum*. Was this impressive discourse on mutability (ll. 179–236 are the most important), which meant so much to Spenser and other Elizabethans, introduced mainly in order to display Ovid's learning, or was it intended, despite much intervening matter, to recur to the reader's memory when he reached the epilogue and to add weight to that final exaltation of poetry as the only conqueror of Time? Whatever be the right answer to this question, there can be no doubt that both passages were very much in Shakespeare's memory and imagination when he was writing these sonnets about poetry as the defier of Time.

The remaining *loci* may be more summarily treated. In Ovid's *Amores* there are two passages concerned with the immortality which the poet himself can achieve, as distinct from that which he can confer: in I. xv, in reply to those who accuse him of idleness, he gives a long list of poets who have achieved eternal fame, and concludes

> Ergo etiam cum me supremus adederit ignis,
> vivam, parsque mei multa superstes erit—

lines which contain an audacious and obvious imitation of a passage in Horace's epilogue to the Third Book:

> non omnis moriar multaque pars mei
> vitabit Libitinam.

In III. ix, the beautiful funeral elegy on Tibullus, the two themes are in some sort combined in the lines (27–30) declaring that, although Homer too has perished, his fame, and the fame of those he has celebrated, have survived:

> Hunc quoque summa dies nigro submersit Averno.
> defugiunt avidos carmina sola rogos.
> durat, opus vatum, Troiani fama laboris
> tardaque nocturno tela retexta dolo.

And then come two lines (39–40) memorably imitated by Herrick:

> Carminibus confide bonis; iacet, ecce, Tibullus,
> vix manet e toto parva quod urna capit.

In those passages where the elegiac poets promise, if not eternal, at least contemporary fame to their mistresses and their 'lovely boys' the emphasis is mainly upon the enduringness of poetry in general, for a Roman poet could not publicly exalt the object of a purely personal affection with the weight and resonance with which Horace could celebrate the public virtues of Lollius and the achievements of Augustus. Great revolutions had to take place in European civilization and sensibility before a Petrarch could speak as he did of his Laura or a Shakespeare of his friend. The theme of Horace's Censorinus Ode, *Donarem pateras*, often reappears: the mistress or the boy may indeed find many lovers able to bestow more costly gifts, but the gifts bestowed by the poet will endure for ever. Thus in *Amores*, I. x (59–62), Ovid declares that, while garments will get torn and gold and gems get broken, the fame conferred by his songs will be everlasting, and in II. xvii (27–28) that his *carmina* supply the place of a large fortune and that many women long to be celebrated by him. In the fourth elegy of Tibullus's First Book (61 ff.) Priapus, having declared, in reply to the poet's question, that kindness and compliance are the best ways to win a boy's affection, recollects that in these bad days boys expect presents, and urges them to love poets and the Muses and to disdain golden gifts:

> Quem referent Musae, vivet, dum robura tellus,
> dum caelum stellas, dum vehet amnis aquas.

Only Propertius, I think, and he only in a single passage, has achieved something of an Horatian, almost, one might say, of a Shakespearian, resonance on this topic of the contrast between the poverty of the poet and the uniqueness of what he can bestow when, at the end of the second elegy of his Third Book (17 ff.), he declares that his *carmina* shall be so many monuments to Cynthia's beauty and that, while pyramids and temples and costly tombs are destroyed by fire or weather or time, the fame his *ingenium* has achieved shall endure for ever:

> Fortunata, meo si qua est celebrata libello!
>   carmina erunt formae tot monumenta tuae.
> nam neque Pyramidum sumptus ad sidera ducti,
>   nec Iovis Elei caelum imitata domus,
> nec Mausolei dives fortuna sepulcri
>   mortis ab extrema condicione vacant.
> aut illis flamma aut imber subducit honores,
>   annorum aut ictus pondere victa ruent.
> at non ingenio quaesitum nomen ab aevo
>   excidet: ingenio stat sine morte decus.[1]

In *Amores*, III. xii, Ovid professes to regret having celebrated Corinna's beauty, since by so doing he has turned her into a prostitute, made himself her bawd and pandar, and himself opened the door to other lovers, but Propertius, so far as I know, and again only in a single passage (III. xxiv. 1–8) is the only ancient poet who has declared, in a fit of anger, that his mistress's reputation for beauty is an illusion that has been created entirely by himself:

> Falsa est ista tuae, mulier, fiducia formae,
>   olim oculis nimium facta superba meis.
> noster amor tales tribuit tibi, Cynthia, laudes.
>   versibus insignem te pudet esse meis.
> mixtam te varia laudavi saepe figura,
>   ut, quod non esses, esse putaret amor;
> et color est totiens roseo collatus Eoo,
>   cum tibi quaesitus candor in ore foret.[2]

---

[1] Since these lines are not easy, I give H. E. Butler's translation: 'Happy she that book of mine hath praised! My songs shall be so many memorials of thy beauty. For neither the Pyramids built skyward at such cost, nor the house of Jove at Elis that matches heaven, nor the wealth of Mausolus' tomb are exempt from the end imposed by death. Their glory is stolen away by fire or rain, or the strokes of time whelm them to ruin crushed by their own weight. But the fame that my wit hath won shall never perish: for wit renown endureth deathless.'

[2] In Butler's translation: 'False, woman, is the trust thou puttest in thy beauty;

See Miltons sonnet on Shakespeare.
also Chapmans references to Cynthia

It was no doubt this passage which suggested to Thomas Carew his famous

> Know *Celia*, (since thou art so proud,)
> 'Twas I that gave thee thy renowne,

where (again, so far as I know) the topic makes its first reappearance in modern vernacular poetry. On its absolute incompatibility with Petrarch's sonnets to Laura and Shakespeare's sonnets to his friend it is unnecessary to insist; although it is not, perhaps, so utterly remote from the mood of some of Shakespeare's sonnets to or about the Dark Lady. It also sufficiently illustrates the contrast between the general light-heartedness, lack of reverence, and comparative superficiality in the promises, or proffers, of immortality which the elegiac poets make to their 'flames' and the *gravitas* with which Horace declares that he will not allow the public virtues of Lollius to be lost in oblivion. Indeed, except for some of the things which they are sometimes led on to say about poetry in general, the love-poets' verses on this topic of the poor but powerful poet seem, at least to a modern reader, to be continually approaching the territory of comic opera, or even of the music-hall joke ('You stick to me, Dolores—immortality's worth more than a mink coat').

III

I will now turn to Petrarch, whose influence, direct or indirect, upon all Renaissance sonneteers was so inescapable and, to a considerable extent, determining. I cannot claim to have noticed every passage in his sonnets and canzoni where he speaks of the fame which his poetry has achieved, or may achieve, for Laura and for himself, but those which I have noticed among the 366 poems of the *Canzoniere*, and which I will briefly mention, are remarkably few and, for the most part, so modest and tremulous and muted that they might easily escape attention, and perhaps few students of Petrarch who had not been attentively looking for them would be able to remember that they were there. Shakespeare's treatments of this topic

long since the partial judgment of mine eyes hath made thee overproud. Such praises of old my love bestowed on thee, and now it shames me that thou hast glory from my song. Oft did I praise the varied beauty of thy blending charms, and love deemed thee to be that which thou wert not. Oft was thy hue compared to the rosy star of dawn, though the splendour of thy face owed naught to Nature.' At the end of line 4 in the Latin of the Loeb edition there is a question mark: if this is not a misprint, Butler has not translated the text he has given, which could only mean 'Are you ashamed of being renowned by my verses?'

form an unforgettable and inseparable portion of our total impression
of his sonnets, but Petrarch's require to be pointed out and do not
significantly modify our total impression of the *Canzoniere*. Since
few poets have thought more about posthumous fame than did
Petrarch, 'the laureat poete', as Chaucer called him, this might at
first sight seem surprising, but there are, I think, two convincing
explanations. In the first place, Petrarch's hopes of poetic immortality were based, not upon his vernacular, but upon his Latin poetry;
and, in the second place (and perhaps far more importantly), the
whole tradition, the whole manner of thinking and feeling, behind
his poetry to and about Laura was absolutely incompatible with
anything like resonant self-confidence or boastfulness. For Petrarch
may be regarded as the first great popularizer of that characteristic
combination of Courtly Love and partly philosophic, partly Christian idealism, unworldliness, and 'spirituality' which had been more
reconditely expressed by Dante and some of his early Italian
predecessors.

It is significant that in none of the Laura poems does Petrarch
venture to speak of poetry as he does in 104,[1] 'L'aspettata vertù,
che'n voi fioriva', a sonnet addressed to Pandolfo Malatesta, Lord of
Rimini, who had already begun his distinguished military career,
and for whom Petrarch declares that he wishes to write something
that will make his name mount into esteem, since not even marble
statues can be as permanent as writings. In the sestet the influence
of Horace's Censorinus Ode and Ovid's *Amores*, I. x (59–62), is
sufficiently obvious:

> Credete voi che Cesare o Marcello
>   O Paulo od Affrican fossin cotali
>   Per incude già mai né per martello?
> Pandolfo mio, quest' opere son frali
>   Al lungo andar; ma 'l nostro studio è quello
>   Che fa per fama gli uomini immortali.[2]

In nearly all the Laura poems his allusions to *fama* are far more
humble than this, and are often, as it were, merely slipped in. Thus,

---

[1] In my references to the *Canzoniere* I give the numbering in the edition by Carducci and Ferrari, which is that of most of the best modern editions, and I discard
the cumbrous use of Roman numerals. I also give, in each case, the first line.

[2] 'Do you believe that Caesar or Marcellus or Aemilius Paulus or Scipio Africanus
could ever have become what they are for us through bronzes or hammered marble?
My Pandolf, these works are frail for long continuance, but the art we study is that
which, through fame, makes men immortal.'

in 61, 'Benedetto sia 'l giorno e 'l mese e l'anno', after blessing the time and place of his first sight of her and all the sweet pain that followed, he concludes:

> E benedette sian tutte le carte[1]
> Ov' io fama le acquisto, e 'l pensier mio
> Ch' è sol di lei sí ch'áltra non v'ha parte.[2]

In 71, 'Perchè la vita è breve', the first of three canzoni on Laura's eyes, he attributes to their power whatever merit his verse may possess (ll. 7–13):

> Occhi leggiadri dov' Amor fa nido,
> A voi rivolgo il mio debile stile
> Pigro da sé, ma 'l gran piacer lo sprona:
> E chi di voi ragiona
> Tien dal suggetto un abito gentile,
> Che con l'ale amorose
> Levando il parte d'ogni pensier vile.[3]

In 146, 'O d'ardente vertute ornata e calda', he seems to make a definite distinction between what he might have achieved in Latin and what he must be content with achieving in the vernacular. After apostrophizing, in the octave, Laura's spiritual and physical beauty, he declares that, if his rhymes could be understood so far away, he would fill the remotest corners of the world with her praise, but that, since he cannot reach so far, he will make sure that Italy hears it,

> udrallo il bel paese
> Ch' Appennin parte e 'l mar circonda e l'Alpe.

In 186, 'Se Virgilio et Omero avessin visto', he declares that if

---

[1] Was Petrarch's habitual use of the word *carte*, in which he was followed by other poets, including Tasso, a Latinism imitated from Horace's declarations that he would not keep an unadorning silence about Lollius in his *chartae*:

> non ego te meis
> chartis inornatum silebo (IV. ix. 30–31)

and that Censorinus's well-doing would not receive its due reward if *chartae* remained silent about it:

> neque
> si chartae sileant quod bene feceris,
> mercedem tuleris (IV. viii. 20–22)?

[2] 'And blessed be all those parchments where I acquire fame for her, and (blessed be) my thought which is so entirely of her that no other woman has any part therein.'
[3] 'Charming eyes where Love makes his nest, to you I apply my feeble style, inert in itself, but great delight spurs it; and he who discourses of you draws from the subject a gentle habit which, with amorous wings exalting, withdraws him from all ignoble thought.'

Virgil and Homer had seen Laura they would have devoted all their powers to her celebration, to the discomfiture of Aeneas, Achilles, Ulysses, Augustus, and Agamemnon. Scipio Africanus, 'that ancient flower of virtues and of arms, what a resembling star he would have had in this new flower of honesties and beauties. Ennius of him sang a rugged song, of this other I: and, oh, if only my wit be not tiresome to her and she do not disdain my praise!' In 187, 'Giunto Alessandro a la famosa tomba', Petrarch alludes to what was to become for Renaissance writers perhaps the most memorable of all *loci* on poetic immortality, the description by Plutarch in his *Life* and by Cicero in the *Pro Archia* of Alexander's visit to the tomb of Achilles, where he exclaimed, according to Cicero, 'O fortunate adolescens, qui tuae virtutis Homerum praeconem inveneris!'[1] Petrarch regrets that the incomparable Laura

> Nel mio stil frale assai poco rimbomba,

'achieves so little resonance in my feeble style'. Worthy of Homer, Orpheus, or Virgil, fate has committed her to one who adores her but whose telling of her perhaps diminishes her praise. In 194, 'L'aura gentil che rasserena i poggi', returning from Tuscany to the neighbourhood of Laura's Avignon and, it would seem, punning (in a manner often imitated by Tasso) upon *l'aura*, the breeze, and *Laura*, he declares that by its sweet breathing he recognizes the gentle breeze which is unclouding the hills and awakening the flowers as that through which it is decreed that he should mount into torment and into fame,

> Per cui conven che 'n pena e 'n fama poggi.

203, 'Lasso, ch'i' ardo, et altri non me 'l crede', contains the nearest approach to something like an Horatian or Shakespearian proclamation. He reproaches her for pretending not to be aware of his love for her, which is so apparent to all others:

> Quest' arder mio, di che vi cal sí poco,
>   E i vostri onori in mie rime diffusi
>   Ne porian infiammar fors' ancor mille;
> Ch' io veggio nel pensier, dolce mio foco,

---

[1] Imitated by Spenser in *The Teares of the Muses*, 433–4. Petrarch's lines were quoted by E. K. at l. 65 of the October eclogue of the *Shepheardes Calendar*. The story was retold by Amyot in the Preface to his translation of Plutarch's *Lives* and by Du Bellay in his *Deffense et illustration de la langue française*, II. v.

> Fredda una lingua e duo belli occhi chiusi
> Rimaner dopo noi pien di faville.[1]

Here it seems probable that Petrarch had in mind Horace's beautiful lines about Sappho in the great roll-call of Greek lyric poets in the Lollius Ode:

> spirat adhuc amor
> vivuntque commissi calores
> Aeoliae fidibus puellae.[2]

In 205, 'Dolci ire, dolci sdegni e dolci paci', after having comforted his soul, in the preceding sonnet, with the thought that Laura is leading it to God and the bliss of heaven, he now declares that she is also leading it to fame on earth: 'Do not repine, but endure and be silent, and temper the sweet bitterness which has distressed us with the sweet honour which you have received through the loving of her to whom I said: You alone delight me.' Some of the utterances we have already considered might be regarded as variations upon that familiar topic of panegyrical poetry and oratory, the author's apology for his inability to do justice to his subject, although on the lips of a courtly lover such professions can vibrate with a meaningfulness and a genuine humility that widely separate them from the tones of a courtly flatterer. Thus in 261, 'Qual donna attende a glorïosa fama', after declaring that other ladies can learn from Laura what true virtue is, Petrarch continues:

> Ivi 'l parlar che nullo stile aguaglia,
> E 'l bel tacere, e quei cari costumi
> Che 'ngegno uman non po spiegar in carte.[3]

And in what he says of 'fame' in the *Canzoniere* Petrarch often conveys the impression (perhaps, indeed, it is the total impression left by these passages) that to acquire it for Laura is a kind of religious duty, and that any fame he himself may acquire thereby is to be regarded as something more or less incidental, or at best as a kind of reward conceded to human frailty rather than as a personal achievement. Thus at the conclusion (ll. 73–76) of 268, 'Che

[1] 'This ardour of mine, for which you care so little, and your glories promulgated in my rhymes may yet perhaps be able to inflame thousands; for I behold in thought, sweet my fire, one cold tongue and two fair closed eyes remaining behind us full of sparks.'
[2] 'The love still breathes and the ardours still live that were confided to the Lesbian maiden's lyre.'
[3] 'Here is the speech which no style equals, and the lovely silence, and those dear manners which human wit cannot display in parchments.'

debb' io far? che mi consigli, Amore?', a canzone written after the death of Laura, Love commands him not to be transported by his grief to suicide and thus lose Heaven where Laura is, sighing only for him:

> E sua fama, che spira
> In molte parti ancor per la tua lingua,
> Prega che non estingua,
> Anzi la voce al suo nome rischiari,
> Se gli occhi suoi ti fûr dolci né cari.[1]

It would seem that it was only gradually that Petrarch came to perceive that his poetry about Laura was achieving fame both for her and for himself. In 293, 'S' io avesse pensato che sí care', one of the sonnets written after her death, he declares that had he known that his 'rhymed sighings' ('le voci de' sospir miei in rima') would become so cherished, he would have written more of them and in a better style:

> E certo ogni mio studio in quel tempo era
> Pur di sfogare il doloroso core
> In qualche modo, non d'acquistar fama.
> Pianger cercai, non già del pianto onore.[2]

Indeed, in the *Canzoniere* Petrarch seldom professes to regard his own fame (as distinct from any he may have won for Laura) as more than a consolation. In what I think is the last allusion to it, in 360, 'Quell' antiquo mio dolce empio signore', a canzone in which the poet cites Love before the tribunal of Reason, Love declares in his defence that it has been solely through him, who raised his intellect to where it would never have been raised by itself, that the poet has risen into some degree of fame (ll. 88–90):

> Salito in qualche fama
> Solo per me, che 'l suo intelletto alzai
> Ov' alzato per sé non fôra mai.

It is fascinating and illuminating to attempt to define more closely certain resemblances and differences between, on the one hand,

---

[1] 'And for her fame, which [still]breathes in many places through your tongue [Horace's *spirat adhuc amor* yet again], she prays that it may not be extinguished, but rather that your voice may brighten at her name, if to you her eyes were sweet or dear.'

[2] 'And truly all my study at that time was to find some means of discharging my sad heart, not to win fame. Weeping I sought, by no means honour through weeping.'

Shakespeare and Petrarch and, on the other hand, between each of them and the ancients, in their treatment of this topic of poetic fame. While the emphasis of Horace and Ovid and the rest is almost wholly upon the monumental and monumentalizing quality of poetry in general and of their own poetry in particular, as an individual achievement that will be inseparably associated with themselves, and only secondarily, and in their love-poetry, one might almost say, only trivially, upon those whom they condescend to honour, Shakespeare and Petrarch alike never speak of their own poetry other than as a thing wholly dedicated, wholly subordinated, to the person it professes to honour. Shakespeare, like Petrarch, sometimes declares (though not, it must be admitted, in his very finest sonnets), and perhaps always implies, that his friend has been the sole inspirer of his verse, and only once, I think (in 107, the 'mortal moon' sonnet), does he use the pronoun 'I' in such a context and speak of the perpetuation of himself and of his friend on, as it were, equal terms:

> Now with the drops of this most balmy time
> My love looks fresh, and Death to me subscribes,
> Since, spite of him, I'll live in this poor rime,
> While he insults o'er dull and speechless tribes:
>> And thou in this shalt find thy monument
>> When tyrants' crests and tombs of brass are spent.

Some, no doubt, would say that even Shakespeare, when he wrote sonnets, was compelled, perhaps almost unconsciously, to conform to what might be called the Sonnet tradition, which Petrarch himself had done so much to establish, and in which what was most central and unalterable was the tone and attitude, which must remain predominantly, despite any temporary backslidings and rebelliousnesses, one of humility and adoration. But Shakespeare, after all, was writing these sonnets over a period during which the vogue of the English sonnet was declining, and the young men of the Inns of Court, stimulated no doubt by the example of Donne, together with some of the young disciples of Ben Jonson, were rejecting and satirizing all that Petrarch represented, and were attempting to revive, sometimes agreeably enough, but often, in what they doubtless regarded as achievements of the true Roman *sal* and *facetia*, with an embarrassing mixture of crudeness and caddishness, all those specifically pagan elements in ancient love-poetry which find no echo in either Petrarch or in Shakespeare.

If Shakespeare remained, to a considerable extent, within the tradition of Petrarch, it was because of a certain spiritual affinity. 'Spirituality', indeed, a quality almost completely absent from ancient love-poetry, is perhaps the best single word to describe what the sonnets of Petrarch and of Shakespeare have in common. In a certain sense, perhaps, Shakespeare's sonnets to his friend are even more 'spiritual' than Petrarch's about Laura; for, while Petrarch, after all, has told us quite a lot about Laura, and all his contemporary readers knew, and were intended to know, who she was, how wholly inward and invisible in Shakespeare's sonnets is that 'life' which he promises to perpetuate! What was it in his friend that 'lives' there? We do not even know his name, and, if he was in any sense a public man, we have not a single allusion to any of his public acts, whether as courtier, soldier, statesman, or ruler of a great house or great estate. All we know of him is what he 'meant' to Shakespeare, which amounts to no more (and no less) than knowing something of what love and friendship meant to Shakespeare. How little here remains of the ancient conception of fame, of κλέος, or, if anything of it remains, what a strange metamorphosis it has undergone! That generalization of the particular and particularization of the general which becomes so increasingly characteristic of Shakespeare's dramatic verse is here, perhaps, most recognizably and persistently at work. All those qualities which make a person lovable, all those, perhaps, which for Shakespeare made life itself lovable and livable, are particularized, incarnated, in an individual, and that individual is generalized into their unique but, alas! so transient incarnation. It is as though Shakespeare could only apprehend the meaningfulness of life when it was, for him, incarnated in a person, and as though he could only really love a person as the incarnation of that meaningfulness. (How enormous is the gulf between the most characteristic, that is to say, the most whole-hearted, of Shakespeare's sonnets to his friend and those to or about the Dark Lady, with their continual admissions of recognized and hated self-deception, of the degradation of love into lust, and of the enslavement of the spirit to the flesh!) *Et incarnatus est*: whatever may have been Shakespeare's intellectual attitude towards that mystery, whether he 'died a Papist' or remained no more than a kind of half-believer, it inescapably and unconsciously influenced all his thinking and feeling. The 'inwardness' of his sonnets, in comparison with the 'outwardness' of the odes of Pindar and

never!

Horace, reflects not merely a difference in genius and temperament, but also certain characteristic differences between the Pagan and the Christian worlds. For Christianity, as Rudolf Kassner has finely said, gave a new depth-dimension to the human consciousness.

And yet, despite their affinity in spirituality and inwardness and in their dedication of their verse to the service of the beloved, whom both declare to have inspired it, how different are the manners in which Petrarch and Shakespeare speak of their poetry and of its purpose! Why does Petrarch habitually speak of it so humbly, and, as it were, inconspicuously, while Shakespeare so often speaks with an unforgettable and Horatian resonance of his 'powerful rime'? The reason is, I think, that Shakespeare is undertaking a larger, a more tremendous, a more desperate task. Petrarch conceives, or professes to conceive, it his duty to proclaim what one might almost call the gospel of Laura in order that her 'fame', her good fame, may increase among mankind at large the love of goodness and of gentleness; but, although he must try to ensure that her terrestrial life lives on in his verse as an 'example', he never suggests that her whole life is dependent upon him for its continuance, or that he alone stands between it and devouring Time. During her lifetime he is fully convinced that her soul will find a place in Heaven, and, after her death, he conceives himself to be pleasing her soul in Heaven by continuing to spread the fame of what was heavenly in her among men on earth. Whether Shakespeare in any sense, if at all, 'believed' in the Christian doctrine of immortality I find impossible to decide; nevertheless, and although I should hesitate to pronounce with any confidence what non-metaphorical meanings may or may not be implicit in the utterances of one who so habitually thought in metaphors, I can only record my impression that from Shakespeare's sonnets no less than from Horace's odes there breathes the conviction that it is only in his poetry that anything of his friend and of himself beyond *pulvis et umbra* will survive. Survive in this world, survive among men? The distinction and the implication *may* be present, but they are not, I am inclined to say, meaningfully and poetically present. Shakespeare's sonnets, like Petrarch's, are unworldly, but not, like Petrarch's, other-worldly, and they are filled with a sadness different from Petrarch's and resembling that which breathes from so much of the great poetry of the ancient world: an almost overwhelming sadness at the fact of human transience.

to save a life

IV

Of Italian poetry and, more particularly, of the Italian sonnet from Petrarch to Tasso I cannot claim more than a slight and superficial knowledge. On this topic of poetic immortality the only really memorable utterances that I have been able to discover are in three sonnets of Tasso: one addressed to Alfonso II, Duke of Ferrara, and two in the *Rime d'Amore*. The first declares, as the title has it, 'that there is on earth no truer image of eternity than the glory obtained through writers'. The latter part of the sonnet may well have owed something to Du Bellay's *Antiquitez de Rome*, which had been published in 1558, but it is perhaps the most memorable of all Renaissance poems on the 'outlastingness' of poetry and by far the finest of those all too numerous sonnets in which the unhappy poet appealed from his confinement to the various grandees of Italy:

> Quando nel ciel tra mille aurate sedi
>   Che piene son de' tuoi grandi avi illustri,
>   T'innalzerà dopo girar di lustri
>   Chi comparte le pene e le mercedi,
> Sorger vedrai sotto gl'invitti piedi
>   Gl'imperi e poi cader quasi ligustri
>   Frali, e capanne ti parran palustri
>   Gli eccelsi tetti de' tuoi regi eredi;
> Di Menfi e di Babel cadute e sparte
>   Le meraviglie barbare e sepolta
>   Roma fra le ruine onde s'ammira:
> Solo in terra vedrai farsi le carte
>   Del cielo imago, e 'n lor tua gloria accolta
>   Qual vivo sol se tua pietà m'aspira.[1]

The two sonnets from the *Rime d'Amore* were printed consecutively and are among the later sonnets to Lucrezia Bendidio, for whom Tasso's long passion was now drawing to a close. In the first of them there enters for the first time into what has hitherto been a

---

[1] 'When into Heaven amidst thousand gilded seats which are filled with your great illustrious ancestors shall exalt you after revolving of lustres He who allots the penalties and the rewards, you shall see rising beneath your invincible feet the empires and then falling like frail privets, and marsh cabins shall appear to you the lofty roofs of your royal heirs; of Memphis and of Babylon fallen and scattered the barbarian marvels and Rome buried among the ruins from whence she is admired: on earth you shall see parchments alone acting as an image of Heaven, and in them your glory welcomed like a living sun if your pity lifts me up.' *Rime*, ed. Solerti, iii. 235.

predominantly Petrarchan world the specifically classical and pagan topic, alien both to Petrarch and to Shakespeare, of 'ingrateful beauty threatened'.

> Vedrò da gli anni in mia vendetta ancora
> Far di queste bellezze alte rapine,
> Vedrò starsi negletto e bianco il crine
> Che la natura e l'arte increspa e dora;
> E su le rose, ond' ella il viso infiora,
> Spargere il verno poi nevi e pruine:
> Cosí il fasto e l' orgoglio avrà pur fine
> Di costei, ch' odia piú chi piú l' onora.
> Sol penitenza allor di sua bellezza
> Le rimarrà, vedendo ogni alma sciolta
> De gli aspri nodi suoi ch' ordía per gioco;
> E, se pur tanto or mi disdegna e sprezza,
> Poi bramerà, ne le mie rime accolta,
> Rinnovellarsi qual fenice in foco.[1]

> Quando avran queste luci e queste chiome
> Perduto l' oro e le faville ardenti,
> E l'arme de' begli occhi or sí pungenti
> Saran dal tempo rintuzzate e dome,
> Fresche vedrai le piaghe mie, né, come
> In te le fiamme, in me gli ardori spenti;
> E rinnovando gli amorosi accenti
> Alzerò questa voce al tuo bel nome.
> E 'n guisa di pittor che il vizio emende
> Del tempo, mostrerò ne gli alti carmi
> Le tue bellezze in nulla parte offese:
> Fia noto allor ch' a lo spuntar de l' armi
> Piaga non sana e l' esca un foco apprende
> Che vive quando spento è chi l' accese.[2]

[1] 'I shall yet see in my requital rapine made by the years of these lofty beauties, shall see standing neglected and white the hair that nature and art curl and gild; and upon the roses with which nature beflowers that face, winter then scattering snows and frosts: thus shall they too have end, the pomp and pride of her who hates most him who most honours her. Then only repentance of her beauty shall remain with her, beholding every soul loosed from those hard knots of hers she wove for sport; and, even though now she so disdains and despises me, she then shall long, received into my rimes, to be renewed like phoenix in fire.'

[2] 'When these eyes and this hair shall have lost the gold and the glowing sparks, and the weapons of the fair eyes now so piercing shall be by time blunted and tamed, fresh shall you see my wounds, nor, as in you the flames, extinguished in me the ardours, and, renewing the amorous accents, I shall uplift this voice at your fair name. And, like painter who emends the blemish of time, I shall show in lofty songs your beauties in no part harmed: then shall be manifest that at the unpointing of the weapons

Even in the second of these two sonnets there is a certain Roman *superbia*, a certain self-exaltation on the part of the poet and a certain condescension towards the object of his affection, which reveals, I think, the influence of ancient love-poetry (although I cannot recall any ancient love-poet's having declared that his love would outlast his mistress's beauty), and which is alien to the Petrarchan tradition. The tone and spirit of it is also subtly but profoundly different from Shakespeare's greatest and, so far as I know, both literally and metaphorically *incomparable*, utterance on the topic of 'eternity in love protested', an utterance in which even the greatest of poets seems to have become completely merged into something greater, and in which we seem to hear, no longer merely the poet, but love itself defying Time:

> Let me not to the marriage of true minds
> Admit impediments. Love is not love
> Which alters when it alteration finds,
> Or bends with the remover to remove:
> O, no! it is an ever-fixed mark,
> That looks on tempests and is never shaken;
> It is the star to every wandering bark,
> Whose worth's unknown, although his height be taken.
> Love's not Time's fool, though rosy lips and cheeks
> Within his bending sickle's compass come;
> Love alters not with his brief hours and weeks,
> But bears it out even to the edge of doom.
>   If this be error and upon me proved,
>   I never writ, nor no man ever loved.   (116)

Perhaps, though, it is not quite fair to Tasso, perhaps it would not be quite fair to any poet, to make him stand the push of this comparison.

V

The young Ronsard not only imitated almost everything that any ancient poet had ever said about the enduringness of poetry, but also, and often in a quite breath-taking manner, spoke of his own poetry and his own immortality much as Pindar, Horace, and the

[sc. that caused it] wound does not heal and the fuel is seized by a fire that lives when extinct is what kindled it.' *Rime*, ed. Solerti, ii. 109–11. These two sonnets, together with thirty-five other sonnets by Tasso, were first printed in *Rime degli Academici Eterei*, dedicated to Marguerite de Valois, in 1567, a copy of which must very soon have come into the hands of Ronsard, whose most famous sonnet probably owes something to these two by Tasso.

rest had spoken of theirs. Thus, at the end of the Fourth Book of his Odes, published in 1550 when he was twenty-five, he inserted a kind of epilogue *A sa Muse* (later transferred to the end of the Fifth Book when, by the addition of that, he had over-topped Horace's four-book monument), beginning

> Plus dur que fer, j'ai fini mon ouvrage;[1]

and in the ode 'De l'Election de son Sepulchre' he declared that the shepherds would visit every year his tomb on an island in the Loire and would exclaim:

> Que tu es renommée
> D'estre tumbeau nommée
> D'un de qui l'univers
> Ouira [later: chante] les vers—[2]

one of these passages where, for an English reader, the short lines become irresistibly reminiscent of eighteenth-century opera libretto and emphasize the difference between the vastness of the claim and the triviality of its expression. There is a contrast between the youthful *hybris* of the odes and the comparatively sober and infrequent appearances of this topic in his love-sonnets, of which he must have written upwards of 500. It is a contrast which seems to me strong evidence for the restraining and prescribing influence of what I have called the Sonnet tradition. Nevertheless, even in his sonnets Ronsard's utterances on this topic are restrained only in comparison with those in his odes; and although, in proportion to the number of his sonnets, they are comparatively infrequent, they produce, when placed together, a total impression of self-exaltation that would have shocked Petrarch and which is quite different from that exaltation of poetry as the defier of Time and eternalizer of transient beauty that we find in Shakespeare. Of Petrarch's worshipping and evangelizing and of Shakespeare's selfless devotion and sadness over human transience, and of what I have called the 'spirituality' of both these poets, there is little trace in Ronsard;[3] and the general im-

---

[1] Laumonier, ii. 152. I shall quote Ronsard's poetry partly from the still uncompleted edition begun by the late Paul Laumonier for the Société des Textes Français Modernes (1924–), in which the poems, with the later variants, are given in the text and chronological sequence of their first printing, and partly from the complete edition by Hugues Vaganay (1923), in which the text, except for poems printed after that date, is Ronsard's own 1578 edition of his *Œuvres*.

[2] Laumonier, ii. 99.

[3] Ronsard was a devout, and even fanatical, Catholic, while Shakespeare, for all we know, may have been almost an unbeliever; nevertheless, in a profound sense,

pression conveyed by his own utterances about it is that even in his love-poetry he was primarily concerned with building yet further monuments to his own glory—by which I do not mean to imply that the monuments are not often splendid or the glory unachieved.

To the first collection of his *Amours* (1552), celebrating mainly his 'Cassandre', he prefixed a sonnet dedicated to the Muses, which, like so many of his poems, underwent much alteration in later editions, and of which the sestet (printed in capitals which it does not seem necessary to reproduce) reads as follows in the text of 1578:

> Ronsard, afin que le siècle avenir
> Maugré le temps en puisse souvenir
> Que sa jeunesse à l'amour fist homage:
> De la main dextre apand à vostre autel
> L'humble présent de son livre immortel,
> Son cœur de l'autre aux pieds de ceste image.

There are indeed a few professions of humility in Ronsard's sonnets, but, like the use of the word *humble* in the penultimate line of this dedication, they have a hollow ring and the appearance of mere concessions to a convention he is only pretending to accept. In two of the *Cassandre* sonnets where he is partly imitating some of Petrarch's professions of poetic insufficiency there are characteristic and significant differences. In 72,

> Amour, que n'ay-je en escrivant, la grace
> Divine autant que j'ay la volonté,[1]

he declares that if only he could achieve the height of style he longs for he would surpass Orpheus. Loftier even than Pindar and Horace, he would dedicate to her divinity a book so weighty that even Du Bellay would give place. Not even Laura would fly so alive through the world in Tuscan verse as she would in French. This was clearly suggested by Petrarch's 146, 'O d'ardente vertute ornata e calda', but while Petrarch is merely saying (in so many words) that, since

---

Shakespeare is far more Christian. Indeed, greatly as I admire Ronsard's finest poetry, I am sometimes tempted to wonder whether there does not remain, after all, a certain superficiality that excludes him from what Matthew Arnold used to call 'the glorious class of the best'.

[1] Ronsard continued to add to, rearrange, and revise his Cassandre and Marie sonnets and eventually entitled them, respectively, the First and the Second *Livres des amours*. To them, in the edition of 1578, he added for the first time the *Sonets pour Helene*. They are all contained in the first two volumes of Vaganay's edition, to which, giving the number and the first line, I shall henceforth refer, and from which (in the text of 1578) I shall quote.

he is writing in the vernacular and not in Latin, he must be content
with an Italian audience, Ronsard has no doubt either about the
universality of the French language or about his own ultimate
ability to surpass Pindar and Horace—as his friend Du Bellay already
has done! 1587,

> Si l'escrivain de la Gregeoise armée
> Eust vu tes yeux, qui serf me tiennent pris,

was clearly suggested by Petrarch's 186, 'Se Virgilio et Omero avessin
visto', and 187, 'Giunto Alessandro a la famosa tomba', but while
Petrarch professes to regret that his style, unlike those of Homer
and Virgil, is unworthy of his subject, Ronsard declares that if only
he is able to celebrate Cassandre worthily,

> Il n'y aura ny myrthe ny laurier
> Digne de toy, ny digne de ma teste.

In 199,

> Pille, Garçon, d'une main larronnesse
> Le bel esmail de la verte saison,

he tells his page to gather flowers for his room, to fetch him his
'lyre', so that he may soothe his torment, and also to give him ink
and paper:

> En cent papiers tesmoins de mon souci,
> Je veux tracer la peine que j'endure:
> En cent papiers plus durs que diamant,
> Afin qu'un jour nostre race future
> Juge du mal que je souffre en aimant.

Ronsard, I think, was the first poet to introduce, often with splendid
effectiveness, such pieces of self-dramatization into his sonnets, and
I am inclined to think that Sidney learnt the device from him and
that Ronsard himself learnt it from some of Horace's odes. I have
no doubt whatever that the 'Garçon' in this sonnet is the equivalent
of that *puer* whom Horace tells not to spend time searching for some
last rose for a chaplet, or to cool some Falernian, or to run and
fetch Lyde with her lyre or Neaera with her chestnut hair.

In the sonnets and poems inspired by simple Marie of Bourgueil
the immortality theme occurs only in a sonnet, first printed in the
Bocage of 1554, which, in the editions from 1560 onwards, served as
an epilogue to the second *Livre des amours*, where it was preceded by
an *Elegie à Marie*, a charming poem, with some notable imitations

of ancient poets. The passage about the temple which, if he were a great king, Ronsard would build on the banks of the Loire, with statues of Marie and of himself, is imitated and elaborated from Theocritus's twelfth Idyll, and the concluding lines, expressing the wish that after their deaths a spirit may descend to him in the Shades, and tell him that his songs about their love are still on the lips of men, are imitated from the tenth Idyll; while the opening lines bring Ronsard, for once at any rate, into the company of Shakespeare, for they were certainly, as I think Shakespeare's 74th sonnet was almost certainly, inspired by Ovid's epilogue to the *Metamorphoses*, and for Ovid's

> parte tamen meliore mei super alta perennis
> astra ferar

Ronsard has found an equivalent not less memorable than Shakespeare's

> My spirit in thine, the better part of me.

> Marie, à celle fin que le siecle advenir
> De noz jeunes amours se puisse souvenir,
> Et que vostre beauté que j'ay long temps aimée,
> Ne se perde au tombeau par les ans consumée,
> Sans laisser quelque marque apres elle de soy:
> Je vous consacre icy le plus gaillard de moy,
> L'esprit de mon esprit, qui vous fera revivre
> Ou long temps, ou jamais, par l'âge de ce livre.[1]

That in lines inspired, or partly inspired, by the same passage in Ovid both Ronsard and Shakespeare should have used, respectively, the words *consacre* and *consecrate* ('The very part was consecrate to thee') is surely a rather remarkable coincidence, even though not, perhaps, in itself sufficient to prove that Shakespeare had read Ronsard. Partly, it may be, because of his violent anti-Protestantism, Ronsard (except, perhaps, by Sidney) seems to have been far less widely read in England than either Du Bellay or Desportes. Ronsard imitated the Ovidian *locus* again in an elegy *Au Roy* (Henri III), beginning 'Je resemble, mon Prince, au Prestre d'Apollon', first printed in the 1584 edition of his *Œuvres*, in a passage concluding with a line which (as we shall see) had already concluded one of the Hélène sonnets:

[1] Vaganay, ii. 145.

> Ne vous arrestez point à la vieille prison
> Qui enferme mon corps, ny à mon poil grison,
> A mon menton fleuri: mon corps n'est que l'escorce.
> Servez-vous de l'esprit, mon esprit est ma force.
> Le corps doit bien tost rendre en un tombeau poudreux
> Aux premiers Elements cela qu'il a pris d'eux.
> L'esprit vivra tousjours qui vous doit faire vivre,
> Au moins tant que vivront les plumes et le livre.[1]

Here again the Shakespearian resemblances are striking:

> The earth can have but earth, which is his due;
> My spirit is thine, the better part of me. (74)

> So long as men can breathe or eyes can see,
> So long lives this and this gives life to thee. (18)

I find it hard not to give at least serious consideration to the possibility that Ronsard may have helped Shakespeare to find a new meaningfulness in Ovid's lines, and even that it may have been mainly a reading of Ronsard which suggested to him, as a main topic, the theme of poetic immortality, though Shakespeare treated that topic in his own far less egotistical fashion. The absence, except perhaps in the passages I have just quoted, of any striking resemblances in phraseology is not in itself against this possibility, since Shakespeare transfigured and Shakespearianized his reading to a far greater extent than any other Renaissance poet. All that we can be really certain about is that he had read far more poetry than we shall ever be able to demonstrate.

In the sonnet (74) which serves as an epilogue to the second *Livre des amours*, and which begins

> Cesse tes pleurs, mon livre: il n'est pas ordonné
> Du destin, que moy vif tu sois riche de gloire,

Ronsard promises immortality, not to Marie, but to his book, and imitates, with a characteristic piece of outdoing, a passage at the conclusion of the *Amores* (III. xv. 11–14), where Ovid imagines a stranger in days to come contemplating the walls of little Sulmo (now Sulmona), his birthplace:

> Atque aliquis spectans hospes Sulmonis aquosi
>   moenia, quae campi iugera pauca tenent,
> 'Quae tantum,' dicet, 'potuistis ferre poetam,
>   quantulacumque estis, vos ego magna voco.'

---

[1] Vaganay, v. 233.

Horace and Virgil and Ovid, with a local patriotism that still
survives in Italy, all proudly referred to their humble birthplaces as
places where they would be for ever remembered, but it was more
than problems of scansion that prevented them from introducing
into these and similar contexts their own names.[1] Ronsard, I think,
was the first, and perhaps the last, great poet to commit this final
arrogance:

> Quelqu'un apres mille ans de mes vers estonné
> Viendra dedans mon Loir, comme en Permesse, boire:
> Et voyant mon pays, à peine pourra croire
> Que d'un si petit champ Ronsard se vante né.

In the *Sonets pour Helene*, written in late middle age and containing
some of Ronsard's finest verse, the immortality theme makes three
notable appearances, although in each case, it must be admitted, in
a manner and with an emphasis strongly suggesting that Hélène de
Surgères was but the occasion for the erection of further monuments to the glory of Pierre Ronsard. In II. 2, beginning

> Afin qu'à tout jamais de siecle en siecle vivre
> La parfaite amitié que Ronsard vous portoit,

he sends her a 'sempervive', or sengreen:

> Elle vit longuement en sa jeune verdeur.
> Long temps apres la mort je vous feray revivre,
> Tant peut le docte soin d'un gentil serviteur,
>   Qui veut, en vous servant, toutes vertus ensuivre.
> Vous vivrez (croyez-moy) comme Laure en grandeur,
> Au moins tant que vivront les plumes et le livre.

II. 49, beginning

> Ceste fleur de Vertu, pour qui cent mille larmes
> Je verse nuict et jour sans m'en pouvoir souler,

was clearly suggested by those two sonnets of Petrarch, already
referred to, in which he professes to regret that Laura did not live
in the days of Homer and Virgil; but while Petrarch dares not hope
to do more for Laura, that 'new flower of honesties and beauties',
than what Ennius, in his rugged song, was able to do for that

---

[1] The signings, as it were, of their own names by Horace at the end of *Odes* IV.
vi and by Virgil at the end of the *Georgics* are not accompanied by predictions of
their own poetic immortality and have affinity with the simple σφραγίς (seal), in
which, at the conclusion of poems or collections of poems, various Hellenistic poets
had inserted their own names.

'ancient flower of virtues and of arms' Scipio Africanus, Ronsard
not only has no hesitation in declaring that he will do for Hélène
what Homer did for Achilles, but even implies, in his concluding
lines, that she ought to be very grateful to him for doing it, since,
whatever he may have condescended to say in praise of her, 'this
creature', in the words of Shakespeare's Cleopatra, 'is no such
thing':

> Il eut pour sa prouësse un excellent sonneur:
> Tu as pour tes vertuz en mes vers un honneur,
> Qui malgré le tombeau suivra ta renommée.
> Les Dames de ce temps n'envient ta beauté,
> Mais ton nom tant de fois par les Muses chanté,
> Qui languiroit d'oubly, si je ne t'eusse aimée.

The implication in the concluding lines is quite unambiguously
expressed in the fifth of the eight Hélène sonnets first published in
1609, long after Ronsard's death, a sonnet in which he reproaches
her with her ingratitude towards him, who has raised her from
comparative obscurity to a fame equal to that of Marguerite de
Valois, Queen of Navarre, whom the young Desportes had celebrated in his *Hippolyte* sonnets:

> Quand au commencement j'admiré ton merite,
> Tu vivois à la Court sans louange et sans bruit:
> Maintenant un renom par la France te suit,
> Egallant en grandeur la Royalle Hypolite.
> Liberal j'envoyay les Muses à ta suite,
> Je fis loin de ton chef evanouïr la nuit,
> Je fis flamber ton nom comme un astre qui luit,
> J'ay dans l'azur du Ciel ta loüange décrite.[1]

Ronsard, here and elsewhere, comes very close to that original
variation on the theme of 'ingrateful beauty threatened' which, as I
have already remarked, seems to have been first fully developed by
Carew. Ronsard does not, indeed, go so far as to declare (though he
very often seems to imply) that, as Propertius had declared in one
of his elegies, his mistress's reputation for beauty is an illusion
created by himself, nor does he, like Carew, threaten to 'uncreate'
what he has created; nevertheless, the mixture of condescension and
self-exaltation, the insolence, one might almost say, that is present
in almost every one of the utterances on poetic fame in his love-

[1] Vaganay, ii. 473.

poetry is far closer to the second stanza of Carew's famous poem than to anything in Petrarch or in Shakespeare:

> That killing power is none of thine,
> I gave it to thy voyce and eyes:
> Thy sweets, thy graces, all are mine;
> Thou art my starre, shin'st in my skies;
> Then dart not from thy borrowed sphere
> Lightenings on him, that fixt thee there.

While there is a certain spiritual affinity between Petrarch and Shakespeare, there is scarcely any more real spiritual affinity between Petrarch and Ronsard than there is between Petrarch and Carew.

I have deferred until now my consideration of II. 24. This sonnet is perhaps the most wonderful single result of the Renaissance theory and practice of 'imitation'; for although, except for the characteristic insolence and dramatization and introduction, not merely once but twice, of the poet's own name, there is literary precedent for almost every detail, precedent without which the sonnet could not have been what it is, it yet remains in the truest sense original and such as no other poet but Ronsard could have written. The central 'idea', if one may so call it, that of an ageing mistress reviewing in the poet's verses, as in a mirror, her former beauty and reproaching herself with her unresponsiveness to his love, was, I think, first expressed, or first memorably expressed, and in such a manner as to excite many imitations, by Tasso in the two sonnets which I have already quoted; although, while Tasso imagines himself as still living and 'serving', Ronsard imagines himself as dead. The subsidiary ideas or topics, with which this central idea is combined, those of 'ingrateful beauty threatened' and what might be called *carpe florem*, had been frequently handled by the poets of the Greek Anthology and by Horace and the Roman elegiac poets, when they threatened an unresponsive mistress or 'lovely boy' with the loneliness and the regret for lost opportunities of pleasure that would come with the all too swift disappearance of transient beauty. Perhaps the most elaborate, most famous, and, by Renaissance poets, most imitated of all ancient treatments of the topic *carpe florem* was the fourteenth Idyll, 'Rosae', of Ausonius, with an imitation of whose concluding lines Ronsard himself concludes his sonnet:

> collige, virgo, rosas, dum flos novus et nova pubes:
> et memor esto aevum sic properare tuum.

There remains the setting, the dramatically and almost realistically imagined situation of the ageing mistress, *au soir à la chandelle*, unwinding and spinning flax with her women and murmuring Ronsard's poems about her, mention of whose name rouses them all from their half-somnolent labours. Even this was suggested to Ronsard by one of the most memorable things of its kind in Latin poetry, the concluding portion of an elegy of Tibullus (I. iii), which contains two other passages (of a more conventional kind) often imitated by Renaissance poets. Tibullus addresses the elegy to his friend Messala from a sick-bed in Phaeacia, and, professing to fear that he may die in this foreign land without proper funeral rites, curses seafaring and introduces an elaborate description of the Golden Age, when seafaring was unknown. Then he declares that, even if he is doomed to perish here, Venus will conduct him to the Lovers' Elysium, with which he contrasts the place of punishment to which he prays that all interrupters and profaners of his love may come. In the concluding lines (83 ff.) he addresses his mistress Delia:

But for you, I pray that you may remain chaste, and that, as guardian of holy honour, the old woman may ever sit sedulously at your side. Let her tell you stories when the lamp has been set in its place and draw the long skeins from the full distaff, while around you the maids, bending over their toilsome tasks, gradually grow heavy with sleep and drop their work. Then may I suddenly come, all unannounced, so that I may seem to have been sent from heaven into your presence.

This passage of almost Homeric simplicity, so different from the social backgrounds and scenes which Ovid so often evokes in the *Amores* and *Ars amatoria*, must suddenly have suggested to Ronsard one of those dramatic situations which he was peculiarly able to exploit, and it is above all his brilliant transposition and modification of it that makes the familiar topics it enshrines appear as things almost wholly new.

> Quand vous serez bien vieille, au soir à la chandelle,
> Assise aupres du feu, devidant[1] et filant,

[1] *Devidant*, 'winding or unwinding from a reel or distaff', is the reading of the editions both of 1578 and 1584, and I think it must stand, although many modern scholars and anthologists seem to prefer *devisant*, 'chatting', which appeared for the first time in some of the posthumous editions. The corresponding lines of Tibullus are

> haec tibi fabellas referat positaque lucerna
> deducat plena stamina longa colu.

Devisant, it is true, is nearer to *fabellas referat*, but what corresponds to that in

Direz, chantant mes vers, en vous esmerveillant,
Ronsard me celebroit du temps que j'estois belle.
    Lors vous n'aurez servante oyant telle nouvelle,
Desja sous le labeur à demi sommeillant,
Qui au bruit de Ronsard ne s'aille resveillant,
Benissant vostre nom de louange immortelle.
    Je seray sous la terre, et fantaume sans os:
Par les ombres Myrtheux je prendray mon repos:
Vous serez au fouyer une vieille accroupie,
    Regrettant mon amour, et vostre fier desdain.
Vivez, si m'en croyez, n'attendez à demain:
Cueillez dès aujourd'huy les roses de la vie.

As a love-poem, this great sonnet is in some ways nearer to the ancients and in some ways nearer to the moderns than to either Petrarch or Shakespeare. That splendid *superbia*, sometimes amounting almost to insolence, and that exaltation of the poet, which elsewhere often blends so incongruously with passages that Ronsard has imitated from Petrarch, is an ancient, and, above all, a Roman thing; although in ancient love-poetry such exaltation of the poet is never *integrated* in this way. It is not in love-poetry, but in poetry celebrating public achievements—certain passages in Pindar and Horace's Lollius Ode—that we find a similar integration, and even there, although poetry is exalted, the poet does not venture to exalt himself above his subject or to transpose, as it were, from love-poetry the topic of 'ingrateful beauty threatened' and introduce it as 'ingrateful eminence threatened'. In their numerous passages on the topic of 'ingrateful beauty threatened' the ancient love-poets spoke in the main merely as men, not specifically as poets: an ancient poet might declare that the day would come when his mistress would look in her glass and be sorry, but Tasso, so far as I know, was the first poet to declare that the day would come when she would look in his verses and be sorry; and, as I have already remarked, I think it was probably Tasso who suggested the possibilities of this topic to Ronsard. And in this sonnet of Ronsard's not only is there no trace of that humble and religious adoration, that spirituality, and even, at times, 'metaphysicality', that we find both in Petrarch and in Shakespeare: even that profound sadness at the fact of human transience which is so strong both in the ancients and

Ronsard is *chantant mes vers*, and Hélène could not be both *chantant* and *devisant* at the same time. *Devidant*, on the other hand, exactly corresponds to *deducat*, 'unwinding (flax from the distaff) and spinning'.

in Shakespeare seems in Ronsard to have been completely swallowed up in his contemplation of the glory of poetry and his own glory as a poet. When I said that this sonnet was in some ways nearer, not only to the ancients, but also to the moderns, than to either Petrarch or Shakespeare, it was chiefly one modern poet I had in mind, W. B. Yeats. The comparatively early

> When you are old and grey and full of sleep,
> And nodding by the fire, take down this book,

one of his first really great poems, was clearly inspired by Ronsard's sonnet. There are indeed obvious differences: there is far less self-exaltation, far more sadness, tenderness, and adoration in Yeats's poem, as there is also, for that matter, in the later and greater 'The Folly of being comforted'; but they are both magnificent examples of that 'dramatic lyrical expression' which Yeats so admired in Ronsard, who, he declared, like Villon, had made splendid drama out of his own life. In the sonnets of our greatest dramatist, no less than in the sonnets of Petrarch, there is nothing that can properly be called 'self-dramatization'—not, at any rate, in the sense in which we so often have it in Ronsard, in Yeats, and in Donne.

VI

To turn from the great European poets we have been considering to the sonnets of Shakespeare's English contemporaries is to enter a region of comparative provinciality and amateurishness. There are indeed a few sonnets, more of them by Sidney than by any other poet, which may be 'let alone for the comparison', but both in sheer genius and sheer craftsmanship the general level is far below that of the Italians and the French. Indeed, despite his immense genius and immense achievement, Shakespeare's own craftsmanship, sometimes even in his finest sonnets, is too often slovenly and very far from Coleridge's *desideratum* of 'the best words in the best order': there are too many inversions merely for the sake of rhyme, too many syllable-supplying expletives such as 'do', 'did', and 'doth', and too many rhymes on the final syllable of weak past participles, such as 'remember-ed' and on the final syllable of words like 're-lat-i-on'. Perfection still remains perfection, even though it be Shakespeare himself who sometimes falls short of it.

In the sonnets of Shakespeare's English predecessors the theme of poetic immortality makes occasional appearances only, I think, in Spenser, whose *Amoretti* were published in 1595; in Daniel, whose *Delia* sonnets were first printed as an independent collection in 1592 and continued to reappear, with various revisions and small 'augmentations', in volumes containing other poems by Daniel between 1594 and 1623; and in single sonnets in Constable's *Diana* (1592) and Drayton's *Ideas Mirrour* (1594). Spenser, in his only memorable sonnet on this topic (75), uses a kind of emblem or allegory which, so far as I know, is original:

> One day I wrote her name upon the strand,
>   but came the waues and washed it away:
> agayne I wrote it with a second hand,
>   but came the tyde, and made my paynes his pray.
> Vayne man, sayd she, that doest in vaine assay,
>   a mortall thing so to immortalize:
> for I my selue shall lyke to this decay,
>   and eek my name be wyped out lykewize.
> Not so, (quod I) let baser things deuize
>   to dy in dust, but you shall liue by fame:
> my verse your vertues rare shall eternize,
>   and in the heuens wryte your glorious name,
> Where, whenas death shall all the world subdew,
>   our loue shall liue, and later life renew.

This, although perhaps a more confident and resonant declaration than Petrarch would have ventured to make in a sonnet to Laura, is closer to the proud humility (as one might almost call it) of Shakespeare than to the condescension and self-exaltation of Ronsard.

Daniel has no less than six sonnets on this topic, some of them of considerable merit, and sufficient in themselves to have directed Shakespeare's attention to it—if, indeed, his attention required directing, and if the topic had not already been suggested to him by his own reading of the Latin poets and, perhaps, of Ronsard. Two of them, 36 and 40,[1] are obvious imitations of those two famous (already quoted) sonnets of Tasso, a poet whom Daniel greatly admired; and although these remain, what Shakespeare's sonnets to his friend never are, poems of courtship, with allusions to his 'wrong' and her 'pride', they contain less of what I have called Roman *superbia*

---

[1] I refer to the numbering in the convenient edition (1908) of Daniel's *Delia* and Drayton's *Idea* by Arundell Esdaile, which is that of the 1623 edition of Daniel's *Works*.

(perhaps only because Daniel's style could not achieve it) than do Tasso's two sonnets, and more of Shakespearian humility. The first, beginning 'I once may see when years shall wreak my wrong', concludes:

> When, if she grieve to gaze her in her glass,
> Which then presents her winter-withered hue,
> Go you, my verse, go, tell her what she was,
> For what she was she best shall find in you.
> Your fiery heat lets not her glory pass,
> But, Phoenix-like, shall make her live anew.

The second is a good example of that decent and dignified, though almost never really splendid or memorable, plainness which Daniel sometimes achieves when he has a good model behind him:

> When Winter snows upon thy sable hairs,
> And frost of age hath nipped thy beauties near,
> When dark shall seem thy day that never clears,
> And all lies withered that was held so dear;
> Then take this picture which I here present thee
> Limnèd with a pencil not all unworthy;[1]
> Here see the gifts that God and Nature lent thee,
> Here read thyself and what I suffered for thee.
> This may remain thy lasting monument,
> Which happily posterity may cherish;
> These colours with thy fading are not spent,
> These may remain when thou and I shall perish.
>   If they remain, then thou shalt live thereby;
>   They will remain, and so thou canst not die.

In 41, together with a very un-Petrarchan and un-Shakespearian humbleness of style, there is something of Petrarchan and Shakespearian humility and some thematic resemblance to Shakespeare's magnificent Sonnet 32, concluding

> But since he died, and poets better prove,
> Theirs for their style I'll read, his for his love';

although in that sonnet Shakespeare is not specifically promising immortality either to his friend or to himself.

> Thou canst not die while any zeal abound
> In feeling hearts that can conceive these lines;

---

[1] This is far from being the only line in Daniel's sonnets that defies all attempts at scansion.

Though thou, a Laura, hast no Petrarch found,
In base attire yet clearly beauty shines.
And I, though born within a colder clime,
Do feel mine inward heat as great, I know it;
He never had more faith, although more rhyme;
I love as well, though he could better show it.
But I may add one feather to thy fame,
To help her flight throughout the fairest isle;
And if my pen could more enlarge thy name,
Thou should'st then live in an immortal style.
  For though that Laura better limnèd be,
  Suffice, thou shalt be loved as well as she.

Sonnet 42, beginning

Be not displeased that these my papers should
Bewray unto the world how fair thou art,

is a very feeble sonnet, partly imitated from Guarini; 43 is a much
more notable achievement, inspired not, it would seem, by any
particular model, but by any or all of those great commonplaces
about poetry as more enduring than buildings, pyramids, marbles,
and bronzes of which I have already cited so many examples from
both classical and Renaissance poets:

Delia, these eyes that so admireth thine
Have seen those walls which proud ambition reared
To check the world, how they entombed have lien
Within themselves, and on them ploughs have eared,
Yet never found that barbarous hand attained
The spoil of fame deserved by virtuous men,
Whose glorious actions luckily had gained
The eternal annals of a happy pen.
And therefore grieve not if thy beauties die;
Though time do spoil thee of the fairest veil
That ever yet covered mortality,
And must instar the needle and the rail;[1]
  That grace which doth more than enwoman thee
  Lives in my lines and must eternal be.

Here too there is something of Shakespeare's subordination of
himself and his poetic gift to the task of rescuing all that is rescuable
in the beloved from oblivion and devouring Time. And the same is
true of 53, where the topic of perpetuation is combined with a

---

[1] 'trayle' (ed. 1592) seems the better reading.

characteristically Petrarchan and occasionally Shakespearian profession that the poet's verses have been inspired entirely by the
person to whom they are dedicated:

> Let others sing of knights and paladins
> In aged accents and untimely words,
> Paint shadows in imaginary lines
> Which well the reach of their high wits records.
> But I must sing of thee, and those fair eyes
> Authentic shall my verse in time to come,
> When yet the unborn shall say, 'Lo, where she lies,
> Whose beauty made him speak that else was dumb'.
> These are the arks, the trophies, I erect,
> That fortify thy name against old age,
> And these thy sacred virtues must protect
> Against the dark and Time's consuming rage.
> Though the error of my youth in them appear,
> Suffice they show I lived and loved thee dear.

In these six sonnets it is only occasionally that Daniel achieves
something like the Shakespearian resonance and the Shakespearian
phrase. They do not communicate anything like the range and
intensity of inner vibration that Shakespeare's do, and they seem
almost shallow in comparison with that profound concernment, not
only about the friend's transience but about human transience in
general, that we feel in Shakespeare's. Nevertheless, they constitute
the fullest and finest treatment of this topic in English poetry before
Shakespeare, and, although their tone is so much fainter, their
accent is not perhaps greatly different from Shakespeare's own.

Shakespeare's use of Popular Song

FREDERICK W. STERNFELD

THE Elizabethan playwright was wont to make use of the treasury of popular song whenever it suited the humour of his plot. An allusion by title or first line; the quotation of one or more stanzas with, perhaps, minor variations suited to the occasion; even the refashioning of a well-known model almost, but never entirely, beyond recognition—these were the alternative means by which ballad and song might play their parts in the repertoire and so achieve an added immortality.

Of these three methods, the second is well known. Annotated editions of Shakespeare's plays illuminate the background of the lyrics of Ophelia, Lear's fool, and Autolycus. But the extremes of Shakespeare's range—mere allusion or significant variation—are less easily detected. An example of each is the subject of the present essay: the allusion to an Irish ballad and the parody of a popular Elizabethan song.[1]

Shakespeare's *Henry V* has been a favourite hunting ground for commentators for well over two centuries. The emendation of a number of passages in the Folio text has been vexatious, the more so when the phrase in question does not occur in any of the quartos; but the perspicacity of certain eighteenth-century editors elicits our admiration, in particular that brilliant emendation of IV. iv. 4 by Malone, worthy to be compared with Theobald's 'and a' babbled of green fields'.

Theobald's correction of an obscure phrase is justly famous both for its ingenuity and its illumination of a pathetic passage in which the popular figure of Falstaff is put into its grave. A similar enigma confronts us when the French soldier's 'Vous estes le Gentilhome de bon qualitee' evokes Pistol's disdainful: 'Qualtitie calmie custure me.' This championship of the native tongue is echoed in the *Satiromastix* when Asinius must swear not to 'carry Lattin poets about you, till you can write and read English at most'. Dekker's thrust at Ben Jonson is without ambiguity, but the scene in *Henry V*

---

[1] Both allusion and parody appear in the Folio of 1623 only, not in the quartos.

must accommodate the popular attitude to Pistol's swaggering role and his propensity for expressing himself in well-worn phrases and clichés. 'Custure me' is not as celebrated as Quickly's 'green fields', but its solution proved equally challenging and had to await Malone's discovery in 1790 that 'Calen o custure me' was the burden of an Irish folk-song.

In 1723 Pope had quietly emended 'Qualtitie' to 'Quality',

> Quality calmy custure me

and so it remained (without emendation by Theobald) until Warburton, Pope's literary executor, took it upon himself to publish an edition 'by Mr. Pope and Mr. Warburton' in which he haughtily emended 'custure' to 'construe'. But the printer's devil that had produced 'qualtitie' in the Folio was still dogging the passage which emerged as 'We should read this nonsense thus, *Quality*, cality, consture me, art thou a gentleman? i.e., tell me, let me understand whether thou be'st a gentleman.' Needless to say, the combined arrogance of Pope and Warburton provoked many a counter-invective. Warburton's title had immodestly promised 'The Genuine Text . . . is here settled: Being restored from the Blunders of the first Editors and the Interpolations of the two Last.' Thomas Edwards of Lincoln's Inn was quick to respond with *A Supplement to Mr. Warburton's Edition of Shakespeare. Being the Canons of Criticism.* . . . Canon XIII ironically advises the critic: 'He need not attend to the low accuracy of orthography or pointing, but may ridicule such trivial criticisms in others . . . consture, IV. 399. for construe. . . .'[1]

Edwards suggested a further emendation, namely, 'calmie' to 'call you me', which Dr. Johnson adopted in 1765 along with Warburton's 'construe'. In the Johnson–Stevens editions of 1773, 1778, and 1785, the emendations of Warburton and Edwards were combined and the passage read

> Quality, call you me?—Construe me, art thou a gentleman?

The Malone edition in 1790 made no further emendations. But the appendix of afterthoughts has the following note (vol. x, p. 645): 'the old copy [folio text] is very nearly right, and . . . a much slighter emendation . . . will suffice.' Malone then quotes the rubric

---

[1] 1st edn., 1748, p. 44; 3rd edn., 1750, p. 102; *The Canons of Criticism*, 1765, p. 174. All three editions in Bodleian. It is amusing that Edwards too became the victim of a printer's error. The index of the 1765 edition lists the corrections of Warburton, referring to p. 136, instead of 174.

'to Calen o custure me, sung at every line's end' from the *Handful of Pleasant Delights*, 1584, and concludes that Pistol 'is only repeating the burden of an old song'. He notes further that Pistol 'elsewhere has quoted the old ballad beginning "Where is the life that late I led?" ' This reference is a credit to Malone's comprehensive knowledge, for it is, in fact, the only other ballad to which Pistol alludes,[1] although his master Falstaff and Silence quote them frequently.

Descended of a family that had long lived in Ireland, and a graduate of Trinity College, Dublin, Malone was in an advantageous position to comprehend the passage. Once the connexion between the Folio's 'Calmie custure me' of 1623 and the tune 'Calen o custure me' in the rubric of 1584 had been recognized, the song, with one spelling or another, was found in a number of contemporary and later sources. There is no doubt that English audiences considered the title 'Callino' as foreign: Davies of Hereford characterizes the burden as 'from a foreign land, which English people do not understand'; and Playford dubs the tune 'Irish'. This fact, in conjunction with the usual vagaries of Elizabethan orthography, accounts for the multiple variations in spelling.[2] Even so, the tune was named thirteen times at least during Shakespeare's lifetime, a frequency that suggests a reasonable amount of general popularity.

(1) 1582 *Stationers' Register* (Arber, ii. 407): '. . . twoe ballads whereof thone intituled CALLIN O CUSTURE ME. . . .'[3]

(2) 1584 *Handful of Pleasant Delights* (ed. Rollins, p. 38): 'A Sonet of a Louer in the praise of his lady. To CALEN O CUSTURE ME: sung at everie lines end.'

(3) *Stationers' Register* (Arber, ii. 457): 'CALLINO SHRYLL OVER GADDESHILL. . . .'

(4) 1588–1611 Six musical MSS.

    (*a*)   Cambridge U.L.: Dd. 4. 23: CALLINO ROBYNSON for cittern.

---

[1] 'O Death rock me asleep' (*2 Henry IV*, II. iv. 211) can hardly be termed a ballad.

[2] The English 'Quality' appeared as 'Qualtitie' in the 1623 Folio, 'Qualtity' in the Folios of 1632 and 1664. 'Quality', correctly spelled, first appeared in the Folio of 1685. Malone, referring to the Folio text in 1790, misspells it 'Qualitee' in vol. v and 'Qualitie' in vol. x. Considering as well the misprints in Warburton and Edwards, it begins to look as though an Irish charm bewitched the scholars working on Shakespeare's line.

There are also several Scottish versions of the ubiquitous refrain. Cf. M. Kennedy-Fraser and K. Macleod, edd., *Songs of the Hebrides*, 3 vols., 1909–21, iii. 69. Mr. and Mrs. John Campbell, Isle of Canna, have two other versions, and there is a note on the song by Mr. Campbell in *T.L.S.*, 27 June 1958.

[3] The name of the song is in capitals for the sake of quick reference.

(*b*)   Trinity College, Dublin: D. 1. 21: CALLENO for lute.

(*c*)   Cambridge U.L.: Dd. 3. 18: CALLINOE for lute.

(*d*) (*e*) (*f*) William Byrd's CALLINO CASTURAME, for virginals, transmitted in three MSS: cf. Fellowes's edition of Byrd's *Works*, xx. 5.

(5) 1599 Shakespeare, *Henry V*, IV. iv. 4: Qualtitie CALMIE CUSTURE ME.

(6) 1599 Nashe, *Lenten Stuff* (ed. McKerrow and Wilson, iii. 177): '. . . amongst our harmonious English CALINOS. . . .'

(7) *c*. 1601 Dekker (ed. Bowers, i. 380), *Satiromastix*, v. ii. 235: 'Nay, your oohs, nor your CALLIN-OES. . . .'

(8) *c*. 1611 Davies of Hereford (ed. Grosart, ii. 16), *Scourge of Folly*: 'But it was like the burden of a song call'd CALLINO. . . .'

(9) 1667 Playford's *Catch that catch can, or the Musical Companion*, p. 231: CALLINO CASTORE ME, entitled 'An Irish tune'.

Also 1847 Robert Southey, *The Doctor* (7 vols., 1834–47; here quoted from the 1853 ed., one vol., p. 385): 'And he had one [ballad] of Irish growth . . . CALLINO CASTORE ME. . . .'

Of the six manuscripts transmitting the music (Item 4), the best known is the keyboard version by William Byrd, in the so-called Fitzwilliam Virginal Book. An arrangement for lute is to be found in the so-called Ballet Lute Book (Dublin), whereas Thomas Robinson's version for a four-stringed cittern is preserved in Cambridge Dd. 4. 23. (Thomas Robinson published instruction books for both lute and cittern in 1603 and 1609—*S.T.C.* nos. 21127 and 21128.) The melodies of these three variants are tabulated in Fig. 1 and abbreviated as Byrd, Ballet, and Robinson. Whilst the soft, aristocratic lute was favoured by English gentlemen and sophisticates over the louder, more popular cittern, it must be admitted that in a metrical sense Robinson's cittern version better fits the poem from the *Handful of Pleasant Delights* than does either the Ballet or the Byrd version. The differences are only slight, however, as the transcriptions show. The fourth version illustrated is that printed by Playford. It is obviously a different tune, notwithstanding certain similarities. Cambridge Dd. 3. 18 preserves only the lute part of an arrangement for consort and is, therefore, incomplete.

The interpretation of the phrase has varied from time to time. James Boswell the Younger, in his revised edition of Malone's *Shakespeare* (1821), offered 'Little girl of my heart for ever and ever'. The credit for establishing the original meaning must go to Gerard

Murphy, whose careful and sympathetic study deduced 'The girl from beside the [river] Suir'.[1] Of the recent Celtic studies which yielded the ultimate solution, the Elizabethan playwrights Dekker and Shakespeare had no advantage. For them it was simply a popular tune and a foreign one. Its lure lay not in the meaning of the words but in its acoustical associations: qualité—quality—calino; ohs—calinoes. Allusion to a foreign burden was part of the dramatic scheme, and 'Calino' fitted well into Pistol's gibes at the Frenchman and his foreign tongue. In much the same way Dekker alludes to it toward the end of the *Satiromastix*. When Horace, alias Jonson, under Tucca's scourging, cries 'Ooh', Sir Vaughan retorts with 'Nay, your oohs, nor your Callin-oes cannot serve your turn'.[2]

The 'Willow Song', far from being a mere allusion, was actually performed on the stage by a singing boy in the role of Desdemona. The burden 'Willow, willow, willow' reoccurs some 400 lines later, when it is hummed by the dying Emilia:

> I will play the Swan
> And die in Music. *Willow, willow, willow*.[3]

About the model for the song there has been a good deal of understandable confusion, since many poems of the sixteenth and seventeenth centuries have a 'willow' refrain. Four early examples appear, at first glance, to offer valid material for a gloss on Desdemona's song. The first, called 'The Willow Tree', occurs as an air in the Scottish Skene MS. In his nineteenth-century edition Dauney[4] fitted it appropriately to a seventeenth-century text printed in Aberdeen by John Forbes:

> (Willy) How now shepherd, what means that?
> Why wearst thou willow in thy hat?

---

[1] *Eigse: A Journal of Irish Studies*, 1939–40, i. 127–9.

[2] Cf. *English Institute Essays for 1956*, pp. 16 ff. (particularly pp. 26–32) for a study of the popularity of the tune in the nineteenth and twentieth centuries.

[3] The stage direction 'Singing', clearly implied by the italics in the Folio text, was inserted by Dyce before the burden (v. ii. 248). Modern editors usually (and rightly) follow Dyce, e.g. G. L. Kittredge (1936), A. Walker (1957), and M. R. Ridley (1958).

[4] The principal musical reprints of various willow songs, hereafter referred to by editor, are: W. Chappell, *Popular Music of the Olden Time*, 2 vols., 1859, i. 206–8; ii. 774; W. Dauney, *Ancient Scottish Melodies from a manuscript of the Reign of King James VI*, 1838, pp. 248 and 301 (cf. also *Grove's Dictionary of Music*, 5th edn., 1954, vii. 677; Percy's *Reliques*, book VIII, no. 9; and Wooldridge, i. 157); E. H. Fellowes, ed., *English School of Lutenist Song Writers*, 2nd ser., vol. 15; *The Muses' Garden*, 1610, by Robert Jones, pp. 24–26; E. H. Fellowes, 'The Willow Song' [B.M. Add. MS. 15117] in Richmond Noble, *Shakespeare's Use of Song*, 1923, pp. 152–4; P. Warlock and P. Wilson, *English Ayres*, 6 vols., vol. i (1st ed., 1922), 2nd ed., 1927, pp. 19 ff.; H. E. Wooldridge, *Old English Popular Music*, 2 vols., 1893, i. 106–10.

> Are thy scarfs of red and yellow
> Turned to branches of green willow?
(Cuddy) . . . It is Phyllis only she
> That makes me wear the willow tree.

In the famous British Museum MS. Add. 15117 (f. 16) the colours are changed to blue and tawny, but the beloved girl (with the exception of Shakespeare's song the idol is female) remains Phyllis, and the lyric shares with the burden of the Forbes text the characteristic threefold repetition of 'willow' to form a line in the stanza:

> Since my joys through Phyllis' frowns
> Are extinguished and thrown down . . .
> I will lay away my weeds of blue
> And take me to my tawny hue . . .
> My garland is the willow-tree
> Willow willow willow   [this line repeated 6 times]

The text of Robert Jones's lute song (reprinted by Fellowes) also introduces the word 'willow' in the body of the stanza with several threefold repetitions in the burden:

> I am so far from pitying thee
> That wear'st a branch of willow-tree . . .
> O willow willow willow [this line repeated 3 times]
> O willow willow-tree
> I would thou didst belong to me.

And in the comedy of *Sir Giles Goosecap*[1] the foolish knight 'for merry form's sake' is crowned with the emblem of sadness, whilst the remainder of the company are decorated with the nuptial rosemary. Again the line 'willow, willow, willow' appears three times:

> Willow, willow, willow,
> Our captain goes down,
> Willow, willow, willow,
> His valour doth crown.
> The rest with rosemary we grace . . .
> Willow, willow, willow,
> We chant to the skies.

These quotations are pertinent in so far as they show that the willow tree and its doleful associations were as often met in lyrics as in other branches of literature. But prosodically and musically they

---

[1] *Tudor Facsimile Texts*, vol. 43, 1912, last page; cf. also *The Comedies of Chapman*, ed. T. M. Parrott, 1914, p. 670.

cannot be analogues for Shakespeare because of their iambic rhythm.[1]
Desdemona's doleful knell is couched in the anapaestic rhythm
made popular by Tusser in the sixteenth century; and justly so, for
the two unstressed syllables intervening between the accents give
a characteristic lilt to text and tune. By subdividing crotchets into
quavers or quavers into semi-quavers it would be possible mechani-
cally to accommodate the greater number of syllables of an anapaestic text to the tune of the air in the Skene MS.; but the result
would be a forced, unnatural rhythm, in contrast to willow-texts
that trip on the tongue like this:

John Heywood

> [Heading] All a green willow willow willow willow
> Alas by what mean may I make ye to know
> The unkindness for kindness that to me doth grow . . .
> For all a green willow is my garland.[2]

Gorgeous Gallery of Gallant Inventions

> My love what misliking in me do you find,
> Sing all a green willow:
> That on such a sudden you alter your mind,
> Sing willow willow willow.
>
> (Ed. Rollins, 1926, p. 83)

Howell's *Devises, 1581*

> [Heading] All of green Willow, Willow, Willow, Willow
> Embrace your bays sweetly that smile in love's sight . . .
> To me most unhappy, still spurned by despite,
> Is given writhed willows to express my state right.
>
> (Ed. Raleigh, 1906, p. 23)

Howell's *Devises, 1581*

> [Heading] All of green laurel
> Look up to the laurel, and let willow go,
> And trust to the true friend, embrace not thy foe,
> Sing all of green laurel.
>
> (Ibid., ll. 9–14. The first half (ll. 1–8) is iambic)

Thomas Deloney

> When fancy first framéd our likings in love,
> Sing all of green willow:

---

[1] Other iambic willow songs are to be found in *Roxeburghe Ballads*, ed. Chappell-
Ebsworth, 9 vols., vii. 355; and *Pepys Ballads*, ed. Rollins, 8 vols., ii. 202.
[2] B.M. Add. MS. 15233, f. 48, facsimile of first stanza in J. O. Halliwell Phillipps,
ed., *The Moral Play of Wit and Science and early Poetical Miscellanies*, 1848. Redford's
play of *Wit and Science* and Heywood's verse have been variously edited since.

> And faithful affection such motions did move
> For willow, willow, willow.
>> (*Works*, ed. Mann, 1912, p. 165)

B.M. Add. MS. 15117, f. 18
> The poor soul sat sighing by a sycamore tree,
> Sing willow, willow, willow,
> With his hand in his bosom and his head upon his knee,
> O willow willow willow willow.
>> (Reproduced in facs. in F. Bridge,
>> *Shakespearean Music*, 1923, p. 23)

Pelham Humfrey (1647–74)
> A young man sat sighing by a sycamore tree,
> Sing willow willow,
> With his hand in his bosom, his head on his knee,
> O willow willow, o willow willow.
>> (Reprinted Stafford Smith's *Musica*
>> *Antiqua*, 1812, p. 171)

Playford's *Pleasant Musical Companion*, 1686
> A poor soul sat sighing near a gingerbread stall,
> O gingerbread, oh, oh, gingerbread, oh.
>> (Third Part, no. 17, *The Second Book*
>> *of the Pleasant . . .*: Wing S2261)

Gilbert and Sullivan
> On a tree by a river a little tomtit
> Sang 'Willow, titwillow, titwillow'.

'The poor soul sat sighing', recorded in B.M. Add. MS. 15117,[1] evidently caught and held the popular ear far more surely than any of its predecessors. Not only did it become the ancestor of the Humfrey, Playford, and Gilbert lyrics, but its vogue in the seventeenth century is further attested by the variants given in the *Roxburghe Ballads* and Percy's *Reliques*.

Shakespeare's first stanza follows the popular lyric closely when allowance is made for the necessary change of sex. Early issues of the Folio of 1623, such as the Chatsworth copy (facs. Clarendon Press, 1902) print

> The poore Sonle set sining, by a Sicamour tree
> Her hand on her bosome, her head on her knee.

The corrector at the printing house properly amended 'Sonle' and

---

[1] For convenience' sake this manuscript will be designated here as the London Book.

'set' but seems to have had insufficient familiarity with balladry to realize the error in 'sining'. Later issues like the Huth copy (facs. Yale Press, 1954) have

> The poore Soule sat singing . . .

a pardonable mistake and one perpetuated by early editors, among them Rowe, Pope, and Johnson. But once again Malone restored the line to its proper reading.

As Desdemona's song proceeds the scope of the verbal alterations broadens. In the following comparisons of the Folio text with the London Book only the couplets are given and the well-known refrain is omitted. It would be labouring the obvious to argue the excellence of the poetic changes which Shakespeare wrought on his models:

London Book, Stanza III

> The mute bird sat by him, was made tame by his moans,
> The true tears fell from him, would have melted the stones

becomes Shakespeare, Stanza II

> The fresh streams ran by her, and murmur'd her moans,
> Her salt tears fell from her, and softened the stones.

The subsequent alterations show a concern with dramatic verity rather than poetic beauty:

London Book VII

> Let nobody chide her, her scorns I approve,
> She was born to be false, and I to die for love.

Shakespeare III

> Let nobody blame him, his scorn I approve
> (Nay, that's not next . . .).

Desdemona's false start is an obvious way of conveying her frame of mind to the audience. But thus far the distortion is only in the sequence of stanzas, the position of the line within the stanza is unchanged. Not so in the next:

London Book IV

> Come all you forsaken, and mourn you with me,
> Who speaks of a false love, mine's falser than she.

Shakespeare IV
>   I called my love false love: but what said he then?
>   If I court moe women, you'll couch with moe men.

The climax of the song has the most significant variation. That the first line is in effect the second line of the model is unimportant in comparison with the acid reproach of promiscuity that rankles in Desdemona and comes to the fore, destroying the lyric integrity of the original. At this point her version is less song than unwitting self-expression. How ironical and touching that the dying Emilia, in Act V, should return to the burden, 'willow, willow, willow'. The swan song, turned leitmotif, is the only quotation of its kind in Shakespeare where a fragment of a song is repeated in the same play. Emilia's coda thus becomes an act of transfiguration. Desdemona's variation, on the other hand, depends for its effectiveness on the playgoer's knowledge of the model. By starting with a well-known text to a well-known tune, her deviations become significant. To suggest that Desdemona is made to entertain the audience with a familiar song by way of an appropriate interlude would be to misconceive Shakespeare's dramatic plan. It would be equally mistaken, however, to assume that the dramatic and symbolic meaning of the Willow Song could come across without the actual singing.

We know of two Elizabethan pieces of music that would be suitable for anapaestic couplets. The first occurs in the Dallis Book (Trinity College, Dublin, MS. D. 3. 30), an English collection of solo lute music, 'begun by the pupils of Master Thomas Dallis, Cambridge, in 1583'. A variant of this melody also occurs in the Lodge Book (Folger Library, Washington, MS. 448. 16) under the title 'All of green willow'.

In the Dallis Lute Book compositions are usually identified by a title; there are no texts. However, we find attached to one of the pieces the rubric, 'Finis all a greene willow M[aster] T[homas] Dallis'. Similar phrases, 'All a green willow', 'All of green Willow', 'Ay me the green willow', occur in the anapaestic poems quoted above, ranging from John Heywood to the London Book. In fact, Shakespeare employs the phrase twice, both as a second line and at the end of the burden.

London Book
>   The poor soul sat sighing by a sycamore tree,
>   Sing willow willow willow,

> With his hand in his bosom and his head upon his knee . . .
> Ay me, the green willow must be my garland.

Shakespeare

> The poor soul sat sighing by a sycamore tree,
> Sing all a green willow,
> Her hand on her bosom, her head on her knee . . .
> Sing all a green willow must be my garland.

A complete transcription[1] of the charming song in the Dallis Book is given in Fig. 2, fitted both to John Heywood's 'All a green willow' (the earliest surviving text) and to Shakespeare's text. The first offers little or no difficulty, its quatrain fits bars 1–8 and the burden bars 9–16. The square brackets, inserted after the first note of bar 4, will accommodate Shakespeare's second line, 'Sing all a green willow' (there being no such need in the case of Heywood). This arbitrary insertion could be argued on internal grounds but, fortunately, the extra notes do occur in the Lodge Book which the late Otto Gombosi termed 'one of the oldest and most appealing musical settings of the Willow Song'. Unlike the Dallis, which is a straight reduction for the lute, similar to a modern piano score, the Lodge version repeats each strain, the repetitions being in slightly ornamented fashion. We shall probably never know if the Heywood or Shakespeare stanzas were sung to the music recorded by Dallis. Tunes of the same rhythmic shape are easily interchangeable, whether in ballad metre or anapaests. Since the Dallis tune was undoubtedly popular, it is likely that a variant of the Willow Song was sung to it in the sixteenth century, though not necessarily by the boy singer in Shakespeare's Company.

A more likely alternative for the company of the King's Men occurs in the London Book. This version is justly famous. The melody has been printed by Chappell and by Wooldridge (with nineteenth-century harmonizations), and a complete transcription has been made by Peter Warlock.[2] That it 'once "sighed along" the traverses of the Globe Theatre', as Furness thought, we do not know, but it is closer to Shakespeare's verbal text than any other known

---

[1] I am indebted to Miss M. C. Crum (Bodleian) and Mr. Ian Harwood (Lute Society) for assisting me in reading and transcribing the microfilm.

[2] Warlock makes two logical emendations in the accompaniment, at bars 21 and 27. In his book *The English Ayre*, 1926, p. 128, he offers the hypothesis that the music 'might conceivably be the work of Robert Parsons who died in 1570'. Recently Alfred Deller has made a gramophone recording with the original, not Shakespeare's, text.

variant. The differences are trivial, as will be seen in Fig. 3. Shakespeare's words have been placed under those of the manuscript text whenever there is a dissimilarity. The adaptation of the first sixteen bars is, indeed, simple. However, scholars have disagreed on the completeness of the burden following the couplet which, in the London Book, occupies bars 14–29. At the end of the first stanza Shakespeare's Folio text merely indicates 'Sing willow willow willow'. This induced E. H. Fellowes (whose adaptation was published in 1923) to finish the first stanza at bar 16, second beat, and return to bar 1 to begin the next stanza. But I believe that 'Willow willow willow' is merely the beginning of a refrain which it was unnecessary to print in full in the Folio. When there was a need to indicate the interspersion of spoken words (in roman type) the printer included more of the burden (in italics).

1 *The fresh streams ran by her, and murmur'd her moans,*
2 *Sing willow; etc.*
3 *Her salt tears fell from her, and softened the stones,*
4 *Sing willow, etc.* (Lay by these)
5 *Willow, willow.* (Prithee high thee; he'll come anon)
6 *Sing all a green willow must be my garland.*

This I interpret to mean that lines 1 and 2 occupy bars 1–10. Lines 3 and 4 take bars 10–16, at which point the first insertion intervenes 'Lay by these'. Line 5 (Willow, willow) would be a printer's abbreviation for bars 16–24, followed by the next interruption (Prithee . . .), after which the last line of the burden is spelled out in full. Shakespeare's final stanza, by contrast, is cut off after Desdemona has grafted her incongruous second line on to the model, and there is no refrain. Seventeenth-century singers in a Shakespearian play could not by any means have used the Folio text as copy for performance, nor can they do so now; see Lucius's song in *Julius Caesar*. On the other hand, the impact of the poet's gradual dismantling of the well-known ballad depends on Desdemona's singing the first two stanzas *in toto*; only then are we properly moved by the false start of the third stanza and shocked by the fourth.

The manuscript represents several chronological layers of songs which were universally popular in the early seventeenth century. The mixture of psalms and playhouse songs would imply that its owner or user was a professional musician rather than one performing exclusively in the theatre. The manuscript is written in various hands and was probably not completed until 1616, as it contains 'Have you seen but a white lily grow' from Jonson's *The Devil is an Ass*. Another song, 'Come my Celia', from *Volpone*, may be dated as of 1606. But there are included as well compositions which clearly originated before 1600: Richard Edwards's 'Awake ye woeful knights' from *Damon and Pythias* and the anonymous 'O death rock me asleep', which has been ascribed alternately to Edwards and to Rochford. Another song, 'In youthful years', which is certainly by Edwards, was printed along with two other lyrics from the London Book,[1] in an early miscellany, *Paradise of Dainty Devices*, 1576. There are several compositions by Byrd and one by his teacher Tallis, 'I call and cry to thee o Lord'. It is certain proof of the popularity of these ancients to find them in company with the later works of Jonson and Campion.

The manuscript offers little help as a source for a critical apparatus: the Folio text, 'Sing all a green willow', is no less authoritative than the manuscript 'Sing willow willow willow'. On the other hand, the setting in the London Book has the virtue of preserving for posterity the attractive irregularity that is so much a part of the web of poetry and music in that age. When we contemplate verse and tune together we become conscious of the charming interplay between half-lines of only two musical accents (bars 7–9 and 14–16) and lines of four musical accents—a togetherness which belongs to the age of Byrd and Morley rather than that of Humfrey and Purcell.

[1] Hunnis's 'Alack when I look back' and (?) Kinwelmarsh's 'O heavenly God', both with music by William Byrd.

APPENDIX I

Byrd

Ballet

Robinson

When as I view—your come - ly grace, — Ca - len o — cus-

Playford

Cal - li - no   Cal - li - no   Cal - li - no Cas - to - re me

By

Ba

Ro

-tu - re me, Your gol - den hair—your an - gels face—

Pl

E - va Ee   E - va Ee   loo   loo— loo —

By

Ba

Ro

Ca - len o— cus - tu - re me

Pl

— loo   lee

APPENDIX II

(1) [lay by these] Bar 16

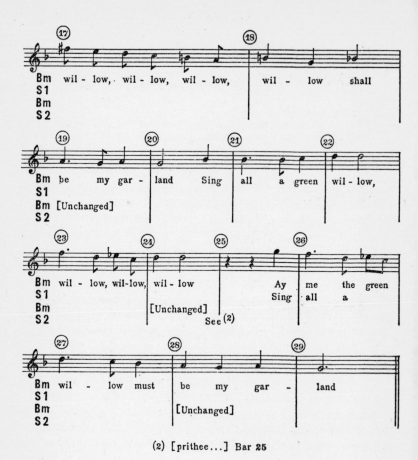

(2) [prithee...] Bar **25**

'Under which king, Bezonian?'

PETER ALEXANDER

CHARLES LAMB in his *Preface* to *Specimens of English Dramatic Poets* explains the principle governing his selection in these words:

> My leading design has been to illustrate what may be called the moral sense of our ancestors. To show in what manner they felt, when they placed themselves by the power of imagination in trying situations, in the conflicts of duty and passion, or the strife of contending duties; what sort of loves and enmities theirs were; how their griefs were tempered, and their full-swoln joys abated: how much of Shakespeare shines in the great men his contemporaries, and how far in his divine mind and manners he surpassed them and all mankind.

Lamb's notes throughout show us how in his choice of scenes he has this design continuously before him; it is difficult therefore to understand how Mr. T. S. Eliot came to say that 'the *Specimens* made it possible to read the plays as poetry while neglecting their function on the stage'.[1] As it is possible for us to misunderstand almost any work that was ever written without our being justified in attributing our error to the author, we must suppose Mr. Eliot to imply that the *Specimens* somehow lead even the judicious reader to look on drama from some uncritical point of view, for he continues, 'all modern opinion of the Elizabethans seems to spring from Lamb, for all modern opinion rests upon the admission that poetry and drama are two separate things'. As representatives of the opposing but equally erroneous schools of criticism Mr. Eliot cites Swinburne and Archer, one preferring Elizabethan drama in spite of its admitted dramatic defects, the other modern drama although it had no claims to poetic worth. For Mr. Eliot's argument, however, the differences between these opposites are unimportant compared with their agreement that poetry and drama are two different things, the common basic assumption made possible, he feels, by Lamb.

Archer's opinions about Elizabethan drama were mistaken from the first, as Mr. O'Casey has often reminded us. Error is always

---

[1] T. S. Eliot, *Elizabethan Essays*, 1934, p. 8.

with us, but particular forms of error have their day, and it is perhaps not too much to say that Archer's opinions, if one may borrow an American phrase that once delighted Mr. O'Casey, are as out of date as Stonewall Jackson's socks.

To fasten Archer's errors about the Elizabethan drama on Lamb, who emphasizes those elements in drama without which stage productions are merely spectacle or opportunity for elocutionists, is a strange miscarriage of critical justice especially on the part of one who is like Lamb himself a critic primarily concerned about the moral sense that gives its significance to a dramatic situation. That such a concern is the basis of Mr. Eliot's interpretation of drama may be illustrated by what he has to say on the final situation of *Othello*.

In his well-known essay *Shakespeare and the Stoicism of Seneca* Mr. Eliot detects in Shakespeare 'a new attitude' somehow derived from Seneca, the attitude of self-dramatization that Shakespeare's heroes sometimes assume in moments of exceptional intensity. Of this new attitude he takes Othello's last speech as an outstanding illustration, and comments on what may be called the moral sense that prompts it in these words:

I have always felt that I have never read a more terrible exposure of human weakness—of universal human weakness—than the last great speech of Othello. (I am ignorant whether anyone else has ever adopted this view, and it may appear subjective and fantastic in the extreme.) It is usually taken on its face value, as expressing the greatness in defeat of a noble but erring nature.

For what he takes to be the common misconception of the speech Mr. Eliot would substitute an entirely contrary interpretation:

What Othello seems to me to be doing in making this speech is *cheering himself up*. He is endeavouring to escape reality, he has ceased to think about Desdemona, and is thinking about himself.

To quote further is unnecessary, since Mr. Eliot's words have awakened so many and such prolonged echoes in contemporary criticism: that Othello is adopting 'an *aesthetic* rather than a moral attitude', and that Shakespeare is exposing 'this *bovarysme*, the human will to see things as they are not', are propositions that are now regarded by some commentators as self-evident.

For a writer to expose the *bovarysme* of mankind is no doubt a legitimate exercise of his art and a revelation of his moral sense; if, however, we are to suppose that this was the final rung of the climax provided for us by Shakespeare in the successive scenes of *Othello* or *Hamlet*, we shall have to change entirely our conception of the nature of Shakespearian tragedy, and perhaps of tragedy generally, although Mr. Eliot regards the tragedy of Corneille and Racine as distinguished from Shakespeare's by its lack of this modern attitude which he characterizes as that of Nietzsche.

It is not an attitude that Mr. Eliot, in spite of his high estimate of Shakespeare as poet and dramatist, can approve of, and he wonders if Shakespeare adopted it because of its 'theatrical utility'.

If Mr. Eliot's attitude here is somewhat ambiguous he has a predecessor in this way of thinking who has left us in no doubt about his disapproval of an art based on 'theatrical utility' rather than sound moral sense. Mr. Eliot, when he told his readers that he feared his views might be judged fantastic and merely idiosyncratic, had not yet read or had forgotten Tolstoy's essay on Shakespeare where he would find an interpretation of the final situation in *Othello* much like his own.

Tolstoy compares *Othello* unfavourably throughout with its Italian source, and, though he allows that Othello's suicide may be effective in a theatrical kind of way, judges it as a manifestation of a weakness of character that ruins our conception of the man. Alymer Maude here translates as follows:

However effective may be his suicide (which does not occur in the romance) it quite destroys the conception of his firm character. If he really suffers from grief and remorse then, when intending to kill himself, he would not utter phrases about his own services, about a pearl, about his eyes dropping tears 'as fast as the Arabian trees their medicinable gum', and still less could he talk about the way a Turk scolded a Venetian, and how 'thus' he punished him for it! So that . . . our conception of his character is constantly infringed by false pathos.[1]

To some such view Mr. Eliot has unconsciously subscribed, although he has not ventured to develop it in the logical way that leads to Tolstoy's total rejection of Shakespeare's art as based on a faulty moral sense. While the fact that Tolstoy and Mr. Eliot come to agree in their judgement of the final scene in *Othello* opens up most important critical questions, for the present it will be sufficient to ask what a man in Othello's position should have done to escape the charge of weakness or of adopting an *aesthetic* pose.

[1] Leo Tolstoy, *Recollections and Essays* (World's Classics), p. 347.

The question might be partially resolved if we could find a play with a final situation very similar to that in *Othello* and an outcome entirely different. A comparison of the attitudes adopted by the protagonists would perhaps help to define more sharply the features that distinguish a moral from an *aesthetic* attitude. And here I must beg the indulgence of Spanish scholars and especially of Professor Parker, for I propose to follow him into a region where I could not venture without his guidance and yet once there ask him a question that may suggest that I do not understand how moral sense may vary with the change of language and latitude.

In his *Approach to Spanish Drama of the Golden Age*[1] Professor Parker invites us to enter on the subject by considering the action of Calderon's *El médico de su honra*. The hero, for so I suppose we may describe him, suspects his wife of infidelity and to preserve his honour has her murdered secretly by a professional blood-letter. In some sense he seems to resemble Othello, for he can say 'My soul adores you and my honour hates you'. On learning of the death of the lady the King, Pedro the Cruel or the Just, orders the widower to marry Leonor, a lady whom he would in earlier times have married had he not suspected her of dishonourable conduct. The hero has now to admit more or less the true position; the King, however, instead of punishing him for the murder of an innocent woman confirms the order for the marriage, and, as the pair take hands before the King, we hear the man who has just supervised the bleeding to death of his innocent wife say that, since he traffics in honour, he displays a bloody hand, and the lady who takes it express her entire satisfaction at its condition.

In using this play of Calderon to give us our first impression of Spanish drama Professor Parker finds himself, or at least puts his readers, in a difficulty; for he finds himself forced to tell us that, in spite of what we may call the *aesthetic* justification of the hero's conduct to be found in other critics, he himself believes that Calderon intended us to view the action as a cruel and inhuman one. Yet having established this impression at the beginning of his study, he asks us in the end to believe that the structure of Spanish drama shows 'the subordination of the theme to a moral purpose through the principle of poetic justice'. It is true, he adds, that this justice is not exemplified 'only by the death of the wrongdoer', but this leaves us wondering if in his first example the hero's second

[1] 1957.

marriage is to be regarded as a form of punishment worse than death.[1]

As a comment on the Spanish hero's words as he takes the hand of Leonor, 'I traffic in honour and so I display a hand bathed in blood', we might fairly use Mr. Eliot's words, 'Humility is the most difficult of all virtues to achieve; nothing dies harder than the desire to think well of oneself'. It is a pity that Tolstoy did not let us have his comments on Calderon's hero. Tolstoy naturally could enter into the conflicting feelings that drove Othello and the Spanish hero to what the sequel proved to be murder. In *Anna Karenina* Tolstoy lets us hear how Anna despises her husband because he lacks the urge of an Othello: 'He is not a man, not a human being. He is . . . a doll! No one else knows it, but I do. Oh, if I were he, I should long since have killed, have torn in pieces, a wife such as I, and not have called her "Ma chère Anna". He is not a man.' But if Tolstoy regarded Othello's suicide after such a deed as weakness, would he have regarded the boast of the trader in honour as the proof of a firm mind? Would he have argued that the Spaniard had at least the courage of his convictions in being prepared to justify his murder as Othello was not?

But Othello does try to justify himself, it may be observed, and in this lies the very point of Mr. Eliot's charge. It is here, however, that we can make the vital distinction that Othello's conduct enforces. He will not offer any justification of his act to the eternal judge before whom he feels he stands; he welcomes the only sentence he can think adequate, and that is damnation; he does, however, have something to say to what we may for the moment call the spectators in court. How we should understand what he says may be made clear by a simpler but parallel situation.

In Scott's tale of *The Two Drovers* Robin Oig has slain his chosen friend, Harry Wakefield, compelled by what he feels to be an irresistible obligation of honour. At his trial Robin Oig does not try to excuse himself for an act that had seemed to him as grievous as it was necessary; what he did protest against in court the judge makes clear to us as he comments on counsel's suggestion that the Highlander had acted in stabbing an unarmed man like a coward. 'I observed', said the judge, 'the prisoner shrink from this part of the

---

[1] My colleague Miss McClelland, to whom I am greatly indebted for guidance through this play, wishes to dissociate herself from all opinions about Spanish drama expressed by those who are as unfamiliar with the language and literature as the present writer.

accusation with the abhorrence natural to a brave man.' From what do Shakespeare's protagonists shrink at the end? Not from their fate, certainly; but just from such observations as this by Mr. Eliot himself: 'Hamlet, who has made a pretty considerable mess of things, and occasioned the death of three innocent people, and two more insignificant ones, dies fairly well pleased with himself'—it is from such a garbled account of his actions that Hamlet would protect himself when he entrusts his story to Horatio; and what Othello fears is not death but the name of having acted, as Dr. Leavis and others have not hesitated to declare, from 'an obtuse and brutal egotism'.

Nor is Othello's action in killing himself an endeavour to escape from reality. He is hastening, as he believes, to judgement. 'I give a life for the life I took', said the Highlander, 'and what can I do more?' But the Moor wishes to give not merely his life but his salvation.

Tolstoy and Mr. Eliot are no less insistent than Lamb on making an understanding of the moral sense of the dramatist the basis of their interpretation. Yet the novelist and the poet as they survey the dramatist's world come on what they pronounce to be 'theatrical utility' rather than moral sense. They feel about Shakespeare as perhaps the greatest man of letters of all time sometimes felt about the only drama that can challenge the supremacy of the Elizabethan. It seemed to Plato an exhibition of human weakness. The differences between Mr. Eliot and Lamb are part of a greater debate about the relation of art and morals, and where one stands in the argument can be seen by how one judges the final scenes of Shakespeare's tragedies.

The Rider on the Winged Horse

MARY LASCELLES

OF the various myths which have been pressed into service to convey an impression of the poet's predicament, one at least has followed a strange course, always inviting attention, but often hard to trace. The elements composing it appear, when they are brought into focus together, hardly reconcilable. Nevertheless, since their motion obeys the dictates not of the reason but of the imagination ('a licentious and vagrant faculty', as Johnson calls it), rational compatibility may not be required. It seldom happens that all are present at once; now one predominates, now another, and it is only when they change places that the eye is teazed and delighted by a strange iridescence. The myth I intend is that which, with whatever variety of implication, plainly associates two figures, the poet and the winged horse Pegasus, and the treatment it has received prompts questions which may (at the outset) be framed like this. The usual sources of information—dictionaries and hand-books of myth—agree in calling the association modern (except in so far as it may be inferred from the connexion of both with the Muses). Is the matter indeed so simple? Many, with more assurance, assert that it was Boiardo who, in his *Orlando Innamorato,* first mounted the poet upon Pegasus;[1] but in none of these have I discovered a reference. Was it indeed one man's turn of fancy that conquered a whole realm of figurative allusion so rapidly and so completely as this elusive passage must have done? And from these initial questions others will arise.

I propose therefore to take up a position beside two great English poets and listen when each is saying something about his vocation in terms of this myth of the rider on the winged horse: Spenser, in *The Ruines of Time,* Milton in the proem to the seventh book of *Paradise Lost.* Thence it may prove possible to descry some significant phases in the development of a meaning with which the tale

---

[1] Pauly-Wissowa, *Real-Encyclopädie der Classischen Altertumswissenschaft,* is an exception. S. Reinach drew attention to the stages by which hearsay had hardened into assertion among lesser reference books ('Pégase, l'hippogriffe et les poètes', *Revue Archéologique,* Paris 1920). The process continues.

of horse and rider was not originally charged—even as the links of
a river, itself unseen in the distant landscape, may be traced by the
line of living green accompanying its course.

Of the two passages, Milton's is surely both the more explicit and
the more enigmatic.

> Descend from Heav'n *Urania,* by that name
> If rightly thou art calld, whose Voice divine
> Following, above th'*Olympian* Hill I soare,
> Above the flight of *Pegasean* wing.
> The meaning, not the Name I call: for thou
> Nor of the Muses nine, nor on the top
> Of old *Olympus* dwellst, but Heav'nlie borne,
> Before the Hills appeerd, or Fountain flowd,
> Thou with Eternal wisdom didst converse,
> Wisdom thy Sister, and with her didst play
> In presence of th'Almightie Father, pleas'd
> With thy Celestial Song. Up led by thee
> Into the Heav'n of Heav'ns I have presum'd,
> An Earthlie Guest, and drawn Empyreal Aire,
> Thy tempring; with like safetie guided down
> Return me to my Native Element:
> Least from this flying Steed unreind, (as once
> Bellerophon, though from a lower Clime)
> Dismounted, on th'*Aleian* Field I fall,
> Erroneous there to wander and forlorne.[1]

This is explicit in so far as the allusion to the story of Bellerophon's
fall, though intricately woven of strands from Homer and Pindar,
does not appear to be complicated by medieval accretions of allegory. Nevertheless, it perplexes by those overtones of fear which
are surely audible in the analogy between the fallen man and the
poet, tones sharpened by the allusion to Orpheus which follows
hard upon it. I will not ask 'Of what is the poet afraid?' Fear does
not require a definable object; but, when it is expressed by a man so
little fearful as Milton—so sure, moreover, of his poetic vocation—
we must desire to know something of its cause. Furthermore, there
is a turn in the story of Bellerophon as his grandson Glaucus tells
it to Diomedes in *Iliad* VI which puzzles the imagination. Between
the man loved by the gods, saved from the danger into which a false
accusation has brought him, carried triumphantly through his

---

[1] *Paradise Lost,* vii. 1–20, ed. Helen Darbishire, 1952. (Likewise other quotations
from Milton.)

forlorn expedition against the Chimaera—and the man hated by the gods, at whose hands two of his three children perish, forced to end his life alone in the Aleian plain, 'eating his heart out' and shunning the haunts of men, there is, as the story now stands, no *narrative* connexion; only the idea of mortality joins them—Glaucus speaks as survivor of a once flourishing line.

From a mere *modern*, who has all the way between Homer and Milton to travel (and is besides very ill equipped for the journey), no more, I hope, will be expected than a passing reference to Hesiod, who first associated Pegasus with Bellerophon in the conquest of the Chimaera,[1] and an attempt to show the bearing on later developments in this myth of the tale to which Pindar alludes in two odes: Olympian XIII and Isthmian VII. In the first of these, the favour of the gods is intimated by the story that Pallas gave Bellerophon a bridle, by means of which he subdued the winged horse Pegasus and so achieved his quests; their disfavour, by the poet's explicit refusal to tell what became of him when Pegasus went home to an Olympian stable. The second ode darkly suggests what has been withheld by the first: it is not for man to aspire to the dwellings of the gods; that was how Bellerophon fell, thrown by Pegasus. His was the end that waits on forbidden joys. Thus, a connecting thread is drawn by the hint of ὕβρις, between Bellerophon blessed and Bellerophon cursed: the winged horse divinely but (in the event) disastrously given becomes the instrument by which he first escapes danger and then brings destruction on himself.

In one province of the Roman literary world myth shrinks to fable, or even less. Catullus' line

non si Pegaseo ferar volatu[2]

suggests that the winged horse has become a mere figure of speech. For Horace, however, the fable of Bellerophon's fall is capable of being charged afresh with meaning—personal meaning, if lines 25 to 31 in Ode IV. xi may be understood in some such way as this: Bellerophon, like Phaethon, fell by inordinate desire of the unattainable; but there is another sort of failure to come to terms with life—

[1] *Theogony*, l. 325. For the complex origins and intricate early development of the myth, see T. J. Dunbabin, 'Bellerophon, Herakles and Chimaera', in *Studies Presented to David Moore Robinson*, Washington U.P. 1953. Also, H. A. Fischer, *Bellerophon*, Leipzig 1851.
[2] LV. 16. With this use of Pegasus in hyperbole, to suggest fabulous speed, cf. Horace, *Ode*, I. xxvii, Propertius, II. xxx (a).

failure to accept, in face of approaching age, the ebbing of hitherto attainable good.

> terret ambustus Phaethon avaras
> spes, et exemplum grave praebet ales
> Pegasus terrenum equitem gravatus
>   Bellerophontem,
> semper ut te digna sequare et ultra
> quam licet sperare nefas putando
> disparem vites.

Meanwhile, that other tribe of associations which, gathering about the winged horse, was to oust Bellerophon from popular imagination must have been gaining ground. It cannot, we are told, be traced back beyond Hellenistic times; but, when first encountered, it is well enough established to be the object of allusion. In the Idyll known as the Lament for Bion, the Muses are invoked to mourn for the dead poet, who drank from the Pegasean well—παγασίδος κράνας.[1] Pausanias gives it as traditional that Hippocrene, the spring on the slopes of Helicon where the Muses were honoured, had been made by the hoof of Bellerophon's horse.[2] This theme also the Roman poets held themselves at liberty to subdue to a personal application. Thus Propertius opens III. iii by representing himself as a dreamer in the Muses' haunt—

> Visus eram molli recubans Heliconis in umbra,
>   Bellerophontei qua fluit umor equi—

warned by Apollo that his genius is not for great poetic undertakings. Persius' elaboration of this disclaimer, in the Prologue to his Satires, removes the allusion one degree further from the grandeur of myth:

> Nec fonte labra prolui caballino,
> nec in bicipiti somniasse Parnaso
> memini, ut repente sic poeta prodirem.
> Heliconidasque pallidamque Pirenen
> illis remitto, quorum imagines lambunt
> hederae sequaces: ipse semipaganus
> ad sacra vatum carmen adfero nostrum.
> quis expedivit psittaco suum chaere
> picamque docuit nostra verba conari?
> magister artis ingenique largitor

---

[1] *Bucolici Graeci*, ed. Wilamowitz-Moellendorff, 1910, p. 93 (l. 77).
[2] *Description of Greece*, IX. xxxi. 3. See also II. xxxi. 9.

> venter, negatas artifex sequi voces;
> quod si dolosi spes refulgeat nummi,
> corvos poetas et poetridas picas
> cantare credas Pegaseium nectar.

If, among these disclaimers of poetic ambition, there linger any echoes of Bellerophon's tragic fall, they will not be heard again until editions of Greek authors begin to come from the Italian presses in the 1480's. But the repercussions of Persius' Prologue are quite another story. The Satires were known and esteemed in the Middle Ages;[1] and these lines, with their ostensible profession of unworthiness, were evidently regarded as a pattern exordium. It may indeed be said that *not sleeping on Parnassus* became an indispensable piece of literary good manners. Not every one who repeated this formula, however, had an ear for its intonation. Presently, therefore—in England, not later than the beginning of the fifteenth century— irony, with its mingled colours, enters the story: the persons become agents of happenings which they neither intend nor expect. To Chaucer, Persius' intention is of course clearly audible; he captures the import of the whole passage in a glancing allusion, and clinches it with a comparable disclaimer of rhetorical skill:

> I sleep never on the mount of Pernaso,
> Ne lerned Marcus Tullius Cithero. . . .[2]

And, if there is irony in prefixing these lines to a tale in which poetical and rhetorical art are happily allied, we may be sure it is deliberate.

A small circumstance serves to measure the quickness of response on which Chaucer might reckon: the Ellesmere scribe wrote in the margin against the Franklin's apology the first two lines of Persius' Prologue—perhaps from memory, for he is not word-perfect. Later variations on this theme, however, call in question more than verbal accuracy. What are we to make of John Walton's *Prefatio Translatoris* to his version of Boethius?

> Hyt leketh not me to labour nor muse
> Upon these olde poyses derke
> For cristen fayth such thynges moste refuse
> As witneseth Jerom the noble clerke

---

[1] J. E. Sandys, *History of Classical Scholarship*, 1921; E. R. Curtius, *European Literature and the Latin Middle Ages*, tr. W. R. Trask, 1953.
[2] Chaucer, *Works*, ed. Skeat, 1894, iv. 482 (Prologue to the Franklin's Tale).

> Hyt shulde be no cristen mannes worke
> Tho false goddes names to renew . . .
> And certen I have tasted wonder lyte
> As of the welles of calyope
> No wonder though I sympelly endyte
> Yel wyl I nofte un to Tessiphone
> Ne to her susters that in hel be
> Besekynge after craft of eloquence
> But pray to God of hys benignitie
> My spirit to enspyre with hys influence.[1]

If indeed he knew Persius, and had not met his disclaimer already reduced to a commonplace, may we accept Dr. Curtius' pleasant suggestion that to a medieval clerk Persius' *semipaganus* might signify only half a pagan?[2] This would certainly open the way to a *half-Christian* distrust of the Muses, accepted as implicit in any such disclaimer as his. A hundred years later Gavin Douglas, having praised Virgil for drinking deep of Helicon,[3] professes his own independence of such sources:

> Calliope nor payane goddis wyld
> May do to me no thing bot harme, I wene. . . .[4]

Lydgate may have been intermediary between Persius and such allusions as these; his variations on the theme of the Prologue are notable. He appeals, for example, to Clio who dwells with her sisters

> . . . by Elicon the welle,
> Rennyng ful clere with st[r]emys cristallyn,
> And callyd is the welle Caballyn
> That sprang by touche of the Pegasee. . . .[5]

Indeed, he seems to have known all fourteen lines of the Prologue, and valued them as a collection of mythological allusions—on which he drew no fewer than four times.[6] Can he have guessed that the word *caballinus* was chosen to suggest a decidedly underbred horse?

---

[1] *The Boke of Comfort called in Latyn Boecius de Consolatione Phil: . .* 1525. Walton (who wrote in 1410) says, moreover, that he knows himself inferior to Chaucer and Gower.

[2] Op. cit., p. 233.

[3] For the confusion of Helicon with Hippocrene, see pp. 181–2, below.

[4] *Works*, ed. Small, 1874, ii. 5 and 17–18 (*Prolough of the First Buik of Eneados*).

[5] *Troy Book*, ed. Bergen (E.E.T.S.), 1906, p. 2.

[6] Besides the *Troy Book*, these contain allusions of this kind: *The Complaint of the Black Knight*; the *Fall of Princes*; the *Life of St. Alban*. There is sufficient reason for believing that each allusion is Lydgate's own addition to his source.

Its sound was pleasing, its rhyme serviceable; what more could a poet ask than that a fountain should be both caballyn and crystallyn?

Alike as commonplace and allusion, this disclaimer of the Muses' aid long retains one constant characteristic—its personal application: with whatever variations of tone, serious or sardonic, the poet must be understood as referring to himself—as it were, in his professional capacity. Whence it follows that such a passage is most likely to occur in prologue or dedication, or else in some part of a longer work which gives occasion for a reaffirmation of poetic purpose. The implications, however, of this denial of the Muses could be extended. 'Avoid Parnassus', whether this signifies self-admonition or a warning offered to a fellow poet, may mean: 'Withdraw from a barren region.' Thus, to Maynard, at odds with Richelieu, it affords a figure of speech for stinted patronage.

> Descens de la double montagne

is one expression of a favourite theme for epigrammatic complaint;

> Le feu de la Prose & des Vers
> Ne fait plus bouillir la marmite. . . .[1]

So is the more famous epigram which ends:

> Malherbe, en cét âge brutal,
> Pegase est un cheual qui porte
> Les grands hommes à l'Hospital.[2]

From here, a ready way opens downwards to the use of Pegasus as a figure of speech in satire of poetic pretension; and Boileau takes it.[3] This is the mood of Butler's satire, and this the employment to which he puts the winged horse—for example, in his Character of *A Small Poet*: '. . . To what Purpose did the Antients feign *Pegasus* to have Wings, if he must be confined to the Road and Stages like a Pack-Horse, or be forced to be obedient to Hedges and Ditches?'[4] But I doubt whether outright satire was ever the characteristic English response to this myth. To the systematic French mind we must often seem like children who strike out an odd notion by chance and, on hearing others laugh, set up for humorists. Thus,

---

[1] François de Maynard, *Œuvres poétiques*, ed. Garrisson, Paris 1885–8, iii. 109–10.
[2] Ibid., iii. 102–3.
[3] e.g. in *L'Art poétique*, Chants I and III; *Discours au roi*, &c.
[4] Samuel Butler, *Genuine Remains*, ed. R. Thyer, 1759, ii. 115. See also p. 119.

Corbett, a generation earlier, had eased the passage from satiric observation to grave reflection with this gently ironic allusion:

> Away, my Muse, from this base subiect, know
> Thy Pegasus nere strooke his foote soe low.[1]

And these mingled colours had appeared in Thomas Randolph's warning to a friend not to look for 'the Pegasian spring' either by 'the Oxes ford' or 'the bridge through which low Cham doth run'.[2] One more English illustration may be cited for its odd simplicity. *Queen Tragedy Restor'd* is a little piece of drollery for the stage: the Queen, sick almost to death, is rescued from the coma into which quack physicians have thrown her by a pageant, in which Shakespeare rises and speaks:

> At the Behest of *Sol's* bright Charioteer
> Patron of those choice Spirits, who with youthful
> Ardour mount fiery-footed *Pegasus*,
> *Bellerophon's* proud Steed, lo *Shakespear* comes![3]

Despite the pitiable failure of the verse to wake Shakespearian echoes—despite much that is deliberately ludicrous in the context—these four clumsy lines surely imply recognition of the splendour still latent in that outworn figure of speech which was once part of a poetic myth.

It is pleasant to turn back towards some of the numerous references to the Muses in Italy of the fourteenth and fifteenth centuries, and to observe acknowledgement rather than disclaimer as the customary approach. (Disclaimer itself, when it appears, will be softened and brightened by the suavity of Italian poetic manners, until it shines with a lustre not unlike that of acknowledgement.) Among these references are to be found passages which Chaucer knew, and to which he paid his tribute of imitation—for example, the invocation at the opening of the *Teseida*, and the valediction:

> O sorelle Castalie, che nel monte
> Elicona contente dimorate
> dintorno al sacro gorgonëo fonte
> sottesso l'ombra delle frondi amate

---

[1] Richard Corbett, *Iter boreale*, ll. 99–100; *Poems*, ed. J. A. W. Bennett and H. R. Trevor-Roper, 1955, p. 34. Corbett is passing from gibes at tapsters to thoughts stirred by the fall of Richard III.

[2] Thomas Randolph, *Poems*, ed. Thorn-Drury, 1929, p. 97.

[3] I know this 'Dramatick Entertainment' only in the anonymous edition of 1749.

> da Febo, delle quali ancor la fronte
> spero d'ornarmi sol che 'l concediate,
> le sante orecchi a' miei prieghi porgete
> e quelli udite come voi dovete.

—and, after a closing reference to the Muses:

> E però che i porti disïati
> in si lungo peleggio giá tegnamo,
> da varii venti in essi trasportati,
> le vaghe nostre vele qui caliamo,
> e le ghirlande e i don meritati,
> con l'ancore fermati, qui spettiamo,
> lodando l'Orsa che con la sua luce
> qui n'ha condotti, a noi essendo duce.[1]

Chaucer, as his commentators have remarked, gathers images from both these widely separated stanzas, glancing also at a passage, or passages from the *Divine Comedy*, when he frames the invocation to his *Anelida and Arcite*:

> Be favorable eek, thou Polymnia,
> On Parnaso that, with thy sustres glade,
> By Elicon, not fer from Cirrea,
> Singest with vois memorial in the shade,
> Under the laurer which that may not fade,
> And do that I my ship to haven winne. . . .[2]

He could, indeed, have found similar *Helicon* references in the prose of Dante and Boccaccio.[3] I venture to call in question the inference often drawn from such passages that these poets *confused* Helicon with Hippocrene.[4] The springs associated with Pegasus, or with the Muses, or (as the tale grew) with both, were so numerous; the relationships between the mythical beings were so intricate; and both had so long a record of figurative service, that some such explanation as this seems preferable. To the great Italian poets—

---

[1] Boccaccio, *Opere*, iii, ed. A. Roncaglia, Bari 1941; *Teseida*, I. 1, and XII. 86. Propertius likewise had linked his reference to the Muses with this simile of the storm-beaten vessel making into port—whether by coincidence, merely, or a natural train of figurative thought.

[2] Chaucer, *Works*, ed. Skeat, i. 365–6.

[3] e.g. Dante, *De Vulgari Eloquentia*, II. iv; Boccaccio, *De Genealogia Deorum*, XIV, *passim*.

[4] e.g. John Livingston Lowes, 'Chaucer and Dante', in *Modern Philology*, April 1917. His list of sources of misinformation would be conclusive if Chaucer, Dante, or Boccaccio had been writing a manual of information. Since, however, they were writing poetry, it may surely be urged that these sources, if they recollected them, gave them licence, if they needed it, for poetic play.

and to some few others, surely, who had taken them for masters—
one function of myth was to serve as plaything for a craftsman, and
the pleasure of the thing consisted in a bold and happy redisposition
of the figures, whether in pictorial or verbal composition. Where
words compose the pattern, the changes will be rung on names and
the epithets from which they are framed, or with which they are
compounded—with a strong preference, in a literate society, for the
oblique and allusive formation, such as Dante's 'diva Pegasea'[1] or
Boccaccio's 'antrum Gorgoneum'.[2] This latter, with deliberate
artifice, recalls Pegasus' birth from the death-pangs of Medusa, the
dint of his hoof in the rock, and the stream that issued from it, with
the sole purpose of designating the source of poetic inspiration. I
cannot believe that Boccaccio used the phrase 'monte Elicona' in
his invocation, and 'l'Elicone / fonte' in a later passage of the
Teseida,[3] for no better reason than confusion of mind. Here, rather,
is the buoyancy of a poet who regards himself as natural heir to the
treasures of ancient myth. Amongst his remoter followers, the case
may well be different.

This, if it is a just interpretation, should be borne in mind when
approaching a particular fifteenth-century reference which may
prove important in the development of the association between
Pegasus and the poet. I mean the opening to the tenth canto of the
fourth book, in Nicolo delli Agostini's continuation of Boiardo's
Orlando Innamorato. Reinach drew attention to it,[4] and suggested
that here at last was that mysterious turn in the development of the
myth so often attributed to Boiardo.

> Non perchio creda al Eliconeo fõte
> Tuffar el Griffo mio ne le sacre onde
> Et con rime fiorite, terse, & pronte
> Cingermi al capo de le aurate fronde
> Ne con Apollo al bel Pegaso monte
> Seder con le sue muse alte, & feconde
> Che essendo come io sõ di poco p̃ggio
> Salir non spero a si sublime seggio.
>
> Ma sol per dar diletto al Signor mio
> Et qualunque mi stara ascoltare

---

[1] *Paradiso*, XVIII. 82.　　　　　　　　　　[2] *De Genealogia Deorum*, XIV. xx.
[3] XI. 63. This, an elaborate verbal picture, has for subject Apollo and the Muses
depicted on a shield.
[4] Op. cit., p. 229. Though I shall have occasion to disagree with his conclusions,
I should certainly not have found the passage without the help of his mentioning it.

Seguo dou'io lasciai con tal desio
Che piu non si potrebbe imaginare
Sĕza altra inuocatiõ de Euterpe, & Clio
Perch'io so ben che lui mi pol aitare
Et far mia naue gir con prosper uento
Nel desiato porto a saluamento.[1]

That it is in the continuation rather than the poem that we should
look for the modern conception of Pegasus I am indeed convinced,
for in the *Orlando Innamorato* itself I have found no reference but to
grifoni e pegasei as beasts of the chase[2]—and the plural alone would
discredit any attempt to link this passage with the myth of the
Muses' horse. Nevertheless, Reinach was (I believe) hampered by
not having seen the stanzas and attributing the word *Pegaso*, on the
advice of a friend, to a printer's error: a misprint for *Parnaso*. This
seems questionable. Not only is Pegasus present in the editions of
1538 and 1539; he persists in those of 1553, 1584, and 1602—which
exemplify Domenichi's revision;[3] and no edition giving Parnassus
has (so far as I know) been found. Lodovico Domenichi, moreover,
makes himself responsible for more than merely verbal improvements; elsewhere in the poem he corrects mythological allusions
with some rigour. Yet, while carefully supplying the adjectival form
Pegaseo, he appears satisfied with the meaning. May we not say that,
to the sixteenth-century editor, it presented no difficulty, because
the poet was by now airborne? Of this at least I am sure: Agostini's
passage, whether he wrote Parnaso or Pegaseo, observes a traditional
pattern, though newly diversified. From the first to the fifteenth
century, these refrains have been heard in alternation: 'Sleep on
Parnassus? Not I.'—'Be favourable to me, you who dwell on Parnassus or by the sacred spring.' Agostini preserves the pleasantry
in the disclaimer, the true modesty in the acknowledgement, while
giving to both a fresh and agreeable turn: 'Sleep on Parnassus?
Converse with the Muses? No, no—it is enough that I write to
please *you*.' This is the mood in which Sidney—whether prompted
by Agostini or another, or else without any prompting at all—
recalled Persius' prologue in his seventy-fourth sonnet:

[1] Boiardo, *Orlando Innamorato*, Venice 1539. My choice of an edition to quote may,
I am afraid, be arbitrary, but I have made a comparison with others to ensure that it
shall not be misleading.
[2] Matteo Maria Boiardo, *Orlando Innamorato*, ed. A. Scaglione, Turin 1951, ii. 569
(Book III, Canto v, stanza 37).
[3] These five Venetian editions, all I have been able to examine, contain within the
two stanzas I have quoted numerous verbal variants.

> I never dranke of *Aganippe* well,
> Nor never did in shade of *Tempe* sit:
> And Muses scorne with vulgar braines to dwell,
> Poore Lay-man I, for sacred rites unfit—

that last line surely the perfect equivalent of Persius' *semipaganus*. This sonnet, one of several playful assertions that the heart's devotion is of more avail than any help the Muses can give, may (for all we can now tell) have been formerly designed to stand first in the sequence.

From Agostini's continuation onwards,[1] we are frequently aware of that tone—of pleasantry no longer sardonic, of personal application without bravado—which belongs above all to letters, or verse exchanged between friends. Thus, Ariosto (in a verse epistle concerned with the education of his friend's son) complains that, at the time when *he* was fit for the melody of Pegasus (*pegáseo melo*), his father compelled him to read law.[2] And it is with a like pleasant freedom that Gabriel Harvey offers advice to Spenser: '... perhappes it will advaunce the wynges of your Imagination a degree higher: at the least if any thing can be added to the loftinesse of his conceite, whom gentle *Mistresse Rosalinde*, once reported to have all the *Intelligences* at commaundement, and an other time, Christened her *Segnior Pegaso*.'[3] But the happiest of these allusions is Milton's, in a letter to Diodati: 'Multa solicite quæris, etiam quid cogitem. Audi, Theodote, verum in aurem ut ne rubeam, & sinito paulisper apud te grandia loquar; quid cogitem quæris? ita me bonus Deus, immortalitatem. Quid agam vero? πτεροφυῶ, & volare meditor: sed tenellis admodum adhuc pennis evehit se noster Pegasus, humile sapiamus.'[4] Of such intimate communication as this, commendatory verse can be no more than a shadow; but, as a shadow may show whence the light falls, so the sonnet addressed to William Drummond by Sir David Murray of Gorthy, a poet of Prince Henry's household, illustrates the employment of this emblem in formal exchanges of courtesy:

> The sister *Nymphes* who haunt the *Thespian* Springs,
> Ne're did their Gifts more liberally bequeath

---

[1] Said to have been published in 1495. The earliest extant edition appears to be 1506.

[2] *Satires*, VII. 154–9.

[3] *Three proper wittie familiar letters, lately passed betweene two Universitie men* . . .; text from Spenser, *Poems*, ed. E. de Sélincourt, 1912, p. 625.

[4] Columbia edition, xii. 26.

To them who on their Hills suck'd sacred Breath,
Than vnto thee, by which thou sweetly sings.
Ne're did *Apollo* raise on *Pegase* Wings
A *Muse* more neare himselfe, more farre from Earth,
Than thine. . . .

These lines, together with the representation of a winged horse on the title-page of the 1614 *Poems*,[1] provoke a hitherto unspoken question: what did Pegasus mean to the common reader?

It is here that the mythographers must be taken into the reckoning; both because they had something to do with the development of this myth, and because they conditioned the response on which the poets counted. Poetic allusion requires of the reader some knowledge of the matter referred to; and, while I can nowise believe that Milton, for example, pored over dictionaries and handbooks of myth,[2] yet it is evident that he would have been obliged to frame his mythological allusions very differently for an age (like ours) in which the schoolboy's mind is not furnished with the information such books contain. The mythographies, however—ancient, medieval, modern—demand the scope rather of book than essay, even for the tracing of a single myth. They have, fortunately, received attention;[3] yet only an attempt (such as this) to find the answer to a particular question will show how intricate are their relationships —how frequently, for example, successive editions or translations of some one work will introduce significant variations into a single story, or how remote the antecedents of these variations are likely to be. I propose, therefore, to take my stand on two notable works, each (I believe) illustrating a distinct and important development; each, certainly, well known and influential. Boccaccio's *De Genealogia Deorum*[4] may be regarded as the culmination of the medieval tradition in mythography, and Comes's *Mythologiae*[5] as outstanding among modern compilations. The watershed between them is formed by

[1] Drummond, *Poetical Works*, ed. L. E. Kastner, 1913. For the sonnet, see i. 95; for a facsimile of the title-page of the edition (supposedly) of 1614, see plate 6, facing i, p. liv.
[2] See D. T. Starnes and E. W. Talbert, *Classical Myth and Legend in Renaissance Dictionaries*, University of North Carolina Press 1955.
[3] e.g. J. Seznec, *La Survivance des dieux antiques*, Studies of the Warburg Institute, vol. xi, 1940.
[4] First printed in Venice 1472. I shall have occasion to use the Basle edition of 1532, but will note any significant variation from the first edition.
[5] Natalis Comitis (i.e. Natale Conti), *Mythologiae*, published in Venice 1551. I shall have occasion to use the Paris edition of 1583, but will note where it differs from that of Venice 1567, the earliest I have been able to obtain.

the labours of those printers who made available texts (often with scholia) of ancient authors, in the last three decades of the fifteenth, and first three of the sixteenth century, enabling the lesser man's work to supersede that of the greater, and making even Boccaccio's editor and translator more knowledgeable than their author.

If Boccaccio may be accepted as representative of the medieval scholar poet, then it will appear that Bellerophon was known to the Middle Ages[1] as the triumphant hero of a romance of adventure: the man in whom virtue was rewarded; who, though falsely accused, compelled to carry his own death warrant and sent on a forlorn hope, won safety and acclaim with the help of his magic horse. I have indeed found references to Bellerophon's fall in both of the works attributed to Hyginus the Mythographer: according to that known as the *Fabulae*,[2] he fell in the Aleian fields, but was still to attain a happy ending; according to the even more dubious *Poeticon Astronomicon*,[3] he attempted the flight to heaven, but, looking down, was seized with terror, fell and perished. All this is a far cry from Homer. A medieval reader, however, could encounter the Homeric version of Bellerophon's end among the pseudo-Aristotelian *Problemata* (XXX. i), or in Cicero's *Tusculan Disputations* (III. 63)—or, in their derivatives. In this thirtieth *Problem*, Bellerophon is cited among mythical heroes distinguished for their melancholy, and also for eminence in philosophy, politics, poetry, or art, and two and a half lines from the *Iliad*, recounting his disfavour with the gods and wanderings in the Aleian fields, are quoted. In the third *Disputation*, extravagance in grief is censured, Bellerophon, with other mythical figures, instanced, and two lines, the account of his wanderings, quoted. (Both quotations are in Latin.) This allusion is not without reverberations. Petrarch, in the investigation of his own melancholy which he puts into the mouth of St. Augustine (in *De Secreto*), quotes these latter two lines.[4] An indistinct version of the *Problem*, with the Homeric lines loosely translated into French,

---

[1] I have endeavoured to verify this supposition by resort to the sources and analogues of the *De Genealogia*—notably, the Vatican mythographies, *Scriptores rerum mythicarum*, ed. Bode Celle 1834.

[2] The title given to this collection by its editor, J. Micyllus, in whose text of 1535 (Basle) it survives. (*Aleios* is his correction of *alienos*.)

[3] First printed at Ferrara 1475. I have used the text of the 1535 volume, in which it is bound up with the *Fabulae* and other matter, but have compared it with that of the first edition.

[4] In the text of 1489, *Aleis* has become *alienis*, as in the text of Hyginus corrected by Mycillus. In the Italian translation *El Secreto*, Siena 1517, the epithet has become *amoenis*—which suggests forgetfulness of the original story.

is discoverable in *Le Miroir des Melancholicques*—'En ceste question est dispute pourquoy les Melãcholicques sont ingenieux'.[1] It reverberates also in that valley of echoes, Burton's *Anatomy of Melancholy*: 'Why melancholy men are witty, which Aristotle hath long since maintained in his Problems, and that all learned men, famous Philosophers, and Law-givers, *ad unum fere omnes Melancholici*, have still beene melancholy; is a Probleme much controverted.'[2]

These are but fitful and fragmentary recollections of an older, tragic story, such as could hardly be pieced together by a reader who knew nothing else of Bellerophon than the record of triumphant adventures which Boccaccio derived from some four centuries of mythographical tradition. It is with the amplified text of the *De Genealogia* published in 1532 by Jacobus Micyllus at Basle that the old pattern begins to reappear:

> Asclepiades sic tradit: Superbientem eum, ex rerum felici successu, tentasse cum Pegaso in cælum quoꝗ subuolare, quam audaciam cum Iuppiter odisset, immisisse Æstrum Pegaso, à quo agitatus excussit Bellerophontem, ceciditꝗ in campum Lyciæ, qui post ab eodem Aleius dictus est, eo quod cæcus in eo errasset Bellerophontes donec periret.[3]

Presently, in the translation and commentary of Betussi, we recognize that the story could no longer stop short at the victory over some monster: two passages of the *Elucidario poetico*, those under the names of Bellerophon and Pegasus,[4] recount the fall. Pegasus made the spring of Hippocrene, sacred to the Muses: 'Dapoi chinando egli il capo in pirene fonte dolce, Bellerofonte vi sallì sopra volendo volare in cielo, alla fine cadette, ma pegaso giungendo al cielo fu posto tra le stelle.'[5]

It is to Comes, amplified by Linocier and others,[6] that we must turn for such an account of Bellerophon as the diffusion of Greek texts had made possible; full, circumstantial, with references to

---

[1] This purports to be a translation from the Greek, by Meury Riflant, Paris 1543.
[2] 1621, p. 263. Burton seems to have forgotten the poet.
[3] Micyllus' end-note to Boccaccio's account of Bellerophon, p. 346.
[4] In sixteenth-century dictionaries, the entries under these two names are sometimes at variance. For example, in the 1596 edition of the *Dictionarium historicum, geographicum, poeticum*, attributed to Charles Estienne, one (Pegasus) accords with Hyginus, the other (Bellerophon) with Micyllus' note.
[5] Giuseppe Betussi, *Della Geneologia degli dei di Giovanni Boccaccio, Elucidario*, p. 61; first published 1545; but I quote from the edition of 1644 (Venice)—the earliest I have seen.
[6] G. Linocier, Paris 1583. For the labours of other editors, culminating in this edition, see F. L. Schoell, 'Les Mythologistes italiens de la renaissance et la Poésie Elisabéthaine, (*Revue de Litterature Comparée*, 1924), p. 10.

Homer and Pausanias, but coloured by a new morality, apparent in the very telling of the story:

Sed Bellerophon, quale est ingenium plerisque mortalium, tãta rerum gestarum felicitate nimium elatus in cœlum quoque ascendere super equo Pegaso voluit: quam arrogãtiam Iupiter omnis temeritatis grauissimus vindex deprimendam esse ratus, œstrum illi equo immisit, quare Bellerophon præceps in terram deturbatur. Cum in Aleiam Ciliciæ planitiem is cecidisset, cæcúsque factus fuisset, *tamdiu errauit per illam planitiem, quamdiu vixit, donec inedia denique fuit assumptus ac victus penuria, cùm nullam neque domum, neque hominem reperisset:* at Pegasus nũc sublimis, nunc depressus per aëra volans, in cœlum denique rediit in Iouis praesepe, quæ stellae sunt ita vocatæ.[1]

'Quale est ingenium plerisque mortalium'—this is upon us even before we reach the systematic allegorization of the myth; but it is in the full allegory, medieval and modern and the development from one to the other, that we may hope to discover a source for the tragic vision of the poet in his association with Pegasus.

The pattern of allegorical interpretation (traceable from Boccaccio, and even from his sources, to Comes) is threefold. The strands in the plait may be sufficiently distinguished thus: the simplest is that of natural philosophy—for example, Pegasus is explained in terms of air currents. Political philosophy, rooted in the euhemerist tradition, makes Bellerophon's exploits into well-planned campaigns, and Pegasus into a naval vessel—or, as Philemon Holland says (with an eye to Plutarch, Amyot, and the Queen's navy), a pinnace.[2] Thus interpreted, Bellerophon may adventure with Perseus as his fellow knight-errant, or else be equated with him.[3] Since the distinction between this interpretation and that of moral philosophy is not so sharp as that which divides both from natural philosophy, the acts of either hero may afford matter for discourse on man's political or moral attributes. It is this moral allegory that contains the pith of my argument. Boccaccio is here encumbered with an intractable medieval accretion: the description of Pegasus as a monster (hardly less grotesque than the Chimaera) in the *De Imagine Mundi* then attributed to St. Anselm.[4] This work

[1] Op. cit., pp. 955–6. *. . .* not in 1567.

[2] Plutarch (*Moralia*) made the Chimaera a pirate; Amyot, in a note to his translation (Paris 1572), inferred pursuit by means of *un vaisseau fort leger*, and Holland names it.

[3] Boccaccio equates them; Raoul Lefèvre, in his Troy romance, makes them companions. Various arguments have been offered in explanation.

[4] The author was Honorius Augustodunensis—see Migne, *Patr. Lat.*, vol. 172.

must be responsible for the monstrous Pegasus of Henryson and Barclay.[1] Notwithstanding this impediment, Boccaccio expounds the meaning of Pegasus and his riders according to tradition. The flying horse is fame—that is, good repute, earned by deeds neither lucky nor foolhardy, but well judged. He made the spring signifying that poetic utterance by which great deeds are celebrated; hence it is said to be dedicated to the Muses. The theme, more than once repeated, is: fame, in the keeping of the poets.[2] The sources are the medieval mythographies, without discrimination. For the interpretation of Bellerophon, however, Boccaccio turns specifically to Fulgentius, and quotes him word for word: Bellerophon is wise deliberation (*bona consultatio*), appropriately mounted on Pegasus, after whom the eternal spring (of wisdom) is named. 'Sapientia enim bonae cõsultationis aeternus fons est.' And so we return to the association with the Muses.[3]

This interpretation of horse and rider as fame, and the qualities that earn fame, has been too little regarded; but it is not difficult to illustrate. Lydgate, after his customary disclaimer of poetic skill, reflects that the celebration of his hero, St. Albon, does not require it:

> The golden trompet of the house of fame
> With full swyfte wynges of the pegasee
> Hath [blowe] full farre the knyghtly mannes name.[4]

In Hawes's *Pastime of Pleasure*, an allegorical figure, who is not called Fame but leads the dreamer where fame may be won, approaches surrounded with tongues of flame and riding upon a palfrey

> whiche hadde vnto name
> Pegase the swyfte / so fayre in excellence
> Whiche somtyme longed / with his premynence
> To kynge Percyus. . . .[5]

Halle records the appearance, in a masque at Henry VIII's court, of 'a person called Reaport, appareled in Crymosyn satyn full of

---

[1] Henryson, in his Sixth Fable, associates him with the Minotaur, the *Bellerophont* and the Werwolf. Barclay couples him with the Chimaera—monsters to be vanquished—in his Fourth Eclogue. The allusion is not to be found in his sources.

[2] *De Genealogia*, X. xxvii *Pegasus*. The theme is repeated in XII. xxv *Perseus*.

[3] Ibid., XIII. lviii *Bellerophon*. Fulgentius, *Mythologiarum libri tres*, in the 1535 edition of Hyginus: Book III, p. 148.

[4] *The Lyfe of Seint Albon* . . ., St. Albans 1534, Prologue to Book I, ll. 15–17. See also the edition by C. Horstmann, Berlin 1882.

[5] Stephen Hawes, *The Pastime of Pleasure*, ed. W. E. Mead (E.E.T.S.), 1928, ll. 178–81.

tõges, sitting on a flyẽg horse with wynges & fete of gold called, Pegasus'.[1]

As with poetry, so with fame: the figure engaging the imagination may be either horse or rider. The poet may mount the winged horse, or let his own wings grow; likewise, Pegasus may be, or bear, renown. Moreover, so pliant is the myth, so lively the mood in which it was originally applied, that the very shape of the rider is subject to vagaries of the imagination. Now the poet may set in the saddle that Muse whom he chooses to call his own. (Johnson, waked to particular attention by political antipathy, makes merry with Addison's clumsy performance of this feat).[2] Now he may invoke Apollo himself in such a manner as to suggest that Pegasus carries a god:

> O, thou king of flames!
> That with thy music-footed horse dost strike
> The clear light out of crystal on dark earth,
> And hurl'st instructive fire about the world. . . .[3]

For poetry enjoys one freedom denied to pictorial representation: we do not ask that its images shall remain constant when their significance can be conveyed by evoking other modes of sensation. What matters, here, is the sense of airy motion.

Comes, like Boccaccio, offers a threefold interpretation, in terms of natural, political, and moral philosophy; but, in this third kind of allegory, the difference between his age and Boccaccio's makes itself plain, for the moralization of the story now attaches itself not to Bellerophon's triumph but to his fall—he is no longer example, but warning:

Alii vitę humanæ rationem propè omnem sub hac fabula contineri tradiderunt: nam neque aduersis rebus nimis tristari, neque prosperis & felicibus nimis gloriari aut extolli conuenit, quoniam horum omnium denique moderatorem Deum esse experimur. Is enim pro sua singulari clementia & calamitatibus iniquè circumuĕtos adiuuat, quod accidit, dum calamitosus esset, Bellerophonti, & nimis elatos animos deprimit, quare præceps idem postea dicitur de cœlo detrusus.[4]

We may suppose that the triumphant fame-allegory, as Fulgentius and Boccaccio knew it and made it known, would have been to

---

[1] Edward Halle, *The Union of the Two Noble and Illustre Famelies of Lancastre & York* . . ., 1550, fol. lxvi[r].

[2] See his life of Addison (*Lives of the Poets*, ed. Hill, 1905, ii. 128), and Addison's culminating eulogy of King William, in *A Letter from Italy*.

[3] Chapman, *Bussy d'Ambois*, v. i.   [4] Op. cit., p. 956.

Comes mere childishness; and—but for that element of play in the poetic approach to myth—his contemporaries and successors should have rated it no higher. That the medieval interpretation of horse and rider persisted, however, we know, not only from the emblem-books,[1] but also from such compilations as the *Mundus symbolicus* of Picinellus, with its Biblical and Patristic analogies, and the *Hieroglyphica* of J. Pierius Valerianus, in which Pegasus is untouched by any recollection that his soaring flight could tempt the tragic hero to ὕβρις, or the Christian to self-will:

Fama autem ubi primùm genita per hominum ora incipit uolitare, Musarum excitat fontem in Parnasso, quippe quòd illustrium uirorum præclara facinora uatibus scribendi suggerunt argumentum.[2]

This tradition may well explain an allusion in Marvell's *The Loyall Scot*. Promising to the young Douglas a duration of fame beyond that of the ancient heroes, the poet glances at their fame-bearer:

> Skip Sadles: Pegasus thou needst not Bragg,
> Sometimes the Gall'way Proves the better Nagg—

the Scottish breed of horse will endure the longer journey.[3]

Such a passage, elegiac in purpose, reminds us that our reaction to the idea of fame cannot always be so simple and serene as it has appeared in the single strain of medieval allegory hitherto exemplified in this argument. Set aside, for the time being, any malign or ambiguous aspect of *Fama*—rumour, or good and bad repute capriciously allotted; dwell on what is simply benign in the conception and the myths embodying it; and this reflection persists: fame, as preserver of worthy names, claims to outlast life. The word indeed resounds splendidly; but let the imagination be disarmed and the heart laid open to impressions received through the un-

---

[1] Alciati, for example, preserves the tradition attributing to Bellerophon the qualities that earn fame. I must plead want of space, as well as skill, for omitting references to pictorial art; to have included them would have doubled the length of this essay.

[2] Basle 1556, Book IV, fol. 32ᵛ. (In an alternative explanation, on the same page, Pegasus is a symbol of speed.) The passage, which is headed by a cut of a flying horse entitled *Fama*, allegorizes the birth of Pegasus. This is the tradition perpetuated by Bacon in the *De Sapientia Veterum* (also in *De Augmentis*), though his emphasis falls on political allegory—the importance of fame (that is, report of victories) in war. For George Sandys, some sixteen years later, the medieval moralization is still the accepted way of interpreting *Ovid's Metamorphoses Englished, Mythologiz'd, and Represented in Figures*, 1626.

[3] *Poems and Letters*, ed. H. M. Margoliouth, 1952, ii. 173. These lines (63, 64) are part of a passage which Dr. Margoliouth regards as a postscript to the narrative of Douglas' death, designed to conciliate the Scots: a tribute to a valiant breed of men and horses.

guarded ear, and grave overtones will become perceptible. Once aware of these, we are prompted to ask questions as to person and tense. Whose fame is the speaker asserting, and in what tense is the assertion delivered? Is the subject some hero of the mythical or historic past? Then it is fame's function to divert the shadow of death from his effigy, making it shine out amidst the obscurity of those whose names no poet has preserved:

> . . . omnes illacrimabiles
> urgentur ignotique longa
> nocte, carent quia vate sacro.[1]

But what if present merit and future renown compose the theme? To flatter a patron, or a mistress, with promises of deathless poetic memorials is indeed to acknowledge that this shadow must fall; but some element—whether of ceremony or of make-believe— in such flattery distances the event and makes the acknowledgement seem merely formal. Let tense and person be changed once again, however, even but a little, and fame be promised to one lately dead—one, moreover, who has died young, 'inheritor of unfulfilled renown'—and the ear will catch another tone; for the poet now charges himself with the affirmation of faith in a future that should have been.

Recognition of the extent of difference between the idea of fame in simple relation to the tale of Bellerophon's triumphant exploits, and in its complex associations with elegy, may help us to measure the distance between E. K.'s gloss on Spenser's April Eclogue and Spenser's own elaboration of the tradition this represents, in *The Ruines of Time*: Helicon, E. K. comments,

is both the name of a fountaine at the foote of Parnassus, and also of a mounteine in Bæotia, out of which floweth the famous Spring Castalius, dedicate also to the Muses: of which spring it is sayd, that when Pegasus the winged horse of Perseus (whereby is meant fame and flying renowme) strooke the grownde with his hoofe, sodenly thereout sprange a wel of moste cleare and pleasaunte water, which fro thence forth was consecrate to the Muses and Ladies of learning.[2]

Spenser's development of the myth of the winged horse occupies two passages in *The Ruines of Time*: lines 421 to 427, and 645 to 658. How they came to be combined with other parts of this great,

---

[1] Horace, *Ode*, IV. ix.
[2] All Spenserian passages are quoted from E. de Sélincourt's edition, 1909–10.

uneven poem and why they stand in this order need not be discussed here; the interwoven themes of fame, the preserver of heroic reputation, Pegasus, the bearer of fame, and Sidney, who was both hero and poet, are sufficient for consideration. Nevertheless, the particular contexts of these stanzas must be briefly indicated.

> But fame with golden wings aloft doth flie,
> Aboue the reach of ruinous decay,
> And with braue plumes doth beate the azure skie,
> Admir'd of base-borne men from farre away:
> Then who so will with vertuous deeds assay
> To mount to heauen, on *Pegasus* must ride,
> And with sweete Poets verse be glorifide.   (ll. 421–7)

This is the climax of some sixteen stanzas on the theme of the Muses and their servants the poets as guardians of worthy reputation; and these stanzas have followed directly on the first of those two passages of lament for Sidney which focus and define the elegiac purpose of the poem: lines 281 to 343.[1]

> Still as I gazed, I beheld where stood
> A Knight all arm'd, vpon a winged steed,
> The same that was bred of *Medusaes* blood,
> On which *Dan Perseus* borne of heauenly seed,
> The faire Andromeda from perill freed:
> Full mortally this Knight ywounded was,
> That streames of blood foorth flowed on the gras.
>
> Yet was he deckt (small ioy to him alas)
> With manie garlands for his victories,
> And with rich spoyles, which late he did purchas
> Through braue atcheiuements from his enemies:
> Fainting at last through long infirmities,
> He smote his steed, that straight to heauen him bore,
> And left me here his losse for to deplore.   (ll. 645–58)

These two stanzas compose the eleventh of twelve 'tragic pageants'. The pageants, or visions, like the preceding lament of the Genius of *Verlame*, illustrate the transience of earthly glory and happiness, and fall into two groups, the second devoted to Sidney; each of these latter six being an emblem 'developed . . . from these poetic symbols which are also constellations, to celebrate the

---

[1] I accept the dedication and envoy as intimations of the central purpose of the poem as it now stands.

entrance into immortality of the poet Philip Sidney, *Philisides, Astrophel,* the Star-lover'.[1]

Spenser's use of mythology—a poet's use—has been censured by some of his commentators.[2] I doubt whether it would have hindered the imaginative response of his first readers. The winged horse was already accustomed to bearing, now the fame of heroes, now the poets who cherished that fame; why not the heroic poet? Sidney's claim on that power which can stay the ruinous hand of time was twofold:

> So there thou liuest, singing euermore,
> And here thou liuest, being euer song
> Of vs, which liuing loued thee afore,
> And now thee worship, mongst that blessed throng
> Of heauenlie Poets and Heroes strong.
> So thou both here and there immortal art,
> And euerie where through excellent desart.   (ll. 337–43)

And the emblem of that power was traditionally wing-borne.[3] Pegasus had soared to heaven and shone there as a constellation: an apt figure, in a world familiar with the allegorization of myth, for the heavenly comfort which must conclude a Christian elegy. As to the choice of Perseus rather than Bellerophon as symbol for Sidney's soldiership, Spenser had not only Boccaccio's warrant for supposing himself free to choose, but also cogent poetic reasons for his preference. Whereas the story of Bellerophon runs contrary to any notion of courtly love,[4] Perseus' rescue of Andromeda is congruous with the romantic element in that tradition, and he therefore a not incongruous counterpart to Astrophel. Moreover, Perseus and Andromeda, with Pegasus hard by, are among the constellations. Not only is Bellerophon absent from this starry company; he fell in endeavouring to reach it; and that flight ended (as readers of Comes knew) with the arrival of Pegasus at the heavenly stable, riderless.

The idea of Sidney seems to run, like a twisted thread of black and gold, through the variously coloured web of *The Ruines of Time.* So intricate a pattern, so strange an alternation of themes one with

---

[1] W. L. Renwick's commentary, in his edition of the *Complaints,* 1928, p. 201. The *star* symbol (as Professor Renwick observes) has not been traced in all six, but may surely be called the dominant figure throughout the group.

[2] e.g. those quoted in the Variorum edition, Johns Hopkins Press *Minor Poems,* vol. ii, 1947—excepting W. L. Renwick.

[3] Hence the winged figure, or figures, in ll. 421–7.

[4] The part of it which seems to have lingered in popular memory is of the same pattern as the story of Joseph and the wife of Potiphar.

another, each vanishing from sight only to recur, and all expressed obliquely, whether in terms of myth, allegory, or heraldry—this may indeed baffle or alienate the modern reader. But we need not suppose it to have been difficult or displeasing to Mary Sidney.

I suggested, in my opening juxtaposition of this poem with the proem to the seventh book of *Paradise Lost*, that medieval accretions might not be observable on the surface of this latter passage. Yet, having now approached it by way of earlier developments in the idea of the winged horse and his burden, we must surely be conscious of its complex and subtle texture of allusion. Milton gathers up, in twenty lines, Homeric, Pindaric, and quite other elements in the story of Bellerophon's fall; glances at widely dispersed interpretations of the myth of Hippocrene;[1] subdues both to his poetic undertaking, and gives to the whole a personal application—not unsupported by tradition, but with a new poignancy.

Here the path of my argument grows suddenly much steeper. What hope can there ever be of translating into critical prose the purpose, even so much of it as is apparent at a single juncture, of such a poem? As for the personal application we divine here, the youngest reader of Milton can tell that he often refers to himself in his poetry; the oldest may well hesitate to define the scope of any particular reference. Indeed, I am dismayed at my temerity; and, but that so substantial a part of the material for this essay has been given me,[2] I should hesitate to proceed.

Among the elements of Milton's purpose in *Paradise Lost*, one surely is beyond dispute: he is to bring us to a point at which we must launch out from the imagined—what poets have feigned—to the almost unimaginable truth he has to relate. In this passage, for example, the Muses are recalled, only to be disclaimed—not flippantly, nor with the hesitation belonging to modesty—but as myth that must give way before revelation. Sometimes indeed fable foreshadows what he intends; but there are times when his intention is of such magnitude that human language has never been able to approach it more nearly than by saying what it was not. His truth may outgo fable or stand opposed to it. Thus, Bellerophon

---

[1] 'Sapientia enim bonae consultationis aeternus fons est . . . Sapientia enim dat musis fontem.' Fulgentius *et al*.

[2] I am particularly indebted to Mrs. Henderson, Miss Labowsky, Miss Syfret, Mrs. Roaf, and Miss Hubbard. The responsibility for what I have made of the references they have given me, and their help in reading them, is of course entirely mine.

does not signify Milton even to the degree that Perseus signifies Sidney. Nevertheless, reference to him here has these two kinds of relevance: he would have invaded celestial regions; but that exploit (even if attained) would have been but a shadow of the poet's aspiration in writing of heavenly transactions; he climbed unbidden and was not saved from the consequences; but the poet, sure of vocation, may implore protection. Both comparison and contrast demand analogy. There seems no reason to suppose that Milton saw Bellerophon as symbol of the poet—though I believe this to have been in Meredith's mind, as it is certainly in that of Mr. Day Lewis.[1] For him, Pegasus alone afforded intimations of analogy sufficient for his purpose—that is, to suggest both comparison and contrast with the famous ascent to heaven of the poets' horse, in a manner intelligible to the common reader, who might be trusted for some recollection of Comes, of Micyllus' edition of Boccaccio or his collection of mythographies, or at least the dictionaries compiled from these sources.

The personal application likewise shows *one* face turned towards Milton's audience, all of whom would recollect that a disclaimer of the Muses' aid was customary, not only in prologues but also in passages requiring the reaffirmation of poetic purpose. To those in sympathy with him, something more would be discernible: the proclaimed independence—no longer merely of patronage, but even of all human approbation; the new and tremendous meaning in the old assertion 'It is enough that I write to please Thee'. There is, however, another aspect of this personal application, which we may perhaps seek to descry—though interpretation must be tentative, and fall far short of the whole. A younger and happier Milton had written to his closest friend: 'Audi, Theodote, verum in aurem ut ne rubeam, & sinito paulisper apud te grandia loquar; quid cogitem quaeris? ita me bonus Deus, immortalitatem. Quid agam vero? πτεροφυῶ & volare meditor. . . .' Let this confession be read in conjunction with certain passages, some of them earlier still, all forerunning *Paradise Lost*. Of the theme of fame in *Lycidas* little need be said: the poem has been closely investigated;[2] but one plain observation must nevertheless be offered here, as relevant to this argument. Of the man who is *called*, much is demanded; yet death may intervene, and

[1] Meredith's *Bellerophon*; C. Day Lewis, *Pegasus and Other Poems*, 1957.
[2] See Rosemond Tuve, *Images and Themes in Five Poems by Milton*, Harvard U.P., 1957.

against death his calling is no defence. ('What could the Muse herself that Orpheus bore . . .' '. . . nor could the Muse defend / Her son.') The answer given in *Lycidas* is that proper to an elegy on a man whom this has befallen: promise of continuity—not as to existence merely, but also as to function, continuance in service. Death, however, is not the only, nor the most fearful threat. The Parable of the Talents haunted Milton's thought. That he had it in mind when he wrote

> How soon hath Time the suttle theef of youth,
> Stoln on his wing my three and twentith yeer!

we know from the draft of a letter which accompanies this sonnet in the Trinity College Manuscript and contains a reference to 'the terrible seasure of him that hid his talent'.[1] It is implicit in the closing lines:

> All is, if I have grace to use it so,
> As ever in my great task-Masters eye.

In the sonnet on his blindness, it becomes explicit—

> . . . that one Talent which is death to hide,
> Lodg'd with me useless—

for a fear like this, reassurance must be found elsewhere than in such thoughts as properly conclude an elegy. Its magnitude can be measured by the change that it works in the story of the unprofitable servant. Parable, like myth, stirs deep responses—so deep that not even veneration for scriptural text will prevent a man from reading his own thoughts into it. Milton having in mind his own poetic endowment, 'that one talent' grows from the single opportunity supposed too meagre to be worth cultivation into something known to be uniquely precious. He has, moreover, given a new and dreadful conclusion to the story, by making death, not deprivation, the penalty for failure. In this sonnet, another answer than that of *Lycidas* is vouchsafed. Yet the question, though it undergoes change, persists, and here, at the mid-point of *Paradise Lost*, Milton discovers a reply to satisfy a poet in the very heart of a great undertaking.

> Up led by thee
> Into the Heav'n of Heav'ns I have presum'd,

[1] Facsimile, Cambridge 1899, p. 6. Milton evidently had St. Matthew's version in mind.

An Earthlie Guest, and drawn Empyreal Aire,
Thy tempring; with like safetie guided down
Return me to my Native Element:
Least from this flying Steed unreind, (as once
Bellerophon, though from a lower Clime)
Dismounted, on th'*Aleian* Field I fall,
Erroneous there to wander and forlorne.

The crucial phase of the story lies still ahead; but the equipoise of hope and fear has been tilted. Undaunted by all that appears unpropitious in the circumstances—in the very endeavour—Milton faces forwards. Celestial matters of more moment and greater delicacy than the war in heaven will presently confront him. This return to earth is not a simple event, nor escape from the field of error made once and for all; the petition for safety is not so to be understood:

The meaning, not the Name I call . . .

Yet the name *is used*; for the meaning could never be fully communicated without it. Moreover, since this name, or group of names, is charged with the associations of a myth, one often related, and usually with some accession of significance, the means by which we are made to understand all that is implied cannot be separated one from another without loss. Story cannot be translated into other terms. *Pegasean wing*, *Bellerophon*—these signify what no interpretation can hope to catch. And yet, as wrack upon the surface of the river shows which hay-fields have been plundered upstream and allows the eye to measure the force of the current, so these scattered fragments of myth and allegory to which I have here drawn attention may tell us something about the antecedents of a poem—even of one so well known as this—and enhance our sense of its volume and power.

Sir Walter Ralegh's *Instructions to his Son*

AGNES M. C. LATHAM

LETTERS of advice to a child seem to be rooted as much in human nature as in literary tradition. In so far as they may be considered a literary kind they are a subdivision of the Conduct Book, which the dawn of a new civility, together with the humanist faith in education, had made a favourite with the Renaissance. The conduct books can show a long and respectable history, going back through Italy to Greece and Rome.[1] The Advices, when they are not simply conduct books in disguise, have not such markedly literary affiliations. They are essentially private and personal, the wisdom of the adviser strained in part through his own experience, and only in part through literary filters. He helps himself to what suits his own purpose, and is likely to be more indebted to a common tradition than to any specific book of manners. Fathers must for centuries have counselled their children without being aware to what literary genre they were conforming.

The private nature of the Advices tends to set them in the direction of realism. When the world is not supposed to be listening there is no need to pretend. Moreover, it matters very much to the father that the advice should be practical and productive. That is why he is giving it. It is therefore no accident that the two most familiar Advices, Polonius to Laertes and Lord Chesterfield to his son, are of a prudential and courtly kind, more concerned with how men are than how they ought to be. Nor is it accidental that it was the seventeenth century which first saw much of this kind of matter in print. In the preface to the revised fourth edition of his *Advice to a Son*, Francis Osborne congratulated himself that 'the liberty of these times hath afforded wisdome a larger Pasport to travell, then was ever able formerly to be obtained, when the world kept her fettered in an implicit Obedience, by the three-fold cord of Custome, Education and Ignorance'.[2]

[1] See, among others, R. Kelso, *The Doctrine of the English Gentleman*, 1929; J. E. Mason, *Gentlefolk in the Making*, 1935; V. Heltzel, 'Chesterfield and the Ideal Gentleman', unpublished thesis, 1925.

[2] F. Osborne, *Advice to a Son, or Directions for your better Conduct, through the various and most important Encounters of this Life* (4th edn.), 1656, sig. A2 verso.

Osborne, taking advantage of the freedom of fathers 'to teach their Children to manage an Hobby-horse', offers a collection of provocative essays, in a style at once witty and casual, under the headings *Studies, Love and Marriage, Travell, Government,* and *Religion.* It is plain that he wrote with a wider public in mind than his son. At any rate, when he published the book (as the introductory matter makes it clear that he did) he put his intentions to an acid test. He knew, too, that he was challenging orthodox positions and was doubtless quite aware that his book sold all the better for the storm of indignation aroused by his essay on Love and Marriage.

More libertine than the sixteenth century, the seventeenth permitted the publication of a book such as Osborne's, which is acknowledged to have paved the way for Chesterfield. At the same time, the powerful puritan bent of the times encouraged the composition of Advices in which religious zeal is dominant, and personal experience is subordinated to spiritual discipline. One of the most attractive examples of this kind came from the firebrand Hugh Peters, in his very touching *Advice to his Daughter,*[1] first published in 1660 after the author had been executed as a regicide. This is personal at least in so far as it is deeply affectionate. It ends with a brief account of the writer's life and troubles, so that the recipient 'may wipe off some Dirt, or be the more content to carry it'.[2] But the most precious bequest that Hugh Peters can leave his child is directions for her soul's salvation rather than a guide to Vanity Fair. Whether he intended his work for the press is not clear. He apologizes for 'the feebleness of what I have sent, being writ under much, yea very much discomposure of spirit'.[3] One may assume, however, that an impassioned pamphleteer and preacher, such as Peters, had little self-consciousness about listeners-in. The sectaries, with their emphasis upon the inner life, made a wide breach in privacy.

Between the two extremes of the worldly and the other-worldly, as instanced by Osborne and Peters, and exercising a particularly powerful influence upon the genre, comes His Majesty King James, whose accession to the English throne in 1603 coincided with the

---

[1] *A Dying Fathers Last Legacy to an Onely Child: or, Mr. Hugh Peters Advice to his Daughter: Written by his own Hand, during his late Imprisonment in the Tower of London; And given her a little before his Death, 1661.* This is the second edition. The British Museum has mislaid its first.
[2] Ibid., p. 97.
[3] Ibid., p. 118.

publication of *Basilicon Doron,* his advice to Prince Henry.[1] He instructs him in three books, in his duty towards God, his duty in his office, and his behaviour in indifferent things. Although King James comes at the end of a long line of writers who prepared blueprints for the Perfect King, his third book, in which he takes proper cognizance of the fact that the Prince is also a man, is so homely, practical, and pious, that it became a major source of seventeenth-century conduct books. A king is, perhaps, exempt, by his position, from requiring the arts of the courtier.

The story of how King James's book came to be published is instructive. He undertook it with an entirely practical purpose in view, during a period of ill health and depression. Convinced that Elizabeth would outlive him, he wanted to leave his son some counsel which would assist him when he was called to the English throne. But King James was an author. He made a Work of it. And having made a Work of it, he arranged to have a few copies privately printed for distribution to favoured persons. Once the manuscript left the King's closet its contents became known, in more or less garbled versions, and its 'Anglo-pisco-papisticall'[2] tendencies caused considerable scandal to the Church of Scotland. In self-defence His Majesty, like many a common author, had 'to publishe and spred the true copies thereof, for defacing of the false copies that are alreadie spred, as I am informed: as likewayes, by this preface, to cleare suche parts thereof, as in respect of the concised shortnesse of my style, may be mis-interpreted therein'.[3]

This is not untypical of the way in which a work genuinely intended to be private could become public; and could, moreover, be written from the first in so serious and stately a vein that one feels that the author had always a secret audience in view. The man who took up a pen in the sixteenth century was apt to find himself, almost without his own collusion, composing for posterity.

Of the three kinds of instructions listed, the spiritual, the pious and practical, and the worldly-wise, there is no difficulty in assigning Ralegh's to the third. Mr. W. Lee Ustick characterizes it as 'the prudential maxims of a cautious, disillusioned man, to whom the sweet of life has turned to sour'.[4] It was not published till 1632,

---

[1] *Basilikon Doron, or his Maiesties Instructions to his Dearest Sonne, Henry the Prince,* 1603.
[2] *The Basilicon Doron of King James VI,* ed. James Craigie, Scottish Text Society, 1950, ii. 10.   [3] Ibid., 1944, i. 13.
[4] W. Lee Ustick, *S.P.,* 1932, xxix. 437. 'Advice to a Son: a type of seventeenth century conduct book.'

fourteen years after the writer's death. I take it to be one of the earliest instances of such a publication; of a document, that is, never intended to be anything but private. It was licensed to Benjamin Fisher on 13 April 1632, as 'a booke called Sir WALTER RAWLEIGH *Ten Chapters conteyning Morall preceptes to his Sonn* by Sir W: R:'.[1] The title-page reads SIR / *Walter Raleighs* / INSTRVCTIONS / to his SONNE, and / to Posterity. / *Whereunto is added* / A Religious and / Dutifull Advice of a / loving SONNE to / his aged FA- / THER. / LONDON: / Printed for *Beniamin Fisher,* / dwelling in Aldersgate-street / at the *Talbot.* 1632. / The reference to 'Posterity' is the printer's way of recommending the work to a wider public. In his address to the reader he says:

It was not perhaps, intended by the renowned Author, that these Instructions shold be made publique: they were directed to his Sonne, who doth make iust and due use of them. But such is the lustre of Wisdome, that it cannot be hidden. Men may bequeath their Wealth to their Children in particular, but their Wisedome was given them for more general Good. . . . Could his noble Sonne bee hereby any way impaired, He shold still have impropriated it. But now He shall gain thus much; The World shall see that the most secret Counsels of his Father were Iust and religious, and hath good cause to hope that a Sonne so instructed can be no otherwise.

The world seems to have greeted the publication with some enthusiasm, since there were six editions by 1636, including one issued in Edinburgh.[2] Afterwards the *Instructions* were incorporated in the little collections of Ralegh's minor works which began to appear in the fifties.[3] There was clearly a market for such ware. The subject-matter was attractive—how to make a success of your life— and the writer was eminent. These were not tips from Sir Politick Would-Be. However tragic his end, Ralegh had kept his footing for a considerable time in very high places indeed. It was possible to see him as a brilliant writer, scholar, and thinker—he had compiled *The History of the World* and compounded a sovereign cordial; as a great courtier, adventurer, and hero, he had received the highest honours in the golden days of Elizabeth, planted colonies, captured galleons,

[1] Arber, *Stationers' Register,* 1877, iv. 242.
[2] *S.T.C.* 20642–6; and T. N. Brushfield, *A Bibliography of Sir Walter Ralegh,* 1908, pp. 137, 138. The editions listed are 1632 (2), 1633 (2), 1634, 1636.
[3] Wing, R 174–6, 180–5; and Brushfield, op. cit., pp. 77–83. The editions listed are *Maxims of State,* 1650, 1651, 1656, 1657 (a reissue); *Remains of Sir Walter Ralegh,* 1657, 1661, 1664, 1669, 1675, 1681, 1702.

explored the large, rich, and beautiful empire of Guiana, and
implacably opposed the Spaniard. In the end he was a kind of
martyr, victim of a rigged trial and the tyranny of a Stuart king.
Some less agreeable facets of his character disappeared in this
general glow. In any case he had been dead fourteen years and his
ambitions were no longer a threat to anybody. People read *Basilicon
Doron* because they wanted to know what James I thought about
being a king and what sort of a king he was likely to be. They read
Ralegh's *Instructions* because they wanted to know what Sir Walter
thought about being a great man and what kind of great man he
had been. In 1899 the work could still be spoken of as a 'celebrated
treatise'.[1]

The printer, Benjamin Fisher, made as pretty a little volume as he
could conveniently contrive. It is a 16mo in eights, carrying fourteen lines to the page, all inset within ruled margins, each line taking
up something less than two inches. There is an engraved portrait of
the author, under which an awkward quatrain pays tribute to 'the
great worth and sharpenesse of his minde'. The text occupies 96
pages. The book concludes with 57 more pages, numbered afresh,
with fresh signatures and title-page, The dutifull / ADVICE / *of a
loving* / SONNE / To his aged / FATHER. / LONDON, / Printed for
Beniamin Fisher / and are to be sold at his shop / in Aldersgate-street
at the / signe of the *Talbot.* / 1632.

The second treatise is not in so many words attributed to Ralegh
nor generally accepted as his. It may be as well to dispose of it at
this point, before going on to the undisputed work. I find it difficult
to read it as a libel against Ralegh,[2] or as ironic.[3] It is completely
impersonal. The father is represented as having led a worldly life
and come to a time when it behoves him to think of his latter end
and make his peace with the Church. We are told that the world has
treated him unkindly. 'It never gave you but an unhappy welcome,
a hurtfull entertainment, and now doth abandon you with an unfortunate farewell.'[4] This, like the insistence that his sins are heavy,
need be no more than a commonplace, a way of recommending
the securer comforts of heaven. The tone throughout is serious
and earnest, a little rhetorical, and more than a little reminiscent of

[1] W. Stebbing, *Sir Walter Ralegh*, 1899, p. 268.
[2] T. Birch, *Works of Ralegh*, 1751, vol. ii, p. cv.
[3] E. A. Strathmann, 'A Survey of the Ralegh Cannon', read before the Modern
Language Association of America, Dec. 1953.
[4] *Advice*, p. 8.

a sermon. There is much imagery, and the comparison of life to a sea-voyage and the soul to a ship is particularly frequent. If the address was in fact directed to Sir Walter by someone who felt he had special need of it, it was in a spirit of good rather than of ill will. If it was a jest of young Walter's (and he was a jester) it is singularly lacking in humour. Surely an attack must at some point indicate upon whom it is scoring a hit, and there must be a moment when an ironist lets us into his secret? It is hard to see at what point we are to take this advice other than literally.

It seems more likely that it was a makeweight of uncertain provenance. The *Instructions* alone are too slight in bulk to make a book. Son to father neatly parallels father to son, though the work itself suggests nothing of filial or paternal relationship. It is simply an exhortation to an ageing man to repent before it is too late. The title-pages begin by describing it non-committally as 'A Religious and Dutifull Advice of a loving Sonne to his aged Father'. Not till it is incorporated in Ralegh's *Remains* in 1657 does the printer devise a general title-page upon which it figures as 'Advise to his Son: his Sons advise to his Father'. The separate title-page of *Maxims of State*, which immediately follows, reads 'With Instructions to his Son, and the Sons advice to his aged Father'. Finally, on p. 108, the work itself appears, with its usual half-title, 'The dutifull Advice of a Loving Son to his Aged Father'. The progress from *a*, to *the*, to *his* would seem to have occurred in the printing-house and to have no real bearing on the authorship of the work. The earliest printer was presumably not averse to a reader supposing that the whole volume was concerned with Ralegh, and later editions heighten the suggestive ambiguity.[1]

The Edinburgh edition, 'Printed by Iohn Wreittoun, 1634', adds a third piece, 'A Meditation upon the XXIIth Chapter of Genesis'. It reproduces the first edition of the *Instructions* and therefore carries on its title-page 'Whereunto is added a Religious and Dutifull Advice of a loving Sonne'. It may be significant that these words no longer appear on the title-page of the fourth edition of 1633, which is described as 'Corrected and enlarged according to the Authors owne Coppy'. It is true that the claim to have better copy takes up some space on the page, but it is conceivable that the readers who objected to the first text of the *Instructions* may also have objected

---

[1] I do not know whether Wing R 160 is really distinct from the 1650 edition of *Maxims of State*.

to the implied authorship of *The dutifull Advice of a Loving Sonne*. This, in the copy of the fourth edition in the British Museum, retains its own full title-page, its half-title, the date 1632, and the pagination of the first edition. There are some slight variations in the ornaments. The text is not emended. The Bodleian fourth edition has a fresh title-page dated 1633.

The assurance in the preface to Ralegh's work that the author's noble son is not in any way impaired by the publication suggests that the source of the manuscript was not the family, whom the printer is obviously trying to placate. Further evidence is supplied by the appearance of an emended text in later editions. Fisher explains to the readers that objections have been made to the first edition, which had 'not only divers omissions, but some errors also'. He now professes to offer a new copy, 'Perfect, Compleat, and most corrected'. He still finds it necessary to add that Sir Walter's surviving son is in no way injured by the publication, and the general tenor of his address does not suggest that it was the family who intervened and supplied the true copy. Had they done so it is hard to believe that Fisher would have failed to exploit a situation so valuable for publicity.

According to T. N. Brushfield's *Ralegh Bibliography*, the emended text was introduced in the second edition of 1632. I have seen no exemplar. The British Museum and the Bodleian have editions of 1632, which I take to be first editions. The British Museum copy corrects misprints which appear in the Bodleian copy. There is a third edition, dated 1633, in Chicago. The British Museum and the Bodleian have copies of the fourth edition of 1633. They are not identical. The title-page of the British Museum copy reads SIR / *Walter Raleigh's* / INSTRVCTIONS / TO HIS / SONNE: and to / Posterity. / *The fourth Edition*, / Corrected and enlarged / according to the Authors / owne Coppy. / LONDON: / Printed for *Beniamin Fisher*, / dwelling in Alders-grate- / street, at the signe of the / Talbot. 1633. / My quotations are from the British Museum copy of the fourth edition, unless I am quoting material which appears in the first edition only, in which case I use the British Museum first edition.

Upon collation it becomes apparent that the early copy was marred by what are presumably scribal errors, mostly small omissions, and some disordered punctuation which spoils the sense. It also bowdlerizes Ralegh's observations upon the advantage of a young man taking a mistress rather than a wife. 'Mistress' is a term the first edition will not permit. It prefers 'how many lewd Women thou hast acquaintance withall', to 'how many Mistresses soever thou hast'.[1] Ralegh appears to have said, 'when thy humour shal change thou art yet free to chuse againe (if thou give thy selfe that vaine libertie)'. This is typical of the way in which he allows for human frailty while recognizing it for what it is. The first edition carries quite a different sense. 'Nor giue thy humour libertie, in accompaning light Women; for though that humour may change in thee againe, yet the blot it leaues on thy honour will euer remaine.'[2]

The new copy is superior, though in its turn not faultless. I see no reason, therefore, to think that it derives directly from Ralegh's autograph. It has no substantially new material to offer. More interesting results come of collating the printed copies with one of the manuscript versions, MS. Additional 22587, in the British Museum. The manuscript omits Chapter X of the printed book, 'Let God be thy protector and director in all thy Actions'; it omits to translate the Latin in Chapter IX; and it inserts a curious political and personal allusion in Chapter I. If this was in Fisher's copy, editorial discretion may well have prompted him to suppress it. I am not aware that any modern editor has called attention to it.

Ralegh is advising his son to 'remember alwaies that thou venter not thy estate with any of those great ones, that shall attempt unlawfull things, for such men labor for themselves, and not for thee; thou shalt bee sure to part with them in the danger, but not in the honour'.[3] He goes on, 'I could give thee a thousand examples, and I my selfe know it, and have tasted it, in all the course of my life; when thou shalt read and observe the stories of all nations, thou shalt finde innumerable examples of the like.'[4] Thus the printed copies. MS. Additional reads: '. . . in all the Course of my life. Remember when thou art younge that the Earle of Southampton was saved and Davers his friend beheaded. Remember att the same tyme that Essex in hope to save his owne life accused all his friends and servants and destroyed them whoe had ventred all for his sake. I name these to thee because they are best in memorye. But when

---

[1] *Instructions*, 1632, pp. 30–31; 1633, p. 30.
[2] *Instructions*, 1632, pp. 14–15; 1633, p. 15.
[3] *Instructions*, 1633, p. 8.
[4] p. 10.

thou shalt reade. . . .'[1] Sir Charles Danvers died on the scaffold in 1601 after making a full confession of his implication in the Essex conspiracy, into which he had been drawn by his great devotion to Southampton.

Another peculiar feature of MS. Additional, which seems also to have passed unnoticed by Ralegh's biographers and editors, is the letter or address to his son which I reproduce below. It does not appear to be part of an ordinary correspondence, but a formal composition, possibly designed either to open or to close the *Instructions*. Alternatively, it may have been the germ from which they grew, a farewell letter which the writer decided to expand further. The style and the sentiments are surely Ralegh's. It appears again, with very little difference, in MS. Petyt 538.18, f. 215, in the library of the Inner Temple, where it follows a transcript of Ralegh's farewell letter to his wife in 1603. In MS. Additional it precedes the same letter, ff. 16^v-17.

MS. Additional 22587 contains transcripts of miscellaneous documents of the sixteenth and seventeenth century. The Ralegh material, comprising some of the better-known letters and the *Instructions*, is all in the same secretary hand, which continues through the bulk of the manuscript. There is nothing in the text of the letters to suggest a particularly authoritative source. The standard of transcription is not high, and the version of the *Instructions* is marred by blatant copyist's errors. The scribe, as is usual with scribes, has his idiosyncrasies, notably an aversion to the use of the full stop. I have inserted stops where they are required by the sense and implied by the fact that the new sentence begins with a capital letter. There are places where the scribe omits the capital and lets the sentence run on in a way that is natural in manuscript but awkward in print. Here I have normalized his punctuation, inserting sometimes full stops and sometimes semicolons. I have also expanded contractions.

Sir Walter Rawleigh to his sonn.

I would have thee my sonne awaken thy self to industrye and Rowse vpp thy spiritts for the world. Greate possessions would make thee lazie, I would have thee to be the sonne of thyne owne fortunes as well as my sonne. I have ever aymed at a Competencye and God hath fitted mee thereafter; nevertheles I deny not but that I have affected

---

[1] f. 11^v.

promocion but it hath beene with a mynd as, God knoweth, to honor him and to doe good in the Common wealth and the same holy and iust ambition I bequeath to thee my deare and wellbeloved sonne.

I feele noe more perturbacion within mee to departe this world then I have donne in my best health to arise from table when I have well dyned and thence to retyre to a pleasant walke. I have had my parte in this world and nowe must give place to fresh gamesters. Farewell. All is vanity and wearynes yet such a wearynes and vanitye that wee shall ever complayne of it and love it for all that. And in all vanityes oure owne imaginacions are most yrkesome and of all oure imagynacions that the most foolish when being by God and nature sized out to be a vessell of smalle Content wee yett stryve to hold either as much of vnderstandinge or fortune as larger vessells and therein strive against Gods ordinance and providence; but see wee rather that wee make that measure that is ours full and that the falt is not in vs though wee bee but pinte whereas others are pottle. Oure heades swymme and our harts beate within vs as if wee were att sea. It is enough that oure owne thoughts perplexe vs but wee ever and anon are shipwrackt and sea sicke. Wee are toyled and hazarded with tempests and stormes that arise abroad. Oure good or ill depends not simply in oure owne Counsells and resolucions but more often vpon adventures that lye not in oure management. Publicke affaires are rockes, private conversacions are whirlepooles and quickesandes. Itt is a like perilous to doe well and to doe ill. Opinion befoggs vs and faire and smooth calemenes befooll vs. Nevertheles my sonne take harte and Courage to thee. Thy adventure lyes in this troublesome barque; strive if thou Canst to make good thy station in the vpper decke; those that live vnder hatches are ordained to be drudges and slaves. Endeavoure rather to be parte of the tymber of the house then lath or mudwall; but be beame tymber not threshould stuffe. Farewell. God only is sure and true evermore to those that are true to him. Noe Gospell truer then this in proofe.

There is a melancholy note in this and a suggestion that the author has not long to live. It is a fact that the composition of such a work as instructions to a son was often the result of premonitions of approaching death. It is difficult to select from the career of a man who habitually lived dangerously any one moment more notably perilous than another. As for moods of melancholy and depression, which might be more instrumental in the matter than assessable peril, Ralegh was notably subject to those. It would be a help, however, in assigning a date of composition, to look for a time when the writer's outlook was sombre and when he might well be inclined to stocktaking.

The work, though short, was not necessarily written all at the same time. Assuming that the reference to the fall of Essex was not a later addition, we must date it some time after February 1601. At least twice after that date Ralegh's life hung in the balance, and he was perfectly aware of the fact. In 1603 he was actually condemned to death and watched his associates brought to execution before he was told of his reprieve. And fifteen years later, on returning empty-handed from Guiana, he was warned by his friends that he would be called to account for it. The last occasion allowed him no leisure for composition, could he conceivably in the circumstances have had the heart for it. He had to practise the most extraordinary tricks, feigning sickness and even madness, to gain time to write his own defence of his proceedings.

Much the same objections apply to the treason trial of 1603. There is extant from this period the text of a farewell letter which Ralegh addressed to his wife from the Tower, the night before his appointed execution. It affords a kind of touchstone for his mood and language at that time. The mood was one of courageous resignation imposed upon a desperate despair. 'I cannot write much. God hee knowes, how hardly I steale this tyme, while others sleepe; and itt is alsoe high tyme, that I should seperate my thoughtes from the world. . . . My deare wife farewell. Blesse my poore Boye. Pray for mee, and Lett my Good god hold you both in his armes. Written with the dyeing hand of sometyme thy Husband, but now (alasse) ouerthrowne.'[1] This was not the time for compiling 'cold prudential maxims', nor even, I think, for the proliferating metaphors of the letter in MS. Additional, though they show a kind of excitement and immediacy and even a kinship to the letter of 1603 which is foreign to the *Instructions*. It is not beyond belief that Ralegh, after his reprieve, set himself to write the farewell letter to his son for which there was not time when death was imminent.

The long period of imprisonment in the Tower, from 1603 till 1616, afforded ample leisure, but the time when ideas of approaching death must have haunted him most persistently was presumably the time which immediately followed his reprieve. Not only were the stresses of trial and conviction still operative, the reprieve itself, though it was to last fifteen years, must at first have seemed precarious. This was a time when a man could be expected to survey his past life and attempt a summary of his own errors. He

[1] From a contemporary transcript in the British Museum, MS. Sloane 3520, f. 14.

was beginning to realize that with the forfeiture of his lands upon attainder he would have nothing to leave his son but such wisdom as the world had taught him, and to which, now he was sequestered from it, he was not likely to be able to add. Moreover, having stumbled so badly in his own walking he had reason to be acutely aware of the dangers the boy must face.

In 1603 Ralegh had one son, Walter, born in 1593. By all accounts he was a wild, irreverent scamp. He was to die in 1617, in the attack on San Thome in Guiana, characteristically pressing ahead of the rest. His father grieved terribly. A second son, Carew, was baptized in the Tower in February 1605. He is the surviving son to whom the printer refers in his address to the reader. It is inconceivable that Ralegh should have drawn up instructions for the second son while the first was still alive. If Carew took the instructions to himself it was in reversion from his elder brother.

A last fragment of evidence which could be used to establish a date early in Ralegh's imprisonment is the fact that the writer's mind is clearly running on Ecclesiasticus and the Book of Proverbs.[1] The Bible is the natural book for a man to turn to when worldly comforts slip away, and one of the few books a close prisoner is likely to have by him. Later, as Ralegh accustomed himself to his situation, he gathered his library around him, not to mention his wife and friends, and his life, though much confined, was in many ways comparatively normal.

Anything like a precise date seems impossible. Conjectural dates depend upon whether one sees the work as the result of a severe shock, in which case it must be dated somewhere near 1603, or of enforced leisure and depression of spirits, in which case it may be dated any time between 1603 and 1616,[2] when Ralegh was released. The Earl of Northumberland, who became a fellow prisoner with him in 1606, upon suspicion of implication in the Gunpowder Plot, waited till 1609 to take up an old manuscript work on the education of a son and add to it some further practical notes drawn from his experience of life. 'He has become', says his modern editor, 'a kind

---

[1] Prof. S. A. E. Betz makes this connexion clear. See 'Francis Osborn's Advice to a Son', *Seventeenth Century Studies*, Second Series, ed. R. Shafer, 1937.

[2] I can find no support in the manuscript for T. N. Brushfield's assertion (*Ralegh Bibliog.*, 1908, p. 137) that the summary which appears in MS. Harley 6534, f. 102, is dated 1609. It plainly originates from the printed text and occurs among other abstracts of books and sermons of the 1630's. Folio 86 of the manuscript bears the inscription, 'Begun heere the 2ᵈ of Julye, 1633'.

of cynical Prospero, contemplating his own failure from the confines of a cell'.[1]

Northumberland and Ralegh were friends long before they were thrown into one another's company in the Tower. It seems likely that the one knew how the other employed his time, but whether they were indebted to one another in compiling their instructions it is not possible to say. There is no obvious borrowing. The works have this in common; they are drawn from personal experience, the writers are disillusioned men of the world, and they are concerned with practical problems of managing an estate, a wife, and servants. Of the two, Northumberland's is the more overtly autobiographical. It was not published until some extracts appeared in 1838, in *Archaeologia*, vol. xxvii. In 1930 G. B. Harrison published a complete text from a manuscript transcript in his possession.

Closest in many ways to Ralegh is a collection of observations by Lord Treasurer Burghley, first printed in 1617.[2] They are very concise, digested into ten Precepts, which, with an introductory letter to his son, fill only 16 pages. The printer has added some further matter, of a rather trifling kind, to make a volume. Ralegh could not be indebted to a book published when he was in Guiana, but Burghley's precepts were evidently circulating in manuscript, and Ralegh had been at one time very intimate with Robert Cecil. Burghley's outlook is utilitarian. He differs from Ralegh, Osborne, and Northumberland in giving no consideration to the extra-marital relationships which they take for granted. In this he agrees with King James who, though possibly for different reasons, recommends strict chastity in both husband and wife.

Although from time to time Ralegh professes in so many words to be deducing his maxims from his own experience, and it is the characteristic of Advice literature to do this, he does not narrate the experiences to which they refer. This gives the impression that he is vague, conventional, and platitudinous, and the autobiographical value of the work is lessened. At times his advice is startlingly at

---

[1] *Advice to his Son: by Henry Percy, Ninth Earl of Northumberland*, ed. G. B. Harrison, 1930, p. 45.

[2] *Certaine Precepts, or Directions for the Well ordering and carriage of a mans life: as also oeconomicall Discipline for the gouerment of his house: with a platforme to a good foundation thereof, in the aduised choice of a Wife: Left by a Father to his son at his death, who was sometimes of eminent Note and Place in this Kingdome. And Published from a more perfect Copy, then ordinary those pocket Manuscripts goe warranted by. With some other Precepts and Sentences of the same nature added: taken from a person of like place, and qualitie*, 1617.

variance with his practice. What, knowing Ralegh, are we to make
of the contemptuous brevity of Chapter VII, 'Exceed not in the
humor of ragges and Bravery, for these will soon weare out of
fashion, but Money in thy purse will ever be in fashion, and no man
is esteemed for gay Garments, but by Fooles and women'? His sour-
ness with regard to friendship is partly, perhaps, a scar left by the
treason trial of 1603, in which he was implicated through an indiscreet attachment to the guilty Lord Cobham, and from which his
old friend Robert Cecil was at pains not to save him. He shares it
with another disgraced prisoner, awaiting execution. Hugh Peters
warns his daughter that a friend 'is a Commoditie so very scarce,
that it will be your wisdom so to look upon a Friend this day, as
likely to be an Enemy tomorrow. How manie sad Experiences can I
witness to of this kind, yea in these times and changes? Fair Dove-
coats have most Pigeons; Lost Estates know no Friends.'[1] Yet in
Peters one feels that there is an ideal of friendship injured. Ralegh
merely does a sum which comes out with an unsatisfactory answer.

There is no evidence that had the situation been reversed Ralegh
would have exerted himself much to save Cobham or Cecil, and the
contents of Chapter I, 'Vertuous persons to be made choyce of for
friends', is probably a fair guide to one about to venture his fortunes
in court intrigue. The title poorly represents the kind of advice
which follows. 'Make election rather of thy Betters than thy In-
feriours, shunning always such as are poore and needy.'[2] 'Great
men forget such as have done them service, when they have obtained
what they would, and will rather hate thee for saying, thou hast
beene a meane of their advancement, then acknowledge it.'[3] 'The
Fancies of men change, and hee that loves today, hateth tomorrow;
but let Reason bee thy Schoolemistris which shall ever guide thee
aright.'[4] Of real friends, of whom to the end he had many, Ralegh
has nothing to say.

Friendship having been related thus firmly to the head rather
than the heart, Ralegh embarks in no different spirit upon Chapter
II, 'Great care to be had in the choosing of a Wife'. He detaches
himself from passion, coldly assesses its power, and makes due
allowance for it in his calculations. 'Everie man preferres his fantasie
in that Appetite before all other worldly desires, leaving the care
of Honour, credit, and safety in respect thereof.'[5] 'Have therfore

---

[1] H. Peters, op. cit., pp. 48, 49.   [2] *Instructions*, 1633, p. 2.
[3] P. 9.   [4] P. 11.   [5] Pp. 13, 14.

ever more care, that thou be beloved of thy wife, rather then thy selfe besotted on her.'[1] 'Let thy time of marriage bee in thy young, and strong yeeres; for beleeve it, ever the young Wife betrayeth the old Husband.'[2] 'Leave thy Wife no more than of necessitie thou must, but onelie during her widdowhood.'[3] Much of this seems to be contradicted by what we know of Ralegh's own marriage. Imprudent in the extreme, because of his position as royal favourite, when it was discovered it lost him the Queen's favour. The farewell letter of 1603 and the letters to his wife from Guiana in 1618 show how close was the bond between them. Though he writes of marriage as though it were a question of discretion controlling appetite, with side references to the breeding of bloodstock, that is not how he lived himself. The calculating tone, the insistence upon the treachery of women, and the disadvantages of whoring, are common-places of the time, as is the attack on the bravery of rags.

It is some relief, after the very materialistic treatment of human relationships in the first two chapters, to see in later ones an ideal of personal honour beginning to emerge, and some warmth in the condemnation of the unworthy. Flatterers 'are ever base, creeping, cowardly persons, for thou shalt not find a valiant friend that wil venter his life for thee a flatterer, but such creeping knaues as is good for nothing else'.[4] 'Doe not accuse any man of any crime, if it bee not to save thy selfe, thy Prince, or Countrie; for there is nothing more dishonorable (next to treason it selfe) then to be an accuser.'[5] Was Ralegh thinking perhaps of the accusations and cross-accusa-tions which had passed between him and Lord Cobham in 1603? A man, he says, must not be a liar, 'lying being opposite to the nature of God . . . and for the world, beleeve it, that it never did any Man good (except in the extremitie of saving life) for a lyar is of a base, vnworthy, and cowardly spirit'.[6] That clause, 'in the extremitie of saving life', is typical of the realism which keeps breaking in, in both Ralegh's precepts and his practice. He could lie roundly in what he considered a good cause—as, for instance, when he wrote to Cecil, trying desperately to keep the secret of his unpolitic marriage. 'If any such Thing weare, I would have imparted it unto your sealf before any Man livinge; and therefore I pray believe it not, and I beseich yow to suppress what you can any such mallicious Report.

[1] *Instructions,* 1633, p. 21.   [2] Pp. 27, 28.   [3] P. 25.
[4] Ed. 1632, p. 37. Ed. 1633 is imperfect here.
[5] P. 46.   [6] Pp. 59, 60.

For I protest before God, ther is none on the Face of the Yearth, that I would be fastned unto.'[1] At the same time he had an intellectual love of truth, as conformable 'to the nature of God', and preferred daring speculation to securer orthodoxies.

Something of this may lie behind his stress, in Chapter IV, upon avoiding quarrels and upon restraint in speech. His notorious 'atheism' can have become a public reproach only through his own indiscreet conversation, as for instance in his dinner-table talk with the Rev. Ralph Ironside upon the nature of the soul, which became the basis for a Star Chamber charge in 1592.[2] A great deal of the evidence against him in 1603 depended upon reported speech, both what Ralegh himself is alleged to have said and what he listened to Lord Cobham saying. Cobham was a wild and dangerous talker, and Ralegh, in his own way, was careless in that respect. At the new King's accession he made the fatal mistake of being seen to be openly discontented, again, unless his enemies belied him, a fault of his unruly tongue. All this lends point to his 'be advised what thou dost discourse of, what thou maintaynest; whether touching Religion, State, or vanitie; for if thou erre in the first, thou shalt bee accounted prophan, if in the second dangerous, in the third undiscreet, and foolish'.[3] He repeats this advice in his letter when he says 'private conversacions are whirlepooles and quickesandes'.

The advice not to trust servants too far can be paralleled in Ralegh's own experience; witness his furious quarrels with John Meere, his bailiff, at Sherborne.[4] It is, of course, a very commonplace experience and a commonplace precept. When he says that having trusted a servant with his money he has 'for tediousnesse' neglected to take prompt account of it, we can well believe him. 'I myself', he adds ruefully, 'have lost therby more than I am worth.'[5] Here for once he openly admits that his advice is based upon his own mistakes.

The warnings against harassing the honest poor are less expectable, not because they are in themselves anything more than moral commonplaces, but because Chapter VIII, 'Riches not to bee sought

[1] W. Murdin, *Burghley Papers*, 1759, p. 664, from the original then at Hatfield House.

[2] See G. B. Harrison, ed., *Willobie His Avisa*, 1926, and E. A. Strathmann, *Sir Walter Ralegh. A Study in Elizabethan Skepticism*, 1951.

[3] Pp. 51, 52.

[4] See *The Gentleman's Magazine*, N.S., vols. xl (1853) and xli (1854), 'Sir Walter Raleigh at Sherborne'.

[5] P. 74.

by euill meanes', is one of the very few in which self-interest is not paramount. Even so, the burden of it is that 'God will never prosper thee in ought, if thou offend therein', and 'Hee that hath mercy on the poore, lendeth unto the Lord'.[1] In the farewell letter of 1603 Ralegh begs his wife, 'howsoeuer you doe, for my soules sake, pay all poore men'.[2]

The one chapter which it is difficult to relate closely to anything we know of the writer is the very long, very biblical ninth chapter, 'What inconveniences happen to such as delight in Wine'. Perhaps Sir Walter for once felt that he was upon ground where he could thank God he was not as other men were. It has been suggested that he had his son's proclivities in mind, but there is no solid evidence to support this idea.

It is my belief that under its impersonal surface Ralegh's advice to his son is closely linked to his own experience of life, but it does not represent the whole man. It does not even adequately represent its genre, for though it is an educative work in itself, upon the subject of education its silence is complete. Not one book is recommended to the reader. Ralegh was himself widely read, historian, scientist, economist, poet. Yet he does not envisage his son's having any cultivated interests at all. Perhaps he felt that books speak loud enough with their own tongues and that the unique contribution he could make to his son's upbringing was his readings in the book of human conduct, for that is essentially what his advice is about—personal relationships, how to avoid making friends and being influenced by people.

It is highly specialized. Looked at from one point of view, friends and marriages alike were pawns in the game of preferment. Love itself was a pawn to hazard with Elizabeth I. Ralegh played this game all his days—if play is the word for something in which one risked reputation, estates, and life itself. 'I deny not', he admits, 'but that I have affected promocion.'[3] Yet with some frequency he neglected his own maxims and suffered for it. Of what he thought about relationships in areas outside the politic and prudential he has little to say. Business is business. If we knew no more about him than we see here we should picture him as a very different man from the one we know, through other sources, that he was. That would be our error. Reserve was characteristic of the time. Few people had as yet acquired an adequate means of charting, assessing, and

---

[1] *Instructions*, 1633, pp. 77 and 79.   [2] MS. Sloane 3520.   [3] MS. Add. 22587.

displaying their own personality. Hence we are puzzled and re-
pelled by much that we know about the men of the Renaissance,
and so expert an analyst as Lytton Strachey is reduced to something
like impotence before the character of Queen Elizabeth and of her
relationship with Essex.

The interesting thing about Ralegh is that his character has
come down to us with more of the ambience of life than most, partly
because we have so many of his letters (even the letter quoted in
this article is sufficient to show how differently the world could
present itself to him when he was not compartmentalizing experience and composing precepts) and partly because he seems to have
had a particularly vivid, impulsive, outgoing nature, so that some
of its warmth is appreciable even today. In his own day it is clear
that he struck sparks off everyone he encountered. He was loved
or hated, but never ignored. That he was frequently left out of the
more sober business of the day—the Queen, for instance, would
never make him a privy councillor—shows that his contemporaries,
though they enjoyed him, were a little uneasy with him. He did not
conform.

There is something, though not by any means all of Ralegh's
complex character, to be read in his *Instructions to his Son*. There is
support for the opinion that he was not by nature mealy-mouthed
or tied to conventions. He had the incisiveness and ruthlessness
displayed there, and the determination to survive at no matter what
cost. Was he also so hard, so wary, and above all so small-minded?
At least he does not aggravate the pettiness by making excuses for
it. At the very end he brings his reading of life suddenly and
characteristically under the eye of God, and we see how much of
contemptus mundi there has been in his worldly wisdom. 'Serve God,
let him be the Authour of all thy actions, commend al thy endevours
to him that must either wither or prosper them, please him with
praier, lest if he frowne, he confound all thy fortunes and labors like
drops of Rayne on the sandy ground.'[1] He is aware of his own limitations. 'All is vanity and wearynes, yet'—the realist intrudes as
ever—'such a wearynes and vanitye that wee shall ever complayne
of it and love it for all that.'[2]

From the seventeenth to the early nineteenth century the treatise
seems to have been accepted without question as edifying. This is
what the printer intended. It was to prove that the writer, even in

[1] *Instructions*, 1633, pp. 98, 99.   [2] MS. Add. 22587.

his 'most secret Counsels' was 'Iust and religious'. The cynicism which shocks the twentieth century apparently passed unnoticed under cover of the practical, didactic tone, and the occasional religious references. Ralegh holds first place in *Instructions for Youth, Gentlemen and Noblemen*, in 1722, followed by Lord Burghley, Cardinal Sermonetta, and Edward Walsingham; and as late as 1824 his work appeared in another anonymous collection which was published under the general title of *Practical Wisdom*. The editor rapturously accepts Ralegh, Burghley, and Osborne, though he silently suppresses all Osborne's scandalous observations on women and marriage and some of Ralegh's.

Recent commentators are more critical. 'The treatise makes an unpleasant impression', says Stebbing, 'with its hard, selfish, and somewhat sensual dogmatism. In extenuation it must be recollected that it was addressed to a hot and impetuous youth.'[1] Lee Ustick characterizes Ralegh as 'thoroughly pessimistic and at the same time coldly prudential'.[2] Professor Betz finds it 'a strange mixture of ruthless worldliness and of simple, practical piety'.[3] Professor Strathmann grants that it 'neither neglects nor obscures ethical considerations', but emphasizes its disillusion.[4] Philip Edwards frankly wishes Ralegh had not written it, 'not that it is always faulty or overprudent, but that the motivating spirit is worldly, politic, and calculating'. He relates it, however, to 'a limited end and narrow sphere of operation'.[5]

In all this there is no mention of a quality which I think is outstanding in the work, and which like others we find in it is paradoxical—the opposite of the caution and prudence and self-preservation which it recommends—and that quality is courage. The man who wrote the *Instructions* was pushing and not very scrupulous. He was realistic and without illusions. In so far as we feel any moral quality to be in the ascendant it is a mixture of the proud and the indomitable, a determination not to be exploited, derided, fooled, and not above all to be a 'base, creeping, cowardly person'. Unlike the *Instructions*, Ralegh's letter to his son is alive with feeling, and that feeling, too, is courage in the face of whatever life may bring. 'Nevertheles my sonne take harte and Courage to thee. Thy

[1] *Sir Walter Ralegh*, 1899, p. 268.
[2] *S.P.*, 1932, xxix. 434.
[3] *Seventeenth Century Studies*, ed. Shafer, 1937, p. 61.
[4] *Sir Walter Ralegh*, 1951, p. 155.
[5] *Sir Walter Ralegh*, 1953, p. 141.

adventure lyes in this troublesome barque; strive if thou Canst to make good thy station in the vpper decke; those that live vnder hatches are ordained to be drudges and slaves. Endeavoure rather to be parte of the tymber of the house then lath and mudwall; but be beame tymber not threshould stuffe.' Those are the words of a man not easily to be daunted. If they were written by Ralegh in 1603 it was at a time when he urgently needed all the moral resources which he could command.

Elizabeth, Essex, and James

JAMES MCMANAWAY

IT does not seem to have been noticed that the device invented by the nobility of England to assure Queen Elizabeth the safe enjoyment of her crown was later adapted, with a minimum of variation, by James VI of Scotland to help assure his eventual succession to that crown. A series of events began in the 1580's that has a remarkable parallel in 1958. Philip II of Spain set a price on the head of William of Orange, and in March 1582 a fanatic shot and almost killed him. In the spring of 1583 it was learned in England that the murder of Elizabeth was being planned by the Duke of Guise. And in July 1584 a second fanatic shot William of Orange and succeeded in killing him. The alarm in England can be understood by those who remember the assassination of King Feisal of Iraq in July 1958 and General Nasser's denunciation by radio of King Hussein of Jordan that was followed by an attempt upon his life.

To English Protestants, whose sole shield was the life of their Queen, the assassination of William the Silent administered the severest shock they had yet received. The powers of darkness appeared to be concentrating against them: villainy without limit or scruple. And as though to emphasize the alarm and horror, a few weeks later, when the Jesuit Creighton was seized aboard a ship bound for Scotland, further details came to light of the wide-flung Catholic conspiracy.

The crisis called for new legislation. But as statesmen reflected on the situation, they decided that delay was dangerous. Something must be done at once. The outlook was indeed preposterous. If the Queen were slain before Parliament met, there would be a constitutional vacuum in the land. Royal officials would immediately lose their positions and all authority derived from the Queen's commission would lapse. There would be no Privy Council, no judges, no Lords Lieutenant, no justices. With the government in eclipse, the way would be open for the organized forces of conspiracy, centred on the Catholic Mary Queen of Scots. It was an invitation to speedy murder.[1]

Within a few weeks, the Privy Council devised a Bond of Associa-

[1] J. E. Neale, *Elizabeth I and her Parliaments 1584–1601*, pp. 15–16.

tion that was circulated throughout the country, the signers of which pledged their lives, their fortunes, and their sacred honours to defend the Queen and to pursue implacably anyone who might attempt to assassinate Elizabeth or remotely benefit by such an attempt.

Put bluntly, this meant that should an attempt be made on Elizabeth's life, Mary Queen of Scots was to be destroyed, whether a party to the action or not. And not only Mary: though the wording may seem ambiguous, it was held to involve the destruction also of her son, certainly if he claimed the throne. The inclusion of James is sufficiently explained by his place in the scheme of the conspirators and by the distrust his actions bred in England. (Neale, p. 17.)

A copy of the Bond dated 19 October at Hampton Court bears the signatures of thirteen members of the Privy Council, and many other manuscript copies are extant.[1] It appeared in print first in 1598 in the second part of *A Pithie Exhortation*, a posthumously published book by Peter Wentworth that will be discussed later. The Bond being informal and extra-legal, when Parliament met in November its gravest concern was for the drafting and adoption of legislation that would embody the main purposes of the Bond.[2] The bill provided, in effect, that any attempt upon the life of Elizabeth for the purpose of advancing the claims of Mary Stuart would disable the Queen of Scots and would authorize pursuit of her to the death, whether or not she were a party to the plot. It provided, further, that her heir, James VI, would be disabled in his claim, but it did not make his assassination mandatory—indeed, Elizabeth might in certain conditions restore his title.

It is not a little ironic that when Elizabeth's age and infirmity aroused the hopes of all pretenders to the succession, James VI should have turned to the English Bond of Association that touched him so nearly and should have fashioned from it an instrument to support his claim.

[1] C.S.P. Dom. Elizabeth, vol. clxxiv, no. 1. See also nos. 2–18; vol. clxxv, nos. 4 and 9, dated 6 and 20 Nov.; vol. clxxvi, no. 11, dated 15 Jan. 1585; Addenda, vol. xxviii, nos. 101, 102, and 108, of various dates. The original minute corrected by Walsingham is in vol. clxxiii, no. 81; no. 82 is a revised draft; no. 83, with Walsingham's corrections, is described as the final version. Other copies are in no. 87. The reasons for revision are discussed by Neale, pp. 16–17. The copy among the Egerton papers, bearing the contemporaneous endorsement 'Lincolnes Inne' is printed in vol. 12 of the Camden Society Publications, 1840, pp. 108–11. It is signed by Thomas Egerton and ninety-four others.

[2] See Neale, pp. 28 ff., for an account of the debates and a discussion of the statute as adopted.

The similarity of the documents came to my attention when examining Folger MS. 6185.1, a large folio, compiled by someone deeply interested in the affairs of the Earl of Essex, perhaps by one of his clerks. Inserted after folio 201, which has on its verso the conclusion of the Scottish Bond, is a fold of smaller paper bearing the text of the English Bond. The insert was whipstitched into the book at a very early date, for both Bonds are listed on the contents leaf, the handwriting of which is largely the same as that of the document transcribed on folio 214.[1] The volume contains transcripts in several hands. The first nine items listed in the table of contents are theological, relating chiefly to the Bishops' Articles. Then follow thirty-four other numbered items, most of which relate directly or indirectly to Robert Devereux, Earl of Essex. Among the exceptions are two sermons, an oration by the Queen, a letter from the Queen to Lady Norris, Sir Henry Savile's oration to the Queen, two memoranda by Thomas Digges, Spenser's *View of the Present State of Ireland* (which, it will be recalled, has a specific reference to Essex), and three letters of members of the Howard family. Following the items listed in the table are some twenty-five documents, many of them copies of letters from Essex to Elizabeth or the Privy Council, or from them to him about affairs in Ireland. One exception is a transcript of the instructions left by Philip II of Spain to his son, and another outlines a plan to permit Catholic worship in England. The volume concludes with a letter from Abdie Ashton, Essex's chaplain, to Sir Henry Wotton, dated from St. John's College on 3 June 1601.[2]

Several names are scribbled inside the front cover, on the contents

[1] The insert consists of a single sheet of paper, folded once. Each folio leaf measures about 200 × 275 mm. The paper, which has no watermark, is much lighter in weight than that of the book. Before being inserted, if one may judge by the darkening of the paper from wear and exposure, the document had existed independently for a considerable length of time. For convenience in filing or carrying about the person, it had been folded twice along the horizontal axis; then, at a later date, it was folded a third time, along the vertical axis. There is nothing to contradict the supposition that the transcript dates from 1584 or 1585.

[2] The volume is in the original calf binding, blind tooled on both covers. The paper is heavy and of uniform quality. The several watermarks are variants of Briquet's 11383 or 11387, a hand and flower *c.* 87 mm. tall, with a '3' at the base of the palm and below it the initials 'PB' or 'PR' (Neuberg, 1537; Hamburg, 1544–6; Coudenberg, Belg., 1550). The first leaf contains an incomplete table of contents; the last leaf appears to be conjugate with the pastedown on the back cover. Leaves 1–3, 6, 110, 167, and 168 are wanting, as is a leaf between 198 and 199; the bottom of leaf 109 was torn away at an early date, but not before item 32, Sir Edward Dyer's letter to Sir Christopher Hatton, had been transcribed, for this title is listed in the table of contents and then marked through; what remains of the letter is likewise marked for cancellation.

leaf, and on the otherwise blank verso of the last leaf, and inside the back cover: Thomas Scott (four times), G. Scott, Melton, Thomas Payne, Iacob Silver, and John Knatchbull. Some of the signatures are in italic; others in secretarial script. John Knatchbull's looks late enough to be the signature of Sir John Knatchbull (1636–96), but there is nothing to identify him. Of greater importance, it would seem, is the italic inscription at the top left corner of the front pastedown: 'Die Veneris Iulij 1° 1601 per me Richardũ Greeneũ.' It would simplify the story if this were the man named by the Earl of Essex in his letter of 11 July 1599 to the Privy Council: 'In my last letter sent by Green from Wicklow, I gave an account of . . . my journey thro' Munster and Leinster. . . .'[1] But this Greene was probably the man mentioned in two letters from Essex's secretary, Henry Cuffe, to Edward Reynolds. In the first, dated 18 July 1599, Cuff writes that: 'In the last part of the journal sent unto you by Francis Greene, in setting down the skirmish near Arkloughe . . .' and in the second, from Dublin on 4 August, he states that: 'Since our last to you we have received from you two despatches, one from Fr. Greene, the other by Mr. Mynne's man.' Though the wording is ambiguous in the letters of Essex and Cuffe, Francis Greene appears to have been only a messenger. Another man named Greene was also attached to Essex, as we learn from two other documents at Hatfield. On 26 February 1601 Captain Thomas Lee wrote to Sir Henry Lee, giving the names of participants in the conspiracy that were in durance, and among those 'To be discharged without bonds, without indictment, arraignment, or fine' is one William Greene. He is referred to in more colourful detail in a letter from William Reynolds to Sir Robert Cecil in February 1601, as follows:

There is one William Green, called Captain Green, in the Counter Poultry, who I hear was in the rebellious troop with the Earl of Essex; which Green (amongst divers of the Earl's men which have quarrelled with me) met me in Thames Street about 2 years ago, where he quarrelled with me. He is generally reported to be a cutpurse, picklock and thief, and lives by cosening shifts.[2]

It seems unlikely that the Richard Greene whose signature appears in the Folger manuscript is the Londoner who was the subject of two letters (7 and 17 October 1599) from Sir John Hart to Sir

---

[1] Thomas Birch, *Memoirs of the Reign of Queen Elizabeth*, 1754, ii. 420.
[2] Historical MSS. Commission, Marquis of Salisbury, Hatfield, pt. ix, pp. 236 and 270; pt. xi, pp. 44, 87, and 93.

Robert Cecil; at some time prior to 7 October, this man had been admitted to 'our hospital', where he 'uttered divers lewd speeches', in consequence of which he had been put in prison to await an expression of Cecil's pleasure.[1] No other man named Richard Greene has been traced in the records of the Earl of Essex or among the papers at Hatfield. The handwriting of the signature in the Folger manuscript occurs again in the italic heading of the Queen's letter to Essex on folio 205ᵛ. It is recognizable in several other places, and, crucially, in the italic heading and in occasional italic words of the Scottish Bond. Since it may be presumed that the man who wrote the italic headings also transcribed the text of these documents in secretarial script, Greene's hand may be identified frequently in the latter part of the volume.

Is it stretching credibility too far to suggest that Essex had three different men named Greene in his employ and that this compilation, containing as it does so many letters to and from the Earl while he was in Ireland, besides numerous other documents that reflect his interests or relate to his activities, belonged to the unhappy favourite and was prepared by his agents?[2] The presence of Ashton's *apologia* to Wotton dated a little more than three months after the execution of Essex need not militate against such a supposition. Its inclusion may have been a last loyal gesture by a faithful servant. And the date of Richard Greene's signature inside the front cover, 1 July 1601, may be a record of the date when the volume came finally into his possession (though *per me* is not particularly appropriate if the phrase was intended to mean other than that Greene's name was written by himself).

It is well known that Essex had an active interest in the problem of the succession and dabbled in private diplomacy. As early as 1589 he sought to open a secret correspondence with James, but the attempt did not prosper. With the passage of years and the intensification of factional rivalries in England, James appears to have moved away from the Cecils and put more dependence in Essex. 'By 1598', writes Helen Georgia Stafford, 'their friendship had grown to such an extent that the French ambassador in London noticed how James entrusted to Essex all that he wished negotiated

---

[1] Hatfield MSS. ix. 367, 373. The writer was almost certainly the Sir John Hart who was Lord Mayor of London in 1589 (Musgrave's *Obituary*).

[2] The frequent departure from chronological order of the Essex papers and the intermixture of extraneous documents are indications that the volume was not the Earl's official letter book.

in the English court'.[1] James could hardly forget the Earl's forth-right avowal of friendship and loyalty:

such as I am, and all whatsoever I am (tho' perhaps a subject of small price) I consecrate unto your regal throne. . . . Neither do I doubt, that the minds of all my countrymen . . . will jointly unite their hopes in your majesty's noble person, as the only center, wherein our rest and happiness consist.[2]

Of all the Englishmen who favoured the pretensions of James, the most outspoken was probably Peter Wentworth, stalwart advocate of the rights of Parliament and vigorous champion of a declaration in favour of James as heir to the crown. The first part of his *A Pithie Exhortation to her Maiestie for Establishing her Successor to the crowne. Whereunto is Added a Discourse containing the Authors opinion of the true and lawfull successor to her Maiestie (S.T.C. 25245)* was probably written in 1587. Copies were made surreptitiously and put into circulation, with the result that Wentworth was examined by the Privy Council in August 1591 and on the 15th of that month was imprisoned in the Gate House, where he remained until 11 February 1592. Wentworth was imprisoned again (25 February 1593) for his stubborn insistence upon a settlement of the succession and was still a prisoner nearly five years later (1597) when death came. It was during his imprisonment that he wrote the Discourse that forms part two of *A Pithie Exhortation*, in answer to N. Doleman's (i.e. the Jesuit Robert Parsons) *A Conference about the Next Succession to the Crowne of Ingland* (1594).[3] Neale writes ('Wentworth', p. 182) that *A Pithie Exhortation* 'was published surreptitiously by his friends in 1598, after his death'. In the light of later investigations, this statement proves to be only partly accurate. The book was indeed printed first in 1598, but since the publication of Pollard and Redgrave's *Short-Title Catalogue* in 1926 it has been known that the place of publication was not London, as Neale seems to have assumed, but Edinburgh. This fact widens the field of conjecture. Wentworth's friends may have brought the manuscript to the attention of Robert Waldegrave, the putative printer,[4]

[1] *James VI of Scotland and the Throne of England*, 1940, p. 203.
[2] Quoted by Stafford, p. 204, from Birch, *Memoirs*, i. 176. The letter, signed with the cipher '7', is dated from London 17 May, with no indication of the year.
[3] J. E. Neale, 'Peter Wentworth', *Eng. Hist. Rev.*, 1924, xxxix. 36–54, 175–205. He cites B.M. Add. MS. 24664, fol. 44b, for the date of part one of *A Pithie Exhortation*. Neale seems not to have known that Doleman was a pseudonym used by Parsons.
[4] Though students of Scottish printing accept the attribution to Waldegrave, it has not been possible for me to confirm the attribution, for the three ornamental

or of James himself. Wentworth's ideas were well known, and a manuscript may have been picked up by one of the Scottish agents in London; Waldegrave may have had no other prompting than the desire for a book that would sell rapidly in Scotland. Or the Earl of Essex may have sent Wentworth's treatise to King James, for when it became impossible for Wentworth to present his treatise to the Queen during the sessions of Parliament in 1589, he considered asking the Earl of Essex to do this.[1] In any case, the book was a potent weapon of propaganda in James's active campaign to win the English crown.

Prompt reports went to London about the King's projects. Late in 1599, Cecil had a letter from George Nicolson in Edinburgh dated 27 November:

I hear, which I beseech your honour to keep close, that there is a general band, subscribed by many, and to be subscribed by all earls, lords, and barons: binding them, by solemn vow and oath, to serve the king with their lives, friends, heritages, goods, and gear; and to be ready in warlike furniture, for the same on all occasions, but especially for his claim to England.[2]

Nicolson's letter adds that a full convention of the estates is to be held on 10 December to adopt a solid course intended to supply the King with money and to provide arms. As news of the bond spread abroad, James appears to have tried dissimulation, for in his report from Liege of 30 May–9 June 1600 J. B., *alias* John Petit, wrote to Peter Halins in London that 'What I wrote you of the King of Scots is true . . . ; but whatsoever he says touching these practices, the association in Scotland . . . shows there is fire that will kindle at the first opportunity.'[3] Copies of the Bond were received in England,[4] and the transcript in the Folger manuscript is proof that at least one copy was in private hands.[5]

James's Bond is certainly a document that the Earl of Essex would have wished to possess, and his agents would have been remiss had they failed to supply one. The presence in the Folger manuscript of

initials, G, M, and S, that occur on A3, B1, and I8 of *A Pithie Exhortation* do not appear in any of Waldegrave's books available to me for examination.

[1] J. E. Neale, *Queen Elizabeth*, 1934, p. 317.

[2] Quoted by Patrick Fraser Tytler, *History of Scotland*, 3rd ed., 1845, vii. 387–8, from a letter in the P.R.O.

[3] C.S.P. Dom. Elizabeth, vol. cclxxiv, p. 439.

[4] Stafford (p. 197) refers to State Papers, Scotland, vol. lxv, nos. 72–75.

[5] Through the kindness of H. N. Blakiston, Esq., it is possible to state that the Folger manuscript was not copied from any of the four documents at the Record Office, though the text is essentially the same.

J. B. also in Chapman papers.

a transcript of the Scottish Bond among documents relating to the Earl is highly significant. And the insertion of the old transcript of the English Bond suggests that the indebtedness of one to the other was recognized.

The Bond was something Essex had to take into account, whether he was a loyal supporter of James or his rival. In his colloquy with Ashton just before his execution, Essex touched on both these matters:

> For the crown, I never affected it. . . .
>
> . . . I knew myself to be bound in conscience, as a Christian, to prevent the subversion of religion, and as an Englishman to have regard to my native country. The only means left to turn away these evils was to procure my access to Her Majesty, with whom I assured myself to have had that gracious hearing, that might have tended to the infinite happiness of this state, . . . and in settling a succession for the Crown, to the preventing of Spanish servitude, and the saving of many thousand Englishmen's lives.[1]

Contemporaries had been somewhat less certain about the goal of Essex's ambition:

> . . . I think that unless some good order be taken, the King of Scots will win the game, if the Earl of Essex be not in his way, whom nevertheless the Scots take to be his greatest friend, but I think that they are deceived.[2]

Throughout the trial of Essex and Southampton, the references to Essex's dabbling in the matter of the succession were few and inconspicuous—presumably upon instructions from the Queen—and there is no trace of them in the official account (Stafford, pp. 210–24). The government could hardly have known how deeply Essex was involved, for his letter to James of 25 December 1600, B.M. Add. MSS. 31022, ff. 107–8, did not come to public attention until modern times (Stafford, pp. 221–4). James's answer is reported to have been carried by the Earl in a little black bag that hung about his neck and was burned before his surrender.[3] Other docu-

---

[1] Quoted by Walter B. Devereux in *Lives and Letters of the Devereux, Earls of Essex. . .*, 1853, ii. 166, 167.

[2] Thomas Fitzherbert, writing 1 Mar. 1599 from Madrid to Sterrell in London, C.S.P. Dom. Elizabeth, vol. cclxx, no. 47. See also Stafford, p. 205, n. 24, citing the warning of Ferdinand of Tuscany to James that Essex was the man most able to hinder a pretender. It is significant that Mountjoy felt it necessary in his letter to James in the summer of 1599 to reassure the latter that Essex was his supporter and not a rival for the crown (Birch, ii. 470).

[3] On 16 Feb. 1601 the Privy Council instructed Sir John Peyton, Lieutenant of the

ments, in a chest, are also reported to have been destroyed as soon as Essex returned from the disastrous ride through London.[1] Incriminating documents were hunted out systematically,[2] and it is remarkable that a volume with so much intimate information about Essex as that of Richard Greene escaped detection. Its contents would have confirmed many suspicions.

Peter Wentworth's name crops up once more before the story ends. On 11 March 1601 the Privy Council dispatched a letter to Mr. Gilpin in the Low Countries, instructing him 'to deale with the Estates' about the printing at Middleburgh of a great number of books in two treatises by Wentworth touching the succession, to the end that the printer might be identified and the books seized and suppressed. Arrangement for the publication had been made by 'some Englishemen of factious humour', with intent to disperse the books 'amongst such as are curious of noveltyes' (*cupidi alicuius novi*, as Cicero would have phrased it). There is no evidence to connect this printing of Wentworth's book with Essex, but it is of a piece with the conspirators' employment of the Lord Chamberlain's Men to perform *Richard II* for the instruction of Londoners in how to deal with a weak king; and no other group of Englishmen are known to which the project may be attributed. The letter of the Council does not indicate that any books had yet reached England; so it may be surmised that information about the edition came from one of the rebels. In this venture, as in his plot to have James send ambassadors to England by 1 February with demands for an immediate recognition of his rights to the succession, Essex's timing would seem to have been fatally upset by the Council's request of 7 February that Essex appear before them.

There is insufficient evidence to prove Essex's complicity in the publication of Peter Wentworth's book in Edinburgh in 1598, in the planning of the Scottish Bond or the adaptation of it from the English document in 1599, or in the printing of Wentworth's book in Middleburgh in the winter of 1600–1. One or more of these ideas may have originated with James VI, or they may have occurred

---

Tower, to make an exhaustive search 'in decent sorte' for 'some paper in a blacke cover'. Although several confessions mentioned it, Essex denied to the Lord Admiral that he had it; but the Council had testimony of its existence (*Acts of the Privy Council*, N.S., xxxi. 166).

[1] 'All his papers, among which was one called a history of his troubles', Devereux, ii. 146.

[2] On 16 Feb. the Council issued a warrant for the search of a trunk belonging to Anthony Rowse, a page to the Earl (*A.P.C.*, N.S., xxxi. 163).

independently to persons unknown. They fall into such a neat pattern, however, that one is tempted to say that if Essex did not plot them he should have.

In putting the Scottish Bond into print for the first time, I have expanded most of the contractions and put into roman type the names of persons and places and the Latin (and a few other) words that are in italic in the Folger manuscript. To show the verbal indebtedness to the English Bond, words that are identical (or substantially the same) are printed in italics; those that are a close paraphrase are printed in small capitals.

A generall band made by the good subiects of the kings *Matie for the preseruation of* his highnes p[er]son, & pursuit of his vndoubted right of the Crowne of England and Ireland. *made.* 1599.

ffor as much as the providence of *god hath* ESTABLISHED KINGDOMEES AND MONARCHIES, and hath APPOYNTED *kinges and princes* to beare *rule over the* same, rep[re]sentinge his devine power in administracōn of Justice to ther *subiects,* and honouring him by establishing *true* and *Cristiane religion according to his word,* In contemplating of which benefits redounding to the people by the lawfull Authoritie of the prince, they are bound to *love, reverence and obaye ther* native sou[er]aignes, to p[ro]cure *to ther vttermost power* ther standing and aduancment, to resist and *withstand all* what soeu[er] practices or attempt[e]s which may be *hurtfull* to there p[er]sones *or states; therfore we* SUBSCRIBING (the *naturall* and loyall *borne subiect*[e]s *of this Realme*) calling to memorie and finding dayly before our eyes, the *greate felicitie* and *estimable comfort,* wher wth all the most happie and *gracious* raigne of our soveraigne hath enriched vs: and the woonderfull QUIETNESSE, wherwith by gods p[ro]vidence, and his highnes prudent *government* in soe vniu[er]sall troubles of all Europe, we have beene blissed: *acknowledging our selves* most *iustly bound wth our bodie, lives, landes, goodes* and geare, *in* HIS *defence and safetie* against what soeu[er], of *what nation degree* or QUALITIE soeu[er] *they be,* that would directlye or indirectly *attempte any* HARME against his most sacred *person,* or estate. Therefore *we and every of vs* CONIUNCTLIE *and severally,* in p[re]sence of the *almightie* POWER, by whome princes rule, whome we call vpon not onely as a Judge, but as a full revenger of suche (as shall violat and contradict or with stand these p[re]sent[e]s) of OUR OWNE FRE MOTIVE, AND WILL, *bindes* and obliges *our selves* MUTUALLYE EACH ONE OF VS TO OTHER, in *firme bond* and whole *societye,* wherby we solemnelye VOWE AND p[ro]*mise before the* GREAT *god with our whole powers, bodies, lives, land*[e]*s, goodes, children and servantes* and all that is vnder our comāndement, truly and *faithfully to serve, and humblye obey our saide soueraigne against all estates, dignities, and earthlie* PRINCES, *what soeuer*, invade or *pursewe by all* manner of hostilitie *as well by force of armes as by all other meanes, all* SORTES *of* p[er]*sones ther* COMPLICES assistant[e]s and p[ar]takers, *as shall attempte* or vndertake *by* DEEDE, *counsell,* or concealment, *to any* PRACTISE *that* may in any respect *tend to the harme of* HIS Maties most *Royall* p[er]*son,* honour estate or dignitie. *And shall neur desiste frome* ANY *manner of* Hostilitie, *pursuites of such* traiterouse tyrant[e]s, till *ther counsellers,* LEADERS, AND PER-TAKERS BE VTTERLIE ROOTED OUT, to the example of others vpon the hope of impunitie to attempt the like. And by cause almightie god amongst diuers his inestimable blessinges which he multiplies vpon our said soveraigne Lord to his glorie & our great comfort, hath established the vndoubted right of the Crownes of England & Ireland in his most royall p[er]son, next to his dear sister Elizabeth nowe Queene of Eng-land, which not withstanding diu[er]se p[er]sons, vpon friuolouse and imp[er]tinent p[re]tences, would goe aboute to impugne, contrarye to his birthright, and the most auncient and allowed lawes of both the Realmes. Wherfore we vpon our bounden dueties to our native soveraigne, and moved in conscience to aduance the righteous succes-sor, solemnly swear and protest by the name of the great god, not onely to ye vttermost of our power & strengthe, to mantaine & defend or soveraigne in his vndoubted right and title to the crowne of England and Ireland against all other p[re]tenders what soeuer, but like wise shall readilie with out any further drifte or excuse, vpon whatsoeue[r] p[re]text, bestowe our selves, our lives, children, servantes frend good[e]s and geare, what soeue[r] else in the *per*suite there of against what soeuer p[er]son, that shall after the death of the Queene of Eng-land, hinder impugn or with stand his Maties heires or successors, in the peaceable getting and enioying, or possessing of the said crownes of England and Ireland. And shall by forceable meanes take the *vttermost revenge* vpon them, ther leaders *Counsellers* PERTAKERS AND ASSIS-TANT[e]s, that *by anie meanes possible we or any of vs cane* excogitat or *devise*: and *neuer desist* till we haue established our dearest sou[er]aigne (or in case of his decease *which god forbid*) his heires and successors, in the Royall Kingdome of England and Ireland, and peaceable fruition of the same, without p[re]iudice All wayes to his Maties dearest sister Queene Elizabeth, during all the dayes of hir life tyme. *And* FOR THE MORE SURE *corroboration of this* o[ur] VOLUNTARIE *bond* & entrie in to soe whole and lawfull a SOCIETIE, *we* and eu[er]ye of vs subscribing *confirme the whole content*[e]s THEROF *by our* solemne and great *othes, taken vpon the holie* SCRIPTURES, *with this expresse condicōn* y^t *none of vs shall* VPON *anye respect of* p[er]*sones, or cause of feare* or daunger, *or hope of reward, separate our selues frome this* CONDICŌN, NOR *fayle* in any p[ar]te the p[re]misses *during* o[ur] *liues.* And if we doe to the contrary (as god forbid) y^t we by our most graciouse sou[er]aigne & his heires and the rest of o[ur] societie, be not onely reputed *as* p[er]*iurd* p[er]*sons*, but also to be p[ro]*secuted* as vnworthie to BEARE OFFICE *in any christian Realme, or civill* COṂON WEALTH. And also to be p[ro]*secuted* as most vile and destestable Traytours, *and publique enimies to god* o[ur] SOU[er]AIGNE *and native Country. To the which paine and punishment we doe voluntarilie submit* o[ur] *selves and every one of vs*, without appellacōn reclamation: which as we are contented that these p[re]sent[e]s be ratified by the states in the nex parliament, and p[re]sentlie inserted and registred in the booke of counsells in futurā rei memoriam. And that executors may be se-created ther vpon in firme effect. *In witnesse* whereof to this p[re]sent bond subscribed with *our handes, and seales* of armes affixed, the yeare of god. 1599 and the 34 yeare of his Maiestie reigne.

Hugh Trevor-Roper's article
"Historical Imagination"
(How about those Diaries eh?)

Hume's History of the Reign of James I

GODFREY DAVIES

THE genesis of David Hume's *History of England* can be briefly traced in the autobiographical note he wrote in order that it should be prefixed to any edition of his works. His appointment in 1752 as head of the Advocates' Library in Edinburgh created the opportunity because it gave him command of a large collection of books. He determined to begin in 1603 with the accession of the house of Stuart to the English throne when, he thought, the 'misrepresentations of faction began chiefly to take place'. The need for impartiality was evident and he was confident that he could supply it. 'I was the only historian, that had at once neglected present power, interest, and authority, and the cry of popular prejudices.'[1] Elsewhere he enlarges upon the need of a history of England. When he has finished the reign of James I he tells a friend: 'You know that there is no post of honour in the English Parnassus more vacant than that of history.'[2]

Harsh criticism of the existing histories of England was general in the first half of the eighteenth century. In the year of Hume's birth the *Spectator* printed a letter which purported to be from a man with a 'strong passion toward falshood'. He proposed to form a society of men of like propensities: 'We might be called *the historians*, for *liar* is become a very harsh word.' Addison is less unkind than Steele, but severe. 'It is a fault very justly found in histories composed by politicians, that they leave nothing to chance or humour, but are still for deriving every action from some plot and contrivance, from drawing up a perpetual scheme of causes and events, and preserving a constant correspondence between the camp and the council-table.' He described how historians could 'please the imagination', though he confessed that this required more art than veracity. He complained that most wrote as if they knew all the secrets of Providence, and that several English ones seemed to have received 'many revelations of this kind'.[3]

[1] I have used the text reprinted in E. C. Mossner's *The Forgotten Hume*, New York 1943, p. 6. Here and elsewhere I have changed the capitalization.

[2] *The Letters of David Hume*, ed. J. Y. T. Greig, 1932, i. 170, 179.

[3] *Spectator*, no. 136, 6 Aug. 1711; no. 170, 14 Sept. 1711; no. 420, 2 July 1712; no. 483, 13 Sept. 1712.

Swift advanced another theory to explain the inferiority of the historical works of his generation. The English language was changing so continuously that historians were discouraged when they realized that their style and vocabulary would soon grow out of fashion and 'in an age or two' require an interpreter to be understood. Nevertheless, he wanted to be appointed historiographer royal in order to deal with Queen Anne's reign, to transmit 'the truth of things . . . to future ages and bear down the falsehood of malicious pens'. This was the purpose of his *Memoirs* of the change of the Queen's ministry in 1710 and *History of the four last years*, but they are rather political pamphlets than histories.[1] That he called his successful rival 'a worthless rogue that nobody knows' is an example of his ignorance or spleen, because Thomas Madox was a learned scholar, two of whose works are still valued by medievalists.[2]

Whether disappointment at his failure to be named historiographer royal was responsible for the passage on historians in *Gulliver's Travels* is a subject for conjecture. Certainly no group suffers a more vitriolic attack. At Glubbdubdrib Gulliver called up the recent dead and commented:

I was chiefly disgusted with modern history. For having strictly examined all the persons of greatest name in the courts of princes for an hundred years past, I found how the world had been misled by prostitute writers, to ascribe the greatest exploits in war to cowards, the wisest counsel to fools, sincerity to flatterers, *Roman* virtue to betrayers of their country, piety to atheists, chastity to sodomites, truth to informers. . . . Here I discovered the roguery and ignorance of those who pretend to write *anecdotes*, or secret history; who send so many kings to their graves with a cup of poison; will repeat the discourse between a prince and chief minister, where no witness was by. . . .[3]

---

[1] His memorial to the Queen, 15 Apr. 1714, is reprinted in *The Prose Works of Jonathan Swift*, ed. Temple Scott, 1911, v. 477. Cf. ibid., p. 367. Swift evidently did not share the view of his friend Archbishop King who had stated: 'History is indeed a serious matter, not to be written carelessly like a letter to a Friend; nor with *Passion*, like a Billet to a Mistress; nor with *Biass*, like a Declamation for a Party at the Bar, or the Remonstrance of a Minister for his Prince; nor in fine, by a Man unacquainted with the World, like Soliloquies and Meditations. It requires a long Experience, a sound Judgement, a close Attention, an unquestionable Integrity, and a Stile without Affectation.' Wiliam King, *Miscellanies in Prose and Verse*, n.d., pp. 463–4. The Huntington Library copy has an inscription by Swift that the book was given to him by the author on 10 Mar. 1708/9.

[2] The two works are *History of the Exchequer*, 1711, and *Firma Burgi*, 1726.

[3] *The Prose Works of Jonathan Swift*, ed. Herbert Davis, 1941, xi. 183.

Lord Hervey, who knew as much backstairs history as Swift, fully shared the dean's opinions. He was as sceptical about the causes of events and as certain that writers did not know them. He thought

> the fortuitous influence of chance so much more decisive of the success or miscarriage of statesmen's schemes, than the skill and dexterity of the most able and artful of them, that I am apt to attribute much less to the one, and much more to the other, than the generality of historians, either from prejudice to their heroes or partiality to their own conjectures, are willing to allow.

Hervey, like Swift, distrusted memoir writers. He related a conversation with the King and Queen about the contributions likely to be made to history by three political opponents of the court. Lords Bolingbroke, Chesterfield, and Carteret will have 'as much truth as the *Mille et une nuits*', said George II, but Bolingbroke was a scoundrel of a higher class than Chesterfield, 'a little tea-table scoundrel'. Caroline was sure all three would tell heaps of lies but of a different kind—Bolingbroke's would be great lies, Chesterfield's little, and Carteret's of both sorts.[1]

A Frenchman who generally praised English literature and philosophy wrote: 'Pour de bons historiens je ne leur en connois pas encore. Il a falu qu'un François ait écrit leur histoire.' He offered two possible explanations. The native genius, which is either cold or impetuous and thus unsuited to 'cette éloquence naïve, & cet air noble & simple de l'histoire', and the party spirit which had discredited all English historians. As an example Voltaire cited the reputation of Mary Queen of Scots, a heroic saint to Jacobites but to others debauched, adulterous, and homicidal. So England had plenty of partisan narratives but no true histories.[2] Bolingbroke defined history as 'philosophy teaching by examples how to conduct ourselves in all the situations of private and public life'. Otherwise it served only to 'render us mere antiquaries and scholars'. He thought that it had been 'purposely and systematically falsified in all ages'. Moreover, the English must yield the palm in writing history 'to the Italians and French and, probably, even to the Germans'.[3]

[1] *Some materials towards memoirs of the reign of King George II. By John, Lord Hervey*, ed. Romney Sedgwick, 1931, iii. 755.
[2] *Lettres escrites de Londres sur les Anglois*, Basle 1734, pp. 200–1.
[3] *The Works of the Late Right Honourable Henry St. John, Lord Viscount Bolingbroke*, 1793, ii. 267, 302, 354.

Such witnesses to the lowly position assigned to history in Hume's formative years suffice to prove that the antiquaries were regarded as dull dogs and the narrators as either ignorant or lying. No hint suggests that Great Britain was about to produce the famous triumvirate of Robertson, Hume, and Gibbon, or that for a century or more British historians were to occupy the foremost seats in the temple of Clio. The inspiration came from France to Scotland, and thence to England. Two French writers changed the very conception of history and revolutionized its aims.

Montesquieu published his *Considérations sur la grandeur et la décadence des Romains* in 1734 and his *Esprit des Lois* in 1748, Voltaire his *Charles XII* in 1732, *Siècle de Louis XIV* in 1751, and *Essai sur l'histoire générale* in 1756. The young Gibbon delighted in 'the frequent perusal of Montesquieu, whose energy of style, and boldness of hypotheses, were powerful to awaken and stimulate the genius of the age'.[1] Hume thanks Montesquieu for a presentation copy of a work 'which has attracted the highest esteem from all nations, and will be the admiration of all ages'. He then adds his reflections on certain passages so that Montesquieu wrote on the original letter that it was 'full of light and good sense'. Eighteen years later Hume's enthusiasm has waned. Yet he still thinks the *Esprit des Lois* has 'considerable merit, notwithstanding the glare of its pointed wit, and notwithstanding its false refinements and its rash and crude positions'.[2]

Voltaire's influence was even greater because he provided a model of the history of an age which other historians could copy. The nature and extent of Voltaire's influence were explained by Hugh Blair in a course of *Lectures on Rhetoric* which he delivered at Edinburgh for twenty years before he published them in 1783. He devoted Lecture XXXVI to history and said in a final paragraph:

I cannot conclude the subject of History, without taking notice of a very great improvement which has, of late years, begun to be introduced into Historical Composition; I mean, a more particular attention than was formerly given to laws, customs, commerce, religion, literature, and every other thing that tends to show the spirit and genius of nations. It is now understood to be the business of an able Historian to exhibit manners, as well as facts and events; and assuredly, whatever displays the state and life of mankind, in different periods, and illustrates

---

[1] *The Memoirs of the life of Edward Gibbon*, ed. G. Birkbeck Hill, New York 1900, p. 96.
[2] Greig, i. 133–8; ii. 133.

the progress of the human mind, is more useful and interesting than the detail of sieges and battles. The person, to whom we are most indebted for the introduction of this improvement into History, is the celebrated M. Voltaire, whose genius has shone with surprising lustre, in so many different parts of literature. His Age of Louis XIV. was one of the first great productions in this taste; and soon drew, throughout all Europe, that general attention, and received that high approbation, which so ingenious and eloquent a production merited.[1]

'Hume', declared Dr. Johnson, 'would never have written history, had not Voltaire written it before him. He is an echo of Voltaire.'[2] Dr. Johnson was undoubtedly expressing the contemporary view. 'In this country', Hume writes to a French correspondent, 'they call me his [Voltaire's] pupil, and think that my history is an imitation of his Siecle de Louis XIV. This opinion flatters very much my vanity; but the truth is, that my history was plan'd, & in a great measure compos'd, before the appearance of that agreeable work.'[3] Apparently Hume was too anxious to deny any possible indebtedness to *Le Siècle de Louis XIV* because he certainly had not composed 'in a great measure' his *History* before the appearance of Voltaire's work. The account, in the autobiographical note already quoted, of his beginning to write the history of the early Stuarts in 1752 is supported by letters written soon afterward. Even if he failed to obtain a copy of the French edition of Voltaire of 1751, he could scarcely have missed the translation of 1752.[4] Yet to assert that he could have imitated Voltaire is by no means to prove that he did. He had a mind far too original to be directly influenced by any man. That he was influenced by the Enlightenment, of which Edinburgh was a centre, as well as a contributor to it, few are likely to deny; but his precise obligations to that intellectual movement cannot be ascertained by a survey of a single reign which is all that is attempted here.

Hitherto a brief survey of the status of history during the first half of the eighteenth century has been followed by a briefer statement of the new conception of its scope and purpose. Henceforth

[1] For another tribute to Voltaire see Lord Chesterfield's letter to his son dated 13 Apr. 1752.
[2] *Boswell's Life of Johnson*, ed. G. Birkbeck Hill and C. F. Powell, 1934, ii. 53 and n. 2.
[3] 5 Nov. 1755. Greig, i. 226.
[4] *The age of Lewis XIV*, 2 vols. (Dublin). As early as 1739 had appeared *An essay on the age of Lewis XIV. . . . Introduction*. For general estimates of Hume as an historian see George H. Sabine, 'Hume's Contributions to the Historical Method', *Philosophical Review*, ed. J. E. Creighton and Ernest Albee, New York 1906, xi. 17–38; and J. B. Black, *The Art of History*, New York 1926, pp. 77–116.

Hume's account of the reign of James I will be examined first by
taking certain episodes in chronological order and then by selecting
certain topics. The aim is not to try to judge Hume as the historian
of England to 1688 with examples drawn from the years 1603 to
1625. The modest purpose is confined to a commentary on his
narrative of those years and no more. On certain crucial issues
Hume's narrative is compared with modern histories, but in general
it is criticized in the light of such authorities as were available at the
time it was written.

Perhaps the most original parts of the history of James's reign
deal with the relations between the King and his puritan subjects.
In Scotland he had found in the Presbyterians 'a violent turn towards republicanism, and a zealous attachment to civil liberty'. Their
ministers used the utmost freedom, disputing his tenets and cen-
suring him to his face, conduct which 'his monarchical pride could
never thoroughly digest'. He feared the popularity Puritans in both
kingdoms enjoyed on account of their austerities, being himself
inclined to 'mirth and wine, and sports of all kinds'. Therefore,
from temperament as well as policy, he was resolved to check the
spread of puritanism in England. But James's policy now as throughout his reign was wiser in purpose than prudent in means. By enter-
ing into 'frivolous disputes' James endowed them with importance
and dignity so that he could not employ 'contempt and ridicule,
the only proper method of appeasing' the quarrel with the Puritans.
After these introductory remarks Hume describes the Hampton
Court conference of 1604.[1] His only comment is that it revealed the
'political considerations which determined the king in his choice
among religious parties'.[2] A more penetrating judgement was
Gardiner's, that James 'had sealed his own fate and the fate of
England for ever', because he had closed the door not merely to
puritan demands but also to Bacon's tolerance.[3]

The first meeting of the new parliament resembled the Hampton
Court conference in that James contrived to show again his dislike
of puritanism, though this time the subject of contention was
constitutional rather than religious. Apart from a notice that the

---

[1] It is noteworthy that Hume relied upon Fuller, a second-hand authority, for his
account and ignored Barlow's *Sum of the Conference*, the sole first-hand authority with
some rather trivial exceptions. See S. R. Gardiner, *History of England 1603–1642*,
1884, i. 155, n. 1.
[2] *History of England*, London 1778, vi. 11 f. (chap. xlv). Subsequent references give
only chapter and pages in this volume.   [3] Gardiner, i. 156–7.

plague had delayed its meeting,[1] Hume plunges straight into the history of the first session. He attempts no preliminary estimate of the part parliament had hitherto taken in national affairs, no account of the representative system then prevailing, and no description of the general election. In candour, however, it should be admitted that all three points were difficult in view of the authorities at his command and the last impossible. His comment on the King's speech might be applied to most of James's utterances from the throne—that it surpassed in style and matter most productions of the age but lacked the brevity and reserve necessary on such an occasion. He then discusses at some length the cases of Goodwin and Shirley, the first establishing the right of the House of Commons to determine the validity of elections and the second the freedom of members from arrest. He introduces a digression on the revolution created in the minds of men by the improvements in the 'arts, both mechanical and liberal'. The sequel in England was that the love of freedom was 'regulated by more enlarged views' and displayed a more 'independent genius in the nation'. The King neither perceived the change nor possessed vigour enough to check its early progress. Instead, he had cherished 'a speculative system of absolute government'. He thought all legal power to be concentrated by divine right in his own person. A modern historian might find little to criticize in this description of the 'opposite disposition of parliament and prince' had it been accompanied by a reference to the new force in politics, the middle classes.

An unfortunate omission from the text was the Apology of 1604, relegated by Hume to a note. Perhaps he underestimated its importance because it was not entered in the *Journals* of the House of Commons or presented to the King. Yet, according to S. R. Gardiner, the Commons assumed in it the position 'they never quitted during eighty-four long and stormy years. To understand this apology is to understand the causes of the success of the English Revolution.'[2] The Commons' attack on the trading com-

---

[1] Hume gives the number of victims in the year 1603 as 'above thirty thousand persons' out of the 150,000 the city contained (p. 14; chap. xlv). If he intended in each case to include only those within the city proper and to ignore the suburbs adjoining he exaggerated the number of deaths. The correct figures for London within and without the walls seem to have been 30,500 (another 5,000 should be added if Westminster and other adjoining parishes are included) deaths out of a population of 250,000. See F. P. Wilson, *The Plague in Shakespeare's London*, 1927, pp. 44, 215.

[2] Gardiner, i. 186. It is odd that no reason is known why it was not presented to the King. That he saw it is evident from his speech at the end of the session.

panies with their monopolies receives more ample treatment, though Hume assumes that the charges were all true.[1] Even if they were justified, the extraordinary risks traders ran might have been enumerated. Monopolies were the more or less inevitable concomitants of mercantilism and sometimes protected key or import industries. Because companies had to bear many burdens now assumed by the government, such as policing the seas and maintaining consuls, they expected privileges which a later age found unreasonable. Monopolies of branches of foreign trade often led to high prices owing to the extortions of the crown, which levied customs and sometimes demanded loans. If, as Hume asserts, English shipping declined during the later years of Elizabeth's reign, the explanation is to be found in the prolonged depression which began in 1586 and lasted until 1604. After a brief survey of wardship and purveyance, a fuller account of the lukewarmness of parliament toward the union of England and Scotland, and a statement of the reason why in spite of its need no new supply was granted the King, Hume brings his account of the first session to a close with a notice of James's rebuke to members. He might well have enlarged on this speech because it illustrated so well the Stuarts' attitude to their parliaments.

In his narrative of the Gunpowder Plot Hume mentions, correctly, the hopes of the Roman Catholics that James, the son of Mary Queen of Scots, would be lenient toward them, but, incorrectly, that on all occasions he had declared he would enforce the penal laws. Then follows a report of a conversation in which Catesby explained to Percy why the King's assassination would be insufficient to help the Catholics, and why blowing up King, Queen, Prince, and all members of Parliament was essential in order to leave Protestants leaderless. This is a fine piece of rhetoric and presents Catesby's arguments accurately enough. Yet an inspection of the authority cited shows that much of the alleged conversation with Percy was actually addressed to a larger group. Furthermore, sentences occur at the end of Hume's account which are not to be found in the tract in question. The reference given is *History of the*

---

[1] In W. R. Scott's opinion (*The constitution and finance of English, Scottish and Irish joint-stock companies to 1720*, 1912, i. 121–8) they contained numerous inaccuracies and many distortions of facts. It is not true that England was exceptional in sanctioning privileged trading companies. '. . . on the whole, contemporary opinion appears to have been justified in regarding a new branch of foreign trade as resembling an invention, and, as such, entitled to a monopoly for a number of years'.

Gunpowder Treason,[1] which was published (and apparently written) in 1679 when Englishmen were in the midst of the excitement engendered by the Popish Plot and the Exclusion Bill to prevent the Roman Catholic heir from succeeding to the throne. Hume also uses the account of the Gunpowder Plot written by James, which was incorporated in the 1616 edition of his works, and the *State Trials*, but not the official version published in 1606 and based upon the examinations of the plotters before their trials.[2]

To turn from episodes to topics, Hume was undoubtedly correct in stressing the significance of finance and the failure of parliament to provide an adequate revenue for the crown. Lacking it, James was driven to various expedients of which the most burdensome was the grant of monopolies. However, the most destructive of these is not mentioned, namely what is generally known as Cockayne's project. This ambitious scheme led to the suspension of the privileges of the Merchant Adventurers and the prohibition of the export of undressed English woollen cloth in order that the new company Cockayne had organized should finish and dye cloth before sending it abroad. The project failed because the number of cloths that could be dyed in England was small and because foreign merchants, especially the Dutch, preferred to buy unfinished cloth and to dye it themselves. Instead of gaining a revenue of £300,000 as he hoped, James found the customs, taxes on exports as well as imports, yielded less than before, and was obliged to cancel the privileges of the new company and to restore those of the Merchant Adventurers, though on onerous terms which hampered the recovery of foreign markets. Indeed, by 1620, the export of cloth was only half of what it had been before Cockayne's project started. Because the cloth trade formed a high proportion of the total exports this interference with its natural course, combined with the harmful effect of other monopolies, was a main contributory cause of the severe depression which began in 1620 and lasted the rest of the reign. The obvious results in parliament were the impeachment of Michell and Mompesson in 1621 and the statute against monopolies in 1624, both of which Hume describes. But he fails to pause and consider whether the proceedings affected the general relations

---

[1] Reprinted in *Smeeton's Historical and Biographical Tracts*, 1820. The relevant passage is on p. 4.

[2] *A true and perfect relation of the whole proceedings against the late most barbarous traitors.* There is another official narrative with the same title except that Garnet is substituted for 'the late . . .'. Hume missed both.

of king and parliament, and whether the financial crisis explains
why members soon showed that they favoured a naval war with
Spain, which they hoped would be self-supporting, or nearly so,
rather than a war on land to recover the Palatinate, which would
cost large and irrecoverable sums.

James's visit to his native land furnishes an opportunity to describe his long struggle with the kirk in order to enlarge episcopal
authority, to establish a few additional ceremonies in public worship, and to render the civil jurisdiction superior to the ecclesiastical.
Hume begins with the reflection that 'the religious spirit, when
it mingles with faction, contains in it something supernatural
and unaccountable; and that, in its operations upon society, effects
correspond less to their known causes, than is found in any other
circumstance of government'. Their zeal for reformation led
preachers to assume a character almost prophetic or apostolic.
The mode of worship established was the simplest possible and
rites and ceremonies were rejected. The sentence of excommunica-
tion, which was passed even by inferior ecclesiastical courts, introduced into Scotland the tyranny of the inquisition without its
orderly procedure. Ministers, not content with their unlimited
jurisdiction in ecclesiastical matters, mingled politics and religion
and uttered 'the most seditious and most turbulent principles'. But
when James had the strength of England at his back he was able to
resist these 'priestly encroachments' and to impose his will upon
the northern kingdom. His 'ill-timed zeal for insignificant ceremonies', though apparently successful, was in reality resented by
all ranks of people. He should have left well alone and trusted to
time to cool fanaticism and restore the influence of 'civil and moral
obligations'.[1]

This picture of the relations of king and presbytery derives its
colour from Hume's reliance upon Archbishop Spottiswoode's *History of the Church of Scotland*. Therefore, his narrative was necessarily
one-sided.[2] Hume was writing at a time when 'the gradual substitution of the secular for the theological spirit in the conduct of
public affairs' had progressed far.[3] He started his history when the
religious group known as the Moderates was beginning to be an

---

[1] Pp. 83–92 (chap. xlvii).

[2] Hume could have used as a check on Spottiswoode the presbyterian Calderwood's *The True history of the church of Scotland*, publ. in an abridged version in 1678
at Rotterdam.

[3] P. Hume Brown, *History of Scotland*, 1902, ii. 443.

influence in the kirk. The emphasis they placed on good works rather than upon faith separated them from the Covenanters of the seventeenth century. Hume's scepticism also was not without its effect upon his treatment of the history of puritanism, and largely accounts for his derogatory remarks on ceremonialism. Nevertheless, the chief criticism of the account of James's reign in Scotland must be that it was too much confined to ecclesiastical questions. The worst fault is the failure to show how James transformed a limited into an absolute monarchy.

Ireland received a briefer treatment than Scotland. James was said to have boasted of his Irish policy as his masterpiece, and his vanity was thought not to be 'altogether without foundation'. Sir John Davies, Solicitor-General and then Attorney-General until 1619 and the only authority cited, felt that in the first nine years of his reign James had done more to reform the Irish than had been accomplished in the previous four centuries. He had abolished the Brehon law, which fixed a money payment as the sole punishment for all crimes, even murder, and the customs of gavelkind and tanistry. By the first all the land of the tribe was divided among the males, and by the second the leader of the tribe was the member of the chieftain's family who seemed best endowed with the qualities thought desirable, and not necessarily the nearest relation. In other words, James was trying to substitute English law for tribal customs. The change was too abrupt and led to the flight abroad of the northern earls of Tyrone and Tyrconnel, not mentioned by Hume, and O'Dogherty's rebellion, to which he devoted one sentence. As a result of the confiscations Ulster became crown property and its plantation followed. Hume thinks this wholly beneficial and gives James full credit for introducing 'humanity and justice among a people who had ever been buried in the most profound barbarism'.[1]

Inasmuch as Davies was one of the commissioners responsible for the scheme for the settlement of Ulster and may well have drafted it, he cannot be considered an impartial witness. Whether Hume ever studied the scheme appears doubtful because his very short account of it has errors of commission as well as of omission. The estates available were of three sizes, 2,000, 1,500, and 1,000 acres, and their new proprietors were bound to erect a castle or walled enclosure for their defence. If they were English or Scottish 'undertakers' they might not have any Irish tenants; but old officers, or

---

[1] Pp. 57–61 (chap. xlvi, at end).

other servants of the crown, 'servitors', might. Neither undertaker nor servitor was permitted to alienate his land to the native Irish, most of whom were to be banished to other parts of Ireland. However, as the number of colonists fell much below expectations, the Irish were often allowed to remain as tenants of land they regarded as rightfully their own. Naturally enough, they saw their new landlords as their oppressors. Being Roman Catholics they hated the colonists, who were often Presbyterians, as their persecutors. They eagerly awaited the day of revenge. It came in 1641.

When dealing with foreign affairs Hume did not have in print the necessary materials for a correct account, and he failed to perceive these imperfections. The page he devotes to the state of Europe in 1603 is superficial and erroneous. It begins with a bad mistake. 'When the dominions of the house of Austria devolved on Philip II, all Europe was struck with terror.' But the empire of Charles V did not pass in its entirety to Philip II. He succeeded only to Spain, the Netherlands, and the Indies,[1] and Ferdinand I was chosen Emperor. It is true that the counter-reformation had progressed so far that in any war of religion the Emperor's hereditary domains, the Catholic princes of the Empire, and the King of Spain would support the Catholic cause, while the divisions among Protestants rendered uncertain the co-operation of Lutherans and Calvinists. As to France, she was said—a little prematurely—to be united in domestic peace by Henry IV, the most 'heroic and most amiable prince that adorns modern story', who is represented as sending Rosny (later Duke of Sully) to England to propose a league to assail the Austrian dominions on every side. Hume relies uncritically upon an untrustworthy version of Sully's *Memoirs*. Actually the mission had a more modest object—to induce James to help relieve Ostend, now enduring the third year of its siege by Spanish forces. It succeeded to a limited extent, because James agreed to the bringing of volunteers, but they were to be paid by Henry, a third of the cost being deductible from the debt he had incurred from Elizabeth. This treaty, Hume concludes, was one of the wisest ratified by James, whose love of peace was 'in the highest degree advantageous to his people'.[2] James's curious notion that having been at peace with Spain as King of Scotland, his accession to the English throne ended the war, evokes

---

[1] Near the end of his reign Philip II transferred the sovereignty of the Netherlands to his eldest daughter Isabella and her husband, the Archduke Albert, a younger brother of the Emperor Rudolph II.

[2] Hume, pp. 6–8 (chap. xlv). Cf. Gardiner, i. 104, n. 1, 106–7.

the comment that he never acquired a knowledge of foreign politics and soon diminished English prestige on the Continent.[1]

The next event noticed was the sale of the cautionary towns to the Dutch which was judged to have been censured by previous historians 'beyond its real weight and importance'. James's surrender of the three fortresses garrisoned by English troops which the Dutch had handed over to Elizabeth as pledge for the repayment of loans was undoubtedly a prudent measure and a good bargain. Why Hume thought that an ambitious prince would have regarded them as his most valued possessions is not clear, especially as Hume first seemed to approve the transaction.[2]

Hume's account of the long-drawn-out negotiations for the Spanish match cannot be examined in any detail. His fundamental defect is to present the Spanish side only from English sources. However, as the historian did not consult the state papers in London, it is not surprising that he did not visit the archives at Madrid and Simancas. Had he explored them, he might have doubted his confident assertions that the 'flattering prospects' of the marriage between Prince Charles and the Spanish princess and of the restoration of Frederick of the Palatinate to his hereditary domains were blasted by Buckingham's temerity in persuading the Prince that the two of them should go in person to Madrid to claim the infanta. Hume relies entirely upon Clarendon's *History of the Rebellion* for his description how James's assent to the journey was obtained, and observes correctly that Clarendon owed his information to Sir Francis Cottington, who was directly concerned. Hardly any additional evidence has since come to light, so an historian today is still in Hume's position and must decide how much to accept of what Clarendon wrote in his old age.[3] One error at least Hume might have avoided—Buckingham did not propose the journey in the hope of overcoming the aversion Charles felt toward him, because he was already the Prince's favourite as well as the King's.[4]

By throwing all the blame on Buckingham, Hume conceals the delaying tactics of Olivares, the Spanish minister of Philip IV, and

---

[1] P. 29 (chap. xlv).   [2] Pp. 80–81 (chap. xlvii).

[3] This part of the *History of the Rebellion* is from the *Life* which Clarendon wrote during his second exile which began in 1667. Perhaps Hume accepted too readily Clarendon's conclusion that the marriage 'was solely broken by that journey' (ed. Macrae, 1888, i. 31).

[4] Clarendon (i. 21) does not assign the removal of the aversion as a cause of Buckingham's proposal, but does assert that it created an entire confidence between the Prince and the Duke after a period of jealousy.

the deceptions practised by Prince Charles. The last had solemnly promised on the eve of his departure from Madrid that the marriage should take place by proxy within ten days of the receipt of the papal dispensation. Before he left Spanish soil he ordered Bristol, the English ambassador, not to use the proxy until he received further orders from England. The excuse was to be the Prince's fear lest his bride should enter a nunnery immediately after the betrothal. This insult to the Spaniard and its timing, after the Prince was safe in the English fleet, were more blameworthy than any of Buckingham's rash acts.[1]

The negotiations ended when James demanded from Philip the restitution of the Palatinate to his son-in-law. When Philip refused to pledge himself to intervene by force of arms—a pledge which had not been required at any time before—the negotiations for a Spanish match ended. Hume refers to the charge the Spanish minister in London, Inojosa, brought against Buckingham, but although it is printed in a translation in the *Cabala* Hume's summary is not very accurate. He was not aware of the suspicion that the Lord Treasurer Middlesex had supplied the information and his ignorance prevented his connecting Inojosa's charge with Middlesex's impeachment, prompted by Charles and Buckingham.

This episode furnishes on a small scale an example of the general defect of Hume's treatment of foreign policy. He was too apt to handle it as a series of separate incidents and not to reveal its dynastic nature. What is more serious, he fails to show how it influenced the whole course of the reign and to demonstrate the interrelation of foreign and domestic policies. In Hume's characterization of James at the close of his reign the sentence occurs that 'he endeavoured, by an exact neutrality, to acquire the goodwill of all his neighbours' but 'was able to preserve the esteem and regard of none'. Whether 'exact neutrality' is the right phrase Hume's own narrative renders doubtful. Peace was preserved for the longest period known in English history before the nineteenth century, and James is entitled to much credit. Perhaps he would deserve even more if he had adopted isolation and refrained from diplomatic intervention when he had neither the intention nor the means of backing his policy with armed force. What Hume calls 'pacific and dilatory measures' raised false hopes on the Continent and irritated James's subjects at home.

[1] See Gardiner, v, chap. xlv, esp. p. 117.

Hume sums up the period of James's rule by the comprehensive verdict that 'in all history, it would be difficult to find a reign less illustrious, yet more unspotted and unblemished than that of James' in Scotland as well as England. Of the royal character he writes that scarcely any of its many virtues were 'far from the contagion of the neighbouring vices. His generosity bordered on profusion, his learning on pedantry, his pacific disposition on pusillanimity, his wisdom on cunning, his friendship on light fancy and lavish fondness.' These are most interesting opinions, worthy to be carefully weighed. Probably Hume's judgement on the reign is more likely to provoke disagreement than his character of the King. No Scottish Presbyterian or English Puritan would have used adjectives like 'unspotted and unblemished', and many an ardent patriot would have found a stronger expression than 'less illustrious'. Hume himself pronounces a severer judgement when he remarks that, except when Parliament was sitting, 'the history of this reign may more properly be called the history of the court than that of the nation'.[1] If James's policy was determined by the predominance of this or that minion (Hume's word for the favourite), it must be *ipso facto* condemned, given the characters of Somerset and Buckingham.

Hume's view of the court was the almost inevitable result of his excessive reliance upon writers like Arthur Wilson and other contemporary or near-contemporary writers who supply many dubious anecdotes about personages but devote few or no pages to underlying causes. Nevertheless, defective as his sources were, some of his omissions are surprising. Whereas S. R. Gardiner entitled his first two volumes the *History of England to the fall of Chief Justice Coke*, Hume does not even mention Coke's dismissal. He does not perceive the significance of the conflicts between the prerogative and the common law. He writes of the growing desire for freedom and attributes it to familiarity with the classics.[2] No doubt they had a share in creating a demand for greater freedom, but it was the common law which erected one of the great barriers to absolutism in Stuart England.[3] Of the common law Coke was the foremost champion and ought to have been praised on this account, the more so as his violent language against Ralegh was recorded to his shame.

[1] Pp. 63–64 (chap. xlvii).
[2] P. 21 (chap. xlv).
[3] Margaret Atwood Judson, *The Crisis of the Constitution, 1603–1645*, New Brunswick 1949, chap. ii, esp. p. 47.

Another result of Hume's concentration upon the court may be his neglect to describe the government of England. At the very end he enumerates some of the chief officers of state but without explaining their functions. He does not account for the decline of the Privy Council when compared with its position under Elizabeth. That he does not mention the committee, the ancestor of the cabinet, is natural, as little was discovered about it until the end of the nineteenth century. He says nothing at all about local government or about the justices of the peace with their significant administrative as well as judicial duties.

At the end of James's reign Hume supplies an appendix on the state of England 'with regard to government, manners, finance, arms, trade, learning. Where a just notion is not formed of these particulars, history can be little instructive, and often will not be intelligible.' No modern historian is likely to cavil at this statement, though he may wonder whether the description of the state of England should not precede rather than follow the chronological account of the reign.

The first subject was the civil government, pronounced to be more arbitrary in 1603 than in 1752 and sustained by the courts of High Commission and Star Chamber, which by themselves sufficed 'to lay the whole kingdom at the mercy of the prince'. The origins and powers of the two courts are dealt with at some length, and it is much to Hume's credit that he avoided the error of dating the Star Chamber from the Act of 1487. As to Parliament, its meetings were so precarious and short that it seemed only 'the ornament of the fabric' of government, which a great many Englishmen thought rested solely in the King. His authority was also bolstered up by the theory of the divine right of kings, a doctrine not invented by the Stuarts but used by them freely when the Puritans began to set forth opposing theories. Here as elsewhere Hume may have underestimated the Tudor parliaments and forgot the Lancastrian precedents which furnished many a weapon to the popular leaders. Perhaps he also overstates the case against the two courts. At least the Star Chamber had been a necessary curb on the powerful barons, and the High Commission probably an equally necessary means of enforcing the Elizabethan church settlement.

The section on religion is noteworthy for the assertions that the Puritans would have rejected a full toleration, and that there were no separatists in the kingdom. It is true that almost all Puritans wished to reform the Church of England rather than to leave it. Presumably if some ministers had been allowed to omit certain ceremonies and to organize themselves on a more or less presbyterian basis they would have tried to impose these innovations on other ministers of contrary views. But it is by no means certain that, if the concessions had been granted as early as the Hampton Court conference, most would not have acquiesced. There were a few separatists, originally called Brownists and later sectaries, as the Pilgrim Fathers proved in this reign and the Independents and others were to prove in the next.

Hume then passes to manners and finds they had changed rapidly between the reigns of James I and George II. The 'violent extremes' of 'industry and debauchery, frugality and scepticism' were unknown in the earlier period, which shared only 'candour, security, modesty' with the later. The nobility and gentry were distinguished from the commonalty by family pride and dignified behaviour. Wealth acquired by trade had not yet confronted all ranks and rendered money as the distinguishing feature of society. Comparisons of this nature are of little worth. What the historian should attempt is to point out the stages and degrees of changes of manners within his chosen field. In the reign of James I the significance of the lavish creations and occasional sale of peerages, the institution of the order of baronets, and the dubbing of many knights, together with the increasing importance of the gentry, might have been estimated. Jacobean art, architecture, furniture, and music deserved a paragraph or two. The rather incidental reference to imprisonment for debt might have been expanded to include some account of the poor law.

At the end of his appendix Hume turns to literature. He begins with the generalization that a very bad taste then prevailed and then furnishes examples of this fault. In Shakespeare many irregularities and even absurdities disfigured his animated scenes. 'In vain we look either for purity or simplicity of diction. His total ignorance of all theatrical art and conduct . . . we can more readily excuse than that want of taste which often prevails in his productions and which gives way only by intervals to the irradiations of genius.' Jonson fared even worse. He possessed all the learning which Shakespeare wanted but none of his genius. Both were equally wanting in taste and elegance, but Shakespeare's rude genius had totally eclipsed Jonson's rude art. Here again the reader should be given a comparison of their respective popularities at the time, not in the 1750's. Donne exhibited some flashes of wit and ingenuity, but these were buried beneath 'the hardest and most uncouth expression that is any where to be met with'. Prose was written with little regard for grammar and with no regard for 'the elegance and harmony of the period. . . . The great glory of literature in this island, during the reign of James, was Lord Bacon.' Yet as an author and philosopher he was inferior to Galileo, perhaps to Keppler. Camden's *History of Queen Elizabeth* was among the best histories written by an Elizabethan, but 'it is well known that the English have not much excelled in that kind of literature'.

Hume was not unique in advancing such opinions on the literature of the first quarter of the seventeenth century, but he belonged to a small minority among the critics of his day. Of course, he was perfectly justified in surveying literature because it formed part of the social history of the time. But he failed to link it up with other cultural manifestations and left his readers to wonder whether 'very bad taste' prevailed in all humanistic activities or even whether it was equally to be found in the 'authorized' translation of the Bible and in the first folio of Shakespeare. But the fundamental question for the historian is not so much whether taste was good or bad, but whether it had been the same under Elizabeth as under James, and, if not, what alterations had been made and what new social or economic conditions had dictated them.[1]

The above examination, necessarily brief, of parts of the history of the reign of James I suggests that Hume is very vulnerable. Sins of omission are probably more numerous than those of commission. Both come mainly from his reliance on printed materials, readily available, to the neglect of manuscripts, including the state papers. Not until 1767 did he seek and obtain permission to inspect 'all the public records and all the papers in the paper-office'.[2] There is no sign that the permission was used in order to revise the history of James I's reign. Yet Hume was conscious of the need for additional materials. When he was engaged on the Caroline age he wrote to a friend:

The more I advance in my undertaking, the more I am convinced that the History of England has not yet been written, not merely for style,

[1] For the chief differences in the literatures of the two reigns see F. P. Wilson, *Elizabethan and Jacobean*, 1946.
[2] To Andrew Miller, 17 July 1767. Greig, ii. 151. Cf. ibid., pp. 162, 172.

He would have found a great deal missing

which is notorious to all the world, but also for matter; such is the ignorance and partiality of all our historians. . . . I may be liable to the reproach of ignorance, but I am certain of escaping that of partiality.[1]

So far as the Jacobean age is concerned, Hume exhibits little partiality for groups or individuals but much prejudice against sects. His likes are less evident than his dislikes. No party is commended as strongly as the Puritans or Presbyterians are condemned.

The reign of James I was Hume's first attempt at writing history. He completed it in less than a year. In spite of its defects, it is still worth reading. In some respects it has the same interest as Bacon's *Henry VII* or Hobbes's *Behemoth*—from it we can discover how a most acute and philosophic mind viewed the history of a given period. It should be judged as a whole and in comparison with its predecessors and contemporaries. Though numerous articles, biographies, monographs, and histories now furnish corrections for every paragraph, yet the general impression of a most significant reign is far from contemptible. The reader may be reminded of an anecdote in Lockhart's *Memoirs of Sir Walter Scott*. There a sculptor, who had completed an equestrian statue of Peter the Great, is said to have given a lecture on the horse of Marcus Aurelius at Rome, during which he pointed out its many faults. In conclusion he compared this statue of a horse with his own and exclaimed, with a sigh: 'Cependant, Messieurs, il faut avouer que cette vilaine bête-là est vivante, et que la mienne est morte.'[2]

Hume's reign of James I represents a point of view which grew unfashionable a century or so ago, but one that should not be wholly neglected. For his appendix on the condition of England Hume deserves all the credit due to a pioneer in unexplored territory. Perhaps Hume's chief merit is his attempt to be comprehensive, to include Scottish and Irish history as well as, for England, foreign policy, the constitution, and economic and social changes. He may merit the criticism of going higher than his authorities allowed him safely to mount. Maybe he did. Yet admiration is due for what he achieved with the means at his disposal. He sometimes overlooked the relationship of facts, but more often connected them and formed a coherent whole. He found much of Jacobean history mere annals or compilations and left it a well-written narrative.

[1] 1882, ii. 223.
[2] To James Oswald, 28 June 1753. Greig, i. 179.

Some Jacobean Catch-Phrases and Some Light on Thomas Bretnor[1]

JOHN CROW

BEN JONSON refers, somewhat cryptically, in *The Diuell is an Asse*, to a number of men in connexion with the raising of the devil. Fitz-Dottrell says,

> I, they doe, now, name *Bretnor*, as before
> They talk'd of *Gresham*, and of Doctor *Fore-man*,
> *Francklin*, and *Fiske*, and *Sauory* (he was in too)
> But there's not one of these, that euer could
> Yet shew a man the Diuell, in true sort.

If one is interested in Bretnor, one finds that the various editors are not notably communicative. One is referred to *A Fair Quarrel*, 1617, by Middleton and William Rowley, to Middleton's *The Inner-Temple Masque*, 1619, and to *The Bloody Brother*, 1639, by Fletcher and others. Here again editors do not help much. In *The Bloody Brother*, one of the 'Five cheating Rogues' or 'Iuglers' is Norbret; it is suggested that he is Bretnor. He is thus described on g1 and g1ᵛ in a part of the play usually attributed to Jonson:

> But there's one *Norbret*, (him I never saw)
> Has made a mirrour, a meere Looking-glasse,
> In shew you'l think't no other; the forme ovall,
> As I am given to understand by letter,
> Which renders you such shapes, and those so differing,
> And some that will be question'd and give answers;
> Then has he sett it in a frame, that wrought
> Unto the revolutions of the Starres,
> And so compact by due proportions
> Unto their harmony, doth move alone

[1] In the preparation of this piece, I worked in the British Museum, in the library of Lambeth Palace, London, in the Bodleian Library, Oxford, and in the Huntington Library, San Marino, California. I desire to thank the courteous staffs of all these libraries and to acknowledge my gratitude to His Grace the Archbishop of Canterbury for permission to reprint from the books in his Palace library. I owe also a great debt of thanks to the trustees of the Huntington Library, as, while I was working there, I was receiving grants-in-aid which made it possible for me to afford to spend two consecutive summers in California.

A true automaton; . . .
He has been about it above twentie yeares,
Three sevens, the powerfull, and the perfect numbers;
And Art and Time, Sir, can produce such things.

In *A Fair Quarrel*, 1617, II^v (Dyce 3.537; Bullen 4.263), Chough says to Trim-Tram, 'What's the word? what sayes *Bretnor*', and Trim-Tram replies, after consulting an almanac, 'The word is sir, *theres a hole in her coate*'.

The quotation from the *Inner-Temple Masque* is from a conversation between the Doctor and New-Year, B4 and onwards (Dyce 5.149+; Bullen 7.211+):

N.Y. How now? What are these?
Doc. These are your Good Dayes, and Bad Dayes, Sir,
Those your Indifferent dayes, nor good, nor bad.
N.Y. But is here all?
Doc. A wonder there's so many.
How these broke loose, euery one stops their passage,
And makes inquiry after 'em.
This Farmer will not cast his seed ith' ground
Before he looke in *Bretnor*, there he finds
Some word which hee hugs happily, as, Ply the Box,
Make Hay betimes, It falls into thy Mouth.
A punctuall Lady will not paint forsooth
Vpon his Criticall dayes, twill not hold well,
Nor a nice Citie-Wedlocke eate fresh Herring,
Nor Perriwinkles;
Although she long for both, if the word be that day,
Gape after Gudgins, or some fishing phrase.
A Scriueners Wife wil not intreat the Mony-master
That lyes ith' house, and gets her Husbands children
To furnish a poore Gentlemans Extremes,
If she find, *Nihil* in a Bagge, that morning,
And so of thousand follies, these suffice
To shew you Good, Bad, and Indifferent Dayes,
And all haue their Inscriptions, here's Cock a Hoop,
This the Geere cottens, and this, Faint Heart, neuer—
These, noted Blacke for Badnesse, Rods in pisse.
This, Post for Puddings, this Put vp thy Pipes,
These blacke and white indifferently inclining
To both their natures, neither Full nor Fasting,
In Dock, out Nettle.

The Days then dance masque and antimasque, the Good Days

wearing inscriptions, 'Cocke a Hoope', 'The Geere Cottens', and 'Faint Heart Never'; the Bad Days wearing 'Rods in Pisse', 'Post for Puddings', and 'Put vp thy Pipes'; and the Indifferent Days wearing 'Neither full nor Fasting' and 'In Docke, out Nettle'.

Almanacs and prognostications by Thomas Bretnor appeared annually for the years 1607 to 1619.[1] His prognostications do not, to the lay eye, appear to differ much from the other prognostications which appeared in such numbers in the early part of the seventeenth century. There are, however, certain points of difference which are observable. All the prognosticators display a certain amount of paranoia: they were, it must be believed, to a certain extent despised and mocked. The despising and the mocking hardly seem adequate to account for the sense of persecution which they displayed. Bretnor seems to think himself more victimized than others. He complains, in the 1617 edition, that 'it was my fortune lately (courteous Reader) among others to be hardly censured, and taxed, of, and for, my good opinion and practise of Astrologie . . .'. In the following year he wrote,

I was purposed (courteous Reader) in regard of my sicknes, and the base estimation of the subiect, to haue written no more in this kind; yet thinking it fit to take my farewell of my honest frends, I am willing (*Tribulis cū factus sim*) to keepe ranke with the rest once more; and the rather to quit my selfe and the Art of an imputation of meere vanity & imposture laid vpon vs by some scrupulous and crack-brain'd sciolists, some of our owne crue also, who write Christian Almanackes forsooth, that haue small matter & lesse worth in thē. . . .

But I know I do but *laterem lauare*, for there are and euer will be some hereticks and miscreants in all professions, whom I leaue to barke at the Moone, while she whirles about the Ocean (as one infers,) and the writing of Almanackes to such or better tempered Artists, and betake my self wholly to the trade of *Hippocrates* and *Galen* . . . and so rest Studious of thy health, *Tho. Bretnor.*

Bretnor did not confine himself to the prose medium: he cultivated even in his prose a nasty lushness and periphrasis that render

---

[1] *S.T.C.* credits the Lambeth Palace Library with a complete run from 1605 to 1617: its set in fact runs from 1609 to 1619, with the year 1611 apparently absent. In the British Museum are the editions for 1607, 1611, 1612, 1615–17. The Bodleian Library has 1613 and 1615 to 1619; in the Huntington Library are 1615–18. University Library, Cambridge, is credited with 1618. The 1630 edition given to the Museum by *S.T.C.* is not by Thomas Bretnor. The libraries here mentioned have enabled me to see a run of the Bretnor almanacs and prognostications from 1607 to 1619, complete but for the year 1608, which I have been unable to trace.

him unlovable to the modern reader. When he desires to say that there will be eclipses, he does it thus: 'Foure times this yeere will part of this Vniuerse be depriued for a small time, of the Sunne his beautious beames, and twise will the Selenean Inhabitants suffer the same accident . . .' and again, '. . . at that very instant will our Grandame *Ops* eclipse and hide the bright beames of sole-shining *Sol*, frō the view of the Lunar Inhabitants . . .' (1613). In 1616 he writes, 'Twise this yeare will most of the Selenian inhabitants, and twise also will some part of our earthy-Orbists, bee depriued of all, or most part of the Sun his sole-heating light; which howsoeuer it may seeme strange and incredible to my friend M. *Dancy*, and others of his ranke and skill (who with *S. Thomas* will beleeue nothing but what they see and feele) . . .', and so on and so forth.

In 1615 he printed the following verses,

> We gape for Gudgions, listen after newes,
>   Are ner'e content with state what er'e it be,
> We blame the times, and seasons doe accuse,
>   When wicked men are cause hereof we see:
> What sinne, what vice, hath reigned heretofore,
> That is not rifer now a great deale more?
>
> Come are the times that *Chaucer* earst foretold,
>   Wherein Ambition beares away the bell,
> The lofty-looker must not be controld,
>   Tis policie the poorer sort to quell.
> He's counted wise that can his neighbour tangle,
> And hee's the man that now a dayes can wrangle.
>
> Most men respect not what they say or doe,
>   Their fist is close, their conscience wide and large,
> If by some quirke in law they can't vndoe,
>   A whit they eare [*lege* care] not how their soule they charge.
> Religion's now a cloake to couer sinne,
> O would to God these days had neuer been!

In 1616 he struck a blow, in verse, at disbelievers in judicial astrology:

> Let *Picus* prate, and let *Pererius* pine,
>   Let *Dauncy* dote, and let *Erastus* frowne,
> Let *Chambers* chafe against the cleere sun-shine,
>   And let *Cavvigny* all his senses drowne:
> Let ech malicious brat that ere was bred
> Disgorge his spleene and rip his idle head.

'Tis out of malice or meere ignorance,
  These Sophisters 'gainst nature so combine:
For had they knowledge, or some little glaunce
  Of her effects, her force, and powers diuine;
Vermillion blushes would their faces die,
Or else, perforce, they must say tongue I lie.

To proue these Buzzards skill, let any man
  At full, or change, or any dire aspect
Of chilly *Saturne* or aduring *Mars,*
  Or sow, or plant, or other thing effect,
And he shall find for all his taken paine,
That cost and labour is but spent in vaine.

Did not the great *Commander* of this Vniuerse
  In one sole day these heauenly Sphears create?
And did he not ordaine by their commerce,
  That like his like should still ingenerate?
He did, he did, with such an awfull hand,
That neuer since no creature could withstand.

Then sith he hath such power to Starres infus'd
  Is't 'gainst his glory they [the] same dilate?
If in their Orbs such vertue be inclus'd,
  Is't fault in vs their forces to relate?
No, God is great and will be prais'd of all,
He's holy too in workes both great and small.

Should we affirme the Planets wanted force
  Or inbred power t'infuse or work at all,
Yet by reflection from that heauenly source
  None dare deny their might Imperiall,
Iehoue hath endow'd bright *Phœbus* with such power
That his effects are seene and felt each hower:
Blush then for shame *Ger. Dauncy* with the rest,
To foole ones selfe in Print it is no iest.

  Soli & vni trino Deo gloria.

Bretnor allowed the rein to his muse on a number of occasions,
but to quote extensively might suggest a prejudice against a no
doubt worthy man. Here finally is one of his poems for the year
1617,

  Now farewell friendship! Charitie *adieu,*
    'Tis not a world to giue, but catch and snatch.
  The vertuous minded mourne, lament and rue,

That in our bosomes we such rancor hatch,
And still our ruines with oppression patch:
For there's no day, no houre, no moment free,
But some distasts by vile ones offered be.

The wily worldling with his cunning shifts
    Out-reacheth farre the seely peasants straine,
O'r-quelling him and all his simple drifts,
    Per fas & nefas, both by might and maine,
    Till all his sources he doe ouer-draine,
And thinkes besides that all's too little too,
For his adherents and their wicked crew.

The soule-her-sweet-synceritie's made sowre,
    With leauen of such hypocrites as leaue her:
Integrity thrust out of her faire bowre
    Mans heart, whereof fowle enuy doth bereaue her,
    And dispossest, where's he that will receiue her?
No Publican, no Parasite, no Knaue,
Can e're conuey a saued soule to graue.

It is not as a poet that I desire to reintroduce Bretnor to the world. Every year, from 1609 to 1618, he gives in his prognostication a list of good days and evill days—those, presumably, on which it would be wise, or unwise, for such buzzards as Ger. Dauncy to 'sow, or plant, or other thing effect'—and for good days and evill days he provides a little motto or catch-phrase. The complete list of these provides a collection of catch-phrases that should be of interest to the student of the colloquial English of the first quarter of the seventeenth century. I have listed them below, arranged by myself into some kind of alphabetical order.[1]

It must not be thought that Bretnor prepared a proverb collection, or even a self-conscious collection of the catch-phrases of his

---

[1] I have placed them in two separate lists, those for the evill days and those for the good days. The order is strictly alphabetical on the assumption that the spelling is modernized, even though I have not modernized it: thus when Bretnor spells as 'thorow' what we should today spell 'through', I have followed his spelling but placed his phrase in its place as though it had been modernized; thus, in the 'good' list I have put in order, after 'A thriftie companion', 'Through the bryers' and then 'Thorow the fire'. Initial articles have been printed but I ignore them in the alphabetical order: I take notice of them when they appear medially in the phrases. After the phrases I note the months in which they appear, using the letters A to L to indicate the twelve months in order. Thus, after 'A trustie Damon' appear the notes '11 F, 12 L': this I intend to mean that the phrase was used by Bretnor in June 1611 and December 1612. 'Thorow the fire' was used twice in the year 1618, in January and in March; I indicate this by '18 AC'.

time. Many of the phrases are not to be regarded as proverbial; some are merely to encourage the believer to do, or not to do, his business on a given day. It does so happen, however, that a number of the encouragements are proverbs (or pieces of proverbs) or catch-phrases. The collection has, therefore, some value to the lexicographer and the collector of proverbs; it may be held, therefore, that the presence of a phrase in a list for any year argues that Bretnor regarded the phrase as being current at the time, in the previous year, when he was composing his list. Many of the phrases are to be found in the stock seventeenth-century proverb-collections, whence they have been collected into the important proverb-dictionaries of the present century, Apperson, the *Oxford Dictionary of Proverbs*, and Tilley. It is, generally speaking, not difficult to search around and find earlier examples for many of the proverbs in Tilley; Bretnor provides a quantity of earlier examples. For 'As kind as a kite', which Bretnor uses for the year 1610, Tilley's first example is in 1639 (Tilley, K 113). Bretnor's 'A bone to gnaw' is, presumably, Tilley's (B 516) 'Gnaw the bone that is fallen to thy lot', first recorded in 1678. I shall not multiply examples.

Many of Bretnor's mottoes are not found in the modern collections. Some are just not proverbs at all (e.g. 'Alas poore fellow'), but many have a convincing ring to them: Tilley's N 316, 'At Nevermass', provides an obvious analogue to Bretnor's 'At Nihilmas' (which he uses not only in his list in 1618 but also in a paranoid attack on Gervase Dauncy in his address to the courteous reader in the same year). Bretnor's '*Nihil* in a bag' is Tilley's N 159, 'Nifles in a bag', or 'Nichils in a bag'; Ray quotes it as 'Nichils in nine pokes'.

I should defend my making of two lists, the 'good' mottoes and the 'evill' mottoes on the ground that the two lists differ in character. The 'good' list contains a far higher proportion of mere short remarks that are neither proverbs nor catch-phrases. It seems to me, also, of interest to allow the 'good' to be inspected separately so that it may be seen how agreeably pessimistic Bretnor was even when he was speaking words of encouragement. It will be seen that a number of his phrases are common to both lists. He was clearly a man with an admirably gloomy turn of thought and it is an invigorating experience to drop the eyes down the 'evill' list and feel the gloom gathering thickly around one. To do this reproduces well Bretnor's obvious feeling that all friends were false friends, that every cloud had a leaden lining, and that apparent success is interesting only as the precursor of disaster.

The 'good' lists tend to contain vapid little *dicta* which remind the modern reader of cracker-mottoes, the notices in 'snakes-and-ladders' boards, and the astrological nonsense which one finds in large-circulation newspapers.

Bretnor's lists appear from the year 1609 to 1618: there are none in the 1607 edition nor in the 1619 edition. It seems unlikely that there were any in the 1608 edition. The idea of having such lists was not original with Bretnor. They are found also in the prognostications of Edward Gresham, examples of whose work for 1604, 1606, and 1607 are given, in *S.T.C.*, as surviving. I print Gresham's list for 1607, and it may be interesting to observe that some of Gresham's 'evill' mottoes reappear as Bretnor's good ones.

EVILL DAYS

January
    Froward, infortunate, and vaine
    Ouer shooes, ouer bootes
    Freends cãnot help it
    Too hote, to last long
    Crosse and cumbersome
    Hardly obtaining
    A lightning before death

February
    Fortune out-runs thee
    Build castles in the ayre
    A mighty Distraction
    Sylla & Charibdis
    It will not goe forward
    A baite for a foole

March
    A wet Eele by the tayle
    From the sunne to the fire
    Sweet meate, sowre sawce
    Thou fishest in the ayre
    Cruell & crafty
    As ill as he can
    A fruitlesse fruite
    Out of his malice
    Much labor lost

April
    Enuie and malice
    A vaine florish
    Both labour and cost
    Much labour, yet loose it
    A dangerous designement
    Suspicious complotting
    A halter comes after
    Fearefull, not fatall
    Crafty companions
    In his power to hurt the
    No hope of good hap

May
    A subtile stratageme
    Some doubtfull difference
    Much adoe about nothing
    All thieves for company
    Nothing will help it
    Combersome Caytifes
    Vntoward and peeuish

June
    No reconciliation
    Mosse and sand
    A *Disdiapason*
    A priuy *Decision*

Vncertaine rouing
Deadly foode
Misery and mischiefe

July

A medley of mischiefe
More hast, worse speede
No evasion
Close complotting
Too small purpose
Falshood in friendship
Haplesse and hopelesse
Crafty and cruell
Doubtful, not desperate
A vaine florish
The sleeping Lion

August

Margery good-cow
A woolfe in a lambs skin
It will not doo
Deall not with edge-tooles
Two heads in one hood
A running sore
The Hare to the kibble
Misery & mischiefe
Vntoward & froward

September

His wits be breecht
A perrilous pause
Thy cap at the wind
Perfidious trechery
The end wil be nought
Dissembled knauerie

Most hast, worse speede
Thou maist be well ducked
A stubborne old knaue
Thy purpose will fayle
Beware thy necke

October

Forbeare for better
Forked, and froward
— No good ankerage
Pride in Prelacie
What mischiefe he can
— A religious cloake
He is not of meanes
From bad to worse

November

It sutes not such a coate
Looke to thine owne state
A vaine enterprise
Double dissembling
Trust no fayre tales
Twixt rocks & syrts

December

Puissant enemies
Idle busines
Scylla & Charibdis
Mischieuous enough
Scornefull disdaine
Proude & presumptuous
Vnkind and peruerse
After the Feast
A vaine attempt
Keepe out of his cloutches

GOOD DAYS

January

Mutuall assent
As it is managed
Better yᵗ, then nothing
Each way good liking
Better at last
Not very secure
Firme, if well followed
Backwards awhile

February

The longer, more lasting
Beginne well, and end well
Pretty deuise, though hardly con-
triued
Close counsell, and cunning
All wil befriend thee
It is for thy good

March

Variety is pleasing
Friendly & fauourable
Hewing wil make it handsome
Wise & good policie
Secrete loue
All alike
Harsh, but harmlesse
Indifferent affecting
Thou shalt recouer it

April

Good if warily handled
Better will come of it
No doubt of good liking
Hart and good will
All speedy successe
Some-thing slow, but sure
All at thy pleasure
Take a true temper
Followe it, and feare not

May

With much a doe
Mutuall consent
A kind combination
Sure and close
Lust if not loue
Meetely well tempered
Friendlie and faithfull

June

A little fresh gayle
Kind entertainement
Friendly aduise
Pretty advancement
Good if it were got
A little reclayming
As kind as can be
Better is toward

July

Loue, though light
Speedy attempt
The sooner the better
Good & worth taking
Iewels and pictures
Light suite

A speedy conclusion
Friendly affection
Industry doth much
Constant enough
Not too forward

August

Well pleased all
As it is followed
A friendly greeting
A princely fauour
Its vnder ground
Shee will not deny thee
Meetly good meaning
As far as in his power
Rouze vp your spirits
A while at the first
A permanent profit

September

Some hope at last
Hote for the while
A great mans fauour
He wil be in case
No great amends
On the mending hand
Something slippery
After a while
What may bee, will bee
More prest then powerfull
Sticke to it, and take it
What one may not, another will

October

When hee comes to his kingdome
Goe to betimes
A sacred synode
When that is doone
Better but for Sycophants
He will bend to thy becke
Firme and stedfast
Forward, if followed
Wily wench
I desire to doo it

November

Latter end better
It is easily got

Doubtfull & difficult
As clean as may be
Good agreement
He is almost fit
Court her in time
Most hartily welcome
Some iewells bee perished, all els is good
Hardly a while
After one brunt better
The world is amending

December
Industry must do it
Firme friendship
Speedy, if profitable
One helps another
Religious and honest
An honorable hart
Wit and great wisdome
On further aduise
Not all expectance
No time too late
It taries the taking
Worse with better

Here, then, is Bretnor's list of Evill days and Good days. I have numbered them in the left-hand margin for convenience when I come briefly to say something about them below. When I do come to make references, if there is any doubt in which list is found the phrase to which I am referring, I place before the number an *e* or a *g* to indicate that it is in the 'evill' or good list.

EVILL DAYS

Aboue thy reach: 11 A
Account not of it: 11 H
Ad grecas Calendas: 12 G, 15 L, 16 J, 17 H, 18 K
Adieu sheats: 09 F
5 Aduenture and loose: 12 E
An afterclappe: 14 H
After death, the phisition: 10 D, 12 F
After mirth mourning: 11 F
After mirth sorrow: 10 J
10 Against the haire: 11 H
Against the streame: 10 E, 11 C, 12 L
Alas poore fellow: 18 D
All a mort: 15 C, 18 H
All blankes: 17 I
15 All by ease: 09 J
All couet, all lose: 11 F, 12 I (couer), 13 C, 16 A
Alls but in vaine: 18 H
All's dasht: 11 F, 18 G
Al's fish that coms to net: 11 G
20 Alls lost: 13 K, 18 E

Alls squat: 14 F
All vpon hands: 11 I
All will not serue: 14 G (Alll ill), 18 B
Almost desperate: 15 E
25 Almost impossible: 09 B, 16 B
Among the bryers: 11 G
An other time, not now: 10 C
As bad as may be: 10 E
As bare as Iob: 10 E
30 As bitter as Gall: 13 E
As false as Iudas: 13 F
As good at home: 09 I
As good be idle: 11 G
As good not: 09 C
35 As good sit still: 09 D, 10 A, 11 A, 14 E, 17 F
As ill as may be: 09 D
As kind as a kite: 10 B, 11 A
As mute as a herring: 16 I
As vnkinde as may be: 10 A
40 At a stand: 11 L, 14 E
At daggers drawing: 12 B, 16 K, 18 K

At his wits ende: 12 C, 13 D, 14 E,
17 CD
At latter Lammas: 16 K, 17 G,
18 F
At least in sight: 11 C
45 At *Nihilmas:* 18 H
At open defiance: 14 H, 16 G,
17 G, 18 CG
At swords point: 14 G, 18 A
At the last gasp: 13 I, 14 K
At too high a rate: 11 H
50 Auoyde his companie: 10 H
Back againe's better: 10 A, 14 D
A backe reckoning: 09 D, 11 I,
13 E, 14 C, 15 H
Backward, and backward: 16 K
Backward and forward: 11 H
55 Backwards is best: 11 D
A bad bargaine: 12 E, 15 G, 16 F
A baite for a foole: 17 K
Bane in the end: 11 C, 12 D, 15 G
A bare excuse: 11 G
60 A barker, no biter: 09 G
Base mettle: 14 H
Beaten with the spit: 10 G
Bee at no cost: 10 A
Be better aduised: 16 DG, 17 F
65 Beggery in the end: 13 C
Beleeue not a word: 15 EK
Be not so hot: 17 C
Be not too bold: 12 C
Be not too busie: 16 I, 18 G
70 Be not too forward: 13 G
Be not too hastie: 11 E
Be not too hot: 09 C
Be not too lusty: 12 F
Bent to do euill: 12 J
75 Bent to do mischiefe: 12 H
Be ruled by reason: 10 H
Better be idle: 10 E
Better not at all: 09 B
Betwixt two extremes: 13 G
80 Betwixt 2, stooles: 14 J
Beware a by-blow: 13 C, 14 G
Beware an afterclap: 14 B
Beware a stab: 16 E
Beware hucksters handling: 11 I
85 Beware the afterclap: 11 E

Beware the halter: 10 F
Beware the next: 09 H
Beware the old one: 09 A, 10 L
Beware the rope: 09 K
90 Beware the stab: 11 G, 12 A, 13 A
Beware the worst: 13 H
Beyond his element: 16 L
Beyond thy reach: 10 D, 16 J
Bid farewell friendship: 17 K
95 Bittersweet: 12 F
Bit with a blacke frost: 11 A, 12 I
Blacke in the mouth: 15 D
Blame none but thy selfe: 10 D
Blesse thee from him: 15 B, 16 B
100 A blind bargaine: 10 CE, 11 A,
12 J, 15 B
A blocke in the way: 13 I, 14 A
A blow on the blind side: 12 G,
13 FJ, 16 K, 17 I
Blowes a breeding: 11 K
A blow with a browne bill: 10 A
105 A blow with a witnes: 15 H
Bould bayard: 09 I
A bone to gnaw: 12 J
A bone to pick: 18 E
A bootles enterprise: 14 K
110 Bootlesse expectation: 11 I
Bootlesse importunitie: 09 D
Boo-peepe: 09 L
A bow too short: 13 J, 14 L, 16 A,
17 J
A braine-sicke humour: 09 L
115 A brain-sicke person: 12 I
A Brazen face: 16 I
Bread and a serpent: 09 B, 10 H,
13 D, 16 K, 17 H
Breath awhile: 10 B, 14 I
Brickle ware: 12 I
120 Bridle thy humour: 12 I
Broyles a breeding: 12 H
Budge not: 11 I
Busy about nothing: 16 F, 17 E,
18 J
Busie to no purpose: 10 D
125 But a brauado: 10 A, 14 L, 15 F
But a dead man: 09 K, 13 G, 15 E
But chaunce medley: 14 C
But crosse carding: 13 A

But hard hap: 15 A
130 But hardly hazarded: 13 H
But harsh entertaynement: 13 H
But ifs and ans: 12 D
But in a hard case: 14 D
But lost labour: 13 A
135 But meere blasts: 13 K
A by-blow: 10 E
By polling and shauing: 11 I
By weeping crosse: 10 B
Care will kill thee: 09 G
140 Care will not cure: 10 E
The case is altered: 10 J, 14 H
A case of vnkindnesses: 17 I
Castles in the aire: 12 E, 15 B,
    16 B, 18 AD
Catch at the Moone: 12 A, 14 A,
    15 C, 16 C
145 Catch at the wind: 18 E
Cauilous carousing: 09 H
Cease thy suite: 14 B
A cholerick caitife: 17 H
Climbe not too high: 10 E
150 Close and counterfeit: 16 L
Close and craftie: 09 A
Close confederacie: 09 E
Close conueyance: 11 L, 14 D
Close practising: 17 A
155 Close vndermining: 11 E
Cold and comfortles: 09 I, 17 L
A cold Christmas: 10 L
Cold comfort: 13 H, 14 E
A cold sute: 11 L, 12 C
160 Come not at Court: 10 I
Come not too neare: 11 K, 16 D
A comfortles Caroll: 09 L
Contend not with him: 12 D
Contention killes thee: 09 A
165 A cooling card: 16 I
Cost ill bestowed: 15 K
A counterfeit Cullion: 16 E, 17 J
A curtesie to blame: 13 K
Crabbed and cruel: 09 A
170 Crabbed and vnkinde: 15 L
A crabbed answere: 13 D
A crabbed carle: 10 B, 14 DI
Crackt in the cariage: 10 D
Craftie conueyance: 09 F

175 Crosse and intricate: 15 J
Crosse carding: 10 G, 11 J, 12 A,
    14 H, 16 AH, 17 A, 18 J
A crosse companion: 09 C
Crosse crabbednes: 09 E
Crosse not his humour: 10 I, 13 A
180 A Crow ith corne: 18 L
A Crow to pull: 09D, 10L, 16L, 18L
A cruell incumbrance: 10 L
Cruelly minded: 09 E
Crueltie is crossed: 10 C
185 Cunning cannot helpe: 12 H
Curst cow short hornes: 12 K
A dangerous designment: 09 A
Dangerous drawing: 11 D
A dangerous incounter: 15 B
190 Danger towards: 12 F
Dasht out of countenance: 14 J,
    17 C
A deadly enemy: 13 C
Dead on the neast: 11 L, 13 K,
    14 GK, 16 F, 17 E
A dead reckoning: 16 H
195 Deale not with him: 10 A
A deepe dissembler: 17 K
Deepe dissimulation: 12 K
De meure vous la: 18 G
Desperat and deadly: 09 H
200 A desperate designe: 12 D
A desperat designment: 16 K
A desperat disease: 09 J
A disastrous enterprise: 09 A
Dishonestly minded: 11 I
205 A displeasing humour: 09 F (vis-
    pleasing)
A doubtfull demurre: 09 K
Doubtfull dissimulation: 09 F
Downe the wind: 12 C, 15 D, 18 C
A dreadfull designe: 17 K
210 Dreame not of it: 10 B
Each way to want: 16 J
An Eele by the taile: 16 G
The end is doubtfull: 13 E
An endles labour: 10 F
215 An endlesse peece of work: 17 A
An intising baite: 11 I
Enuious in the end: 09 A
Euerything goes crosse: 17 A

Euill begin worse end: 12 H

220 Exceeding dismall: 14 E

Faire and softly: 09 G

Faire face, false heart: 12 E

Faire out of square: 12 L

A false *alarum*: 11 I, 15 H, 16 G

225 False harted: 14 D

Falshood in friendship: 11 K, 18 L

Far fetch'd and deare bought: 17 B

Fast in the bryars: 12 F, 13 BH

Fatall in the end: 09 B, 16 D

230 The Fatt's in the Fire: 14 A

Fawning flatterie: 09 F

A feather for a foole: 15 L

Feeble footing: 10 F

A faigned Florish: 10 B

235 A fig for my god sonne: 18 D

Fire and tow: 11 H

Fishing in the aire: 17 H

Fiue and a reach: 09 EL

Flat foolery: 17 D

240 Flie golding: 14 B

Forlorne hope: 12 C, 13 K

Forward & fatall: 12 A

Foundred in the way: 10 G

Frame some excuse: 09 L, 17 A

245 Franticke humours: 09 H

From euill to worse: 09 C, 10 I, 11 C

From piller to post: 18 G

From pomp to pouerty: 18 J

From the teeth outward: 15 L, 16 K

250 A fronting aduersary: 11 D

Froward and fatall: 09 E, 17 A

Froward and feeble: 14 E

A fruitlesse expectation: 09 J

Full of deceipt: 14 A

255 Full of melancholy: 13 F

Gainst wind and tide: 13 G

Gall in the end: 10 A

The gallowes grones: 13 J, 16 G

Gape after gudgions: 14 J, 16 C, 17 F, 18 F

260 Gape not after it: 11 B, 14 G

A graine too light: 12 L

Graple not with him: 11 A

Great boast, small roast: 09 H

A grieuous displace: 10 F

265 Guld in the end: 13 A

Had I wist: 10 K, 11 A

A haggard, no Hawke: 09 H

Hand ouer head: 10 C, 11 E, 14 L, 17 K

A hard bargaine: 09 F, 18 A

270 Hard buckling: 14 F

Hard hap: 09 B, 11 C

Hard is thy hap: 14 H

A hard reckoning: 18 I

Hard to please: 09 E

275 Harme hatch, harme catch: 09 C, 16 H, 17 F

A harsh beginning: 18 A

A harsh farewell: 17 L

Harsh in the handling: 09 D

Haste makes wast: 09 C, 11 H, 12 E, 17 F

280 Haunt not high places: 17 D

Haunt not his company: 11 G

Haunt not his ghost: 15 D

Hearken not to it: 11 D

Hart on his halfe-penny: 09 F, 10 J, 16 F

285 A heauy aduersary: 13 G

Heauie and hartlesse: 09 J

He ieopards a ioynt: 12 G

He lackes wit: 18 B

He lyes at the lurch: 13 L

290 He pleades pouerty: 16 L

He wants performance: 11 L

He will carry no coles: 12 E

He will fob thee off: 10 F

He will looke awry: 16 D

295 He will pleade pouerty: 17 L

He will turne Turke: 10 L, 16 J

The high-way to Tiburne: 16 F

His boult is shot: 09 L

His cake is dow: 15 C, 17 C

300 His credite is crackt: 10 L

His Geese be Swannes: 101 K

His part is pinkes: 17 E, 18 BI

His spirits are spent: 12 L

His wittes are breecht: 10 E, 11 D, 16 F, 17 H

305 Hony and gall: 09 J

Hopefull, yet helples: 09 C
Hopelesse expectatiō: 11 L, 16 G
I am sorry for thee: 14 K
An idle designe: 13 K
310 An idle iourney: 10 I, 11 J, 12 D,
    13 I, 16 B, 17 G, 18 A
An idle pretence: 11 L, 12 A
An idle request: 12 L
Idly disposed: 12 H
Ill luck towards: 16 E
315 In a bottomlesse bag: 14 H, 16 C
In a browne study: 13 I, 16 I, 17 D
In a deepe distraction: 17 C
In a deep melancholy: 16 L
In a desprat case: 10 K, 11 G, 12 B,
    16 A
320 In a franticke fit: 12 L
In a hard case: 18 C
In a heauy case: 15 B, 16 L
In a hurly-burly: 17 E
In a mad taking: 17 C
325 In a melancholy dumpe: 14 A
In an euill temper: 13 E
In a pecke of troubles: 10 G, 11 B,
    12 K, 17 H
In a petty chafe: 16 E
In a pittifull taking: 12 D, 15 E,
    16 I, 18 D
330 In a quandary: 15 H, 17 K, 18 C
In a vile puzzle: 12 B
In a world of woe: 11 B, 17 D
In comber and care: 13 L, 14 EL,
    17 F
In deadly danger: 12 H, 13 BL,
    17 L
335 In desperation: 18 E
In dock out nettle: 16 L
In great extremitie: 14 I
In hope of good-hap: 16 G
In hucksters handling: 10 I, 11 E,
    15 A
340 In shew not in substance: 17 L
Insolent and proud: 09 J
In the way to want: 13 A
In vtter dispaire: 14 C
Inueterate malice: 13 F
345 It bites sore: 18 G
It boads ill luck: 16 F

It bootes not: 11 A, 18 I
It bootes not to brag: 12 D, 13 G,
    14 E
It cannot end well: 17 E
350 It is all in vaine: 16 L
It is base mettall: 10 G
It is but a dream: 12 B, 13 B, 16 C,
    18 K
It is but a flourish: 13 L
It is but a folly: 10 D, 13 C
355 It is but in vaine: 10 C, 12 I, 13 C
It is not for thee: 14 C
It lyes on bleeding: 15 I
It sorts not his humour: 13 G
It will not cotten: 15 D, 17 A
360 It will not fadge: 09 G, 12 I, 15 A,
    17 I
It will not prosper: 13 G
It will not quite cost: 15 C
A Iewish tricke: 18 F
Keepe aloofe: 14 F
365 Keep out of his clutches: 14 A,
    17 B
Keepe out of his reach: 10 K
Keepe thy standing: 09 B
A kisse and a curse: 09 D
Kisse the hares foote: 14 I
370 A knaue in a corner: 10 L
A knaue in graine: 10 H
Labour and lose: 11 E
Labour and loose it: 14 A
Labour in vaine: 10 E
375 A lash at last: 12 F, 14 D, 15 J, 16 I
Laterem lauas: 15 A, 17 I
A lazie mate: 14 F
A lightning before death: 10 C
A lyon in the way: 09 D, 10 I
380 Little hope in it: 16 C
Long haruest, little corn: 12 J,
    13 F
Looke about thee: 09 H, 12 C,
    14 J, 15 G, 16 E, 17 B
Looke ere thou leape: 10 C (you),
    11 G, 12 B
Looke for no goode: 13 H
385 Looke for no mercie: 15 H
Looke not after it: 16 H
Looke not to thriue: 13 E, 14 I

Looke to thy Purse: 10 FL
Looke to thy selfe: 13 A, 14 F
390 Loose time and tide: 14 K
Losse vpon losse: 11 L, 13 I, 15 D,
16 C, 18 B
Lost labour: 13 H, 15 A
Loues labour's lost: 09 L, 11 K,
12ͺE
A lurch at last: 09 E
395 Mad medling: 10 A (hyphen-
ated), 12 K, 14 K, 15 J, 16 B, 17 G
A mad motion: 18 C
Madnesse to meddle: 12 H
Make no great haste: 13 A, 14 G
A malitious baite: 09 H, 12 G
400 Malicious enterprise: 11 I
Maliciously minded: 09 K, 10 B
March not too fast: 10 D
The market is marde: 11 G
Mar'd in the hewing: 16 J
405 Mard in the making: 12 E
The match is marred: 10 F
Meddle not: 09 E
Meddle on nether side: 16 E
Meddle on no hand: 13 E, 14 L,
17 J
410 A meer cheater: 18 J
A mischiefe intended: 16 J
Miserie in the end: 10 D, 15 C
Misse the Cushion: 09 I, 10 A,
12 K, 13 BH, 15 I
More bold thē welcome: 17 J
415 More hast then good speed: 12 J,
13 BE
More haste, worse speed: 15 F,
16 K, 17 J, 18 J
More haste, worst speed: 10 B,
17 D
More then desperat: 15 I
Mountaines turn molehils: 09 F
420 A mournefull departure: 10 J
Much adoe, little sport: 13 D, 16 D
Much boast small roast: 11 F
Much distempered: 12 D
Much ouermatched: 14 F
425 Neither at hom, nor abroad: 10 L
Neither barrel better herring:
10 G

Neither egge nor bird: 11 D
Neyther fish nor flesh: 11 F, 13 D
Neyther full nor fasting: 13 D,
18 B
430 Neither good egge nor bird: 11 D
Neither health nor wealth: 11 J
Neither heere nor there: 09 I,
13 I
Neither late nor early: 12 D
Neither will serue: 11 C
435 Neuer the neere: 12 A
Next to nothing: 15 F
Nihil in a bagge: 17 C, 18 C
A nimming nipper: 11 K
No better: 09 B
440 No boote for thee: 09 G
No braines at all: 16 H
No concord at all: 09 C
No euasion: 11 G
No fast footing: 16 E
445 No fauour at court: 11 C
No fence for it: 17 J
No good āchorage: 14 B
No good meaning: 14 C
No helpe in it: 09 G
450 No hold to be taken: 13 K
No hope in it: 09 J
No hope of recouery: 12 L
No parley at Court: 09 K
No pleasure in it: 10 I
455 No recouery: 18 F
No redemption: 14 D
No such matter: 10 G, 11 K, 12 F
Not all of the best: 09 C
Not as he seemes: 09 C
460 Not at home: 09 E
Not at home nor abroad: 11 B
Not easely acted: 09 L
Not for thy turne: 13 F
Nothing but blowes: 13 D
465 Nothing but frownes: 13 G, 14 I
Nothing but shales: 10 C, 12 B,
15 G
Nothing successful: 09 C
Nothing to the purpose: 12 A,
13 B (to purpose), 15 A
Not one haire to chuse: 16 F
470 No true friendship: 18 I

Not to be found: 09 E
Not to be had: 13 A
Not to be spoken withall: 09 K
Not too fast: 09 A, 11 D, 14 H, 15 E
475 Not too fast for falling: 17 B
Not within compasse: 11 I
Not worth a black dog: 16 A
Not worth a straw: 10 C
Not worth the while: 11 BF, 12 C
480 Not worth whistling: 14 F, 15 H (Nor), 16 D
Nought but disgrace: 11 L, 13 B, 14 B
No way good: 09 A
No way to win: 11 H
On a slippery pin: 10 K
485 Open enmity: 12 E
An opposite enemy: 14 B
Out at elbowes: 12 K
Out at heeles: 15 F
Out of all hope: 10 K, 12 J, 13 CK, 14 C
490 Out of his bias: 14 J
Out of his element: 17 B, 18 C
Out of his wits: 18 H
Ouer head and eares: 11 E, 13 L, 14 L
Ouer the left shoulder: 11 D, 12 E, 15 F, 16 B, 18 I
495 Ouerthrowne by law: 12 K
Paines preuaile not: 09 E
Paines without profit: 10 E
A passionat qualme: 09 K
Past act and recouerie: 09 J, 10 H
500 Past all hope: 15 K
Past all redemption: 10 K, 11 K
Past grace: 18 E
Past God-forbids: 16 D
Past hope of recouery: 15 A
505 Past looking i'th mouth: 17 G, 18 L
Patience perforce: 10 K
Pause a while: 09 J, 11 A
Peeuish and paultrie: 09 A
Pel-mel: 12 L
510 Pernicious plotting: 13 F
Pierce penniles: 09 I, 17 I

A plaine pollicie: 09 B
A point next the worst: 12 BG
Powling and shauing: 10 D
515 Poore and peruerse: 12 G
Post festum: 12 H
Post for a pudding: 16 A, 17 L, 18 A (for puddings)
Post not too fast: 11 A
A potent aduersary: 16 C
520 Presse not too forward: 12 A
Prittily preuented: 11 F
Pride and beggery: 15 L
Pride will haue a fall: 10 C, 11 E, 12 H
Priuily preuented: 12 I (Priuity)
525 A priuy practise: 12 A
Priuy practises: 16 C
A professed enemy: 17 L
Prouoke not his patience: 12 C
Put vp thy Pipes: 18 H
530 Quarrelous quaffing: 09 F
Quite blowne vp: 10 J, 11 K, 12 K, 13 J
Quite Cashierd: 10 F
Quite forlorne: 15 I, 18 E
Quite off the hookes: 16 L
535 Quite out of credit: 11 E
Quite out of his companie: 16 I
Rather do nothing: 09 B
Rather returne: 10 D
Relye not vpon it: 15 K
540 Repent at leisure: 18 D
Reuenge in his breast: 09 K
A reuenging heart: 10 AH
Ride not too deepe: 11 F
Rise and repent: 09 F, 10 B, 11 C
545 Rise vp & fall: 10 H, 11 BJ, 13 D, 14 A
Rods in pisse: 18 K
A rope and a halter: 11 E, 12 L, 13 L, 16 J
A rope and 3 trees: 16 C
A rope for Parrat: 15 H, 17 F
550 Saue shoo-leather: 10 D
Scarse currant: 11 F
Scarse sound at heart: 11 K
Secret complotment: 09 I
Secret malice: 11 J

555 A secret practise: 10 C
Shallowhearted: 11 B
Shame and sorrow: 11 B
A shifting companion: 12 G
Shifts will not serue: 17 G
560 Short shooting: 13 L, 15 I
Shrunke in the weting: 11 C, 12 J, 14 D, 15 J
Sit still and slumber: 13 J
A sleeuelesse answer: 11 L, 13 J
Something desperate: 14 E
565 Somewhat thwarting: 09 E
A sorrowful departure: 09 G
Spare cost: 13 G
Spare cost and charges: 09 K
Spare cost & shooe leather: 12 H
570 Spare labour and cost: 16 E
Spare shoe leather: 09 L
Spend, but speed not: 09 F
Spira poco: 17 E
A stab at least: 12 B
575 Stand shot-free: 12 B
Stay, and stirre not: 13 E
Stay the bels: 12 C, 13 F (the Belles), 15 J, 17 B
Stones against wind: 09 I, 11 K, 12 B, 14 G, 15 E, 16 E, 17 I
Stoope gallant: 18 G
580 Striue not for it: 11 L
A strong aduersarie: 10 J, 11 A
A strong enimie: 09 B
Subtill sophistrie: 10 A
A sodaine qualme: 10 G
585 A swaggering mate: 14 B
Sweet meat, sower sauce: 09 C, 13 I, 16 H
Tagill good-cow: 12 I
Take another time: 15 K
Take deliberation: 10 J
590 Take heed of a lash: 16 J
A Tale of a tub: 15 L
A terrible disgrace: 17 E
There is no redemption: 13 C
They carp at it: 14 J
595 Thou maist go whistle: 16 K
Thou wilt repent it: 16 G
Three to one not: 09 G

Thy cap at it: 09 I, 10 J, 13 J, 14 F, 16 G
Thy footing wil fayle: 09 A
600 Thy suite is cold: 16 K
The tide's past: 12 C
Time is past: 13 E
The time past: 10 G
Toyle to no purpose: 16 J
605 To no effect: 11 J
To no great purpose: 14 C
To no purpose: 09 D, 17 J
Too great a taske: 14 H
Too great ods: 11 G
610 Too high doctrine: 15 B
Too hot and too heauie: 09 L, 10 H (kot), 11 J, 14 K
Too much besotted: 14 J
Topsie turuie: 18 F
To small purpose: 14 L
615 To what purpose?: 17 G
Trouble not thy selfe: 10 H, 11 F
Turn Turke: 12 I
Twixt hawke and buzzard: 11 H
Twixt rockes and sandes: 09 D
620 Twixt rocks and scirt: 18 K
Two faces vnder one hood: 17 I
Two words to one bargaine: 12 F
Vndertake it not: 09 L
Vnkind greeting: 18 B
625 An vnsatiable Miser: 10 K
Vpon a slippery pin: 09 K
Vpside downe: 18 D
Vp to the eares: 15 J
Vayne delusions: 13 I
630 A vaine enterprise: 11 H
A vaine florish: 12 FL
Vaine hopes: 13 B, 14 AD, 15 G
Vaine illusions: 14 H
A vaine offer: 11 J
635 Very vnconstant: 09 B
Very vntoward: 13 B
A violent counterbuffe: 09 G
Walke warily: 10 K, 11 D
Wast, and want: 09 D, 18 J
640 Wast no labour: 09 B, 10 J, 12 A, 14 C
Water in a Sciue: 10 L, 14 J, 16 B, 17 H, 18 H

The weakest to the wall: 12 J
What remedie: 15 C
What to doe?: 09 E
645 A Whip for a Foole: 09 J, 16 H
Wily beguily: 12 J
Wit cannot worke it: 16 I
Without redemption: 09 F
Wit whither wilt thou?: 11 J,
18 E
650 Wofull experience: 18 L

A wolfe by the eares: 10 J, 14 G,
16 A
A word and a blow: 10 CF, 16 D
Worke for the hangman: 11 J,
14 I
The world cannot helpe it: 10 G
655 A worme with a witnes: 14 I
Worse and worse: 09 A
Worse then a Halter: 09 H

GOOD DAYS

Abide the brunt: 14 C
Accesse and recesse: 09 K
Aduancement to the end: 12 E
Aduantage offered: 13 G
5 After a long pause: 16 A
After a while: 18 I
After better aduise: 17 E
After good aduice: 15 D
After some parle: 17 H
10 After the first assault: 13 K
After tryall: 11 K
All at thy commaund: 13 J
All Courtly kindnesse: 14 G
All for thy good: 09 K, 15 C, 16 G
15 All for thy loue: 13 C, 14 A, 16 D,
17 I
All friends: 11 L, 14 I
All hayle: 09 G, 11 H
All heart: 10 F
All he can doe: 14 E
20 All possible fauour: 13 E
All possible pleasure: 11 B, 13 F
Als not gold that glisters: 13 K,
14 H
All that and more: 14 L, 17 EG,
18 H
All that he can: 12 L, 15 A
25 All that may be: 16 C
All things to nothing: 10 G, 16 C,
18 D
All thou demandest: 14 C
Almost at a stand: 18 L
Amends at last: 14 I
30 Amendes for all: 09 H, 10 L, 18 A
Amendes in the ende: 14 A

The amends is making: 13 H,
15 E
As big as his word: 17 J
As fit as may be: 10 D
35 As friendly as may be: 09 C, 13 G
As good as his word: 10 H, 11 I,
13 K
As good thou as another: 09 K
As hard as flint: 13 K
As heart can wish: 10 E, 13 A,
17 A, 18 F
40 As he is humored: 12 C
As it is caryed: 09 I
As it is handled: 15 L (it
handled), 16 D
As it is managed: 10 H, 11 C
Aske and haue: 09 C
45 As she is handled: 11 G
As soone as thou please: 09 A
As sure as a club: 10 F, 11 A, 15 K
As sure as check: 11 D (a check),
12 K, 13 K, 16 L
As tame as a lamb: 11 D
50 As thou wouldst haue it: 12 J,
16 J (would)
As thou wouldst wish: 14 H
As true as steele: 10 IK, 11 B,
15 L
As welcome as the best: 09 L,
13 B
As well as wished: 17 K
55 As willing as wished: 10 G
At a becke: 13 J
At a dead lift: 17 F, 18 E
At a stand: 12 L

At better leisure: 17 I
60 At first word: 12 L
At noone, not before: 13 C
At the first assault: 12 J
At the first dash: 14 F, 16 I
At the first word: 12 B
65 At thy choyce: 10 B
At thy commaund: 10 J, 11 I
At thy gentle dispose: 16 B
Backwards at first: 17 K
Be bould of it: 10 F, 12 C
70 Be bold to aduenture: 17 F
Be briefe about it: 13 I
A becke will suffice: 13 L
Be constant and feare not, 16 G
Be earnest for it: 11 H (or it)
75 Be forward & feare not: 13 AH
Begin well and end well: 16 H
Beleeue her not: 10 F
Be merry and wise: 10 J, 11 A
Be not dismaied: 11 H, 14 D
80 Be not faint hearted: 09 B, 11 L,
   12 F, 13 I, 14 H, 15 G
Be not foyld at the first: 11 J
Be not out-braued: 12 D
Be not ouerdanted: 13 E
Be not too briefe: 13 E
85 Be not too confident: 12 G, 16 L
Be ruled by reason: 16 K
Best in the end: 09 A
Be stirring betimes: 11 D
Best to performe: 09 G
90 Betime or not: 09 H
Better a breeding: 17 D
Better and better: 14 L, 16 D,
   18 B
Better cannot be wished: 12 H
Better hopes then before: 16 I
95 Better is a breeding: 18 A
Better late, then neuer: 10 E,
   11 K, 13 BG
Better may follow: 11 B
Better then his word: 15 H
Better then it seemes: 13 G
100 Better then nothing: 18 J
Better that then nothing: 13 H,
   17 B
Better will follow: 10 B

Better would do well: 09 K
Bet well and warily: 12 J
105 Be well aduised: 15 G
Beyond expectation: 12 D
A bird in hand: 09 I
Bitter-sweet: 11 J, 15 F
Blame none but thy selfe: 11 E
110 Boast not before conquest: 10 K
A boult or a shaft: 12 J, 15 C,
   18 L
Boote and the better: 09 L, 11 G
Both cup and couer: 11 H
Both cup & couer too: 14 J, 16 B
115 Both fauour & friendship: 15 F
Both hand and heart: 10 B
Both heart and hand: 09 D, 11 I,
   12 E, 15 A
Both sweet and sower: 14 C
Both wit and wealth: 10 G
120 Both witty and willing: 12 E
Bound to see it: 15 C
Breath a while: 18 L
Brickle ware: 09 E
Brooke no delayes: 10 C
125 Build vpon it: 15 K
But a hard shift: 11 E
But an aduenture: 16 A
But chance medly: 12 C, 13 B,
   15 B
But cold comfort: 11 B, 12 A
130 But cold entertainement: 10 B
But hap hazard: 15 E
But hard carding: 17 G
But hold vp thy fingar: 12 I
But in a weak case: 14 L
135 By carke and care: 14 G
By carking & caring: 12 G, 16 F
By carriage and craft: 15 L
By hook or crook: 17 D
By line and leisure: 18 B
140 By little and little: 12 K, 14 B
By meane strength: 14 A
By meere mediation: 18 B
By might & maine: 13 AL, 14 BE,
   16 C, 17 H
By plaine pleading: 12 D
145 By plaine plodding: 11 F, 13 H,
   14 C, 15 B, 16 AI, 17 BF

By some pretty plot: 16 L
By suite and seruice: 10 D, 11 J,
12 E, 13 B, 14 I
By wit & warinesse: 13 F
Calme after a storme: 11 D
150 Canst thou please him?: 09 D
Cappe and curtesie: 10 A, 16 A
The case is altered: 11 C, 17 G
Catch hold betimes: 12 G
Catch that can: 13 L
155 Catch that catch can: 16 A, 17 L
Chameleon like: 11 H
Chance medley: 10 C, 12 J
Changing is no robbery: 09 L
Cleanly conueyed: 09 G
160 A clenly shift: 18 G
The coast is cleare: 11 C
Cocke oth hoope: 18 I
Cocke-sure: 15 G
Come and welcome: 09 D, 13 A
165 A comfort at Court: 12 E
Conquest in the end: 10 F, 11 FK,
12 D
Countenance carries it: 17 E,
18 J (will carry)
Courtious and kind: 09 I
The courtier is kind: 09 A
170 A courtiers promise: 10 A
A courtiers welcome: 11 L
Court it that can: 13 L, 14 F
Coy, yet constant: 11 F, 17 K
(but), 18 K
Craftily handled: 09 B
175 Craft in the catching: 09 GL, 10 J
A craftie companion: 11 I
A crafty foxe: 16 L
Craue and haue: 09 D
A crosse before a Crowne: 09 C
180 Cunning in daubing: 16 F
Cup and couer too: 10 A, 13 E
Cut and choose: 17 H
A day for the onc't: 16 F
Delay breedes danger: 09 B, 11 C
185 Delay is good farewell: 11 C (??)
Delaies are dangerous: 12 A
Demaund and haue: 09 K
Depend not much vpon it: 11 L
Depend vpon it: 18 I

190 Diligence doth it: 09 C, 13 F
(does)
Dispatch betime: 09 K
Done, if demaunded: 09 C
Down vpon the naile: 15 K
Early is best: 09 B, 18 E
195 Easily acted: 10 G
Easily intreated: 10 L, 11 K, 15 F
Easily graunted: 09 D
Easily obtayned: 13 F
Easily perswaded: 16 E
200 Easie and familiar: 09 C
Easy to obtaine: 12 H
Either now, or neuer: 09 A, 11 H,
12 C
Indeauour doth it: 10 E
The end will prooue better:
10 L, 12 B
205 A faint heart: 10 K
A faire promise: 14 E
Fall back, fall edge: 16 H
Fall to it betime: 10 B
Fast bind, fast find: 10 K, 14 L,
16 J, 18 K
210 A fast friend: 14 G, 15 AB
The Fates fauour thee: 09 J
A fatherly friend: 10 E
Fauoured of prince & prelate:
09 I
Feare no cullours: 09 C, 11 J, 12 C,
14 K
215 Fetcht out of the fire: 17 D
Firme, if followed: 09 L, 16 H (if
well followed), 17 C
First come, first seru'd: 13 G,
14 C, 17 I, 18 J
First speak first speed: 17 K
Fit for thy purpose: 15 F
220 Fits thy humour: 09 F
Fit thee for her: 18 G
Follow and feare not: 14 E (*omits
not*), 15 J, 16 H (Follow it and),
17 C
Forward if followed: 09 A
For what will you giue me: 10 C
225 Fresh and fasting: 18 F (end fast-
ing)
Fresh and fasting, or not: 11 G

A friend at last: 14 A
A friend in a corner: 11 I, 16 J
A friend in the Court: 10 G
230 Friendly and fauourable: 17 D
A friendly greeting: 17 K
A friendly welcome: 13 L, 16 B,
17 H
A fri: only in shew: 14 J
Freends in court & country:
13 F
235 From the teeth outward: 12 H
Full of complements: 12 G
Full of expectation: 14 F
Get the start of him: 10 K, 11 J
Gouldinges will gaine it: 10 B
240 A good beginning: 10 A
Good catching in time: 10 C
A good foundation: 12 F, 17 J
A good friend helps: 14 J
Good grapling: 14 K
245 Good in the wearing: 18 J
Good lucke at last: 12 K
Good lucke towards: 18 H
A good match in hand: 09 H
A good pate helpes: 09 C, 10 H,
11 G, 16 F
250 Good preferment: 09 E, 10 L
A good resolution: 16 D
Graced with the greatest: 10 K,
11 E (of)
Gratiously graunted: 09 B
A graine too light: 10 J
255 Great men grace thee: 09 C
Great possibility: 12 B
Handsomly handled: 11 J
Hap-hazard: 09D, 10 D, 18 D
Happily attempted: 18 C
260 A happy chance: 16 H
Hard hammering: 17 H
Hardly attained: 17 B
Hardly come by: 18 A
Hardly contriued: 16 H
265 Hardly effected: 11 H
Hardly obtayning: 09 C
Hardly preuailing: 16 D
A hard taske: 16 E
Hard to obtaine: 17 F
270 Haue at all: 18 F

Haue patience & a prise: 17 F
Health and happinesse: 12 J
Heart and good will: 10 AF
Heartily welcome: 12 F
275 A hearty well-wisher: 16 I
He cannot choose: 09 A
He is for thee: 09 D
He is no starter: 10 I
Help at a pinch: 14 I
280 He may doe much: 14 E
He needs no broker: 09 J, 10 J,
11 B, 12 D, 16 F, 17 L
He will fit thee: 09 E
He will not deny: 09 D
He will stand vpon poynts:
10 D, 11 E
285 Highly esteemed: 16 J
His countenance carries it: 15 J
His heart is good: 13 C
His will is good: 09A, 12 K, 16 E
His wit is his warrant: 11 D
290 His wits must worke it: 14 A
Hold fast, and feare not: 18 J
Honestly minded: 10 I (Hou-
estly)
An honest shift: 16 J
An honest shift may serue: 10 E
295 Honey and gall: 11 D
A hopefull designe: 14 B
A hopefull enterprise: 17 A
A hopefull issue: 11 H
Hope in the end: 11 E, 14 GI
300 Hope wel and haue wel: 12 H,
13 D, 17 B
Husband it well: 18 F
If cleanly carried: 17 J
If handsomly handled: 14 B, 15 G,
16 E
If he had it: 09 D, 12 B
305 If it were in his power: 13 B
If mildnesse marre not: 10 I
If plyed in time: 13 G
If thou canst please him: 10 L
If wittily handled: 17 B
310 In a doubtfull case: 12 J, 13 F
In a good humour: 13 J
In a good veine: 17 C
In a merry humour: 10 L, 14 F

In an excellent humor: 15 H, 16 E
315 In a reasonable hope: 16 I
In docke out nettle: 12 G, 18 H
Industry may do it: 12 B
In hope of good hap: 17 I
In space growes grace: 17 A
320 In the euening is best: 12 A
In the euening, or not: 10 D
In the morning, or not: 09 F, 13 E
In the way of amendmēt: 11 G
In the way of preferment: 11 I,
13 D
325 In the way to winne: 14 E
Is good farewell: 11 C (?? *lege* De-
lay is . . .)
It bodes good lucke: 17 A
It cannot come amisse: 11 L
It cannot fall amisse: 17 I
330 It cottons well: 14 A, 16 G, 18 G
It fals in his mouth: 11 G
It fals into thy mouth: 11 A, 12 E
(in), 12 G, 13 F, 14 H (month),
14 I, 15 CH, 17 J, 18 C
It falles out pat: 16 D, 18 A
It falles pat: 15 J
335 It fits thy turne: 10 H, 11 CG, 12 C,
13 C, 14 A, 17 J, 18 L
It is hardly to be had: 13 C
It is ready tempered: 09 B, 12 I
It lyes a bleeding: 10 I, 11 G, 14 G,
16 C
It makes vp thy mouth: 16 L
340 It may do well: 16 G
It requires cost: 12 A, 13 L
It smels well: 10 A
It smiles on thee: 14 I
It sounds well: 18 K
345 It stands vpon thornes: 18 D
It will come at last: 13 E, 14 K,
16 L
It will cotten well: 12 A
It will doe well: 10 G
It will fadge at last: 13 B
350 It will fadge well: 14 D, 17 C
It will square well: 11 E
It workes like waxe: 10 J, 15 B,
16 C, 18 L
Iacke indifferent: 09 E

Iacke on both sides: 18 D
355 A kind farewell: 09 L
Kind greeting: 10 A, 10 H (A
kind)
Kindly embraced: 16 J
A kindly welcome: 13 E
A kisse before a curse: 11 K
360 Labour or lose all: 13 J
A large offer: 14 B
Large promises: 09 F, 11 I
The later the better: 10 C, 11 A
Lay hold in time: 12 L
365 Lay waite in time: 16 L
Let no time passe: 11 E
Let no time slip: 12 F
Let slip no time: 09 D
Let the spice work: 16 G, 17 D
370 Let thy case be knowne: 11 I
Like company, like credite: 10 D
Like to prooue well: 13 A
Like to thriue well: 16 E
Liuely and liberall: 12 G
375 Long before he thriue: 12 J
Long before thrift: 16 K
Long ere he thriue: 14 K
Long ere it fade: 11 G
Long lookt for, comes at last:
13 L
380 Looke before thou leape: 12 K
Looke narrowly to it: 13 K
Looke to it betime: 13 K
Looke to it in time: 13 B
Make account of it: 16 K
385 Make hay while the Sun shines:
12 G, 13 E, 16 G, 18 I (Hay be-
time)
Make no bones at it: 13 D, 14 L,
18 F
Make thy case knowne: 10 C
Make vp thy mouth: 15 L, 17 J
A match well made: 12 F, 14 GJ,
15 BI, 16 D, 18 F
390 Meete him betimes: 10 E
Merrily disposed: 17 B
Might may do much: 12 B
Mirth in the hall: 09 L
More hope then before: 11 D
395 More labour then lucre: 11 J

More prattle then practise: 11 F
More shifts then one: 11 K
More willing thē powerful: 17 G
Most voices: 11 A
400 Mount not too high: 12 I
Moue thy Counsell: 09 B
Much adoe: 09 E
Much adoe, little sport: 10 E
(adoe, & litle), 12 C, 13 C, 14 H
Much curtesie much craft: 09 K
405 Much labour little profit: 12 G
Much may be done: 14 H, 17 A,
18 E
Mutuall assent: 17 E
Mutuall concord: 11 G
Neuer better: 17 A
410 Neuer too-late: 10 G
Next come, next serued: 16 L
A nimble pate helpes: 12 E
No abiding no thriuing: 13 J
No biding no thriuing: 12 E
415 No blushing at it: 09 B
No coyne no coping: 09 E
No contradiction: 09 G, 13 H
No counterfeit: 15 D
No deniall: 09 D, 10 D
420 No dissembler: 16 K
No doubt of acceptance: 17 K
No fayling, if followed: 13 F
No good anchorage: 15 G
No good will wanting: 11 K
425 No great comfort: 10 K, 16 G
No great matter in't: 10 C
No great victorie: 11 I
No matter of importance: 11 L
No paines no gaines: 15 I
430 No penny no paternoster: 09 G,
11 G
No perfect requitall: 16 G
No pleasure without payne: 14 E
No power to deny: 12 H
No question at all: 09 L
435 No question of it: 09 E
No resistance: 09 F
No simple doings: 18 B
No suite denyed: 09 K
Not amisse: 18 E
440 Not easily acted: 13 K, 14 CI

Nothing but want: 10 B
Nothing can hinder: 09 D
Nothing impossible: 09 H, 14 D
Not much amisse: 10 G, 13 J
445 Not so good as his word: 11 L
Not so soone as wished: 12 E
Not very constant: 18 C
Not very forward: 15 D, 16 F
Not very free: 15 J
450 Not very free-hearted: 17 G
Not very pleasing: 17 I
Not very secure: 17 E
Not very steadfast: 10 G
Not very trusty: 09 C, 10 I, 16 J
455 Not without demurres: 13 J
Not without paines: 18 B
Now or neuer: 10 C
Of patience comes ease: 11 B
Of suffrance comes ease: 15 H
460 An olde friend's best: 10 I
On a slippery pin: 11 H
Onely by cunning: 15 B
On the mending hand: 13 A
On the winning side: 15 B, 16 C
465 Open harted: 09 H, 10 C, 14 C
Open house: 09 G
Ouercome with kindnes: 13 H
Past the pikes: 10 H
A pearle among pibble: 11 F
470 Peny wise, pound-foolish: 17 G
Perseuere, and a prize: 09 I
A peece of amends: 12 K
Plant at pleasure: 12 D
Plausible acceptance: 09 K
475 Pleasant and profitable: 09 H
Pleasant in the end: 13 F
Pleasantly conceyted: 09 L
Pleased on al sides: 13 L
Please one, please all: 09 J
480 Please the old fellow: 10 C
Please the old one: 11 C, 12 A,
13 A, 17 F
Pleasing if applyed: 11 K
Pleasingly affected: 14 A
Pleasure and profit: 09 G
485 Plucke vp thy spirits: 18 K
Ply the box: 15 I, 18 K
Policie may preuaile: 17 L

Pollicie preuayleth: 09 E
Policie will preuaile: 14 F
490 A politicke deuise: 10 L
A politicke pate: 13 E, 14 B
Possible in the end: 12 L
Prayer may preuaile: 09 C, 11 E
A present for a Prince: 11 E
495 Present performance: 11 J
Present preferment: 11 E
A present well accepted: 11 A
A present well preferd: 12 C
A present well profered: 16 A
500 Presse for preferment: 11 H, 12 A,
13 BH
Presse on and preuaile: 12 C
Presume vpon it: 11 K
Pretily handled: 09 E, 11 A
A pretty deuice: 11 K
505 Prettie, if it would last: 10 E
Preuent him in time: 13 F
Princely fauour: 12 F, 13 K
A prize at hand: 18 C
A prize if practised: 11 H
510 Put to his trumps: 18 G
A question in Law: 09 G
Ready tempered: 14 C, 15 E,
16 K
A reasonable change: 10 J
A reasonable reckoning: 11 I
515 Reasonable toward: 11 D
Redeeme the time: 11 D
A religious intent: 09 I
Respect the time: 09 F
Rub it out: 18 E
520 A saint in show: 10 A, 12 K
Say and hold: 09 I
Say but the word: 09 E
Say nay, and take it: 09 J, 10 K
Scant cater-cozens: 11 A
525 Scarce cater cozens: 12 L, 16 H,
17 G
Scarse currant: 09 H
Scarce his words maister: 14 D
Scarce out of the bryars: 11 B
Selfe do, selfe haue: 11 K
530 Set a good face on't: 16 F
Set wits awork: 13 J, 18 G
Set wits aworking: 15 I, 17 L

She is for thee: 09 E
Shee staies thy comming: 16 K
535 Shoot not too short: 12 H
Sine numine nihil: 18 H
Slacke, and sure: 10 A, 11 D, 15 C
Slacke no time: 09 C, 10 H, 13 I
Slacke not thy tide: 16 G
540 Sleepe not thy tide: 12 C, 14 D,
15 G, 17 A, 18 H
A slender shift: 11 F
Slippe no aduantage: 14 E
Slip not occasion: 16 I
Slow, and sure: 09 J
545 A smyling Tonge: 09 A
Some comfort in it: 13 I
Something distasting: 10 F
Somthing hollow-harted: 15 J
Something in time: 17 I
550 Something to the purpose: 10 J,
13 I, 14 H, 18 E
Something vncertaine: 10 J
Something vnconstant: 17 K
Something vnprouided: 12 K
Something vntoward: 13 D
555 Somewhat coy: 09 E
Somewhat distasting: 09 F
Somwhat too high doctrine:
14 K
Somewhat to the purpose: 16 I
A sound card: 11 J, 13 G
560 A sound deuice: 09 C
Spare for no cost: 16 F
Spare to speak, spare to speed:
16 L
Speake and spare not: 12 G, 16 C
Speake and speed: 09 A, 10 H,
12 B, 13 I
565 Speake betime: 10 F, 11 L, 16 J
Stand not on termes: 14 F
Stand not vpon points: 14 K,
16 C
Stay and take it: 09 I
Stay for no mans pleasure: 14 I
570 Stay his leisure: 18 B
Step before him: 17 G
Stick to it close: 14 J, 16 H
Stoope and take it: 11B, 12 AJ,
14 K, 17 J

Strange at the first: 10 L
575 Strike while 'tis hot: 09 B, 10 A,
11 E, 13 CJ, 14 B, 15 D, 16 F
Striue to attayne: 13 C
Suttle and polliticke: 09 A
A subtile Foxe: 11 E
A sure Card: 15 L
580 Surpassing expectation: 10 D
Sweet meate sower sauce: 12 F
Take counsell vpon it: 16 K
Take his good offer: 15 F
Take warning in time: 12 I
585 That or nothing: 09 G, 15 K
There is no dallying: 16 E
Thine owne by Law: 09 B, 11 E,
12 E, 16 J, 17 L, 18 C
Thou art in the way: 09 E
Thou hast thy wish: 18 D
590 Though long, yet at length:
09 H, 10 G, 11 I, 12 B
Thou shalt be welcome: 09 G
A thriftie companion: 11 L
Through the bryers: 10 D, 14 C,
15 A, 16 L
Thorow the fire: 12 J, 18 AC
595 Thorow the Pikes: 12 I, 13 D,
14 L
Thorow the stone wal: 13 a
Thy hearts desire: 15 C
Thy suite is graunted: 09 I, 10 K,
14 H
'Tis worth the noting: 17 C
600 Time is precious: 11 B
Too-too familiar: 09 H
Touch and take: 15 E, 16 B
The towne is ours: 13 D, 17 F
(towne's)
Trust to thy wits: 11 K
605 A trustie Damon: 11 F, 12 L
Try before you trust: 12 D
Try, then trust: 09 J, 17 H (and
then)
Try the old fellow: 09 B
Twixt hawke and buzard: 10 H
610 Vn-crost vn-blest: 15 H
Vnperfect friendship: 09 B
Vp and ride: 12 H
Vpon a doubtfull point: 11 C

Vpon further liking: 17 D
615 Vpon the good abearance: 17 B
Vpon thy good abearing: 14 F
Vsque ad aras: 10 I, 16 E, 18 J
Venture and vanquish: 17 C
A very good offer: 14 J
620 Very hopefull: 18 I
Very tractable: 09 A
Victorie in the end: 11 J, 16 B
Vincit qui patitur: 17 C
Want spoyles all: 09 H
625 Warinesse may win it: 16 B
The way is made: 10 F, 12 I, 18 H
Welcome at a word: 14 J, 15 J,
16 A
A welcome guest: 10 H, 11 A,
12 G
The welcomst aliue: 12 K
630 Welcome still: 10 E
Welcome to the Court: 09 K
Well aduentured: 16 K
Well affected: 11 C
Well attempted: 15 D
635 Well disposed: 14 G
Well, if it end so: 09 I
Well, if warily: 09 F, 14 I, 15 I
Well managed: 09 A
Well met: 11 D
640 Well resolued: 14 D
Well ventred: 15 A
What thou desirest: 15 A
What thou wilt: 09 E
What thou wilt aske: 11 C
645 What thou wilt desire: 12 F
When thy turne comes: 11 F
While it is hot: 09 F
Whether for a penny: 09 A
(Wheter), 12 BI, 14 H
Why not?: 18 F
650 A wily Py: 09 A
Winne it and weare it: 10 L, 11 B,
12 H, 13 H, 15 E, 16 D
Winke at smal faults: 09 J, 10 C,
17 H
Wise and wary: 09 I
With heart & good will: 13
655 With little labour: 09 K
With much adoe: 10 F, 11 D

With much labour: 17 L
Without any great suite: 10 F
Without welt or gard: 12 K
660 With small intreaty: 12 L
With some difficulty: 13 E, 14 D, 17 H
Wit may win her: 13 E, 15 K
Wit may worke it: 16 E
Wit rather then wealth: 10 L
665 Wittily handled: 16 J
Wittie and wealthie: 09 L

A witty shift: 13 D
Witt whither wilt thou?: 09 J
Wit will wear it out: 13 C
670 Wonne with a feather: 14 L
Worke, or win not: 09 H
Worke wel and win: 12 F
The world is amending: 10 B, 11 B, 12 D, 13 D (mending), 14 F (worlds)
Yeelding affection: 09 D

Lavish annotation of these lists would profit little. Many of the phrases will need no elucidation for anyone who has a reasonable knowledge of colloquial seventeenth-century English and if I have said nothing about any phrase, it may be inferred that I thought nothing needed to be said. When ignorance has prevented me from being able to elucidate something which seemed to me mysterious, I have said so. Bretnor has a habit of splitting proverbs and producing a baffling result by using one half only. 'Beaten with the spit' (*e*62) refers to Tilley's M 147, 'Give a man roast meat and beat him with the spit'. 'Better to be idle than not well occupied' (I7) explains *e*77; 'Better sit still than rise up and fall' (S 491) has both its halves used, as 'As good sit still' (*e*35) and 'Rise vp & fall' (*e*545). 'To make a shaft or a bolt of it' (S 264), a Shakespearian proverb, is referred to in *g*111. 'A crafty knave needs no broker' (K 122) explains *g*251. Bretnor uses 'Brickle ware' as both evill and good (*e*119, *g*123): the reference here is, I fancy, to W 646, 'A woman and a glass are ever in danger', quoted in Kelly's *Scottish Proverbs* (1721) as 'Glasses and Lasses are bruckle ware'.

Some of Bretnor's special alliterative phrases may be annotated. I suggest that they are frequently non-proverbial coinages—e.g. 'Cavilous carousing' (*e*146), 'Crabbed carle' (*e*172), 'Quarrelous quaffing' (*e*530). 'Cold Christmas' (*e*157) and 'A comfortless Caroll' (*e*162) both appear in the month of December. With them may be compared other topical entries: an 'evill' entry at the end of December is 'A harsh farewell' (*e*277); a similar 'good' entry is 'A kind farewell' (*g*355). A number of the phrases for good days refer to earliness and lateness: these, I think, are particular instructions to do business at a time of day and have no general significance (see 61, 90, 194, 320, 321, 322, 363, and 390).

In places emendation may be desired. 'By meane strength'

(*g*141) is possible, 'main' seems more probable; similarly, I suspect that, in *g*144, we should, as in *g*145, read 'plodding'. The word 'catch' has, I think, dropped out in *g*154. 'Follow and feare' is a phrase for May 1614: this should, no doubt, read 'feare not' as in other examples quoted in *g*222. For 'A present well preferd' (*g*498), '. . . proffered' is probably intended (see *g*499). The mysterious 'Is good farewell' (*g*326) immediately follows, in March 1611, 'Delay breedes danger', and I have guessed that *g*326 should read 'Delay is good farewell' (*g*185), whatever it may mean. It may be suspected that either 'Gall in the end' (*e*257) or 'Guld in the end' (*e*265) is misprinted: either, however, makes good enough sense.

It will be noted that Thomas Middleton apparently had a copy of the 1618 Bretnor open before him when he was writing his masque: the phrase quoted in 'A Fair Quarrel' is not found in Bretnor.

OTHER NOTES

(References like 'N 136' are to Tilley's dictionary)

*e*45   Compare N 136.

*e*88   Compare *g*480: *g*481, *g*608. I read these as being non-proverbial phrases giving special advice for the day.

*e*173   I take it that *carriage* means *carrying*.

*e*193   I do not find this agreeably gloomy phrase elsewhere. Bretnor three times uses it seasonally, in November and December.

*e*198   The charitable will lay this and *e*573 on the compositor's doorstep.

*e*240   'Goldings' here and at *g*239 are, I take it, gold coins.

*e*275   An admirable variant of 'Harm watch harm catch' (H 167).

*e*302   I take this mysterious phrase (used three times) to mean 'stabbing is his fate'; cf. the phrase, 'I'll stab thee', as in Samuel Rowlands's 'Looke to it; for Ile Stabbe ye'. This suggestion could hardly be more tentative.

*e*362   *quite = quit, requite.*

*e*421   (= *g*403) This sounds genuine, though I do not remember to have found it elsewhere.

*e*466   *shales* are the shells of nuts.

*e*477   Tilley knows only of those who blush like a black dog (D 507), like Aaron in *Titus Andronicus*.

*e*517   I take this to mean 'Go an elaborate journey to secure a worthless prize'.

*e*573   See *e*198.

*e*587   M 661, 'Margery, good cow, gives a good meal of milk but throws it down with her heels' does not seem to help much in the elucidation of this baffling phrase. Gresham has the phrase 'Margery good-cow' as an 'evill' motto in August 1607.

g163 It hardly needs the saying that this means not 'over-confident' but 'utterly safe'.

g239 See e240.

g386 See B 527. 'Make no bones *at it*' seems to be the earlier form; Tilley quotes it from Gabriel Harvey in 1573; his earliest 'make no bones *of . . .*' is 1640.

g403 See e421.

g469 This rings genuine enough: I do not know of it elsewhere.

g648 The cry of the Thames watermen.

I confess with candour that I can make no profitable suggestion about the meaning of the following.

e4   Adieu sheats.   *the sails lost*
e21   All's squat.
e22   All vpon hands.
e97   Blacke in the mouth.   *not a pure bred*
e238 Fiue and a reach.
e282 Haunt not his ghost.
e587 Tagill good-cow.
g183 A day for the onc't.
g486 Ply the box.   *seed box?*

The Argument about 'The Ecstasy'

HELEN GARDNER

WHENEVER opinion is sharply divided on a question it is worth asking what the opponents are agreed upon. This will usually show what are the genuine grounds of disagreement and narrow the dispute to particular points. But sometimes such an inquiry has a more interesting result. It may show that the opponents are arguing from a common position which is itself false; and correction of this common basic misconception may make it possible to put forward a new view which can take into account elements in the opposing views which had appeared irreconcilable. The dispute over the significance of 'The Ecstasy' is, I think, a case in point. There is no short poem of comparable merit over which such completely divergent views have been expressed, and no lover of Donne's poetry can be happy to leave the question in its present state of deadlock. For it is obvious that those who assert that the poem is the supreme expression of Donne's 'philosophy of love' and those who declare that it is a quasi-dramatic piece of special pleading have now no hope of converting each other. The one side merely adduces fresh parallels from various Italian Neo-Platonists and from Donne's own works; the other continues to insist on the sexual overtones of the imagery and to point out sophistries in the argument. Neither side will recognize that there are elements in the poem which contradict its interpretation.

To Coleridge 'The Ecstasy' was the quintessential 'metaphysical poem': 'I should never find fault with metaphysical poems', he wrote, 'were they all like this, or but half as excellent'.[1] And to a poet-critic of our own day, Ezra Pound, it is equally, beyond question, a great 'metaphysical poem' in the truest sense. After printing the poem in his *ABC of Reading*, he commented: 'Platonism believed. The decadence of trying to make pretty speeches and of hunting for something to say temporarily checked. Absolute belief in the existence of an extra-corporal soul, and of its incarnation, Donne stating a thesis in precise and even technical terms.'[2] But among

[1] *Coleridge's Miscellaneous Criticism*, ed. T. M. Raysor, 1936, p. 138.
[2] *ABC of Reading*, 1934, p. 126.

scholars there has been flat disagreement over the genuineness of the poem's 'Platonism'; and, even among those who regard it as seriously intended, there has been a recurrent note of reserve in their praise of the poem. Thus Sir Herbert Grierson, in his chapter on Donne in the *Cambridge History of English Literature*, declared that 'The Ecstasy' 'blends and strives to reconcile the material and the spiritual elements of his realistic and Platonic strains'; but added the comment, 'Subtle and highly wrought as that poem is, its reconciliation is more metaphysical than satisfying'. Three years later, in his introduction to his edition of Donne's poems, he expanded this view in a passage which may be taken as the classic statement of the orthodox view of the poem:

The justification of natural love as fullness of joy and life is the deepest thought in Donne's love-poems, far deeper and sincerer than the Platonic conceptions of the affinity and identity of souls with which he plays in some of the verses addressed to Mrs. Herbert. The nearest approach that he makes to anything like a reasoned statement of the thought latent rather than expressed in *The Anniversarie* is in *The Extasie*, a poem which, like the *Nocturnall*, only Donne could have written. Here, with the same intensity of feeling, and in the same abstract, dialectical, erudite strain he emphasizes the interdependence of soul and body.

But, after quoting some lines, he added:

It may be that Donne has not entirely succeeded in what he here attempts. There hangs about the poem just a suspicion of the conventional and unreal Platonism of the seventeenth century. In attempting to state and vindicate the relation of soul and body he falls perhaps inevitably into the appearance, at any rate, of the dualism which he is trying to transcend. He places them over against each other as separate entities and the lower bulks unduly.[1]

Against Ezra Pound's 'Platonism believed' we have to set Grierson's 'Platonism modified and transcended, and yet perhaps not fully believed'.

A wholly different view was put forward by Professor Pierre Legouis in *Donne the Craftsman* in 1928. He denied that the poem had any philosophic intention and declared that it was, within a narrative framework, quasi-dramatic, the representation of a very skilful piece of seduction. He regarded the Platonism as a transparently cynical device by which a clever young man, pretending that their

---

[1] *Poems of John Donne*, 1912, vol. ii, pp. xlvi–xlvii.

minds are wholly at one, is persuading a bemused young woman that there can be nothing wrong in her yielding to him. After a detailed examination of the poem, Professor Legouis summarized his view of it by saying:

> Donne does not set out to solve once for all the difficult problem of the relations of the soul and body in love. He considers the particular case of a couple who have been playing at Platonic love, sincerely enough on the woman's part, and imagines how they would pass from it to carnal enjoyment; whether he thinks this *in abstracto* a natural consummation or a sad falling-off matters little; the chief interest of the piece is psychological, and, character being represented here in action, dramatic. The heroine remains indeed for the reader to shape, but the hero stands before us, self-revealed in his hypocritical game.[1]

M. Legouis's interpretation was strongly contested by many scholars, notably by Professor Merritt Hughes and by the late Professor G. R. Potter.[2] Professor Hughes contested it by referring to Italian and French Neo-Platonists. He showed that the argument for the body's rights in love was a common topic in writers such as Benedetto Varchi, and declared that Donne's poem clearly descended from the casuistry of the Italian Neo-Platonists. Professor Potter supported Grierson's interpretation by a mass of quotations from Donne's poetry and prose to prove that Donne did indeed hold the views which Grierson said that the poem put forward. Neither of these writers, nor, as far as I am aware, any other opponent of M. Legouis, attempted to refute in detail his close analysis of the poem and his criticism of the sophistries of its supposed argument.

The controversy flared up in a slightly different form when Professor C. S. Lewis and Mrs. Joan Bennett skirmished over 'The Ecstasy' in the course of a general battle over Donne's merits as a love-poet.[3] Professor Lewis, classing the poem with 'poems of ostentatiously virtuous love', declared that it was 'nasty'. If the idea of 'pure' passion has any meaning, he said, 'it is not like that'; and he concluded by exclaiming, 'What any sensible woman would make of such a wooing it is difficult to imagine'. Mrs. Bennett took up the challenge and reaffirmed Grierson's view of the poem's

---

[1] *Donne the Craftsman*, Paris 1928, pp. 68–69.

[2] Merrit Y. Hughes, 'The Lineage of "The Extasie"', *M.L.R.* xxvii, Jan. 1932, and 'Kidnapping Donne', *Essays in Criticism*, Berkeley 1934, pp. 83–89; G. R. Potter, 'Donne's *Extasie*, Contra Legouis', *P.Q.* xv, 1936.

[3] In *Seventeenth-Century Studies presented to Sir Herbert Grierson*, 1938, pp. 64–104; see particularly pp. 76 and 96–97.

philosophy. The debate had rather shifted its ground here to the value of the philosophic views put forward, or assumed to be put forward, by the poem; but Professor Lewis appeared to take for granted that we may disregard, as M. Legouis does, the poem's statement that the man and the woman thought as one and take it that the poem, in fact, presents a 'wooing'. Later, Professor Lewis, while 'still unable to agree with those who find a valuable "philosophy" of love in "The Ecstasy" ', confessed that he had 'erred equally in the past by criticizing the supposed "philosophy" '. Asserting that ideas in Donne's poetry 'have no value or even existence except as they articulate and render more fully self-conscious the passion' of a particular moment, he declared that the real question was 'how that particular progression of thoughts works to make apprehensible the mood of that particular poem'.[1]

In spite of all the parallels from Italian Neo-Platonists and all the references to Donne's views on the relation of soul and body which have been brought against him, M. Legouis has not retracted. On the contrary he has more than once reaffirmed his view. He must have been encouraged in this obstinacy by the accession of a notable recruit in Professor Frank Kermode who, in his British Council pamphlet on Donne, informs the general public, as if the case did not need arguing, that 'The Ecstasy' may be classed with 'The Flea' as an example of Donne's 'original way of wooing by false syllogisms'. He says of 'The Ecstasy': 'The argument, a tissue of fallacies, sounds solemnly convincing and consecutive, so that it is surprising to find it ending with an immodest proposal. The highest powers of the mind are put to base uses, but enchantingly demonstrated in the process.'[2]

Professor Kermode's quip that the whole argument leads to 'an immodest proposal' finds certain echoes among those who claim that the poem's Platonism is seriously intended. Thus, Professor Mario Praz, who spoke of 'The Ecstasy' as 'un compendio della metafisica d'amore quale la concepiva il Donne', and repeated Grierson's view that 'Questa poesia tratta della mutua dipendenza del corpo e dell' anima', confessed to finding disconcerting notes in the Platonic poetry of Donne and cited, as an example, 'il contrasto tra la macchinosa argomentazione metafisica e il pratico realismo della perorazione' in 'The Ecstasy'. He thought that one would be

---

[1] *English Literature in the Sixteenth Century*, 1954, p. 549.
[2] *John Donne* (Writers and their Work, no. 86), 1957, p. 12.

inclined to think this the invention of a mocking spirit if one did not recall parallel statements from Donne's letters.[1] Even Professor Merrit Hughes, by using such a phrase as 'the casuistic idealism of the Italians', and by calling Donne's poem 'frankly carnal', shows that he believes the poem finds its culmination in a plea, or a 'proposal', that the lovers should turn from the enjoyment of spiritual communion to the pleasures of physical. This is the common ground on which the dispute about the poem's meaning has arisen. Both sides take it for granted that the main point of the poem is a justification of physical love as not incompatible with the highest form of ideal love. The point of disagreement is whether the justification is seriously meant (and, if so, is it to be taken seriously or is it worthless), or whether the whole argument is intentionally sophisticated and the poem shows somebody 'being led up the garden path'.

The whole dispute has arisen, in my opinion, from a misreading of the last section of the poem (ll. 49–76). The only 'proposal' which is made in these lines is the perfectly modest one that the lovers' souls, having enjoyed the rare privilege of union outside the body, should now resume possession of their separate bodies and re-animate these virtual corpses. The phrases

> But O alas, so long, so farre
> Our bodies why doe wee forbeare?

> To'our bodies turne wee then,

and

> ... when we'are to bodies gone,

have as their obvious and main meaning, and this we must establish before we start listening for overtones, or hunting for ambiguities, the sense 'But, O alas, why do we for so long and to such a degree shun the company of our bodies?', 'Let us then return to our bodies', and 'When we are gone back to (our) bodies'. The final *and*, one must suppose from its position, the conclusive reason for such a return of the separated souls is not that it will in any way benefit the lovers; but that only in the body can they manifest love to 'weake men'.[2] The fact that an ideal lover is invited to 'marke'

---

[1] *Secentismo e Marinismo in Inghilterra*, Florence 1925, pp. 28 and 27.

[2] In his 'Platonic' poems Donne constantly, as here, makes distinctions between himself and his mistress, who are 'saints of love', worthy of canonization and capable of performing miracles; those who are capable of understanding these mysteries, Doctors, as it were, of Amorous Theology; and the 'laity', who either need simple instruction, or to whom it would be 'prophanation of our joyes' to speak.

them when they are 'to bodies gone' surely makes the notion that the poem culminates in an 'immodest proposal' absolutely impossible.[1] M. Legouis himself thought it particularly shocking that 'the hypothetical listener of the prelude re-appears and turns spectator at a time when the lovers as well as we could wish him away'. But the lovers, far from wishing him away, actually invite his presence. They wish to display the mystery of their love to one of 'love's clergie' as well as to the 'laity', to one who is 'so by love refin'd' that he can understand 'soules language', as well as to 'weake men', who can only glimpse these mysteries through the reports of their senses, and who need, therefore, the body for their book.

My own position combines elements from both views. I regard the poem as wholly serious in intention. (Whether it is wholly successful I must leave undiscussed for the moment.) But if the conclusion really meant what it has been supposed to mean, I should be on M. Legouis's side, since the arguments put forward, regarded as arguments leading to the supposed conclusion, are beneath contempt. None of the analogies work if taken as elements in an argument designed to justify the body's claims in love. I am not, on the other hand, wishing to deny that, as a corollary to its main line of thought, the poem implies the lawfulness and value of physical love. I should also not deny that separate lines and stanzas of the poem, if taken in isolation, are susceptible of a fuller and richer meaning than they have within the limits of the poem, and that we can legitimately quote them as expressing more than the lovers in the poem intend. I am only denying that the poem is in the least concerned to argue to this particular point. In other poems, as in the passages which have been quoted from his letters and sermons, Donne does declare that

> as all else, being elemented too,
> Love sometimes would contemplate, sometimes do;

but in this poem he is concerned with something else. As Professor Lewis justly says, one of Donne's greatest gifts as a lyric poet is the intensity with which he abandons himself to the exploration of a

---

[1] It is one thing for a narrative poet to describe two lovers in passionate embrace oblivious of a bystander, as Spenser does at the original ending of Book III of the *Faerie Queene*; it is quite another for lovers themselves to call for an audience at their coupling.

particular mood, or experience, or theme. In this poem, as the title[1] tells us, his subject is ecstasy. He is attempting to imagine and make intellectually conceivable the Neo-Platonic conception of ecstasy as the union of the soul with the object of its desire, attained by the abandonment of the body. Unlike the great majority of Donne's lyrics 'The Ecstasy' is a narrative, relating an experience which took place in the past. But by means of the hypothetical listener it turns into a poem in the dramatic present, Donne's habitual tense, in the long 'speech' of the lovers, which occupies two-thirds of the poem. Both the unusual narrative form, with its exceptionally detailed setting and its description of the lovers' poses, first seated, then prone in ecstasy, and the introduction of the hypothetical listener are made necessary by the nature of the experience which Donne is trying to render. It is the essence of ecstasy that while it lasts the normal powers of soul and body are suspended, including the power of speech, and the soul learns and communicates itself by other means than the natural. Ecstasy can then only be spoken about in the past tense. Donne has shown both a characteristic daring and a characteristic ingenuity in attempting, by means of his ideal listener, to render the illumination of the soul in ecstasy as a present experience. The conception of such a listener being refined, beyond even his own high stage of refinement, by his contact with the lovers in their ecstatic union is in keeping with a recurrent note in those lyrics of Donne which deal with the mysteries of mutual love: the claim that he and his mistress can give 'rule and example' to other lovers, that they have a kind of mission. If we take the poem as concerned with ecstasy and read its arguments as designed to illuminate the conception of love as a union by which two become one, we can explain the meaning of passages which have baffled commentators and have been passed over silently by most disputants over the poem's meaning. I hope to demonstrate that my hypothesis as to the poem's central intention[2] can, as the older one could not, thus 'save the phenomena'.

[1] 'The Ecstasy' always occurs with a title, and the same title in manuscript. We are, therefore, justified in assuming, as we cannot with most of Donne's poems, that the title is the author's.

[2] In declaring that the poem does not conclude with a proposal to 'prove, while we may, the sweets of love', I have been anticipated by one critic, Donaphan Louthan, in *The Poetry of John Donne, an Explication*, New York 1951. I regret that I cannot agree with the details of his analysis.

I

Before considering the poem in detail I wish to establish that Donne derived his conception of 'amorous ecstasy' from a definite source. Donne actually wrote two poems on the ecstasy of lovers. Ironically, Gosse, who has been the butt of scholars for his fantastic attempt to treat Donne's love poetry as autobiographical, saw the connexion between them. There is often much sense in Gosse's nonsense and in a single sentence on 'The Ecstasy' he hit the mark twice. He connected it with the poem which has, since the edition of 1635, been printed as the tenth elegy, under the title 'The Dreame', and he owned to being puzzled by 'the obsession with the word "violet" ', which he thought 'had, unquestionably, at the time of its (the poem's) composition an illuminating meaning which time has completely obscured'.[1] The tenth elegy is not, in fact, an elegy at all, but a lyric. It should be printed in stanza form, and its title, given to it by whoever edited the edition of 1635 and placed it with the Elegies, should be altered. I wish it could be called simply 'The Image'; but a wholly new title would be inconvenient. I propose, therefore, to call it 'Image and Dream', which both preserves a link with the older title and serves to connect the poem with, and differentiate it from, the poem called 'The Dream' which appears among the Songs and Sonnets. The poem puzzled Grierson, who was misled by the title 'The Picture' which is given to it by one unreliable manuscript. His error in taking the opening words, 'Image of her', to mean 'picture of her', instead of 'intellectual idea of her',[2] led him to dismiss the poem in his commentary as 'somewhat obscure', and it has never received much attention. Since it is not generally familiar, I print it in full.

Image and Dream

Image of her whom I love, more then she,
    Whose faire impression in my faithfull heart,
Makes mee her *Medall,* and makes her love mee,
    As Kings do coynes, to which their stamps impart
The value: goe, and take my heart from hence,
    Which now is growne too great and good for me:
Honours oppresse weake spirits, and our sense
    Strong objects dull; the more, the lesse wee see.

---

[1] *Life and Letters of John Donne,* 1899, i. 75–76.
[2] The right interpretation was put forward by E. Glyn Lewis, the only critic who has discussed the poem at length; see *M.L.R.,* vol. xxix, Oct. 1934.

When you are gone, and *Reason* gone with you,
    Then *Fantasie* is Queene and Soule, and all;
She can present joyes meaner then you do;
    Convenient, and more proportionall.
So, if I dreame I have you, I have you,
    For, all our joyes are but fantasticall.
And so I scape the paine, for paine is true;
    And sleepe which locks up sense, doth lock out all.

After a such fruition I shall wake,
    And, but the waking, nothing shall repent;
And shall to love more thankfull Sonnets make,
    Then if more *honour, teares,* and *paines* were spent.
But dearest heart, and dearer image stay;
    Alas, true joyes at best are *dreame* enough;
Though you stay here you passe too fast away:
    For even at first lifes *Taper* is a snuffe.

Fill'd with her love, may I be rather grown
Mad with much *heart,* then *ideott* with none.

The importance of this poem to my argument is that it can be shown to depend directly upon a source, and the same source lies, I believe, behind 'The Ecstasy'.

I cannot believe that Donne could have written 'Image and Dream' if he had not very recently been reading one of the most famous and beautiful works of the Italian Renaissance, Leone Ebreo's *Dialoghi d'Amore*.[1] Written about 1502 and published in 1535, the *Dialoghi d'Amore*, if we judge by the number of editions, rivalled Ficino's commentary on the *Symposium* (*De Amore*) and Pico's commentary on some sonnets by Beneviente as a main source of sixteenth-century Neo-Platonism. It was twice translated into Spanish, and twice into French, as well as into Latin and Hebrew. The distinction which 'Image and Dream' turns on, between the 'dulling' of the senses by 'strong objects' and the 'locking up' of the senses in sleep, is handled at length in the third and last of the dialogues in which Philo instructs his mistress Sophia in the mysteries of love.

---

[1] Translated, under the title *The Philosophy of Love*, by F. Friedeberg-Seeley and Jean H. Barnes, 1937. Page references are to this translation. Quotations in Italian are from the edition by S. Caramella, Bari 1929. The translators, in attempting to render the Italian into modern English, are often nearer to Donne's words than a literal translation would be. For a discussion of Leone Ebreo as a philosopher see Heinz Pflaum, *Die Idee von Liebe. Leone Ebreo*, Tübingen 1926.

The dialogue opens with the lover, Philo, being reproached by Sophia for being oblivious of her presence. He excuses himself by saying that his mind was rapt in contemplation of her beauty, whose image 'impressed' upon it has made him dispense with his external senses.[1] Sophia asks how something so effectively impressed on the mind cannot, when present, enter the eyes. Philo acknowledges that it was through the eyes that her radiant beauty pierced into the very midst of his heart and the depth of his mind ('nel centro del cuore e nel cuore de la mente'). Sophia recurs to her point later, when in reply to Philo's saying that if she must complain she should complain against herself, since she has 'locked the door' against herself, she answers, 'Nay, I lament rather that the image of my person has more sway over you than my person itself': the paradox with which Donne begins his poem. Philo agrees that the image has more power, since an image within the mind is stronger than one from without.[2] This is stock Neo-Platonic doctrine and parallels could be adduced from Ficino, Pico, Bembo, and many others. What makes it certain that Donne read it in Leone Ebreo is that Philo's first defence against Sophia is that she would not have blamed him for being unaware of her presence if he had been asleep. She owns that sleep would have excused him, since its custom is to remove all sense-perception (*che suole i sentimenti levare*). He declares that he has a better excuse than sleep and she asks what can blot out perception more than sleep which is a semi-death (*che è mezza morte*). He retorts that ecstasy brought about by a lover's meditation is more than semi-death. When she protests that thought cannot divorce a man from his senses more than sleep does, which lays him on the ground like a body without life, he answers that sleep restores life rather than destroys it, which is not true of ecstasy.[3] This leads to a long comparison between the physiology of ecstasy and the physiology of sleep. In the one, the mind withdraws, taking with it the greater part of its powers and spirits ('la maggior parte de le sue virtú e spiriti'), leaving only the vital spirit to keep the body

[1] P. 198: 'La mente mia, ritirata a contemplar, come suole, quella formata in te bellezza, e in lei per immagine impressa e sempre desiderata, m'ha fatto lassare i sensi esteriori' (p. 172).

[2] P. 229, *Filone*. 'Si che se lamentar ti vuoi, lamentati pur di te, che a te stessa hai serrate le porte.' *Sofia*. 'Pur mi lamento che possi e vagli in te, piú che mia persona, l'immagine di quella.' *Filone*. 'Può piú, perché giá la rappresentazione di dentro a l'animo precede a quella di fuore' (p. 197).

[3] P. 199, *Sofia*. 'Come può la cogitazione astrare piú l'uomo de' sensi che 'l sonno, che getta per terra come corpo senza vita?' *Filone*. 'Il sonno piú presto causa vita, che la toglia: qual no fa l'estasi amorosa' (p. 173).

just alive. In the other, the spirits are drawn to the lower regions of the body to perform the work of nutrition, the mind is deprived of its reasoning power, and the imagination (*la fantasia*) is disturbed by dreams engendered by vapours arising from the concoction of food.[1] Both sleep and ecstasy, that is to say, discard and inhibit sense and motion; but in the one case the spirits are withdrawn and collected, either in the midst of the head, the seat of all knowledge, or in the centre of the heart, the abode of desire ('in mezzo de la testa, ove è la cogitazione, o al centro del cuore, ove è il desiderio'); in the other they are drawn down to the lower regions of the body. The heart is the link between the head and the belly, and is the seat of the soul, the intermediary between the intellectual and the corporal in man. The vital power of the heart preserves the mind and body from dissolution. But in ardent ecstasy it may happen that the soul will wholly enfranchise itself from the body, and the spirits, the soul's instruments, will be dissolved, or loosened or untied (*resolvendosi i spiriti*), by reason of the force and closeness with which they have been gathered together.[2] This is the blessed death of ecstasy. Philo, whose mistress will not confess that she loves him, declares that her image is acting upon him like poison, which goes straight to the heart and will not leave until it has consumed all the spirits. Her image, which he contemplates in ecstasy, arouses in him insatiable desire, and this desire would destroy the spirits which it has gathered in his heart, if her presence did not save him from death by restoring his spirits and senses to their natural functions. But the return to waking life does not take away the pain of desire which her beauty, contemplated or perceived, arouses.[3]

In his poem Donne has combined the conception of the image in

[1] Pp. 200–3. See particularly p. 201: 'Ma quando la mente se raccoglie dentro se medesima per contemplare con somma efficacia e unione una cosa amata, fugge da le parti esteriori, e abbandonando i sensi e movimenti, si ritira con la maggior parte de le sue virtú e spiriti in quella meditazione, senza lassare nel corpo altra virtú che quella senza la quale non potrebbe sustentarsi la vita . . .; questo solamente resta, con qualche poco de la virtú notritiva, perché la maggior parte di quella ne le profonda cogitazione è impedita, e perciò poco cibo longo tempo i contemplatori sostiene. E cosi come nel sonno, facendosi forte con virtú notritiva, arrobba, priva e occupa la retta cogitazione de la mente, perturbando la fantasia per l'ascensione de' vapori al cerebro del cibo che si cuoce, quali cansano le varie e inordinate sonniazioni, cosi l'intima ed efficace cogitazione arrobba e occupa il sonno, nutrimento e digestione del cibo' (p. 174).

[2] P. 205: 'Cosi pungitivo potrebbe essere il desiderio e tanto intima la contemplazione, che del tutto discarcasse e retirasse l'anima dal corpo, resolvendosi i spiriti per la forte e ristretta loro unione in modo che, afferandosi l'anima affettuosamente col desiderato e contemplato oggetto, potria prestamente lassare il corpo esanimato del tutto' (pp. 177–8). [3] Pp. 230–1; pp. 198–9 in Italian.

the lover's heart, greater than the beloved in her person, whose contemplation 'shuts out' sense, and which 'oppresses the spirits', with an old familiar poetic theme, deriving from Petrarch: the theme of the sensual love-dream, in which the lover finds in sleep the satisfaction which his mistress denies him waking. The image is 'too great and good', and the lover turns from contemplation which may destroy life to sleep which restores it, bidding farewell to his heart as seat of reason and rational desire and allowing 'fantasy' and sensual appetite to reign. But at the close he decides that of the two ways of being 'out of one's senses', he prefers the madness of ecstasy, born of rational contemplation of her image, to the irrationality of sleep, in which he may enjoy the pleasures of fantasy and escape the pain of truth.

In discussing this poem we can point to a definite passage which provided Donne with his basic idea, the likeness and difference between ecstasy and sleep, as well as with certain phrases. The relation of 'The Ecstasy' to the Italian treatise is less immediately obvious but more interesting. The long discussion of the physiology of ecstasy, culminating in the description of the 'blessed death of ecstasy' and including an analysis of the nature of the soul and of its relation to the spirits, is patently the source of Donne's conception of ecstasy, as will be apparent shortly when I use it to explicate the poem. But Donne found much more than this in the *Dialoghi d'Amore*. The discussion of ecstasy does not arise out of the experience of an ecstatic union of the lovers, but from the lover's experience of an ecstatic union with the idea of the beauty of his beloved. The charm and strangeness of Leone Ebreo's book lies in its combination of metaphysical, theological, and cosmological speculation of the most daring kind with a delightful battle of wits between two persons; for Philo, while instructing Sophia in the mysteries of love,[1] is also wooing her, and Sophia is both the very clever pupil, asking leading and often awkward questions, and also the mistress who denies. The work, as it was printed, is unfinished. The close of the third and last dialogue looks forward to a fourth, in which Philo will teach his mistress about the effects of love.[2] It is clear

---

[1] In spite of her name, she needs a great deal of instruction; but I suppose that we can take it that she is instructing her lover in Socratic fashion.

[2] It is uncertain whether the fourth dialogue, which contemporaries inquired for in vain, was ever written. The last record of Leone Ebreo is in 1520, so that, since he was born about 1460, he had probably been dead for some time when his book was published in 1535.

from the close of the third dialogue that Sophia is weakening fast and that the whole work was intended to move towards the blissful moment when Philo and Sophia will be no longer the one the Lover and the other the Beloved, but both will be equally Lover and Beloved. This happy consummation is continually looked forward to and anticipated throughout the work as we have it; but it has not been achieved by the time the book ends. There is then no single passage describing an ecstatic union of lovers to which we can point as the source of 'The Ecstasy'. Instead, we find scattered through the whole work ideas and phrases which have been woven into the substance of the poem.[1]

The first dialogue, which is much the shortest, handles the fundamental problem of the relation of love to desire. Although short, it ranges over the whole subject of love, raising the questions which are to be treated extensively in the subsequent dialogues. The second dialogue deals with the universality of love and is concerned with love throughout the cosmos; the third is on the origin of love, and treats of the love of God. Love between human beings is left to be treated in the missing fourth dialogue, on the effects of love. We can form a good idea of what it was to contain, for the first dialogue contains a brief treatment of love between human beings, and there are references in the others which relate human love to Leone Ebreo's definition of love as the desire for union: 'an affect of the will to enjoy through union the thing judged good'.[2] Thus in the first dialogue he proceeds from this general definition to define 'the perfect love of a man for a woman' as 'the conversion of the lover into the beloved together with a desire for the conversion of the beloved into the lover'. And he adds 'when such love is equal on both sides, it is defined as the conversion of each lover into the other'.[3] This mutual and equal love is the love which Donne is writing about in 'The Ecstasy'.

What has convinced me that the poem was directly inspired by the reading of the *Dialoghi d'Amore* is that phrases which have puzzled me and other commentators and readers cease to be obscure or doubtful in meaning when we read similar phrases in Leone

[1] Parallels for most of these can be found separately in other Neo-Platonic writers. It is the collocation of these ideas in Leone Ebreo which is striking.

[2] P. 12: 'affetto volontario di fruire con unione la cosa stimata buona' (p. 13).

[3] P. 55: 'La propria diffinizione del perfetto amore de l'uomo e de la donna è la conversione de l'amante ne l'amato, con desiderio che si converti l'amato ne l'amante. E quando tal amore è eguale in ciascuna de le parti, si diffinisce conversione de l'uno amante ne l'altro' (p. 50).

Ebreo, and that, while it is possible to find illustrative and explanatory parallels for separate ideas referred to in the poem in a wide variety of authors, once an editor can turn to Leone Ebreo the task of annotating 'The Ecstasy' is child's play. Almost all the *idées reçues* to which Donne refers in the poem are referred to or handled at length by Leone Ebreo. Finally, one of the most striking statements of Donne's lovers echoes a fundamental and distinctive idea of Leone Ebreo. This idea, which is directly opposed to the orthodox view as it appears in the writings of such Platonic doctors as Ficino and Pico and such popularizers of Platonism as Bembo, is exactly what is usually referred to as 'Donne's philosophy of love'.

The best example of a difficulty which can be solved by reference to the *Dialoghi d'Amore* is the doubt which most readers in my experience feel as to what Donne's lovers mean by saying that love mixes souls

> And makes both one, each this and that.

In the first dialogue Philo, at Sophia's request, speaks briefly of human friendship, differentiating those lesser friendships which are for the sake of utility or pleasure from true friendship which generates the good and conjoins the virtuous. This is the 'friendship of perfect union':

> Such union and conjunction must be based on the mutual virtue or wisdom of both friends; which wisdom, being spiritual, and so alien to matter and free from corporeal limitations, overrides the distinction of persons and bodily individuality, engendering in such friends a peculiar mental essence, preserved by their joint wisdoms, loves and wills, unmarred by divisions and distinctions, exactly as if this love governed but a single soul and being, embracing,—not divided into,—two persons. In conclusion I would say that noble friendships make of one person—two; of two persons—one.[1]

This notion that in the union of love one becomes two and two become one is recurred to in the third dialogue when Philo repeats that 'two persons who love each other mutually are not really two

---

[1] P. 31: 'E la causa di tale unione e colligazione è la reciproca virtú o sapienzia di tutti due gli amici. La quale, per la sua spiritualitá e alienazione da materia e astrazione de le condizione corporee, remuove la diversitá de le persone a l'individuazione corporale; e genera ne gli amici una propria essenzia mentale, conservata con sapere e con amore e volontá comune a tutti due, cosi privata di diversitá e discrepanzia come se veramente il suggetto de l'amore fusse una sola anima ed essenzia, conservata in due persone e non multiplicata in quelle. E in ultima dico questo, che l'amicizia onesta fa d'una persona due, e di due una' (p. 30).

persons'. Sophia, in her role of Dr. Watson, asks how many they are, and receives the answer that they are 'only one or else four', since

> Each one being transformed into the other becomes two, at once lover and beloved; and two multiplied by two makes four, so that each of them is twain, and both together are one and four.

'I like this conception of the union and multiplication of the two lovers', comments Sophia.[1] These mystical mathematics also pleased the author of 'The Primrose', who not only rendered them succinctly in the line

> And makes both one, each this and that,

but also remembered that the union of love was a multiplication when he supplied an analogy from nature in the violet which, when transplanted, 'redoubles still and multiplies'.

As for passages illustrating the poem, the following topics, given in the order in which they occur in the poem, are handled by Leone Ebreo: that sight is by means of rays emitted from the eye;[2] that although the soul is one and indivisible, it is also 'compounded', that is, it contains 'mixture of things'; that intelligences love the spheres which they animate, a conception which is discussed at great length to explain why the spiritual intelligence of man is united to his body. Reference to the *Dialoghi d'Amore* supports Grierson's adoption of the reading of the manuscripts against that of the editions in line 55, where the plural 'forces' renders 'le virtú' in the recurring phrase 'le virtú e i spiriti', and supports an emendation which I had intended to propose independently in line 67. In discussing the soul's relation to the body, Leone Ebreo uses the metaphor of gold and alloy.

More exciting is the fact that the first thing which is revealed to

---

[1] P. 260: *Filone*. 'Li due che mutuamente s'amano non son veri due.' *Sofia*. 'Ma quanti?' *Filone*. 'O solamente uno, o ver quattro.' *Sofia*. 'Che li due siano uno intende, perché l'amore unisce tutti due gli amanti e gli fa uno; ma quattro a che modo?' *Filone*. 'Trasformandosi ognuno di loro nell'altro, ciascuno di loro si fa due, cioè amato e amante insieme: e due volte due fa quattro; si che ciascuno di loro è due, e tutti due sono uno e quattro.' *Sofia*. 'Mi piace l'unione e multiplicazione de li due amanti' (p. 222).

[2] P. 215; pp. 175–6 in Italian. Philo explains that the eye sees by the transmission of rays to the object, but that the representation of the object on the pupil is also necessary, and that, further, the eye must direct its ray a second time on to the object to make the form impressed on the pupil tally with the object. This is a highly characteristic attempt to combine two theories (sight by extramission and sight by intramission), or to reconcile Plato and Aristotle on vision. It has suggested to Donne two conceits: the twisting of the eye-beams and that the lovers were 'looking babies'.

Donne's lovers in their ecstasy is something which Philo was at great pains to teach Sophia:

> This Extasie doth unperplex
> (We said) and tell us what we love,
> We see by this, it was not sexe,
> We see, we saw not what did move.

Philo first 'unperplexes' Sophia by teaching her that love and desire are not opposites. In arguing this Leone Ebreo sets himself against orthodox Platonism, as expressed in Ficino's commentary on the *Symposium* or in Bembo's *Asolani*, where the young man who puts forward this view is corrected later by the wise hermit. Sophia, who ably argues for the view that love and desire, or appetite, are clean contrary, is converted by Philo who explains that there are two kinds of love. Imperfect love is engendered by sensual appetite, and since desire, as soon as it is satisfied, dies, this love, which is the effect of desire, dies with its cause. But perfect love 'itself generates desire of the beloved, instead of being generated by that desire or appetite: in fact we first love perfectly, and then the strength of that love makes us desire spiritual and bodily union with the beloved'.[1] Sophia then asks 'If the love you bear me does not spring from appetite, what is its cause?' and Philo replies:

Perfect and true love, such as I feel for you, begets desire, and is born of reason; and true cognitive reason has engendered it in me. For knowing you to possess virtue, intelligence and beauty, no less admirable than wondrously attractive, my will desired your person, which reason rightly judged in every way noble, excellent and worthy of love. And this, my affection and love, has transformed me into you, begetting in me a desire that you may be fused with me, in order that I, your lover, may form but a single person with you, my beloved, and equal love may make of our two souls one, which may likewise vivify and inform our two bodies. The sensual element in this desire excites a longing for physical union, that the union of bodies may correspond to the unity of spirits wholly compenetrating each other.[2]

[1] P. 56: 'Ma l'altro amore è quello che di esso è generato il desiderio de la persona amata, e non del desiderio o appetito; anzi, amando prima perfettamente, la forza de l'amore fa desiderare l'unione spirituale e corporale con la persona amata' (p. 51).

[2] P. 57: 'Il perfetto e vero amore, che è quello che io ti porto, è padre del desiderio e figlio de la ragione; e in me la retta ragione conoscitiva l'ha prodotto. Che, conoscendo essere in te virtú, ingegno e grazia non manco di mirabile attraizione che di ammirazione, la volontá mia desiderando la tua persona, che rettamente è giudicata per la ragione in ogni cosa essere ottima e eccellente e degna di essere amata; questa affezione e amore ha fatto convertirmi in te, generandomi desiderio che tu in me ti converti, acciò che io amante possa essere una medesima persona con te amata, e in

When the desire which is born of this perfect love is satisfied and ceases, the love which inspired it does not cease, nor is the desire to enjoy the fullest union with the beloved lessened by the temporary satisfaction of physical desire. The first thing which Donne's lovers learn in their ecstasy is that theirs is this 'perfect love', not born of desire or appetite, but of reason.

It may now very well be pointed out that having as I hope proved the close dependence of 'The Ecstasy' on the *Dialoghi d'Amore*, I have ended by producing a passage which makes the same point as it has been assumed that Donne was making in his poem: that lovers who are united in soul must, in order that their union should be complete, unite also in body. Here in Leone Ebreo is what has been called 'Donne's metaphysic of love'. I would agree; but I would not agree that in this particular poem this conclusion is being argued for, although it is implied. I would say that 'The Ecstasy' originated in Donne's interest in Leone Ebreo's long description of the semi-death of ecstasy and in the idea that the force of ecstasy might be so strong that it would break the bond between soul and body and lead to the death of rapture. This death in ecstasy his lovers withdraw from, to return to life in the body. What they are concerned to argue, in the concluding section of the poem, is that the bond of the 'new soul' will still subsist when their souls once more inhabit their separate bodies, and that they have a function to fulfil in the world of men which justifies their retreat from the blessed death of ecstasy.

II

'The Ecstasy' falls into three parts. The first twenty-eight lines are a prelude. They set the scene, the 'pregnant banke' which rests 'the violets reclining head'; they describe the pose of the lovers; they tell how their souls went out from their bodies; and they introduce the hypothetical ideal lover who is capable of 'hearing' the wordless communication of the separated souls. The scene is unusually detailed for Donne, and M. Legouis has commented on it sarcastically as showing Donne's incapacity as a poet of nature: 'Even when for once he lays the scene of his action outdoors, his metaphors take

equale amore facci di due animi un solo, li quali simigliantemente due corpi vivificare e ministrare possino. La sensualitá di questo desiderio fa nascere l'appetito d'ogni altra unione corporea, acciò che li corpi possino conseguire in quella la possibile unione de li penetranti animi' (p. 52).

us back to the boudoir or the rake's den. The epithet "pregnant",
though not voluptuous, is also sexual, and the drooping violets
suggest languor.' The violet, which puzzled Gosse, is not here
because of any symbolic associations; but it may be as well to add
that, although in classical poetry it has erotic associations, in Elizabethan literature it is invariably 'modest', 'pure', and the 'virgin of
the year'. It is here because it is a flower which is found in two
forms, the single and the double violet, and Donne is going to refer
later to this phenomenon of nature in an analogy which he did not
find in Leone Ebreo. The setting is a natural one. It is spring, the
traditional season for a dialogue of lovers. The bank is pregnant with
new life and the wild, or uncultivated, single violet grows upon it.
The word 'entergraft' which is used to describe the clasp of the
lovers' hands, is taken from horticulture; and 'propagation' has
horticultural connotations also. It is to horticulture and not to
boudoirs that we must look for the explanation of the presence of
'the violets reclining head'. The language of the first twelve lines
is 'pregnant' with sexual meanings. The 'balme' which 'ciments' the
lovers' hands, as M. Legouis rightly pointed out, implies that they
are young and fit for all the offices of love. I have no objection at all
to his suggestion that the stanza

> So to'entergraft our hands, as yet
> Was all the meanes to make us one,
> And pictures in our eyes to get
> Was all our propagation[1]

implies that, although these are so far the only physical means which
the lovers have employed, they will soon enjoy that union in the
body which perfect love desires. But the main meaning is that so far
their only union is through the corporal sense of touch and the
spiritual sense of sight. It is by these means, particularly through
their gazing into each others' eyes, that soul is being 'conveyed' to
soul and such an ardent desire for union is being engendered as will
cause the souls of each to abandon their bodies.

This ecstasy, or 'going out' of the souls, is described in the first

---

[1] We may compare, if we choose, Ficino's description of how Lysias gazed on
Phaedrus and Phaedrus on Lysias (*Commentary on the Symposium*, VII. 4); and indeed
Ficino's description of the soul and spirits in ecstatic contemplation is much the same
as Leone Ebreo's. But Ficino would hardly allow the lower, corporal sense of touch
to play a part. Professor Mario Praz drew attention to a sonnet by Petrarch (Sonnet
63, *in vita*) which may have suggested to Donne the idea of two lovers united by the
passionate intensity of their gazing on each other.

of the analogies which Donne found for himself and not in his source. They have all puzzled commentators. Their difficulty lies in the precise sense of the connectives 'as' and 'so'. A paraphrase, 'As Fate suspends uncertain victory between two equal armies, our souls hung between her and me', shows we need to expand 'as'. The parallel is not between Fate's action and the souls hanging in the air. The connexion there is purely verbal—between the old Homeric metaphor of the scales of battle 'hung out' in the heavens and the souls being 'suspended' above their bodies. This is an extra adornment of wit over and above the point of the simile whose sense is 'Just as when two equal armies are locked in battle so that neither side is advancing or retreating, so our souls hung motionless, face to face, in the air.' The point which is being established is the absolute equality of the souls and their immobility. While the souls thus 'negotiate' or confer, the bodies lie inanimate on the ground, like statues on a tomb. They are 'her' and 'me'. This is the only use in the poem of the singular pronouns. Elsewhere there is an almost monotonous insistence on the plural pronouns 'we', 'us', and 'our', repeated, at times within a single line, and continually given metrical stress.

So far there has been no suggestion of a union of souls. Indeed, the implications of the souls being like 'two equall Armies', and of the word 'negotiate', hint at the opposite. The notion that equality implies identity does not occur until line 25, when it is stated that this was no parley between opposing sides, but a 'dialogue of one', as it is called at the close: 'both meant, both spake the same'. In order that we may know what the souls said, the hypothetical bystander, another perfect lover, is introduced. He is sufficiently 'refin'd' to understand; but, even so, he will receive a new 'concoction' from his experience, and 'part farre purer then he came'. This is the language of alchemy. The only other use of the word 'concoction' in Donne's poetry is in *The First Anniversary* (l. 456), where the 'example' and 'virtue' of Elizabeth Drury works upon her 'creatures' to give them 'their last, and best concoction'. But the idea that gold, the perfect metal, can be refined into a tincture which will transmute baser, that is less pure or more mixed, metals to its own perfection is common in his verse. The soul, as Leone Ebreo, citing Plato, teaches in his discussion of ecstasy, is of a mixed nature, 'compounded of spiritual intelligence and corporeal mutability'. But it can at times withdraw from the exercise of its bodily functions and unite itself wholly to its intellectual nature.[1] It is then, as he says elsewhere, like gold without alloy.[2] The souls of Donne's lovers, which have thus withdrawn from their bodies, in order to enjoy 'true intellectual light', can, like tincture of gold, give a new concoction to the soul of anyone capable of receiving it, making it 'farre purer'. The conception of the soul as containing 'mixture of things', which underlies the use of the alchemical terms 'refin'd' and 'concoction', is referred to explicitly in the next section of the poem (ll. 29–48), which contains the illumination which the lovers received in their ecstasy.

The first thing which the lovers learn is 'what they love'. By a supernatural experience they learn what is hidden from the lovers of 'The Relic' who 'loved well and faithfully',

> Yet knew not what they lov'd, nor why;

and from the lovers of the 'Valediction: forbidding Mourning', who loved with a love

> so much refin'd
> That our selves know not what it is.

(It is a Neo-Platonic commonplace that perfect lovers do not know what it is they love.) Donne's lovers here see that it was 'not sexe', the 'difference of sex', what distinguishes man from woman, that each loved in the other. It was something invisible, what they did not see, which drew them to each other, or 'moved' them both. By the mingling of their two souls, the invisible essences which drew them together, there has arisen by the power of love a 'new soule', and this new and 'abler soule' is, unlike all separate and individual souls, gifted with complete self-knowledge. It understands its own essence, or nature. The final ecstatic revelation which the lovers receive is the answer to the question which Lord Herbert of Cherbury's lovers debated in a poem which, as Grierson noted, is plainly

---

[1] P. 206: 'L'anima . . . non è uniforme, anzi per esser mezzo fra il mondo intellettuale e il corporeo . . . bisogna che abbi una natura mista d'intelligenzia spirituale e mutazion corporea, altramente non potrebbe animar i corpi. . . . Pur qualche volta si ritira in sé e torna ne la sua intelligenzia, e si collega e unisce con l'intelletto astratto suo antecessore . . .' (p. 178).

[2] P. 396: 'E così come l'oro quando ha la lega e mescolanza de li rozzi metalli e parte terrestre, non può essere bello perfetto né puro, ché la bontà sua consiste in essere purificato d'ogni lega e netto d'ogni rozza mescolanza: così l'anima mista de l'amor de le bellezze sensuali non può esser bella né pura, né venire in sua beatitudine se non quando sarà purificata e netta de l'incitazioni e bellezze sensuali, e allor viene a possedere la sua propria luce intellettiva senza impedimento alcuno, la quale è la felicità' (p. 333).

inspired by 'The Ecstasy'. They learn that their love 'will continue forever'.

The 'new soul' has come into being through the action of love upon individual souls, which alone or 'separate' contain 'a mixture of things'. 'When the spiritual mind (which is heart of our heart and soul of our soul), through the force of desire, retires within itself to contemplate a beloved and desired object, it draws every part of the soul to itself, gathering it into one indivisible unity.'[1] It is two such 'recollected' or 'reconcocted' souls, 'mixed again' by love or desire for union, which love unites to make of two one and of each one two. This union is indissoluble because it is the union of perfect with perfect, or like with like. It is only those things which are unequally mixed which are subject to decay or mutability. The force of love has united all the diverse parts of each soul wholly to its own intellectual nature, which is its true essence, and the 'new soul' of their union, being wholly intellect, knows itself. The union of the lovers is the union of their intellectual souls, or spiritual minds. In their triumphant certainty the lovers borrow a word from the contrary philosophy of materialism, the Epicurean doctrine that the world came into being and exists through the chance congruence of atoms. It is by 'congruence' that they exist, but the atoms from which they grow are souls, and they have not come together by chance but by the force of love, which is the desire for union. Such a congruence is, according to Leone Ebreo, the secret of the whole universe.

In a parenthesis Donne provides an analogy from the natural world. I take the stanza on the transplanting of violets as parenthetical, pointing to the existence of something in nature which is both one and multiple, and regard the 'so' of the line 'When love, with one another so' as referring back, beyond the parenthesis, to love's making 'both one, each this and that'. Like a modern scientist, trying to explain some scientific mystery to laymen, Donne refers to something rather similar in nature to the union which love effects in souls. The idea, often referred to in this period, that certain flowers, including the violet, will grow double by frequent transplantation is perfectly true: 'It is a curiosity', writes Bacon, 'also to make flowers double, which is effected by often removing

---

[1] P. 204: 'Quando . . . la mente spirituale (che è cuore di nostro cuore e anima di nostra anima) per forza di desiderio si ritira in se stessa a contemplare in uno intimo e desiderato oggetto, raccoglie a sé tutta l'anima, tutta restringendosi in una indivisibile unità' (p. 177).

them into new earth; as on the contrary part, the double flowers, by neglecting and not removing, prove single.'[1] Marvell gives the right reason, in speaking of the 'double pink': 'the nutriment did change the kind'.[2] The richness of the new soil stimulates the growth of a superabundance of petals. But in Elizabethan writers I have found certain hints that the 'doubling' of single flowers, and the production of parti-coloured flowers, such as Perdita calls 'nature's bastards', was the result of the mingling of seeds in the earth, and that the 'double' flower, or the 'streaked' flower, was actually two flowers in one. Since it was not recognized until late in the seventeenth century that stamens and pistils were sex organs, the phenomenon of hybridization was not understood. The passage in *The Winter's Tale* describes grafting as a means of producing pied flowers and Bacon wonders whether 'inoculating', that is grafting, might not make flowers double.[3] But he also refers to another method of making shoots 'incorporate': the putting of divers seeds into a clout and laying it in well-dunged earth.[4] This method of planting seeds together in a bag is referred to by the sixteenth-century botanist, Giambattista Porta, in his *Magia Naturalis.*[5] He appeared to think that by this method parti-coloured flowers could be produced by 'commixtion of seeds'. And Puttenham, who distinguishes between 'aiding nature', by enriching the soil in which plants grow, and 'altering nature and surmounting her skill', gives as an example of the latter the production of double flowers from single, as if more were involved in this than mere mulching.[6] I believe that some such notion of 'commixtion' of seeds in the earth lies behind Donne's reference to the 'single violet' which, when transplanted, 'redoubles still and multiplies'. If so, the analogy is a very good one, because the so-called 'double violet' has far more petals than twice a single violet would produce. Union has produced not 'two violets in one', but something much nearer the 'one and four' of the lovers' union.

With the revelation that their love is immortal, the ecstasy of the lovers reaches its climax. Unless they are to enjoy the 'blessed death' of ecstasy, they must now return to their bodies. The conclusion of

---

[1] *Natural History*, Century VI, section 513.
[2] 'The Mower against Gardens.'
[3] *Natural History*, ibid.
[4] *Natural History*, Century V, section 478.
[5] Translated as *Natural Magick*, printed for Thomas Young and Samuel Speed, 1658; see p. 70.
[6] *The Arte of English Poesie*, edited by G. D. Willcock and A. Walker, 1936, pp. 303–4.

the poem (ll. 49–76) justifies this return by reference to the doctrine of the circle of love. The heart of Leone Ebreo's doctrine is that the world as it exists and was created is such a circle. The inferior desires to unite itself in love with what is superior; but equally the superior desires to unite itself in love with what is inferior. The inferior desires the perfection which it lacks; the superior desires to bestow its own perfection on what lacks it. The final cause of love in each is the desire for perfection, for the union of all the parts of the Universe so that it may perfectly realize the divine Idea of its being, and be itself united to its perfect Source and End. The illustration which Philo gives at some length to show the love which superior bears for inferior is the love of intelligences for the spheres which they move and govern, and Sophia comments: 'I suppose it is for the same reason that the spiritual intelligence of man unites with a body as frail as the human: to execute the divine plan for the coherence and unity of the whole Universe.'[1] The same force, love or the desire for union, which has united the lovers' intellectual souls brings those souls back to their bodies. 'Love is the condition of existence of the world and all in it'; and intelligent souls would not 'unite with human bodies to make them rational, if love did not constrain them thereto'.[2]

The souls of the lovers yearn towards their bodies, which are 'theirs', though not 'they'. They own their debt to them. By the joining of hands and the gazing of the eyes the desire for union became so strong that soul was conveyed to soul. (The word 'thus' in line 53 is meaningless unless we take it that the 'thankes' for the bodies' aid refers to the experience of the poem and not to some remote first meeting.) It was because the bodies yielded up their own faculties, the powers of the senses, and allowed the 'sensible soul' to be wholly united to the intellectual soul, leaving themselves deprived of motion and sense, that the ecstasy came to pass. The lovers turn to their own purpose the metaphor of gold and alloy, to declare that the body is alloy and not dross, and find an analogy to support them in their belief that they need not fear that the descent

[1] P. 189: 'Credo che per questa medesima causa l'anime spirituali intellettive degli uomini si collegano a corpo si fragile come l'umano, per conseguire l'ordine divino nella collegazione e unione di tutto l'universo' (p. 164).

[2] P. 191: 'Siccome niuna cosa non fa unire l'universo con tutte le sue diverse cose se non l'amore, séguita che esso amore è cause de l'essere del mondo e di tutti le sue cose.' Also: 'Né mai l'intelligenzie . . . s'unirebbero con li corpi celesti . . . se non l'amassero; né l'anime intellettive s'uniriano con li corpi umani per farli razionali, se non ve le constringessi l'amore' (p. 165).

of their souls from ecstatic union to inhabit their separate bodies
will make it impossible for soul to flow into soul. Donne is here
referring, I think, to the fundamental Paracelsian doctrine that the
influence of the heavenly bodies, whether good or evil, is the 'smell,
smoke or sweat' of the stars mixed with the air.[1] It is, like the
analogy with violet, an illustrative parallel: 'heavenly bodies
cannot act upon man without the material intermediary of air, so
we may believe that souls which are in the body can communicate
through the body's aid'. The famous lines which follow display the
working of the cosmic principle of the circle of love in the micro-
cosm, or little world of man:

> As our blood labours to beget
>   Spirits, as like soules as it can,
> Because such fingers need to knit
>   That subtile knot, which makes us man:
> So must pure lovers soules descend
>   T'affections, and to faculties,
> That[2] sense may reach and apprehend,
>   Else a great Prince in prison lies.

The blood strives to become spiritual, to produce the spirits, or
powers of the soul, which are necessary to unite the intellectual and
corporal in man. Conversely souls must condescend to the affections
and faculties of the body in order that man's sense organs may become rational. The mind, as Philo teaches Sophia, 'controls the
senses and directs the voluntary movements of men'. 'For this
purpose it must issue from within the body to its external parts and
to the organs of sense and movement, in order that man may
approach the objects of sense in the world around him, and it is
then that we are able to think at the same time as we see, hear and
speak.'[3] If the soul does not thus inform all the activities of the

---

[1] *Paramirum*, I. viii. *Der Bücher und Schrifften*, Basle 1589-90, i. 15.

[2] Although I cannot claim support from the manuscripts, I am reading 'That' for
'Which'. 'Which' gives no sense, because 'sense' does not 'reach and apprehend'
affections and faculties, but 'reaches and apprehends' objects of sense by means of
them. I am assuming that 'which' has been substituted for 'that' under the mistaken
notion that 'that' was a relative. Copyists tend to treat the two forms 'which' and
'that' as interchangeable. If we read 'That', as I do above, the action of the souls
becomes purposeful, so that it parallels the purposeful action of the blood. I had
decided that this emendation was necessary before I came upon the passage quoted
below which supports it.

[3] P. 201: 'La mente è quella che governa i sentimenti e ordina i movimenti volun-
tari degli uomini: onde per far questo offizio bisogna che esca de l'interior del corpo
a le parti esteriori, a trovare l'instrumenti per fare tali opere e per approssimarsi agli
oggetti de' sensi che stanno di fuora, e allor pensando si può vedere, odire e parlare
senza impedimento' (p. 174).

body, it is abandoning its task which is 'rightly to govern the body'.[1] Its duty is to take 'intellectual life and knowledge and the light of God down from the upper world of eternity to the lower world of decay' and thus realize the unity of the Universe. A soul that does not perform this divinely appointed function is like a prince in a prison. The concordance to Donne's poems shows how fond he is of the metaphor of the soul as prince and the body, with its limbs, as his province. If the soul does not thus animate the body in all its parts, it is imprisoned in a carcass instead of reigning in its kingdom. Donne is contrasting the Platonic view of the soul imprisoned in the flesh with the Aristotelian conception of the union of the soul and body in man. A prince is no prince if he does not rule his kingdom and a kingdom without a prince is a chaos. Prince and kingdom need each other and are indeed inconceivable without each other. In the final lines of the poem the lovers find a further justification for life in this world, in the duty to reveal love to men, and declare that, if one of 'love's Divines' has heard their 'dialogue of one', he will not be aware of much difference between their union when 'out of the body' and their union when they have resumed possession of their kingdoms.

III

It remains to ask how successful 'The Ecstasy' is in what it attempts, and this question is connected with the problem of why it has given rise to such contradictory interpretations. 'The Ecstasy' is remarkable among Donne's lyrics for its length and for its lack of metrical interest and variety. Although it has fine lines and fine passages, it lacks, as a whole, Donne's characteristic *élan*, and at times it descends to what can only be described as a dogged plod. It is also remarkable for an excessive use of connectives, such as 'as' and 'so'. It was this which first suggested to me that it depended on a written source. (Anyone who has ever corrected large numbers of *précis* knows how hard these little words can be worked in summarizing discursive arguments.) The word 'argument', I think, holds the clue both to

---

[1] See pp. 189–90; p. 164 in Italian. The soul is able to mount to Paradise 'con rettitudine del suo governo nel corpo'. If it fails, 'resta ne l'infimo inferno, sbandita in eterno dalla unione divina e dalla sua propria beatitudine'. Donne's prison may be this 'lowest hell' to which the soul which has not fulfilled its function as a 'great Prince' is banished; but I prefer the interpretation suggested in the text, because of his use of the present and not the future tense.

the slight sense of dissatisfaction which Grierson expressed and also to the variety of misinterpretations which the poem has suffered. There is a tone of argument throughout the lovers' speech which is out of keeping with the poem's subject. The essence of any illumination received in ecstasy, if we accept the conception of such illumination being possible, is that it is immediate and not arrived at by the normal processes of ratiocination. In ecstasy the rational faculty is laid aside and in a holy stillness the intellect rests in the contemplation of what is, and in the peace of union. Donne's lovers seem very far from this blissful quiet. Their minds are as active as fleas, hopping from one idea to the next. Although we are told that the two souls speak as one and that we are listening to a 'dialogue of one', the tone is that of an ordinary dialogue in which points are being made and objections met. When Donne was inspired by the *Dialoghi d'Amore* to write a poem showing the achievement of union in love, he caught from his source that tone of persuasion which has misled readers. The poem *sounds* as if someone is persuading someone. The defect of 'The Ecstasy' is that it is not sufficiently ecstatic. It is rather too much of an 'argument about an ecstasy'. It suffers from a surfeit of ideas.

For all that it is a wonderful poem and a poem that only Donne could have written; and it holds the key to Donne's greatest love-poetry. No poet has made greater poetry than Donne has on the theme of mutual love. He has no predecessors here and virtually no successors of any stature. The poems which Donne wrote on the subject of love as the union of equals, such poems as 'The Good-morrow', 'The Anniversary', or 'A Valediction: Forbidding Mourning' are his most beautiful and original contribution to the poetry of human love; for poets have written very little of love as fullness of joy. I am in no way depriving Donne of his glory when I suggest that it was in Leone Ebreo's book that he found this conception, which he made so wholly his own, of love as not being love 'till I love her that loves me'. I do not believe that Donne was very deeply moved by the conception of ecstasy. He too often in his sermons disparages the idea of ecstatic revelation for me to feel that it had ever had a strong hold on his imagination. He was, on the other hand, profoundly moved by the conception of love as union. 'Image and Dream' and 'The Ecstasy' would seem, from their closeness to their source, to be the first poems which Donne wrote on this theme. In other poems on the same subject we can explain ideas and phrases

by referring to Leone Ebreo,[1] but we cannot in the same way speak
of the *Dialoghi d'Amore* as a source. I cannot at present suggest
when Donne first read Leone Ebreo, though I think it may be
possible to discover this. But it seems likely that Donne's love
poems, like his divine poems, came in bursts, a new theme leading
to a group of poems, and that we can legitimately think of his poems
on love as 'peace', like his youthful poems, the Elegies, on love as
'rage', as having been written fairly close to each other in time.
More than one of the poems of mutual love assumes the presence of
a king on the throne, and so must have been written after 1603. I do
not wish to follow Gosse in trying to make Donne's love-poetry
autobiographical and deprecate attempts to connect particular lyrics
with Mrs. Herbert or with Lucy, Countess of Bedford. At the same
time I cannot believe that we can divorce a man's intellectual life
and the sources of his creative inspiration from his experience.
Certain books, and certain ideas which we meet with in our reading,
move us deeply and become part of our way of thinking because
they make us conscious of the meaning of our own experience and
reveal us to ourselves. I find it impossible not to connect Donne's
marriage with his discovery of a great new subject for poetry in
Leone Ebreo's discourses on love as union.

It is the fashion today in scholarly circles, in reaction against
earlier idolizing of Donne, to exalt his wit at the expense of his
artistic and intellectual integrity, and to deny that ideas had any
value to him as a poet except as counters to be used in an argument.
Donne's greatness needs restating. One element in that greatness is
that certain ideas mattered to him intensely and that he made them
wholly his own. It is characteristic of his intellectual stature that
his Platonism was derived, not at second-hand from fashionable
poets, but directly, from one of the great books of the early Renaissance. The *Dialoghi d'Amore* is an ambitious attempt to bring into a
synthesis all the intellectual traditions of Europe. It attempts to
include in its doctrine of a living universe, moved and united by
love, the cosmology and physiology of Aristotle, the Platonic doctrine of Ideas, the Neo-Platonic doctrine of the Transcendence of the
One and of procession from and conversion to the One by means of
the Emanations, and the Jewish doctrine of Creation. Anyone who
is familiar with Donne's religious writings knows how deeply he

---

[1] In annotating some of the Songs and Sonnets I have found the *Dialoghi d'Amore*
as useful as I found the Glossed Bible when I was editing the *Divine Poems*.

meditated the doctrine of Creation. It is the stress on this distinctively Judeo-Christian doctrine—that the High and Holy One Himself loves the world which He made—which distinguishes Leone Ebreo from the other masters of Neo-Platonism, Ficino and Pico, making him give the material universe and the body a greater dignity. We are not depriving Donne of his greatness and originality as a poet of love if we think of him as inspired in part by a book which, in its Hebrew translation, was in the library of Spinoza, and from which, it has been suggested, he took the idea which we most associate with him of 'the intellectual love of God'. In 'The Ecstasy' Donne is too tied to his source. It smells a little of the lamp. In other, more wonderful, poems he was able to tell in his own language and in his own way what he had learned in his experience, as illuminated by the Jewish Platonist, of love's power to 'inter-inanimate two souls'.[1]

---

[1] Since this Essay went to press I have read with great interest Mr. A. J. Smith's discussion of 'The Ecstasy' in 'The Metaphysic of Love', *R.E.S.*, Nov. 1958. Mr. Smith gives an admirable summary of amorous philosophizing in sixteenth-century Italy in order to demonstrate how little Donne's 'metaphysic of love' has the right to be called original. Although he makes more use of Leone Ebreo than of any other writer he does not suggest direct dependence, and his interpretation of the last section of Donne's poem differs greatly from mine. I must own that I think he has forced the sense of Donne's words.

Donne's Poetry in the Nineteenth Century (1800–72)

KATHLEEN TILLOTSON

NO serious student is deceived by statements frequently encountered in literary journals that Donne's poetry was 'discovered' forty or fifty years ago; such statements generally signify no more than the writer's emotionally possessive attitude to Donne, with perhaps a vague recollection of the dates of Mr. Eliot's essays of 1921, or Grierson's edition of 1912. But the latter, indeed a landmark in Donne scholarship, was a culmination as well as an initiator of interest in his poetry; publishers cannot afford to be philanthropists, and the edition would not have been undertaken without some assurance of existing demand. The period really notable for a rapid quickening and extension of interest in Donne is the 1890's; the evidence has been well assembled by Joseph E. Duncan in 'The Revival of Metaphysical Poetry, 1872–1912',[1] and some of it will be readily remembered by those who grew up in days when Saintsbury, Dowden, and Gosse were still obvious critics to consult.

Mr. Duncan chose 1872 as the date of the Rev. Alexander Grosart's edition, from which existing demand is not a necessary inference as it was printed for private circulation and Grosart's choice of poets was nearly as undiscriminating as his editorial methods. Nevertheless the interest was there,[2] and it is a mistake to dismiss the forty years before Grosart as a period of neglect or misunderstanding, and to regard Browning's known admiration as merely another instance of his oddity and independence in his time. No doubt what has blocked inquiry is the notorious omission of any poem of Donne's from the most popular and influential of

---

[1] *P.M.L.A.*, 1953, pp. 658–71.

[2] Interest in Donne's text is evident in *Notes and Queries* from the 1860's. In 1868 W. C. Hazlitt wishes that 'some competent person could be found to undertake [an edition] *con amore*'; a correspondent calling himself 'CPL' (doubtless the Rev. T. R. O'Flaherty, vicar of *Capel*, Surrey, and owner of important Donne manuscripts) agrees, and says that he has made large collections but 'cannot find time or courage to carry out my intention' (pp. 483, 614).

Victorian anthologies, Palgrave's *Golden Treasury of Songs and Lyrics* (1861); but Palgrave, as I hope to show, had some excuse, and is not in this respect representative of nineteenth-century anthologists. The forty years before Grosart have their own contribution to the establishment of Donne's poetic reputation, and the true picture is rather one of a gradual (though not steady) recovery than of a revolutionary discovery; so gradual that any starting-point much later than Johnson's *Lives of the Poets* would be arbitrary, and it has seemed best to include the early nineteenth century[1] in this inquiry, although this means recalling some familiar material.

*   *   *   *   *

There is some apparent set-back after that first and best-known phase associated with the 'romantics'. This is understandable; while to the modern reader the evidence of appreciation and insight in Lamb, Coleridge, Hazlitt, Landor, and De Quincey is clear enough to constitute a body of enlightened opinion, their references to Donne are in fact mostly casual, fugitive, or oblique. Lamb seems to have been the first of them to record his appreciation in print and was probably the instigator of Coleridge's interest,[2] certainly of Hazlitt's; but all he has left us is in the long note to *Philaster* in his *Specimens of English Dramatic Poets* (1808), where he quotes the whole of Elegy xvi and commends its sense, wit, and pathos, and a 'fragment of criticism' countering the common antithesis of wit and feeling and defending Donne and Cowley: 'in the very thickest of their conceits,—in the bewildering mazes of tropes and figures, —a warmth of soul and generous feeling shines through'. Most of the other evidence of Lamb's reading of Donne comes from Hazlitt, who in 1820 remembered from twelve years before his reading of that same Elegy 'with suffused features and a faltering tongue' and the 'gusto' with which he quoted Donne's 'most crabbed passages'.[3] Hazlitt, whose remarks on Donne are the

---

[1] A. H. Nethercot, 'The Reputation of the "Metaphysical Poets" during the age of Johnson and the Romantic Revival', *Studies in Philology*, 1925, pp. 81–132, deals mainly with the eighteenth century; see also the same author's 'The Reputation of John Donne as a Metrist', *Sewanee Review*, 1922.

[2] His earliest known reference is in the 'Memoranda for a History of English Poetry' which Dr. Coburn (*Inquiring Spirit*, 1951, p. 120) thinks may be 1796–8. See also the notebook quotations of 1800 and 1803–4 (*Notebooks*, ed. K. Coburn, 1957, i, nos. 698, 1786–7, 1789).

[3] 'Of Persons one would Wish to have Seen' and 'The Conversation of Authors'.

nearest approach to formal criticism in the period, never really assimilated his poetry, which he seems not to have read until 1818. Early in that year, in his *Lectures on the English Poets*, he says he 'know[s] nothing' except Lamb's favourite Elegy and 'some quaint riddles in verse which the sphinx could not unravel'. Some months later, in the third of the lectures on *English Comic Writers*, he quotes from three of the *Songs and Sonets*, with comments emphasizing Donne's unevenness: the second verse of 'The Blossom', for example, is 'but a lame and impotent conclusion from so delightful a beginning'.[1] Coleridge, who had already in 1811 begun annotating volumes borrowed from Lamb, referred to Donne in the *Biographia Literaria* (chaps. i and xviii), and in 1818 projected a lecture on 'Dante, Donne, and Milton' ('the middle name will perhaps puzzle you', he wrote to Cary);[2] but no report survives, and Crabb Robinson's diary records it simply as a lecture on Dante and Milton. Some of Coleridge's comments and marginalia were published in *Table Talk* and *Literary Remains*, but the best of his criticism—the marginalia in Lamb's copy of the *Poems*—not until 1853, in *Notes Theological, Literary, and Miscellaneous*, and (more completely) in the American *Literary World*. De Quincey's reading of Donne is known only from a few penetrating sentences on the 'metaphysical' poets (whom he prefers to call 'Rhetorical') in a review of Whately's *Rhetoric* in *Blackwood's* (1828): 'Few writers have shown a more extraordinary compass of powers than Donne; for he combined—what no other man has ever done—the last sublimation of dialectical subtlety and address with the most impassioned majesty'; and Landor's reading, probably extensive, is known only from the 'Imaginary Conversation'[3] of Walton, Cotton, and Oldways (1829) where the several imaginary quotations indicate what struck him most in Donne; these lines are a comment in themselves:

> She was so beautiful, had God but died
> For her, and none beside,
> Reeling with holy joy from east to west
> Earth would have sunk down blest;
> And, burning with bright zeal, the buoyant Sun
> Cried thro' his worlds *well done*!

---

[1] He included no Donne in his *Select Poets of Great Britain*, 1824.

[2] It would not have done so, for Cary's journal shows him reading Donne's satires in 1800.

[3] There is also a brief and conventional reference to Donne's 'hobbling' verse in 'A Satire on Satirists', 1836.

Leigh Hunt shows some knowledge of Donne in his later writings, and in a review of Tennyson's 1830 poems[1] notes, of 'Love and Sorrow', that 'the author must have been reading Donne. . . . This is the very Analogical Doctor come back again.' The poem is one of those that Tennyson never reprinted; it exemplifies an interest which was evidently current among his undergraduate contemporaries, and which we shall meet again, with a difference, in Henry Alford. Hartley Coleridge has some verses on Donne which quote and expand his father's line on iron pokers; and two more sympathetic notes, buried among his marginalia on Carew in Anderson's *British Poets*:

> Men may joke or quibble till they cannot do otherwise, and yet not have joked away all feeling. . . . Is there any difference in style between Donne's Sacred Poems and his wildest love riddles?
> Carew is far smoother [than Donne]; but where is the strength, the boundless wealth of thought, the heart beating beneath its twisted mail?[2]

Thomas Phillips in a lecture at the Royal Academy in 1827 (published 1833) compares Giotto with Donne; the student of art should forget his 'gothic imperfections' which resemble Donne's 'uncouth phraseology' in being nevertheless 'full of sentiment'—a stock distinction, but an unexpected application. The extent of Wordsworth's knowledge is doubtful; the sermons and poems were in his library, and in the winter of 1830 he was reading the sermons aloud to his wife, but he refers only once to any poem, when urging Dyce to include 'Death be not proud' in his *Specimens of English Sonnets*; Dyce did so, and recorded Wordsworth's plea in his copy of the 1633 poems.[3] Southey was unconverted in 1807, when he collected his *Specimens of the later English Poets*: 'Nothing indeed could have made Donne a Poet, unless as great a change had been worked in the structure of his ears, as was wrought in elongating those of Midas';[4] which possibly provoked Coleridge to his masterly defence of Donne's verse.

---

[1] *Leigh Hunt's Literary Criticism*, ed. L. H. and C. W. Houtchens, 1956, p. 358; see also pp. 498, 526, 561, and for the reference in *The Book of the Sonnet*, p. 318 below. Hunt also annotated a copy of Donne's poems which was borrowed by G. H. Lewes; see below, p. 319.

[2] *Essays and Marginalia*, 2 vols., 1851, ii. 7, 10.

[3] *Letters, Later Years*, i. 469, ii. 652; cf. *Divine Poems*, ed. Helen Gardner, 1952, p. 69.

[4] Compare Nathan Drake, *Literary Hours*, 1798, p. 452, and *Shakespeare and his Times*, 2 vols., 1817, i. 615.

Coleridge's notes, our most valued legacy of Donne criticism from this period, seem not to have been well known save for the line 'wreathes iron pokers into true-love knots'. Nothing came of Barron Field's project of a Percy Society edition incorporating these marginalia[1]—though their publication in the *Literary World* may have stimulated Lowell's interest and his encouragement of the Boston edition of Donne in 1855,[2] the only near-complete and separate collection of Donne's poetry between Tonson's and Grosart's. But American interest goes farther back and Emerson's, as shown in his letters and journals, has a more obvious source. A letter written in 1815, at the age of fifteen, shows him reading Johnson's life of Cowley, and struck (like Ayrton at the evening party of 1808, in 'Of Persons one would Wish to have Seen') by the stanza beginning 'Here lies a he-sun and a she-moon here'. His comment is 'I should like to see the poem it was taken from.'[3]

For many readers meeting Donne for the first time in Johnson's dozen or so of ample quotations, this would be a natural response. We need not go to Johnson to account for Lamb, who had his own 'midnight darlings, [his] folios'; but there is other evidence, some of it on lower levels,[4] that Donne was increasingly read after about 1790, and this almost certainly reflects the popularity of the life of Cowley.[5] Boswell thought it the best of the *Lives*, because Johnson had 'exhibited' the metaphysical poets 'at large, with such happy illustrations from their writings, and in so luminous a manner, that indeed he may be allowed the full merit of novelty, and to have discovered to us, as it were, a new planet in the poetical hemisphere'. This is a tribute often overlooked.

The curious could not pursue their interest in Johnson's edition, which started with Cowley; but Donne's poems were available in

---

[1] Field's comments are quoted from the manuscript in the Houghton Library at Harvard, by Roberta Florence Brinkley in *Coleridge and the Seventeenth Century*, Durham, N.C. 1955, p. 519 n. This book includes some previously unpublished notes on Donne (pp. 527–8).

[2] Lowell's annotated copy of this was used in the Grolier Club edition of 1895.

[3] *Letters*, ed. R. L. Rusk, 6 vols., Columbia 1939, i. 10. On Emerson's interest in the metaphysical poets generally see Norman Brittin, *American Literature*, 1936, pp. 1–21, and Emerson's anthology *Parnassus*, Boston 1875.

[4] Such as an otherwise negligible article on Cowley, Donne, and 'Clieveland' [*sic*] by 'M. M. D.' in the *European Magazine*, Aug. 1822, pp. 108–12.

[5] Johnson knew Donne's poetry very well, and quoted from it constantly throughout his Dictionary, 'for instance, ninety-seven times under Q, R, S' (W. B. C. Watkins, *Johnson and English Poetry before 1660*, Princeton 1936, p. 80) and as the Dictionary long remained a standard work, this may have had considerable influence in familiarizing readers with Donne's poetry.

Bell's edition (1781), and after 1793 in Robert Anderson's *British Poets*, which adds a 'life' based on Granger's in his *Biographical History*, and quotes Johnson. Any Victorian gentleman's library would be likely to include Bell or Anderson or Chalmers (1810), and though the text of Donne is unsatisfactory the collection is reasonably complete,[1] and the lack of any further edition in England until Grosart's is not necessarily an indication of neglect. After the turn of the century, Donne also begins to be represented in anthologies and selections: George Ellis's *Specimens* (1801)[2] has 'Go and catch a falling star' and the first stanza of 'Negative Love', and Capel Lofft's *Laura; or an Anthology of Sonnets* (1814) has three sonnets. Thomas Campbell's *Specimens* (1819) has four poems (two incomplete), Ezekiel Sanford's *Works of the British Poets* (Philadelphia 1819) has fourteen of the *Songs and Sonets* and twenty-three other poems or parts of poems, James Montgomery's *The Christian Poet* (1827)[3] has two Holy Sonnets and the 'Hymn to Christ', Southey's *Select Works of the British Poets* (1831) has five *Songs and Sonets*, all the Holy Sonnets, and sixteen others, Robert F. Housman's *Collection of English Sonnets* [1835] has two sonnets, Richard Cattermole's *Sacred Poetry of the Seventeenth Century* (1836) has seven Holy Sonnets, the First Anniversary, 'Hymn to Christ', and a few others, and Samuel C. Hall's *Book of Gems* (1836) has ten *Songs and Sonets*. The choices rarely coincide; each editor has read Donne for himself, and made his own selection. In the same period, casual quotations from Donne turn up in odd places; the 'Biographical Notice' of Jane Austen by her brother Henry (1818) says that 'her eloquent blood spoke through her modest cheek' (this is in all periods the most frequently quoted passage); Julius and Augustus Hare, *Guesses at Truth* (1827), quote from the third satire (and in the 1838 edition also from a sermon); Hood quotes both the 'he-sun' lines (perhaps caught from Hazlitt or Lamb) and another favourite pun from 'old Donne';[4] Edmund H. Barker, the ill-starred classical scholar, quotes two 'Specimens' from

---

[1] All follow 1719 (which follows 1669), each adding its own misprints. (The 1719 life, in accidental anticipation of the modern scholar to whom this volume is presented, has 1572 as the date of Donne's birth.) Elegy xx was first printed from manuscript in Francis G. Waldron's *Collection of Miscellaneous Poetry*, 1802.

[2] 2nd edition, 3 vols.; these poems were also in the one-volume edition of 1790, and in all later ones (1803, 1811, 1845, 1851).

[3] The Rev. John Mitford's *Sacred Specimens*, 1827, has only the wrongly attributed Psalm 137.

[4] *Atlas*, 25 June and 9 July 1826, and *Whims and Oddities*, 'The Marriage Procession', Nov. 1827 (I owe the Hood and Barker references to Mr. P. F. Morgan). Another wit, Douglas Jerrold, was also, according to his son's 'Memoir', a reader of Donne.

Paradoxes and Problems (1652) in the *Constitutional Magazine* of September 1835 (p. 156); two lines (53–54) of Elegy xvi appear as motto to a story in the annual *Friendship's offering* (1835); and No. 76 (by Newman) of *Tracts for the Times* (1836) quotes a passage from Sermon XXXI. A different kind of knowledge is suggested by Anna Jameson's *The Loves of the Poets* (1829), who quotes 'The Message' as 'long popular, and I can remember when a child, hearing it sung to very beautiful music'.

Most of the selections mentioned also include some criticism, some but not all in stock phrases about harsh versification, obscurity, and cold conceits. 'His ruggedness and whim', says Campbell, 'are almost proverbially known'—testimony at least to common knowledge; 'yet there is a beauty of thought which at intervals rises from his chaotic imagination, like Venus smiling on the waters'. Cattermole thinks that modern readers find Donne obscure only because they prefer 'voluptuous sweetness' to 'depth of sentiment and originality of thought'. S. C. Hall, while taking the usual line about 'beauties and deformities', tilts the balance decisively; his specimens, he says, show that Donne was often 'smooth even to elegance'. 'He was absolutely saturated with learning—his intellect was large and searching . . . his wit playful yet caustic. At times he is full of tenderness; and in spite of himself submits to the mastery of nature.' He believes that Donne's 'name as a poet is largely known and esteemed'—in contrast both to Anna Jameson seven years earlier, who had thought him 'little read, except by those who make our old poetry their study', and probably chiefly known 'from the lines at the bottom of the page in Pope's version'; and also to the egregious Nathan Drake, who in 1817 writes that 'A more refined age, and a more chastized taste, have very justly consigned his poetical labours to the shelf of the philologer.'

'Those who make our old poetry their study' are best represented by an unknown, independent, and at times strikingly perceptive writer in the *Retrospective Review* of 1823.[1] Here indeed are the accents of discovery; if the progress of Donne's reputation is ever to be fully charted, 1823 should be as important a date as 1921.

---

[1] Vol. viii, pt. i, pp. 31–55. The essay is cited by Allibone, and was known to Grosart (*Notes and Queries*, 1870, p. 505), but the only modern critic who speaks of having read it is Wightman F. Melton, *The Rhetoric of Donne's Verse* (Baltimore 1906), and no attempt has ever been made to identify the writer. The editor of the *Retrospective*, Henry Southern (who also edited the *London Magazine* in 1825–8), wrote some articles, and so did Charles Wentworth Dilke, P. G. Patmore, W. J. Fox, and Thomas Noon Talfourd. On present evidence Talfourd seems a possible conjecture. (Since

This essay I propose to describe in some detail. Though headed with the title of the 1669 *Poems*, it is almost entirely concerned with the *Songs and Sonets*, seventeen of which are quoted, either whole or in part. It begins by mocking at Theobald's phrase 'nothing but a continued heap of riddles' but makes no other reference to earlier criticism, and never uses the term 'metaphysical'. At the outset Donne is placed 'at the head of the minor poets of his day', for his learning, his 'active and piercing intellect . . . imagination, if not grasping and comprehensive, most subtle and far-darting—a fancy rich, vivid, and picturesque, and at the same time, highly *fantastical* . . . a mode of expression singularly terse, simple, and condensed . . . a wit, admirable as well for its caustic severity as its playful quickness'.[1] Far from objecting to his verse, the critic finds in Donne 'an exquisite ear'; his only deficiencies are in 'sensibility and taste', and the former is interestingly qualified:

His sensibility was by nature strong, but sluggish and deep-seated. It required to be roused and awakened by the imagination, before it would act; and this process seldom failed to communicate to the action which it created an appearance of affectation (for it was nothing more than the appearance).

His 'scholastic habits . . . without weakening his sensibility', contributed greatly 'to deform and denaturalize its outward manifestations'; feelings and thoughts were heightened and illustrated by a 'host of images and associations', supplied by 'quick-eyed wit' and 'subtle ingenuity'. This is seen as a fault, but a fault of his age and school, springing from a disregard of the principle 'that an idea or a sentiment may be poetical *per se*':

They considered that *man* was the creator of poetry, not Nature; and that any thing might be made poetical, by connecting it, in a certain manner, with something else. A thought or a feeling was, to them, not a thing *to express*, but a theme to write *variations* upon—a nucleus, about which other thoughts and feelings were to be made to crystallize.

Donne's 'school' is then compared with, but distinguished from, the Della Cruscans: superior, because the latter 'tried to make things poetical, by means of words alone', the former, by 'a vast fund of thoughts and images'.

this article was sent to press I have seen the third edition of Keynes's *Bibliography of John Donne*, 1958, where the review is attributed to 'J. Spence'.)

   [1] S. C. Hall borrowed from this passage; see p. 313 above. It is also recalled in some anonymous *Lectures on the English Poets*, 1847, pp. 27–28.

Having thus cleared the ground, the critic announces his main intention: 'to bring to light some of the exquisite beauties which have hitherto lain concealed from the present age'—beauties of every kind, though unaccountably mixed with 'deformities', which perhaps explains the 'total neglect', remarkable in 'an age which boasts that it has revived a knowledge of, and a love for its great predecessor'. The reader of Donne should not judge hastily from transient irritation; he will soon find 'great exercise for his *thinking* faculties (if nothing else) even in the objectionable parts of Donne'. Some pieces are entirely free from this 'mixed character': notably the 'Valediction: forbidding mourning' (quoted complete), which 'for clearness and smoothness of construction, and a passionate sweetness and softness in the music of the versification, might have been written in the present day'—if indeed any modern poet is capable of it. 'The simile of the compasses, notwithstanding its quaintness, is more perfect in its kind, and more beautiful, than anything we are acquainted with.' On other poems, the critic is often felicitous, finding in 'The Good-Morrow' 'an air of serious gaiety . . . as if composed in the very bosom of bliss', and in 'The Message' 'a certain wayward simplicity of thought peculiarly appropriate to such compositions'; in 'The Prohibition' Donne 'bandies a thought about (like a shuttlecock) from one hand to the other, only to let it fall to the ground at last'. No other poet could have made the comparison of the nerves and the braid of hair in 'The Funeral' *tell* as he had done; 'The Will'[1] illustrates 'his infinite fullness of meaning . . . almost every line would furnish matter for a whole treatise in modern times'; 'Negative Love' shows 'a love for the passion excited, rather than the object exciting it . . . that lives by "*chewing the cud* of sweet and bitter fancy" . . . that broods, like the stock-dove, over its own voice, and listens for no other'. Later, this comparison with Wordsworth is made explicit, and his style is called a return to that of the first stanza of 'The Blossom'. Many more poems and passages are quoted and praised, and the divergence from traditional views is evident in the repudiation of Pope's 'brilliant and refined' version of the satires: nearly a hundred lines from the fourth Satire[2] (from 'Towards me did run') are quoted,

[1] This poem later became a favourite; it is in the selections of Southey, Hall, Alford, and in *Chambers's Cyclopaedia*, and is the only poem chosen from Donne in Dyce's *Early English Poems, Chaucer to Pope*, 1863.

[2] Almost the only previous discussion of the satires is in John Payne Collier's *The Poetical Decameron*, 2 vols., 1820, and he is mainly concerned with questions of date.

with the simple comment, 'It strikes us as being nearly the perfection of this kind of writing.' And although the essay concludes with some concessions to the common view of Donne's faults, this enthusiasm is the note of the whole; indeed, the specific comments seem slightly at variance with the general framework, as if the writer were captivated in the act of quoting. His judicious assessment of faults and beauties crumbles before the conviction of Donne's uniqueness—his poems 'bear a mark that we cannot very well expound, even to ourselves, but which we know no one could have placed on them but him'.

*   *   *   *   *

In the Victorian period, 'official' opinion, as represented in histories of literature, encyclopedias, and biographical collections,[1] represents a hardening and simplification of the views of Johnson and of Hazlitt; the term 'metaphysical' is generally objected to,[2] but Donne is associated with his 'school', and the same phrases recur parrot-wise—'remote analogies', 'far-fetched images'—and usually with emphasis on his inequalities—'He mixed up with what was beautiful and true much that was fantastical and false.' But the merely contemptuous tone of Henry Hallam in his *Introduction to the Literature of Europe*[3] is exceptional:

> Donne is the most inharmonious of our versifiers, if he can be said to have deserved such a name by lines too rugged to seem metre. Of his earlier poems many are very licentious. The later are chiefly devout. Few are good for much; the conceits have not even the merit of being intelligible, and it would perhaps be difficult to select three passages that we should care to read again.

To parallel that we must go back to Southey or Theobald. But in the same year, 1839, Henry Alford allows Donne 'a fine musical ear' (with three examples cited in a footnote) and attributes his harshness to that 'laborious condensation' typical of the juvenile poems of great men. The anonymous editor of the *Book of Poets* (1841?), who includes 'His Picture', part of 'The Dissolution', and one sonnet, finds, despite harshness and pedantry, 'an innate vigour

---

[1] Such as G. G. Cunningham, *Lives of the Most Eminent and Illustrious Englishmen*, 4 vols., 1837, iii. 240–2; Robert Bell, *Lives of the Most Eminent Literary and Scientific Men of Great Britain*, 2 vols., 1839, i. 50–53.

[2] The sense in which Johnson used the word (see A. H. Nethercot, 'The term "Metaphysical Poets" before Johnson', *M.L.N.*, 1922, pp. 11–17) is not understood, which is itself an interesting comment on its altered associations.

[3] 4 vols., 1837–9; iii, ch. v.

and freshness which will always ensure [his poems] a high rank in English poetry'. The writer of the article on Donne in *Chambers's Cyclopædia of English Literature* (1844) trims his course; this poet's reputation has 'latterly in some degree revived', and whereas earlier critics spoke of his 'harsh and rugged versification, and his leaving nature for conceit', it is now acknowledged that 'amidst much rubbish, there is much real poetry, and that of a high order'. To show his merits four quotations are given, including the first verse of the 'Valentine' *Epithalamion*,[1] a passage from the fourth satire, the 'Valediction: forbidding mourning', and 'The Will'. (The later fortunes of this entry are not without interest; the 1858 edition merely added a little more information on editions and manuscripts, but the 1876 edition was revised, and 'rubbish' was altered to 'bad taste'.)[2] G. L. Craik in his *Sketches of the History of Literature* (1845) quotes 'Sweetest Love' to illustrate Donne's ear for melody, and thinks the verse of the satires was 'adopted by choice and on system' and is 'not without a deep and subtle music'.

'Why are Donne's sermons not reprinted at Oxford?' Coleridge had asked, and the question was repeated by his nephew, the editor of *Table Talk*, and by the *Quarterly's* reviewer of *Literary Remains* in July 1837. The result was the six-volume edition by the Rev. Henry Alford[3] in 1839, miscalled *Works of Dr. John Donne*; the new interest in Donne's prose was also reflected in *Selections from the Works of John Donne D.D.* (Talboys, 1840), two editions of the *Devotions* (Talboys and Pickering, both 1840), Richard Cattermole, *Literature of the Church of England* (2 vols., 1849), James Brogden, *Illustrations of Liturgy and Ritual* (3 vols., 1842), and Robert Aris Willmott, *Precious Stones, Aids to Reflection* (1850). All this helped to draw further attention to the divine poems. Alford included them all, the 1840 selection had several, and so did another Oxford collection, *Gems of Sacred Poetry* (2 vols., 1841), with an introductory essay which notes 'a great, though gradual revolution' in the taste of the last thirty years, for both the poetry and the theology of Elizabethan and Jacobean writers. Cambridge followed in 1847 with

---

[1] This is probably the reason for its becoming a common quotation; I find it, for instance, in a paper by G. A. Sala in Dickens's *Household Words*, 19 June 1852, and in the Causton edition of Walton's *Life*, 1855.

[2] In 1892 the entry shows no change except a reference to Grosart's edition; it was entirely rewritten, with the help of Edmund Gosse, in 1901.

[3] The edition was prepared in 1838 at the request of the publisher, J. W. Parker; but Alford had been interested in Donne since his undergraduate days at Cambridge (*Life, Letters, and Journals*, edited by his widow, 1873, pp. 75, 112).

Select Poetry Chiefly Sacred of the Reign of James the First, edited by Edward Farr, which has a fuller selection. There are similar later examples (including a very Gothic-looking volume, W. H. Rogers's *Spiritual Conceits, extracted from the Writings of the Fathers, the old English Poets, &c.*, 1862), and one interesting omission; Leigh Hunt's posthumous *Book of the Sonnet* (1867), though praising 'La Corona', refrains from including it because 'Donne's piety, though sincere, was unhealthy.' No extended criticism of the divine poems is found until 1868 when George Macdonald, recently Professor of English Literature at Bedford College, included a chapter on them in *England's Antiphon*, a popular account of English religious poetry. He is perplexed by their 'incongruities', on which he at least is specific, commenting in some detail on 'Hymn to God in my Sickness', which he regards as typical of Donne's 'best and worst'. The 'best' is contained in the first and in the last two stanzas: he explains, and praises, the music image:

To recognize its beauty . . . we must recall the custom of those days to send out for 'a noise of musicians'. Hence he imagines that he has been summoned as one of a band already gone in to play before the king of 'The High Countries': he is now at the door, where he is listening to catch the tone, that he may have his instrument tuned and ready before he enters. But with what a jar the next stanza breaks on heart, mind, and ear!

The sudden shift of comparison of himself from map to navigator is thought 'grotesque and absurd'; still worse is the next stanza, where 'he is alternately a map and a man sailing on the map of himself'. These strictures must have influenced Emerson, who gives only Macdonald's three preferred stanzas, without notice of omission, in his anthology *Parnassus* (1875). In the same year as Macdonald's book, the Archbishop of Dublin (R. C. Trench) brought out his *Household Book of English Poetry*, which included the 'Lecture on the Shadow' and two Holy Sonnets, 'Death, be not proud' and 'As due by many titles', the last of which he describes as 'rough and rugged' but 'the genuine cry of one engaged in that most terrible of all struggles'; he goes on to compare Donne with St. Augustine, 'the same tumultuous youth . . . and then the same passionate and personal grasp of the central truths of Christianity'.

But sometimes the new interest in Donne as divine encouraged the playing-down of his secular poems. Alford apologized for having 'pruned' so 'unsparingly' from them, but 'it seemed to me that the character of this work being theological, the Poems which were to be inserted should be of the same stamp'. He accordingly gave no satires, only three of the *Songs and Sonets*, one elegy, and one epithalamion. The Rev. Augustus Jessopp in his edition of *Essays in Divinity* (1855) regarded Donne as 'the greatest preacher England has ever produced' but thought his powers 'comparatively trifled away' up to 1613—a remark which prepares one for his article on Donne in the *Dictionary of National Biography* (1888), twenty columns long but with only a cursory reference to the poems. To accept Donne whole has been difficult for critics ever since Walton.

That is one reason why there are few attempts at comprehensive criticism, though it is not quite fair to call Donne 'yet unappreciated', as De Quincey did in 1851.[1] In 1838 the youthful G. H. Lewes[2] apostrophizes the poet as 'Honest John Donne—rough—hearty—pointed and sincere' and observes in 'The Good-Morrow' 'the true language of passion, which will appear unnatural only to those who never felt *une grande passion*'. There is true appreciation in an essay in *Lowe's Edinburgh Magazine* of February 1846, the first of a series of three including Herbert and Herrick. Grosart quoted it as 'by Dr. Samuel Brown of Edinburgh, I believe'; it has since been attributed to Coventry Patmore.[3] Whoever the author, his approach is independent and unusual (though there are signs that he has read the *Retrospective* essay), and he has strongly marked views on poetry in general. Some of his preferences in Donne are surprising at that date. The satires are ranked highest, 'the best in the language', and Pope's sophistications exposed by parallel quotations from the fourth satire (this passage is quoted by Grosart). Donne's verse may be rough, 'But who . . . would not . . . prefer climbing, with Donne, these crags where all the air is fresh and wholesome, to gliding, with Thomas Moore, over flats, from beneath the rank verdure of which arises malaria and invisible disease?' Those

---

[1] *Works*, ed. Masson, 1897, xi. 110.

[2] 'Retrospective Reviews—No. VII' in the *National Magazine and Monthly Critic*, Apr. 1838, pp. 373–8. Lewes's name is given at the head of No. 1 of the series, which is unknown to his biographers. He had borrowed a copy of Donne from 'L. H.' and quotes some of the owner's marginalia: this must be Leigh Hunt, whom Lewes knew well by 1837.

[3] See Frederick Page, *Courage in Politics*, 1921, appendix ii, and J. C. Reid, *The Mind and Art of Coventry Patmore*, 1957. Patmore was writing for periodicals in 1845–6, but the evidence here is of the dubious sort called 'internal'. Dr. Samuel Brown contributed an essay on Herbert to *McPhail's Journal* in 1848, which has a slight resemblance to the Herbert article in *Lowe's*; Grosart's recollection probably confused the two.

who submit his poems to 'affectionate reflection' will pardon his worst versification: 'since no sacrifice of meaning is ever made to it,—it thus being so much more palatable to the truly cultivated taste than the expensive melody of some modern versifiers'. The unfavourable contrast with modern poetry is pursued in a rather obscure statement that in Donne's day poets acted unconsciously on their 'instinctive immediate perception . . . without limits imposed by the logical faculty, or the hyperbole-hating decencies of flat conventionality', whereas 'our modern carpet-poets tread their way upon hyperbole as nicely as they would do over ice of an uncertain strength, dreading every moment to be drowned in ridicule'. Donne was also fortunate in living in an age 'when English intellect was at its height' and when religion had 'enhanced poetic liberty' and 'extinguished that false shame which Romanism had attached to the contemplation of the sexual relations'. But his poetry is never likely to be popular, because of its ruggedness and its difficulty; the meaning demands constant attention, and only to the 'most faithful and disciplined lovers of the muse' will he be 'a peculiar favourite'. This aristocratic, rather truculent tone is certainly not unlike that of Patmore's later criticism.

He has not much to say of particular poems. The love-poems show 'the love of love' rather than the passion for its object, and their conceits make them inferior to the satires; but the 'Valediction' is an exception, a 'noble poem', 'exquisite' in versification. It is quoted entire, and there are also short quotations from 'The Ecstasy', 'The Good-Morrow', 'The Blossom', and the first Epithalamion, but the quality of the last is impossible to show in extracts—it has an 'inexplicable, incommunicable aura'. There are quotations from the first *Anniversary*, but the divine poems as a whole are slighted.

His next essay, on Herbert, contrasts Donne's rough strength with Herbert's smooth sweetness, and reveals the writer as an admirer of Tennyson, who is compared with Herbert in his combination of 'activity of thought' with 'native sweetness of feeling and . . . expression'. But he adds, disputing Coleridge's view, that the highest genius is 'masculine', and Herbert's and Tennyson's 'feminine'; which again is reminiscent of Patmore. If he is the writer, we may guess that this early interest was stimulated by Coleridge, and by his father P. G. Patmore, the friend of Lamb and Hazlitt. It may have affected his poetry. Mario Praz (who is unaware of the essay in *Lowe's*) makes a case for Donne's influence,[1] citing similar images ('as turning spirals draw the eyes'), verbal echoes ('some say, "It lightens", some say "No" '), and the movement of the quatrains. Dowden had noted this too, with more moderation: 'The metre of the *Extasie* is the same as that of the *Angel in the House*, and the manner in which meaning and metre move together closely resembles that of Mr. Patmore's *Preludes*.'[2] But if Patmore really was inspired by Donne, the effect is counteracted by his firm narrative line and the deliberate surface simplicity of his style; his contemporaries were not so obtuse as Praz thinks in emphasizing the influence of Tennyson.

Tennyson's only known comment on Donne is on the 'Valediction: forbidding mourning'. But as this poem is quoted in full in Walton's *Life*[3]—which, as the *Lowe's* essay says, had 'a hundred readers' for every one of Donne's poetry—this is not necessarily evidence of wider knowledge of Donne. Such wider knowledge is, however, shown by some of Tennyson's friends and contemporaries, besides Browning: for example, Sir Henry Taylor, who quotes not only the 'Valediction' but twice from the *Elegies* in his *Autobiography*;[4] by Edward Fitzgerald;[5] John Forster, who praised Landor for catching the style of the poet so happily, 'not only its extravagance, but its genius';[6] and George Eliot, who quotes 'The Undertaking' and 'The Good-Morrow' in two chapter-mottoes[7] of *Middlemarch*—chosen, significantly, for chapters concerning Ladislaw and Dorothea, and the latter (ll. 8–11) touchingly forecasting Dorothea's admission of her love.

Palgrave's knowledge of Donne is not in doubt. He quotes him in *The Passionate Pilgrim* (1858); in preparation for the *Golden Treasury* (1861) he went through Chalmers's *English Poets* twice; and he shows his knowledge and his opinion of Donne in a review[8] published in the same year, where he contrasts the 'imaginative con-

---

[1] *The Hero in Eclipse in Victorian Fiction* (translated 1956, first published 1952), pp. 431–9.

[2] *Fortnightly Review*, June 1890, p. 805.

[3] The *Lives* were constantly reprinted, and the edition of 1855 is very fully annotated (by Thomas Edlyne Tomkins) with many additional quotations from Donne's poetry.

[4] Published 1885, but begun in the 1860's; see i. 183, 273, 288.

[5] *Letters*, ii. 26 (letter of 1861).

[6] *Life of Landor*, 1869, ii. 183 n. Forster owned a copy of the 1633 Poems which had been in the Drury family.

[7] Chaps. XXXIX, LXXXIII.

[8] *Quarterly Review*, Oct. 1861, pp. 449–50, 456. His authorship is known from his copy of the article in the British Museum (*Opuscula*, I, press-mark 012274 ee. 1).

ceits' of Ralegh's 'Come live with me' with the 'frostwork in-
genuities of the intellect' in 'The Bait', and notes that 'far-sought
conceits and allusions' and 'strange contorted phraseology' are not
peculiar to Donne and Cowley 'but more or less mark English poetry
from Surrey to Herbert and Crashaw'. In his *Treasury of Sacred Song*
(1889) he included three Holy Sonnets and one hymn, noting in
Donne's poetry generally a 'strange originality almost equally
fascinating and repellent', and a 'strange solemn passionate earnestness' underlying the 'fanciful conceits'.

It was Palgrave who recorded Tennyson's moving recitation of
the last four stanzas of the 'Valediction' and his praise of their
'wonderful ingenuity'.[1] We do not know whether this was before
or after 1860, or whether 'all that stood near admission' to the
Golden Treasury and was submitted to Tennyson for final decision
included any of Donne. The manuscript, Tennyson's notes, and
several marked volumes, survive, but provide no answer, Chalmers's
Poets unfortunately not being among them. But it is interesting to
see from notes on the manuscript that Tennyson, who was an
enthusiast for Marvell and introduced the 'Horatian Ode' to Palgrave, not only approved for inclusion 'The Garden' and 'The
Emigrants' Song' but 'greatly pleaded for the *Lover*' ['To his Coy
Mistress']—'but', adds Palgrave, 'I thought one or two lines too
strong for this age'. We know too that Palgrave omitted Spenser's
Epithalamion 'with great reluctance as not in harmony with modern
manners', and other love-poems which he privately described as
'too high-kilted', and that he thought of a separate collection of the
more 'decidedly amorous'. The original standard for inclusion was
evidently strict; one of the advisers wrote 'too coarse' against 'It
was a lover and his Lass',[2] which was, however, included. This fear
of the 'young person' is one possible reason for omitting many of the
Songs and Sonets;[3] as Grosart says, 'it needs courage to print the
poetry of Dr. John Donne in our day', and even he hesitated long
over Elegy xix. But a nearly contemporary anthologist, J. C. M.
Bellew, who says in the Preface to his *Poets' Corner* (1868) that he
had a 'black list' of authors 'whose works it would be impossible to

[1] 'Personal Recollections', contributed to Hallam Tennyson's *Memoir*, 1905, ii. 503.
[2] Note in Palgrave's copy of Bell's *Songs of the Dramatists*, in the present writer's possession.
[3] Palgrave included two verses of 'Absence' (from Davison's *Poetical Rhapsody*) which was approved by all the selectors, but did not attribute it to Donne until the edition of 1891, on Grosart's authority. In the edition of 1912 the name was removed.

put into the hands of a youth or a schoolgirl', nevertheless managed to find seven poems which could safely represent Donne, mostly divine poems, but one of them 'The Anniversary' from *Songs and Sonets*. Palgrave, however, had narrowed his choice at the outset by explicitly excluding religious lyrics; and some of the other criteria given in his notes and Preface would tend, on his view, to keep Donne out:

a comparative absence of extreme or temporary phases in style . . . will be found throughout.

That a poem shall . . . reach a perfection commensurate with its aim— that we should require finish in proportion to brevity—that passion, colour and originality cannot atone for serious imperfections in clearness, unity or truth . . . above all, that excellence should be looked for in the whole rather than in the parts,—such and other such canons have been always strictly regarded.

If no verses by certain writers who show . . . more thought than mastery of expression are printed in this volume, it should not be imagined that they have been excluded without much hesitation and regret.

Palgrave made many later additions to Books I and II,[1] but he did not take the opportunity to add any of Donne; by 1891, the last revised edition, there could be no doubt of Donne's recovery of fame, and his continued exclusion shows rather Palgrave's firmness in holding to his original principles. But I have found some interesting new evidence of a momentary wavering. He acquired Grosart's edition, and his copy is in the British Museum, with a few markings.[2] He used this for his *Treasury of Sacred Song*, marking with approval five Holy Sonnets (two more than he finally included) and also writing 'fine and pathetic' against the 'Hymn to Christ' and 'spoiled by its own cleverness' against 'The Cross'; but he was evidently also thinking of the revised *Golden Treasury*, for he set a mark of approval on 'Sweetest Love', and also on the first verse of 'The Anniversary', with the words 'Si sic omnia!' That might be taken as his final word on the love-lyrics.

'More *thought* than mastery of expression' was a disqualification for the *Golden Treasury*. But Grosart dedicated his edition of Donne

---

[1] Over thirty poems in all were added; some are mentioned in Colin J. Horne, 'Palgrave's *Golden Treasury*', *English Studies* (English Association, 1949), the best account of the work.

[2] Press-mark 2326 d. 3. It is not catalogued as Palgrave's, and his signature has disappeared in recent rebinding, but the marks are unmistakably his.

'to Robert Browning, the poet of the century for *thinkers* . . . knowing how much his poetry, with every abatement, is valued and assimilated by him'. As Browning's poetry gained in fame and influence in the last quarter of the century, the way was prepared for a wider and truer appreciation of Donne. The extent of the 'assimilation' is less important than the increasing notice taken of the likeness between them, not only by Grosart but by Dowden, Gosse, Schelling, and many others;[1] it is clear from these critics that the movement of their reputation was partly interdependent, like Tennyson's and Keats's in the 1840's, or Mr. Eliot's and Donne's in the 1920's.

At the date of Grosart's dedication, Browning had known Donne's work for over forty years. He was reading it in 1826–8 (fired, perhaps, by the *Retrospective Review?*) and is said by Griffin to have set 'Go and catch a falling star' to music. When writing *Paracelsus*, as he afterwards recalled, he was once light-headed and fancied he had to go through a complete version of the Psalms by Donne. In 1844 he and Miss Barrett, as yet unknown to each other, were applied to by R. H. Horne for mottoes to suit individual writers in *A New Spirit of the Age*, and one for Henry Taylor was an aptly-chosen quotation from Elegy iv.[2] The quotations in his letters to Elizabeth Barrett in 1845–6 show a close familiarity with Donne, and are lightly interwoven with his courtship; he quotes (from memory and inaccurately, but very aptly in the context) from the third stanza of the 'Valentine' *Epithalamion*; in another letter he asks her why she should 'lean and hearken' after Italy. The line 'as an amber drop enwraps the bee', from 'Honour is so sublime perfection', is applied to Carlyle's view of poetry. (It has not previously been noticed, however, that another quotation, from 'Donne's pretty lines about seals', is really from Herbert's 'In Sacram Anchoram Piscatoris'.)[3] Elizabeth Barrett quotes in her turn from 'The Will'

[1] See Joseph E. Duncan, 'The Intellectual Kinship of Browning and Donne', *Studies in Philology*, 1953, p. 81; and Edward Dowden, *Fortnightly Review*, 1890. A writer in *Putnam's Monthly Magazine*, Apr. 1856 (quoted in L. N. Broughton, *Robert Browning. A Bibliography 1830–1950*, 1953, p. 99) may be the first to draw the parallel.
    [2] *Letters of E. B. Browning to R. H. Horne*, 2 vols., 1877, i. 136. But the quotation is not in Browning's letter to Horne (*New Letters*, ed. De Vane and Knickerbocker, 1950) and may have come from Miss Barrett, whose quotations from the Holy Sonnets in *The Seraphim*, 1838, and reference to Donne in *The Book of the Poets* (*Athenaeum*, 1842) show that she had some knowledge of Donne before she met Browning.
    [3] Printed in editions of Donne from 1650 to 1719, and also in Alford, but not in Anderson or Chalmers; this fact, taken with the early date of Browning's reading of Donne, and the presentation to him of a copy of 1719 in 1842, suggests that he used an early edition. (The particular lines are not in Walton's *Life*.)

and the second satire, calling the author 'your Donne'. When Browning writes 'Soule-hydroptique with a sacred thirst' in 'The Grammarian's Funeral' he is again virtually quoting Donne; not, as Mr. Duncan suggests, the Second Anniversary, but 'an hydroptique immoderate desire of human learning and languages', in the well-known letter given by Walton. In 1869 William Rossetti[1] recorded Browning's enthusiasm for 'a poem by Donne named *Metempsychosis*'; by then he had written the poem in which he quotes it, *The Two Poets of Croisic*:

> He's greatest now and to de-struct-i-on
>   *Nearest.* Attend the solemn word I quote,
> O Paul! *There's no pause at perfect-i-on*
>   Thus knolls thy knell the Doctor's bronzed throat!
> *Greatness a period hath, no sta-ti-on!*
>   Better and truer verse none ever wrote
> (Despite the antique outstretched *a-i-on*)
> Than thou, revered and magisterial Donne!

Finally, in a late uncollected poem, 'Epps', he called Donne 'brave' and 'rare', and drew on the supposed sixth satire and Grosart's note on it.

Whether Browning did more than read, quote, and praise is impossible to establish. Readers of both poets—fewer now than fifty years ago—must often be haunted by a fleeting sense of likeness, especially in Donne's satires and *Metempsychosis*, but it is doubtful whether this amounts to influence. Mr. Duncan has collected possible parallels, and also considers the 'kinship' of the two poets under the four general headings of philosophical ideas; casuistical logic, metaphor, and wit; development of the dramatic monologue; and experiments with a conversational metric and idiom. The first seems to me the weakest, the last the strongest part of his case. But, as he justly says in conclusion, the influence was such as 'to supplement and reinforce . . . natural talents and predilections'; and therefore, we might add, virtually impossible to distinguish from them. Both poets were eccentrically learned, restless in thought and fancy, proud, reserved, and independent; free of 'all the four corners' of 'grammar'; and both sometimes harsh and unconciliating

---

[1] D. G. Rossetti was reading Donne, evidently for the first time, in 1880 (*Family Letters*, ii. 356); Swinburne discovered the *Anniversaries* in 1876 (letter to Theodore Watts-Dunton, printed in T. J. Wise, *Autobiographical Notes by A. C. Swinburne*, 1920) and has several interesting references to Donne in his *Study of Ben Jonson*, 1889, e.g. pp. 99, 129, 142.

in their attitude to readers—'this sullen writ / Which just as much courts thee as thou dost it'. But the danger of emphasizing the 'kinship' is that it may blind us to some of the special virtues of each poet: on the one hand, to Donne's control and scrupulosity, the habitual leanness of his style, as opposed to Browning's comparatively slapdash and sprawling exuberance; and on the other, to Browning's dramatic power of penetrating into a great variety of other characters and situations, where Donne is almost wholly confined to his own various but single self. Consider each at his best: though the verse and style of 'My Last Duchess' carry echoes for the reader of Donne, the character and situation lie outside his range; and Browning could never have attained the intensity and formality of the *Holy Sonnets*. It might be hazarded that no later poet has come nearer to Donne than Browning, though the nearness is the measure of an impassable distance.

But this is doubtful ground, and what I have wished to establish is rather the nature of the whole nineteenth-century context of Browning's interest in his 'revered and magisterial Donne'. Unenlightened as many Victorian critics and readers of Donne may appear to our own far more fortunate age, they were not so benighted as it has been the fashion to suppose.

Memories of Harley Granville-Barker and Two of His Friends

J. DOVER WILSON

My dear F. P.   Did you ever meet Granville-Barker?

I KNEW him first as the actor, and I can see him now as Eugene Marchbanks in *Candida*, slinking miserably along the back of the stage while the Rev. Mavor Morell preached at him; then as the dentist in *You Never Can Tell*, leaning triumphantly over the gassed Crampton; later still as Jack Tanner, made up as the young Shaw with a little red beard, bouncing on to the stage with the Revolutionist's Handbook under his arm; and lastly as the mad priest in *John Bull's Other Island*. How he enchanted us! And what a lovely voice he had, given perfect scope in the incantations by the last-named: To my mind that was the finest voice I ever heard on or off the stage, and its owner one of the greatest actors. The performances I speak of took place in 1905, when I was a young schoolmaster in Croydon, shamefully neglecting to correct the Latin exercises of two forms in order to play truant during the Vedrenne-Barker season at the Court Theatre, Sloane Square. You were sixteen then, I reckon, and I think a schoolboy in Birmingham, so that you probably missed my luck. All young London at any rate went mad over Shaw at that time. People who write about Harley today, now that he can't reply, tell us that he owed everything to Shaw. We who can go back to 1905 say to ourselves that Shaw owed everything to him or at any rate that the debt was reciprocal. We had read *Plays Pleasant and Unpleasant* and *Three Plays for Puritans* as undergraduates, volumes in which the plays were fitted out with elaborate stage-directions for the reader because the author couldn't get anybody to risk producing them on the popular stage; and we all said: 'Very brilliant, but of course quite unactable since the characters are points of view, not human beings at all.' It was Harley in Sloane Square who taught us how wrong we were, and Shaw knew it, and felt all the more bitter when the split came.

In January 1906 I went off to Finland as the first English Lector in the University of Helsingfors, and when soon after I got there my professor asked me to put on a course of public lectures about some

modern English author, I naturally chose Shaw. I felt I had chosen
well at the end of the first lecture when an elaborately dressed lady
swam up and exclaimed: 'Ach Lector Vilson, it wass scharming,
scharming'—until I was undeceived by her next sentence, 'You see
the bloom is on your speech, the bloom!' But I had one flattering
tribute. The Finnish theatre put on a performance of *Candida* and
asked me for advice as to costume, furniture, &c., appropriate for
the person and room of a London slum parson. I told them that the
Rev. Mavor Morell was High Church and that in the Church of
England the higher the churchmanship the lower the dog-collar.
But I fear they fell down over this; for when from the box which the
director had kindly placed at my disposal I saw the actor come on,
there was enough collar beneath his chin to have rejoiced a Chad-
band. All was well with the parson's room for the first two acts.
But the company had insisted on having a window at the back,
which I told them must be a sash window with a roller blind;
omitting to add, however, that the blind should be all of one colour.
What was my horror, then, when the curtain went up in Act Three,
to be faced by a backcloth with a large yellow dragon disporting
itself from top to bottom of the blind in the centre. Not that anybody else in the audience was shocked.

Finland, of course, cut me off from the Court Theatre, which the
Vedrenne-Barker company left in 1907; and though I returned to
London in 1909 I was too busy with work as a lecturer at Gold-
smith's College to go often to the theatre. Nor, I think, did I ever
see any of Harley's own plays performed. I wish I had, because I
never found them very readable, and I fancy they may be better on
the stage than in the book.

I can't remember when I first met him personally. Probably it was
at a meeting of the Shakespeare Association held under Gollancz's
auspices in King's College in the Strand when I became Professor
of Education there in 1924. But my letters from him begin in 1928,
the first being connected with a controversy in *R.E.S.* between
Mark Hunter and myself about act- and scene-divisions in Shakespeare—a controversy which was brought to an end, in the way
he had, by Walter Greg, who put the theorists to silence by furnish-
ing the facts. But I am the proud possessor of a copy of *Prefaces to
Shakespeare II (1930)*, inscribed 'For J. Dover Wilson, in gratitude
for much, from Harley Granville-Barker, Paris, December 1929'.
This was an over-generous return for a proof of Faber's Folio fac-

simile of *Antony and Cleopatra* I had sent to save him carting the Oxford Folio about Europe as he worked at his Preface to that play. After that we soon dropped titles and the correspondence became fairly frequent, culminating in letters fast and furious over *Hamlet*. For when I discovered that *Prefaces III* was to be devoted entirely to *Hamlet*, and he learned that I was in the middle of a 'shocker' which he dubbed 'What 'Aitches in 'Aitch', he consented to look at a carbon and to make comments thereon. He was sorry for it later.

What Happens is *vieux jeu* nowadays, but it goes on selling and C.U.P. have just issued another new edition, so that possibly one of your B.Litt. students may be interested in the following letter which Harley wrote after reading the carbon, and which as I came to realize showed great self-restraint. It only expresses too what he thought at the time; his views had changed somewhat when he came to publish in 1937.

Paris. Nov: 7. 1934

My dear J. D. W. Well, I have been a devil of a time—thinks you!—getting through it. But I needed to go carefully and I've only had spare afternoon hours to give (you said there was no great hurry): my own infant Hamlet taking up the mornings, muling and puking as it lies—still!—on my table. I have scribbled recklessly and often ribald-ly, as you said I might, on the pages. What is my perspective view, now that I have just turned—and torn—the last page?

The Ghost business. Immensely valuable. I don't think it can possibly be brought out in all its variety in a modern performance—but neither do you. But much could be done, especially in the first scene by marking the contrast between Horatio and the other two—in their conduct. I don't agree with your *interpretation* of Hamlet's conduct in the 'Cellerage' scene. I think you make it too calculated. But the underlying 'facts' as you put them—most convincing.

The ambition theme. I think all this is very sound. But you surprise me by saying it has been so little remarked on. I have always rather taken it for granted—too much so taken it, doubtless.

The 'lobby' entrance. By Jove, I believe you have convinced me. I didn't think you would. I still don't feel quite sure, for I have not been 'at' that part of the play since I read you. If I am convinced it is because the theory only (forgive me) clarifies what was discernible before—behind cryptic (*too* cryptic for W. S.? there is the question) allusions. And I believe I am—if I am—finally convinced by the sustained metaphor (image) and the *series* of double meanings. But will you take your Bible oath that all these double meanings were obvious to an Elisabethan audience? And don't ride off on your 'Judicious', now. I still, I expect, shan't quite follow you all the way. And, if the word is very farm-yardy, isn't it odd that Polonius should speak of 'loosing' Ophelia?

The play scene. I just think you are utterly wrong. I don't believe for one thing that any true theory which could be successfully put to test on the stage, could need all that explanation and argument. But I see it is no use counter-arguing. You delight too much in your bastard brat. I wish you had strangled it at birth. It will not grow up to do you credit; at least, that is my conviction. By the way, clear up that super-ficial confusion about the First Player. Long tradition has it that this is the gentleman who has grown a beard (see Alleyn's: I give you that point. When *did* he grow his? Nice, if you knew!) recites the Hecuba speech and acts the Player-King but does *not* speak the prologue (which is given for economy to Lucianus but need not and I suppose (anyhow; you apart) should not be.

I think that the identification of the Players with Alleyn's lot may be a sound one. But it does not follow that W. S. would spoil (from my point of view) his play scene by continuing and stressing the matter so far and so heavily as that.

After this I make friends with you again. You give me some fine and most elucidating bits about the *Antic Disposition,* the *Ghost in the Closet* scene, and the *Return*—especially I feel that last. I seldom *quite* agree with you, but the question between us will be one of emphasis mainly. But see—and read if you can—my scribbles.

I'd like, if I may, to keep the MS. a day or so longer. I want to go back over one or two points to make sure I've not misunderstood you. You are going to run me in for a lot of foot-notes in my own book, confound you (and already I can't keep them down). But I expect you'll be 'out' before I shall; so this will be all right, won't it?

I'll launch my revised MS. at your head, if you'll be patient enough to look at it again (or would you rather wait for proof?); but I don't know when. . . I have been largely re-writing and enlarging, trying to gene-ralise a bit about the fellow's stage-craft; and it is troublesome work.

Once I'm through I don't believe I'll ever read a word of W. S. again. Once *you*'re through—oh, my friend, how you face it, right up to *Henry VIII* and *T. of A.*, I don't know!—I'm sure thereafter you'll burst into tears if anyone so much as mentions his name.

But my blessings on you. And forgive me what will seem to you my stupidities about this book. They bulk far larger than they should, for my admiration much outbulks them. You must take that for granted.

H. G.-B.

The ribald marginalia I shall not trouble you with. Let this one suffice, scribbled against the middle section of the chapter about the play scene:

It is 11:30 p.m.! And I am now going to bed!

Sunday, 8 a.m. I have prayed for you *and* taken a walk at Fontaine-bleau. I will face this terrible business once more.

What was so delightful about him was that he never took Shake-spearian criticism *too* seriously, and I think you will agree that it is the long-faced fellows who are most likely to misunderstand our poet. One of them, reviewing my naughty book, wrote:

It is a reconstruction which perhaps no-one could 'disprove'; it simply doesn't help. Not that this will bother Dr. Wilson, since in an introductory letter which some may find embarrassingly personal, he states that it has all been done for the fun of the thing. 'Whether you actually believe your own theory,' he exclaims to Dr. Greg, 'I have never been able to discover; but it was first-rate sport.'

What Happens was published at the end of September 1935 and Harley's *Hamlet* did not appear until the beginning of 1937. It was far too kind to its predecessor, and I re-read it, you may guess, with no less intense interest than the proofs had given; closing the book, however, with some sadness, since it brought to an end what was for me a great experience. As for Harley himself, the inscription on the fly-leaf of the copy he sent me ran as follows:

J. D. W. from H. G.-B.

The rest—please God!—is silence. (Still, there'll always be *Titus Andronicus* to talk about).

Dec: 1936, Paris.

—which seemed to show that he was still in the mood to give up writing prefaces. Fortunately Shakespeare wouldn't let him alone.

Yet though the duel over *Hamlet* was ended, the friendship be-came closer than ever, and we saw one another from time to time, he running over from Paris—where in 1937 he was appointed Director of the British Institute—to meet me for breakfast at the Athenaeum; I having come down by the night train from Edinburgh.

And when Barrie's *The Boy David* (which I irreverently called 'The Girl David' because the title-role was played by Elizabeth Bergner, with a strong German accent) was first launched in Edinburgh, nothing would do but Harley must come over from Paris to see the première. When he told me this I, of course, engaged him for a talk to my Honours class. Barrie never saw the performances at all, since he lay in bed all the time groaning with lumbago at the Caledonian Hotel. There Harley, the morning after his arrival in Edinburgh, went to see him; and there I called to fetch him for my class with a car. As it happened my own car was out of order, so I had to borrow my wife's, a small Austin tourer, not too watertight. This was a nuisance because it was raining as it can only rain in Edinburgh, straight rain, likely to go on for days and days, a 'three days' rain', as Edinburgh calls it. Still, there it was; and we got in together, drove down Princes Street and up the Mound on our way to the University. Unfortunately at the top of the hill there are lights, which turned red as we approached. They turned yellow and then green, but not knowing the little beast I couldn't get the car to start. And we were right on the tramlines, so that presently a queue of trams assembled behind us, gonging furiously. And the rain poured down. At last I said: 'Harley, you must get out, I'm afraid, and help push this bloody machine over the crest.'[1] He was as usual beautifully dressed; but he was a hero. The job was done in a trice, and we were only a few minutes late for the lecture, which was not unusual for the professor. Need I add that we all enjoyed ourselves immensely, while the distinguished visitor told the class what rot that fellow Dover Wilson had written about *Hamlet*?

He had a very deep affection for Barrie who, I suspect, must have befriended him as a young man. At any rate, after Barrie's death in 1935 he came once again all the way from Paris to deliver the funeral oration in the Old Quad. Whether that tribute is extant, I don't know. I could wish it were, as it was a friendship's garland that would have pleased Barrie himself as it delighted all who heard it. It was delivered at the University because Barrie was our Chancellor—though I only once met him. But let me tell you about that.

Soon after I got here I had a ring from Wilkie, the then Professor of Surgery, telling me that Barrie, his old schoolfellow at Kirriemuir, was staying with him and that he was arranging a little 'bachelor party' for him—would I come and join it? I accepted with alacrity. Picture my consternation, however, when I found myself seated next to this formidable person at the table, and guessed (rightly I think) that he wanted to find out what sort of stuffing there was in this Sassenach who was now occupying the Chair that Masson had graced. But my luck was in. I had just been moving to

---

[1] Dorothy would like to have censored all this heavily as a libel upon a member of the family. Our first car was a second-hand baby Austin named 'Hamlet', because I bought it out of what Harry Kessler paid me for his Weimar edition. The second car was a new one of the same make and size which she bought herself and named 'Piglet' after *her* favourite hero in fiction. And it was Piglet that bore Harley to the University.

Balerno; and, arranging my volumes of Meredith on the shelf, I found among them a tiny little booklet by Barrie, to wit, a fantasia occasioned by Meredith's funeral. (You probably don't know it, and I think it is now very rare. But I won't describe it here, because I am sending it to you in the hope that an eminent bibliographer will accept it as a small birthday present.) So tremblingly I opened the ball by reminding him of it, and it started him off talking about Meredith for the rest of the dinner!

Among other things he told us that when he got to London as a young journalist he took the first opportunity to run down to Box Hill, hoping to catch a glimpse of the man whom he almost worshipped at that time; and added, I think, still did. The Chalet, as you know, stood on the side of the hill, with its garden sloping downwards at the back, at the foot of which was a small iron gate. Outside this gate Barrie stationed himself, looking up along a straight path leading to a flight of steps descending to the garden from a door of the house. And to his delight it was not long before the door opened and the familiar figure with a red tie and silver hair appeared. But Meredith came out, walked down the steps, and down the path, growing nearer and nearer to him. 'I can still feel', Barrie finished, 'those iron gateposts in my hands as I clutched them in my excitement—until I could stand it no longer. I turned and fled!'

May I round off about Barrie by adding a reference to another obituary. When a Chancellor of the University dies, a tribute to him is recorded in the minutes of the Senatus. The evening before the meeting at which this should have been read I received a telephone call from the Secretary, informing me that Grierson who had promised to write it had just told him that he had not been well and had nothing to send. Could I supply what was needed? 'My dear Secretary', I exclaimed, 'I'm afraid I'm not much of a Barrie fan. I don't think I've any of his plays on my shelves. But you can't be in a worse position than you are. If I turn up to-morrow with something, your face will be saved, though mine may be for ever disgraced. If I don't, you must make your own apologies.' Yet by another stroke of luck I did find one volume of Barrie's among my books besides the one I am sending you; and it gave me just what I wanted—a vision of little Jimmie with his legs dangling from one of the high benches of the Latin classroom, listening open-mouthed to a lecture. So I had my Minute, and here it is:

With the death of one whose name History has in life already inscribed on the golden roll of English poets and dramatists as 'J. M. Barrie', the University loses not only its Chancellor but also the most distinguished alumnus of the Arts Faculty in the last generation. There was nothing academic about Barrie; he was not of the type that a university exists to foster; and it is clear that he regarded his student days as largely time wasted. Yet it is likely, even probable, that the University gave him, mingled with less appetising courses, exactly the food his imagination needed at that stage of its development, and may therefore claim to have played a decisive part in the shaping of his genius. Indeed, he himself admits as much. Those impressions which he published a few years after graduation, under the title of *An Edinburgh Eleven*, contain 'pencil portraits' of no less than seven Professors of his day, including Blackie, Tait and Sellar. But the first and far the most respectful is that of Masson; and it begins:—

> Though a man might, to my mind, be better employed than in going to college, it is his own fault if he does not strike on some one there who sends his life off at a new angle. If, as I take it, the glory of a professor is to give elastic minds their proper bent, Masson is a name his country will retain a grip of. . . . I seem to remember everything Masson said, and the way he said it.

The wind of the spirit bloweth where it listeth. But something of great moment to Barrie certainly took place in Masson's classroom; and his biographers will do well to take note that the Professor's interpretation of Chatterton—'the marvellous Boy' who never grew up—was, he hints, of peculiar significance to him. The whole essay is a striking testimony to that kindling of mind by mind which is the finest flower of university education.

Of Barrie's standing as a man of letters, and of his special place in the history of literature, it is too early to speak with precision. But two things can be said without fear of contradiction. First, he was the greatest Scottish writer of our time, and succeeded in expressing one aspect of Scotland with remarkable skill and subtilty. And secondly, he is likely to rank with the Irishman Bernard Shaw as one of the two representative 'English' dramatists of the post-Victorian period. For, whereas the corrosive power of Shaw's wit worked as a solvent upon the social and moral ideas of a dying age, the humour and pathos of Barrie caught and fixed for all time the sense of bewilderment and aimlessness—as of a child lost in the dark—which fell upon the spirit of man when the world, in which the Victorians moved with such confidence and comfort, was seen to be fading like an 'insubstantial pageant'. *Courage* is the title of what was perhaps the most memorable of his public addresses. It is a virtue this age stands chiefly in need of; and a message his bereaved University may take specially to heart.

You never know, do you, what a professor of English may do—or, alas, fail to do.

Barrie died before the war; but I think the war came upon us before I met Harley again after his Edinburgh address. He was in Paris, of course, all through the Phoney War, and only just escaped with his American wife an hour or two before Paris fell, getting away through Bordeaux. He soon found work as Director of British Information at New York, but he was intensely patriotic and grew very miserable while the Battle of Britain was going on, so that I had to write to try and cheer him up. In one letter I remember I said: 'Don't *worry*; we're all right. It's true our clothes are wearing out, and I've lost two watches since the war began (one trodden into the mud by the Home Guard in one of the fields near Balerno), so that I now have to borrow a watch from one of my students in case I should lecture too long to them. . . .' The reply came by return. Unfortunately I seem to have lost it. But I remember this sentence very well: 'I wouldn't have your students listen to your pernicious nonsense about Shakespeare one second longer than necessary; I am therefore sending you by the next surface mail—not my second-best bedstead but my second-best watch.' It's a good Geneva chromium wrist-watch which keeps excellent time. The only thing wrong about it is it doesn't like golf, gets out of order if I inadvertently wear it when I am playing. I don't think Harley played games, so it had never been properly trained. But it's one of my proudest possessions, and dearest—as it keeps me still in touch with him.

When he got back to Paris after the war, he found all his books and papers undisturbed, as he had left them, at the British Institute. His faithful concierge had somehow kept the Nazis at bay. We met once or twice again; a memorable lunch at the Ritz comes back to my mind. But he only had a year more of life.

These anecdotes began with Shaw and must end with him. As with Barrie I only met him once; but thereby hangs another tale, and one I may have told you already. If I have, please forgive.

I used to go away with Alfred Pollard for a week or so every summer and on one occasion we decided to take a serial ticket at the Malvern Festival—one of Barry Jackson's enterprises, unhappily now a thing of the past. But you yourself must have been to it several times. It always began, you will remember, with a Miracle or Morality play, followed by some Elizabethan drama or other

(Shakespeare being left to Stratford), continued with a couple of plays from the eighteenth or nineteenth century, and ended up with Shaw's latest. *And*, as cunning Barry knew would be the greatest attraction of all, there was Shaw walking about the place in his ridiculous Victorian Norfolk jacket and knee-breeches with, as I noticed one day when close behind him, a little button at the back of the knee, obviously intended for riding gaiters—though I doubt whether Shaw ever rode a horse in his life. Well, we took our tickets and found that they included afternoon tea on the Monday at a hotel, if one got down from town in time. We did. The tea was provided in a pleasant sort of meadow sloping down from the back of the hotel and approached, rather after the fashion of Meredith's garden at Box Hill, by steps leading down from a door which opened on to a verandah running along the whole length of the building. We were enjoying our ices at a little round tin table, when we suddenly heard a babble of voices from the verandah, and looking up saw it full of people, and in the middle Barry with G. B. S. Presently these two came down; to our amazement made straight for us; and we presently found ourselves being introduced to Shaw. He seized a chair, planted himself at our table, and without more ado or preface of any kind proceeded to tell us exactly what the Elizabethan theatre was like, inside and out. It was an amazing performance; and when it appeared to be drying up at one point I interposed a question by way of a little push to make it flow on. But it was all wrong, from beginning to end, and after a time we realized that it was based on one visit to Oberammergau a few years earlier. Then, having got it off his chest, he rose, gave us a kind of royal farewell, and turned away. I was just going to have a really good laugh with Pollard when I found myself confronted by a little lady. 'You are Professor Dover Wilson, aren't you?' she asked, and then went on, 'I read one of your books once and thought George might like to meet you.' It *was* an afternoon. I had met not only Shaw but his stage-manager!

Was Shaw capable of affection? I think I can say at any rate that he had once adored Harley and regarded him as a kind of son—which was natural, was it not, if the dramatist fell under his spell in Court Theatre days, as the London audiences did? At any rate, when Harley died on the last day of August 1946, Shaw was moved to send to the *Literary Supplement* a photograph he had taken of him with the famous Kodak in 1906, at the height of the Vedrenne-Barker season.

It is an ultra-romantic picture; Harley sits at a table, chin on hand, gazing out through a window with a Father Keegan look in his eyes. And with the photograph, which was reproduced at the head of the *T.L.S.* on 7 September he sent this letter:

Sir,—The enclosed photograph of Harley Granville-Barker, taken by me forty years ago at The Old House, Harmer Green, when our collaboration, now historic, was at its inception, may interest your readers.

We clicked so well together that I regarded him as my contemporary until one day at rehearsal, when someone remarked that I was fifty, he said, 'You are the same age as my father.' After this it seemed impossible that he should die before me. The shock the news gave me made me realize how I had still cherished a hope that our old intimate relation might revive.

But

> Marriage and death and division
> Make barren our lives

and the elderly Professor could have little use for a nonagenarian ex-playwright.

G. Bernard Shaw.

The widow read that in Paris, and he meant her to, for she had robbed him of Harley, and like a true Celt Shaw never forgot or forgave. And with all his genius he was not quite human; that's why he never understood Shakespeare. But Harley did, and in that respect was the greater man of the two. Yet there is genuine grief behind the letter, don't you think?

ever affectionately yours,
Dover

A SELECT LIST OF THE PUBLISHED WRITINGS OF FRANK PERCY WILSON

F.B.A., HON. LL.D. (BIRMINGHAM)

Senior Research Fellow, Merton College
Emeritus Professor of English Literature
in the University of Oxford

ABBREVIATIONS

H.L.Q.	Huntington Library Quarterly
M.S.R.	Malone Society Reprint
M.L.R.	Modern Language Review
R.E.S.	Review of English Studies
T.L.S.	Times Literary Supplement

1914

'Marston, Lodge, and Constable.' Three notes from Add. MS. 11402. *M.L.R.*, ix. 99–100.

Review of F. Aydelotte's *Elizabethan Rogues and Vagabonds*, *M.L.R.*, ix. 391–4.

1918

Note on *A Wonderfull, straunge and miraculous Astrologicall Prognostication* (1591), *M.L.R.*, xiii. 84–85.

'A Pre-Shakespearian use of "twire" ', *T.L.S.*, 18 April.

1920

EVERY MAN OUT OF HIS HUMOUR (1600). Prepared by F. P. W. and W. W. Greg. *M.S.R.*

'An Ironicall Letter.' A note on a hitherto unprinted letter by Jack Roberts to Sir Roger Williams (*c.* 1585). *M.L.R.*, xv. 79–82.

'Three Notes on Thomas Dekker', *M.L.R.*, xv. 82–85.

1922

Review (unsigned) of Dekker's *Seven Deadly Sins* and Congreve's *Incognita* edited by H. F. B. Brett-Smith. *The Oxford Magazine*, 30 November 1922, followed by a letter, 7 December.

1923

'Leigh Hunt and his Work.' Mainly a review of H. S. Milford's edition of the *Poetical Works*. *The Bookman's Journal and Print Collector*, xvii. 169–70.

'Here's lime in this sack', *The Oxford Magazine*, 22 February. Unsigned.

Review (unsigned) of selections from Bacon and Johnson edited respectively by P. E. and E. F. Matheson and R. W. Chapman. *The Oxford Magazine*, 15 March.

Review (unsigned) of selections from Spenser and Fielding edited respectively by W. L. Renwick and L. Rice-Oxley. *The Oxford Magazine*, 29 November.

1924

FOURE BIRDS OF NOAHS ARKE. BY THOMAS DEKKER. Edited by F. P. W. OXFORD: BASIL BLACKWELL.

1925

THE PLAGUE PAMPHLETS OF THOMAS DEKKER. Edited by F. P. W. OXFORD: AT THE CLARENDON PRESS.

Signed article on 'The Jaggards and the First Folio of Shakespeare', *T.L.S.*, 5 November, p. 737, followed by a letter, *T.L.S.*, 12 November, p. 756.

1926

'Spenser and Ireland', *R.E.S.*, ii. 456–7.

'Ralph Crane, Scrivener to the King's Players', *The Library*, Fourth Series, vii. 194–215.

1927

THE PLAGUE IN SHAKESPEARE'S LONDON. OXFORD: AT THE CLARENDON PRESS.

'Notes on the Early Life of John Donne', *R.E.S.*, iii. 272–9.

1929

THE BATCHELARS BANQUET: An Elizabethan Translation of LES QUINZE JOYES DE MARIAGE. Edited by F. P. W. OXFORD: AT THE CLARENDON PRESS.

1931

Review of J. Dover Wilson and May Yardley's edition of L. Lavater's *Of Ghostes and Spirites Walking by Nyght*. *R.E.S.*, vii. 95–97.

1935

'English Letters and the Royal Society in the seventeenth century.' A paper read to the Yorkshire branch of the Mathematical Association, 17 November. *The Mathematical Gazette*, xix. 343–54.

'A Survey of the Brotherton Collection', The *Yorkshire Post*, 1 November.

'Looking Babies.' Letter to the *T.L.S.*, 14 December, p. 859, concerning the phrase 'to look babies'.

1938

'The Tidy', *Philological Quarterly*, xvii. 216–18. (Concerning the name of a bird in Drayton's *Poly-Olbion*, xiii. 79.)

'Some English Mock-Prognostications', *The Library*, Fourth Series, xix. 6–43.

1939

'The English Jestbooks of the Sixteenth and Early Seventeenth Centuries', *H.L.Q.*, ii. 121–58.

Review of R. B. McKerrow's *Prolegomena for the Oxford Shakespeare. A Study in Editorial Method. The Library*, Fourth Series, xx. 234–9.

1940

'Table Talk', *H.L.Q.*, iv. 27–46.

1941

'Shakespeare and the Diction of Common Life'. (The Annual Shakespeare Lecture.) *Proceedings of the British Academy*, xxvii. 167–97.

'Ben Jonson and Ralph Crane', *T.L.S.*, 8 November, p. 555. Identifying Crane as the scribe of Jonson's masque, *Pleasure Reconciled to Virtue*, in a Chatsworth manuscript.

1943

'A Note on George Herbert's "The Quidditie" ', *R.E.S.*, xix. 398–9.

1945

ELIZABETHAN AND JACOBEAN. (The Alexander Lectures, Toronto, 1943.) OXFORD: AT THE CLARENDON PRESS.

'English Proverbs and Dictionaries of Proverbs', *The Library*, Fourth Series, xxvi. 51–71.

'Shakespeare and the "New Bibliography"', *The Bibliographical Society, 1892–1942. Studies in Retrospect*, chapter v, pp. 76–135.

'Some observations on a University.' Extracts from an address given at the College Assembly, 1944, on the College's return to London. *Bedford Writing*, Spring, pp. 6–9.

ESSAYS ON THE EIGHTEENTH CENTURY, PRESENTED TO DAVID NICHOL SMITH IN HONOUR OF HIS SEVENTIETH BIRTHDAY. OXFORD: AT THE CLARENDON PRESS. Edited by James Sutherland and F. P. W. List of D. N. S.'s writings by F. P. W.

THE OXFORD HISTORY OF ENGLISH LITERATURE. Edited by Bonamy Dobrée and F. P. W. Vol. 2, Part 1. OXFORD: AT THE CLARENDON PRESS.

Review of G. E. Bentley's *Shakespeare & Jonson. Their Reputations in the Seventeenth Century Compared. The Library*, Fourth Series, xxvi. 199–202.

1946

'A Supplement to Toynbee's "Dante in English Literature"', *Italian Studies*, iii. 50–64.

1947

PANTAGRUELS PROGNOSTICATION. Reprinted from the translation of *c.* 1660. A Luttrell Society Reprint, edited with an Introduction by F. P. W. OXFORD: BASIL BLACKWELL.

'Shakespeare To-day', *Britain To-day*, no. 131, March, pp. 24–29.

Review of *Surveys of Recent Scholarship* and Archer Taylor's *Renaissance Guides to Books. R.E.S.*, xxiii. 276–7.

1948

'English Proverbs', *Bodleian Library Record*, ii. 219–21.

'Some Notes on Authors and Patrons in Tudor and Stuart Times', *Joseph Quincy Adams Memorial Studies*. Washington: Folger Shakespeare Library, pp. 553–61.

ENGLISH STUDIES 1948. Being volume one of the new series of ESSAYS AND STUDIES collected for the ENGLISH ASSOCIATION by F. P. W.

1949

'A Merie And Pleasant Prognostication (1577)', *The Library*, Fifth Series, iv. 135–6.

1950

'Shakespeare's Reading', *Shakespeare Survey*, iii. 14–21.

GENTLENESS AND NOBILITY. Prepared by A. C. Partridge and F. P. W. *M.S.R.*

LAW TRICKS. BY JOHN DAY. Prepared by John Crow with assistance from W. W. Greg and F. P. W. *M.S.R.*

THE WITCH. BY THOMAS MIDDLETON. Prepared by W. W. Greg and F. P. W. *M.S.R.*

'A list of the published writings of Percy Simpson' edited by F. P. W. OXFORD: AT THE CLARENDON PRESS.

1951

BONDUCA. BY JOHN FLETCHER. Prepared by W. W. Greg and checked by F. P. W. *M.S.R.*

DEMETRIUS AND ENANTHE. BY JOHN FLETCHER. Prepared by M. McLaren Cook and F. P. W. *M.S.R.*

WIT AND SCIENCE. BY JOHN REDFORD. Prepared by A. Brown with assistance from W. W. G. and F. P. W. It has been checked by Charles Sisson. *M.S.R.*

Review of *The Plays and Poems of William Cartwright. Edited with Introduction and Notes by G. Blakemore Evans. The Library*, Fifth Series, vi. 128–9.

Review (unsigned) of W. W. Greg's *Bibliography of the English Printed Drama*, vol. ii. *T.L.S.*, 7 September.

1952

THE CONFLICT OF CONSCIENCE. BY NATHANIEL WOODES. 1581. Prepared by Herbert Davis and F. P. W. *M.S.R.*

WHEN YOU SEE ME, YOU KNOW ME. BY SAMUEL ROWLEY. 1605. Prepared by F. P. W. and checked by John Crow. *M.S.R.*

Review of Stevenson's *Book of Proverbs, Maxims, and Familiar Phrases, The Oxford Dictionary of English Proverbs*, and *Tilley's Dictionary of the Proverbs in England in the Sixteenth and Seventeenth Centuries. R.E.S.*, New Series, iii. 190–8.

THE ARTILLERY GARDEN. BY THOMAS DEKKER. Printed from the unique copy in the library of the University of Göttingen. The text was set up, with a note by F. P. W., by Herbert Davis, L. W. Hanson, and F. P. W. in the New Bodleian over against the King's Arms.

1953

MARLOWE AND THE EARLY SHAKESPEARE. (The Clark Lectures, Cambridge, 1951.) OXFORD: AT THE CLARENDON PRESS.

HONOURABLE ENTERTAINMENTS. 1621. BY THOMAS MIDDLETON. Prepared by R. C. Bald and checked by F. P. W. *M.S.R.*

1954

Review of Alan Keen and Roger Lubbock's *The Annotator. T.L.S.*, 26 March.

Review of Leslie Hotson's *The First Night of 'Twelfth Night'. T.L.S.*, 24 September.

1955

'Dekker, Segar, and Some Others', *H.L.Q.*, xviii. 297–300.

'The Elizabethan Theatre.' The Allard Pierson Lecture, the University of Amsterdam. Reprinted in *Neophilologus*, pp. 40–58.

'Court Payments for Plays 1610–11, 1612–13, 1616–17', *Bodleian Library Record*, v. 217–21.

Review of Peter Alexander's *Hamlet: Father and Son*. *T.L.S.*, 11 March.

Review of Percy Simpson's *Studies in Elizabethan Drama*. *T.L.S.*, 29 April.

1956

JACOB AND ESAU. 1568. Prepared by John Crow and F. P. W. *M.S.R.*

'The Malone Society. The First Fifty Years: 1906–56', Malone Society *Collections*, iv. 1–16.

'More Records from the Remembrancia of the City of London', ibid., pp. 55–65.

1957

'Obituary Notice of Sir Edmund Kerchever Chambers, 1866–1934', by F. P. W. and J. Dover Wilson. *Proceedings of the British Academy*, xlii. 267–85.

'Nicholas Breton's *I Would and Would Not* (1619)', *The Library*, Fifth Series, xii. 273–4.

TEMPORIS FILIA VERITAS. 1589. A Luttrell Society Reprint, edited by F. P. W. OXFORD: BASIL BLACKWELL.

DAMON AND PYTHIAS. BY RICHARD EDWARDS. Prepared by Arthur Brown and F. P. W. *M.S.R.*

THE LIFE AND DEATH OF JACK STRAW. 1594. Prepared by Kenneth Muir and F. P. W. *M.S.R.*

Review of D. B. Quinn's edition of *The Roanoke Voyages 1584–1590*. *R.E.S.*, New Series, viii. 287–8.

1958

THE WORKS OF THOMAS NASHE, edited in five volumes by R. B. McKerrow. OXFORD: BASIL BLACKWELL. A reprint of the original edition with corrections and supplementary notes, edited by F. P. W.

MASTERS OF BRITISH LITERATURE. HOUGHTON MIFFLIN COM-
PANY, BOSTON, MASS. In two volumes. Three plays of Shake-
speare (1 *Henry IV*, *King Lear*, *The Winter's Tale*) edited by
F. P. W. With an Introduction (i. 261–406).

Illustrations of Social Life: 'The Funeral Obsequies of Sir All-in-
New-Fashions', *Shakespeare Survey*, xi. 98–99.

1959

Obituary Notice of Sir Walter Wilson Greg, 1875–1959. *The
Times*, 6 March 1959.

SEVENTEENTH-CENTURY PROSE: FIVE LECTURES. THE UNIVERSITY
OF CALIFORNIA PRESS. The Ewing Lectures, the University of
California at Los Angeles.

Illustrations of Social Life, II: 'A butcher and some social pests',
Shakespeare Survey, xii. 107–9.

INDEX

Addison, Joseph, on historians, 231; *A Letter from Italy*, 190 n.
Advice of a loving Sonne to his aged Father, The dutifull, 203–5.
Agostini, Nicolo delli, continuation of Boiardo's *Orlando Innamorata*, 182.
Alexander the Great, the *Prose Life of*, 22.
Alford, Henry, editor of Donne's *Sermons*, 310, 316 f.
Alfred, King, 105.
Amyot, translation of Plutarch, 188 & n.
Anselm, St., 188.
Archer, William, opinions on Elizabethan drama, 167–8.
Ariosto, Ludovico, 184; *Orlando Furioso*, 43.
Arnold, Matthew, 76.
Ashley, Robert, 17.
Ashton, Abdie, Essex's chaplain, 221, 223, 226.
Astley, John (1) master of the Queen's jewel-house, 39, 40.
Astley, John (2) 36 f.
Aucassin et Nicolette, 104.
Augustodunensis, Honorius, *De Imagine Mundi*, 188.
Ausonius, imitated by Ronsard, 142.
Austen, Henry, 312.
Avignon, 126.

Babington, Anthony, 10.
Bacon, Sir Francis, 55, 66; Hume on, 248; *Henry VII*, 249; *Natural History*, quoted, 299–300.
Baldwin, T. W., 66 n., 77, 84 n.
Baldwin, William, editor of *Mirror for Magistrates*, 2, 3, 14, 15.
Barclay, John, 189 and n.
Barker, Edmund H., 312.
Barrett, Elizabeth, 324.
Barrie, J. M., 331–4.
Bartholomew, St., massacre, 9.
Bellerophon, fall of, 173 f., 194, 195.
Bellew, J. C. M., *Poets' Corner*, 322.
Bembo, Pietro, *Gli Asolani*, 294.
Bennett, Joan, on 'The Ecstasy', 281–2.
Bentley, G. E., *Jacobean and Caroline Stage*, 60.
Bergner, Elizabeth, 331.
Berni, Francisco, *Caccia d'Amore*, 104.
Betussi, Giuseppe, *Della Geneologia degli dei di Giovanni Boccaccio, Elucidario*, 187.
Beverley, Peter, *Historie of Ariodanto and Ieneura*, 43.

Bevis of Hampton, 18, 19, 21.
Bible, Authorized Version, 248; Genesis, 204; Ecclesiasticus, Proverbs, 210.
Bion, *Lament for Adonis*, 101.
Blair, Hugh, *Lectures on Rhetoric*, 234–5.
Blenerhasset, Thomas, his additions to the *Mirror*, 6–7.
Boccaccio, Giovanni, 186, 190–1, 196; *Teseida*, 180–2; *De Genealogia Deorum*, 185, 187.
Boiardo, Matteo Maria, *Orlando Innamorata*, 55, 173, 182–3.
Boileau, Nicolas, 179.
Bond of Association, to defend Queen Elizabeth, 219–20.
Bond, Scottish, 220, 225–6; text of, 228–30.
Book of Poets (?1841), 316–17.
Boswell, James, 311.
Boswell, James, son of above, 153.
Bretnor, Thomas, 250 f.; 'Evill Days', 260–8; 'Good Days', 268–76.
Brinkley, Roberta, *Coleridge and the 17th Century*, 311 n.
Bristol, John Digby, 1st Earl of, ambassador to Spain, 244.
Brogden, James, *Illustrations of Liturgy and Ritual*, 317.
Brooke, Arthur, *Tragical Historye of Romeus and Juliet*, 96–97.
Brooke, Henry, 8th Baron Cobham, 212, 214.
Brown, P. Hume, *History of Scotland*, 240 n.
Brown, Dr. Samuel, 319.
Browning, Robert, 307; *My last Duchess*, 326; *Letters*, 324 f.
Brownists, 247.
Bruno, Giordano, 106.
Buckingham, George Villiers, 1st Duke of, 243–4.
Burghley, Lord, William Cecil, 36, 37, 40; *Certain Precepts etc.*, 211.
Burnell, George, of Staple Inn, 38 f.
Burton, Barbara, 45, 47.
Burton, Robert, *Anatomy of Melancholy*, 187.
Butler, Samuel, 179.
Byrd, William, 43, 153, 162.

Cabala, 244.
Cade, Jack, 16.
Calderon, *El Médico de su honra*, 170.

Calderwood, David, *The True History of the Church of Scotland*, 240 n.
'Callino', an Irish tune, 152–3.
Camden, William, *History of Queen Elizabeth*, 248.
Campbell, Thomas, 312, 313.
Campion, Thomas, 162.
Carew, Thomas, quoted, 123, 141–2.
Carleton, Sir Dudley, 61.
Caroline, Queen, on historians, 233.
Carteret, John, Viscount, afterwards 1st Earl of Granville, 233.
Catesby, Robert, 238.
Cattermole, Richard, 313; *Sacred Poetry of the 17th Century*, 312; *Literature of the Church of England*, 317.
Catullus, 175.
Caucasus, 94–95.
Caxton, William, 28, 32.
Cecil, Sir Robert, afterwards 1st Earl of Salisbury, 211, 222–3, 225.
Chamberlain, John, *Letters*, 60.
Chapman, George, *Bussy d'Ambois*, 190.
Charles, Prince, afterwards Charles I, 243.
Charles V, Emperor and King of Spain, 242.
Chaucer, Geoffrey, 124, 177; and Shakespeare, 98–99; *Anelida and Arcite*, 187; *Hous of Fame*, 93; *Knightes Tale*, 87 f.; *Marchantes Tale*, 90; *Parlement of Foules*, 91; *Squieres Tale*, 97; *Troilus and Criseyde*, 70, 92; *Wyf of Bathe's Tale*, 95, 96.
Chesterfield, Philip Dormer Stanhope, 4th Earl of, 'tea-table scoundrel', 233; *Advice to his Son*, 199–200, 235 n.
Churchyard, Thomas, 2, 5, 6, 7.
Cicero, 126, 186.
Clarendon, Edward Hyde, 1st Earl of, *History of the Rebellion*, 243.
Coke, Sir Edward, 245.
Coleridge, Hartley, 310.
Coleridge, Samuel Taylor, 145; and Donne, 279, 308, 310–11, 320; on Gray's 'reddening Phoebus', 65; *Biographia Literaria*, 309; *Table Talk*, 309.
Collier, John Payne, 315 n.
Comes, Natal, 196; *Mythologiae*, 185, 187, 190.
Copyright, 62 f.
Corbett, Richard, *Iter boreale*, 180.
Corneille, Pierre, 169.
Cottington, Sir Francis, 243.
Court Theatre, Sloane Square, 327.
Courthope, W. J., *History of English Poetry*, 5.
Craik, G. L., *Sketches of the History of Literature*, 317.
Cuffe, Henry, Essex's secretary, 222.

Curtius, E. R., *European Literature and the Latin Middle Ages*, 178.

Dallis, Thomas, lutenist, 159–60.
Damascus, 18.
Daniel, Samuel, 43, 146, 147–9.
Dante Alighieri, 181–2.
Danvers, Sir Charles, 206 f.
Davies, Sir John, Solicitor General of Ireland, 241.
Day Lewis, Cecil, *Pegasus and other Poems*, 196.
Dekker, Thomas, *Satiromastix*, 150, 154.
Deloney, Thomas, 156.
De Quincey, Thomas, 319, 309.
Dictys Cretensis, 27, 29.
Digges, Leonard, 36 f.
Digges, Thomas, 36 f., 221.
Diogenes, Byzantine Emperor, 34.
Dionysius, 103.
Dolman, John, *Lord Hastings*, quoted, 1–2.
Domenichi, Lodovico, 183.
Donne, John, 129, 311, 312; and Ariosto, 51, 55; comments and comparisons, 315–21; Hume's opinion of, 247; *Anniversary*, 304; 'The Blossom', 309; 'The Ecstasy', 279 f.; *Holy Sonnets*, 326; 'The Goodmorrow', 304; 'Image and Dream', 286; *Metempsychosis*, 325; 'The Relic', 298; 'Valediction: forbidding Mourning', 298, 304; *Sermons*, 317.
Dorset, Thomas Sackville, 1st Earl of, 2, 7, 11.
Douglas, Gavin, 27, 178.
Dowden, Edward, 321.
Drake, Sir Francis, 50.
Drake, Nathan, 310 n., 313.
Drummond, William, 184.
Drury, Elizabeth, 297.
Dryden, John, *Conquest of Granada*, 35.
Du Bellay, Guillaume, 7, 132, 136.
Duncan, Joseph E., 307.
Dyce, Alexander, *Specimens of English Sonnets*, 310.

Ebreo, Leone, his *Dialoghi d'Amore* quoted and described, 287–305.
Edinburgh, 'centre of enlightenment', 235.
Edward IV, King of England, 5.
Edward VI, King of England, 5.
Edwards, Richard, *Damon and Pythias*, 162; *Palaemon and Arcyte*, 89, 90.
Edwards, Thomas, *A Supplement to Mr. Warburton's Edition of Shakespeare*, 151.
'Eliot, George', *Middlemarch*, 321.
Eliot, Thomas Stearns, 80, 169–172; on Donne, 307; *Elizabethan Essays*, quoted, 167; *Shakespeare and the Stoicism of Seneca*, quoted, 168.

Elizabeth, Queen of England, 9, 89, 216, 219–25.

Ellis, George, *Specimens*, 312.

Emerson, Ralph Waldo, 311 and n., 318.

England, Courts, 246; Privy Council, 219–20; Parliament, 237, 246.

Epistola Alexandri ad Aristotelem, 24.

Essex, Robert Devereux, 2nd Earl of, 206, 209, 221 f.

Evans, Maurice, *English Poetry in the 16th Century*, 1.

Fabyan, Robert, 12.

Farr, Edward, *Select Poetry of the Reign of James I*, 318.

Ferdinand I, Emperor, 242.

Ferrers, George, 14–15.

Ficino, Marsilio, his commentary on the *Symposium*, 287–8, 294, 296, 306.

Field, Barron, 311.

Finett, John, 60, 61.

Fisher, Benjamin, printer, 202, 203.

Fitzgerald, Edward, 321.

Fletcher, John, *Bloody Brother*, quoted, 250; *The Faithful Shepherdesse*, 61.

Forster, John, on Landor and Donne, 321.

Fraenkel, Eduard, his *Horace* quoted, 115.

Frye, Northrop, 82.

Fulgentius, Fabius Planciades, 189–91.

Galle, Philipp, engraver, 47.

Gardiner, S. R., *History of England*, 236, 237, 245.

Gascoigne, George, 7, 43.

Gems of Sacred Poetry, 317.

Generydes, 23.

Geoffrey of Monmouth, 10, 12.

George II, King of England, on historians, 233.

Gibbon, Edmund, 234.

Gilbert and Sullivan, 157.

Gilpin, George, agent in Low Countries, 227.

Golding, Arthur, 70.

Googe, Barnaby, 74 n., on Chaucer, 86.

Gorgeous Gallery of Gallant Inventions, 156.

Gosse, Sir Edmund, 286, 296.

Grafton, Richard, 12.

Granger, James, *Biographical History*, 312.

Granville Barker, Harley, and Barrie, 332; and Shaw, 327 f.; *Prefaces to Shakespeare*, 328, 331; letter to Dover Wilson, quoted, 329.

Greek Anthology, 142.

Greene, Francis, in Essex's service, 222.

Greene, Richard, 222–3, 227.

Greene, Captain William, 222.

Greg, Sir Walter, 45, 48, 50.

Gresham, Edward, *Prognostications*, 257–60.

Grierson, Sir Herbert, 280, 293, 304, 307.

Grimble, Ian, 45.

Grosart, Rev. Alexander, 307; 'needs courage to print Donne', 322; dedicates his edition to Browning, 324.

Guarini, Battista, 148.

Guido delle Colonne, 27, 29, 30, 31.

Gunpowder Plot, 210, 238, 239.

Guy of Warwick, 19.

Halins, Peter, 225.

Hall, Samuel C., comments on Donne, 313–14; *Book of Gems*, 312.

Hallam, Henry, 316.

Halle, Edward, *The Union of the Two Noble and Illustre Famelies of Lancastre and York*, quoted, 189–90.

Hampton Court Conference, 236, 247.

Handful of Pleasant Delights, 152.

Hankins, J. E., 74 n.

Hannay, Patrick, *Sheretine and Mariana*, 8.

Hare, Julius and Augustus, *Guesses at Truth*, 312.

Harington, Sir John, 42 f.; *An Anatomie of the Metamorpho-sed Ajax*, 43, 53; *Metamorphosis of Ajax*, 43; *Nugae Antiquae*, 54; *Orlando Furioso*, 4, 44 f.; letter to Lord Howard, quoted, 58.

Hart, Sir John, letter to Cecil, 222–3.

Harvey, Gabriel, 184, 278.

Harwood, Sir Edward, 61.

Hawes, Stephen, *Pastime of Pleasure*, 189.

Hazlitt, W. C., 307 n.

Hazlitt, William, 308, 309, 316.

Henry IV, King of France, 242.

Henry, Prince of Wales, 56.

Henryson, Robert, 189 and n.; *Testament of Criseyde*, 6, 93.

Herbert, Edward, first baron Herbert o Cherbury, 298.

Herbert, Sir Henry, *Dramatic Records*, 61.

Herbert, Mrs. Magdalen, 305.

Herrick, Robert, 121.

Hervey, John, Baron Hervey of Ickworth, 233.

Hesiod, 175.

Heywood, John, 156.

Higgins, John, his additions to *A Mirror for Magistrates*, 6, 12 f.

Hind, A. D., *Short History of Engraving and Etching*, 47.

Hippolytus, son of Theseus, 106–7.

Hobbes, Thomas, *Behemoth*, 249.

Holinshed, Raphael, 12.

Holland, Philemon, 188.

Homer, 113 f., 126, 174, 186, 188.

Hood, Thomas, 312.
Horace, 113 f., 175; quoted, 117, 192.
Housman, Robert F., *Collection of English Sonnets*, 312.
Howell, Thomas, *Devises*, 156.
Hughes, Merritt, 281, 283.
Hume, David, account of Ireland, 241; of Europe, 242; on Montesquieu, 234; on Shakespeare and Jonson, 247; merit as historian, 248–9; *History of England*, 231 f.; *Letters*, quoted, 231.
Humfrey, Pelham, 157, 162.
Hunt, Leigh, 310; *Book of the Sonnet*, 318.
Huon of Bordeaux, 19, 22, 24, 34.
Hyginus, the Mythographer, 186.

Independents, under James I, 247.
Inojosa, Spanish minister in London, 244.
Instructions for Youth, Gentlemen and Noblemen, 217.
Ireland, treatment of in Hume's *History*, 241.
Ironside, Rev. Ralph, 214.

James VI, King of Scotland, afterwards, James I, King of England, 200, 211, 219–30; Hume's *History* of, 231 f.; character of, 242–5; manners compared with reign of George II, 247.
Jameson, Anna, *The Loves of the Poets*, 313.
Jessopp, Augustus, *Essays in Divinity*, 319.
Johnson, F. R., 80 n.
Johnson, Samuel, 94, 151, 190; on Donne, 316; 'Hume an echo of Voltaire', 235; 'the imagination a licentious and vagrant faculty', 173; *Lives of the Poets*, 308, 311.
Jones, Robert, lutenist, 155.
Jonson, 59, 129; Dekker's satire of, 150, 154; Hume's opinion of, 247; *The Divell is an Asse* 162, 250; *Hymenaei*, 60; *Masque of Augurs*, 61; *Pleasure reconciled to Virtue*, 61; *Time Vindicated*, 61; *Volpone*, 162.

K., E., gloss on Spenser's April Eclogue, 192 f.
Kassner, Rudolf, 131.
Keare, Leonard, scrivener, 36 f.
Kelly, James, *Scottish Proverbs*, 276.
Kermode, Frank, on Donne, 282.
Keynes, Sir Geoffrey, *Bibliography of Donne*, 314 n.
King, William, *Miscellanies*, quoted, 232 n.
King Horn, 105.
Knatchbull, Sir John, 222.
Knight, G. Wilson, 82.
Kyd, Thomas, *Soliman and Perseda*, quoted, 74; *The Spanish Tragedy*, 62.
Kyng Alisaunder, quoted 24.

Lamb, Charles, 172, 311; *Specimens of English Dramatic Poets*, quoted, 167, 308.
Lament for Bion, 176.
Landor, Walter Savage, 309.
Leavis, F. R., 172.
Lee, Captain Thomas, 222.
Lee, Henry, 222.
Lefevre, Raoul, *Eneydos*, 27.
Legouis, Pierre, 295–6: *Donne the Craftsman*, 280–1.
Leicester, Robert Dudley, Earl of, 37.
Le Miroir des melancholiques, 187.
Lettres escrites de Londres sur les Anglois, quoted, 233.
Levin, Harry, 73.
Lewes, G. H., 310 n., 319.
Lewis, C. S., on 'The Ecstasy', 281–2; *English Literature in the 16th Century*, 1.
Linocier, G., 187.
Livy, Titus, 7.
Lockhart, John Gibson, 249.
Lodge, Thomas, 53.
'Lodge Book, The', 160.
Lofft, Capel, *Laura; or an Anthology of Sonnets*, 312.
'London Book, The', 158–61.
Lorenzo de' Medici, 104.
Louthan, Donaphan, *The Poetry of John Donne, an Explication*, 285 n.
Lowe's Edinburgh Magazine, 319.
Lowell, James Russell, annotated copy of Boston ed. of Donne, 311.
Lydgate, Thomas, translation of Boccaccio, 14; *Lyfe of St. Albon*, 189; *Seege of Thebes*, 32; *Troy Book*, 23, 28 f., 178.

Macdonald, George, *England's Antiphon*, quoted, 318.
Machaut, Guillaume de, 94.
Machiavelli, Niccolo, 17.
Madox, Thomas, historian, 232 and n.
Malone, Edmond, 59, 150.
Malory, Sir Thomas, 20 f.
Mandeville, Sir John, 24, 25.
Marguerite de Valois, Queen of Navarre, 141.
Marie de Bourgueil, 137.
Marlowe, Christopher, classical reading of, 17; and *Godfrey of Boulogne*, 33 f.; and romances, 19 f.; and Troy legend, 27 f.; *Dido*, 23, 27; *Edward II*, 29; *Faustus*, 35; *Hero and Leander*, 25, 102; *Jew of Malta*, 25, 27; *Tamburlaine*, 18, 20 f., 29, 34, 35; *Poems*, 70 n.
Marot, Clement, 104.
Marston, John, on Chaucer, 86.
Marvell, Andrew, 300; *The Loyall Scot*, 191.
Mary, Queen of England, 10.

Mary, Queen of Scots, 9, 220.
'Maske of Flowers', 60.
Maynard, François de, 179.
Meere, John, Ralegh's bailiff, 214.
Meredith, George, 196, 333.
Meres, Francis, 10.
Michell, Sir Francis, impeachment of, 239.
Micyllus, Jacobus, *De Genealogia*, 187.
Middlesex, Lionel Cranfield, 1st Earl of, 244.
Middleton, Thomas, *A Fair Quarrel* and *Inner Temple Masque*, 250, 251, 277.
Milton, John, mythological allusions, 185; *L'Allegro*, 69; *Lycidas*, 196-7; *Of Reformation in England*, 55; *Paradise Lost*, 173-4, 195 f.; *Sonnets*, 197; letter to Diodati, 184.
Mirror for Magistrates, The, 1 f.; 'The Poet Collingbourne', quoted, 4-5.
Mompesson, Sir Giles, impeachment of, 239.
Montaigne, Michel de, 65.
Montesquieu, Charles de Secondat, 234.
Montgomery, James, *The Christian Poet*, 312.
Moore, Thomas, 319.
Morley, Thomas, 162.
Mossner, E. C., *The Forgotten Hume*, 231.
Muir, Kenneth, 77 n., 83 n.
Murray, Sir David, of Gorthy, 184-5.

Newman, John Henry, 313.
Nicolson, George, letter to Cecil, 225.
Nietzsche, Friedrich Wilhelm, 169.
Norfolk, Thomas Howard, 4th Duke of, 9.
Northumberland, Henry Percy, 9th Earl of, 238; *Advice to his Son*, 210-11.
Northumberland, Thomas Percy, 7th Earl of, 9.
Nosworthy, J. M., 82, 84.

O'Casey, Sean, 167-8.
O'Dogherty, rebellion of, 241.
O'Flaherty, T. R., 307 n.
Olivares, Spanish minister of Philip IV, 243.
Orpheus, 100.
Osborne, Francis, 211, 217; *Advice to a Son*, 199.
Ostend, siege of by Spanish forces, 242.
Ovid, 31, 109; myth of Atalanta and Hippomenes, 106; *Amores*, 120 f., 143; *Metamorphoses*, 95, 101, 117, 119 f.; Horologgi's comments on, 110.

Palgrave's *Golden Treasury*, 308, 321-3.
Parabosco, Girolamo, *Delle Lettere Amorose*, 101.

Paracelsus, 302.
Paradise of Dainty Devices, 162.
Parker, Alexander A., *Approach to Spanish Drama of the Golden Age*, 170.
Parrott, T. M., 83.
Parsons, Robert, *A Conference about the next Succession*, 224.
Partonope of Blois, 27.
Passerat, Jean, 107.
Passionate Pilgrim, The, 100.
Patmore, Coventry, 319 and n., 320-1.
Pausanias, 176, 188.
Pegasus, 4, 173 f.
Percy, Thomas, *Reliques*, 157.
Perrett, Wilfrid, 83.
Perseus, and Andromeda, 194.
Persius, *Prologue to Satires*, 176-7.
Peters, Hugh, 212; *Advice to his Daughter*, 200.
Petit, John, 225.
Petrarch, Francis, 121, 290; *De Secreto*, 186; sonnets, 123 f.
Phaethon, 175.
Philip II, of Spain, 219, 221, 242.
Phillips, Thomas, 310.
Philostratus, 105.
Picinellus, *Mundus symbolicus*, 191.
Pico della Mirandola, Giovanni, 287, 288, 306.
Pilgrim Fathers, 247.
Pindar, 119, 174-5; *Odes*, quoted, 113.
Plato, 103, 105, 108, 172, 297, 303.
Playford, Henry, *Pleasant Musical Companion*, 153, 157.
Plutarch, 74 n., 87, 126, 188 and n.
Poeticon Astronomicon, 186.
Poliziano, Angelo, *La Giostra*, 104.
Pollard, Alfred William, 335-6.
Pope, Alexander, 151, 319.
Porta, Giambattista, *Magia Naturalis*, 300.
Potter, G. R., 281.
Pound, Ezra, 279-80.
Practical Wisdom, 217.
Praz, Mario, 282, 296 n., 320-1.
Propertius, 103, 109, 122, 141, 176.
Prynne, William, 62.
Puttenham, George, *The Arte of English Poesie*, 300.
Pythagoras, 120.

Queen Tragedy Restor'd, 1749, 180 and n.
Quiney, Thomas, Shakespeare's son-in-law, 18.

Racine, 169.
Ralegh, Sir Walter, *Instructions to his Son*, 199 f.; MS. of, 207 f.; compared with Northumberland's, 211; opinions of,

217; *History of the World*, 202; letter to his wife, quoted, 209; his sons, Walter and Carew, 210.
Randolph, Thomas, 180.
Reynolds, William, 222.
Rich, Townsend, 44 f.
Richard Cœur de Lyon, 19–26.
Richard, Duke of York, 11.
Ridolfi, Roberto di, 9.
Robertson, William, 234.
Robinson, Crabbe, *Diary*, 309.
Robinson, Thomas, Instruction books for lute and cithern, 153.
Rogers, W. H., *Spiritual Conceits etc.*, 318.
Roman d'Enéas, 25.
Ronsard, 101, 104, 109; quoted, 140, 143–4; compared with Petrarch, 134 f.; influence on Shakespeare, 138 f.; compared with Yeats, 145.
Root, Robert K., 66 n., 80.
Rossetti, William, 325.
Rowlands, Samuel, 277.
Roxburghe Ballads, 157.
Royston, Richard, bookseller, 63.
Russell, Lucy, Countess of Bedford, 305.

St. *Galais*, romance of, 18.
St. John, Henry, Viscount Bolingbroke, 233.
Saints' Legacies, The, 63.
Saintsbury, George, *Caroline Poets*, 8.
Sanford, Ezekiel, *Works of British Poets*, 312.
Sandys, John, *Metamorphosis Englished*, 110, 111 n.
Sappho, 127.
Savile, Sir Henry, 221.
Scott, Sir Walter, 171.
Sermonetta, Cardinal, 217.
Shakespeare, William, act and scene divisions in, 328; classical allusions in Comedies, 68 f., in Histories, 66 f., in Tragedies, 71 f.; and Chaucer, 86 f.; and Horace, 113–19; and the *Mirror for Magistrates*, 13; and Ovid, 65, 89; and Petrarch, 129 f; Hume's opinion of, 247; *All's Well that Ends Well*, 95 f.; *Antony and Cleopatra*, 79 f., 329; *Coriolanus*, 79; *Cymbeline*, 80; *Hamlet*, 73 f. 172, 199; *Henry V*, 150; *Julius Caesar*, 78, 161; *King Lear*, 77 f., 93; *Love's Labour Won*, 98; *Macbeth*, 23, 76 f., 97; *Measure for Measure*, 91; *Merchant of Venice*, 92, 99; *Midsummer Night's Dream*, 88 f., 99; *Othello*, 55, 76, 168; 'Willow Song', 154, 157–161; *Pericles*, 82–84; *Richard II*, 94, 98, 99; *Romeo and Juliet*, 92, 96–97, 99; *Tempest*, 82–85; *Titus Andronicus*, 90, 93, 277;

Troilus and Cressida, 86 f.; *Twelfth Night*, 59 f.; *Two Noble Kinsmen*, 86 f.; *Winter's Tale*, 90, 93, 301; *Sonnets*, 112, 115 f.; contrasted with Pindar and Horace, 130–1; *Venus and Adonis*, 100 f.
Shaw, George Bernard, 327, 335-7.
Shirley, Sir Thomas, 37.
Sidney, Sir Philip, 7, 145; *Astrophel and Stella*, 146; sonnet quoted, 183–4; Spenser's lament for, 193–4.
Sidney, Robert, 56.
Simonides, 113.
Simpson, Percy, 45.
Sir Giles Goosecap, quoted, 155.
Smith, A. J., on 'The Ecstasy', 306 n.
Southampton, Henry Wriothesley, 3rd Earl of, 206 f., 226.
Southey, Robert, on Donne, 310, 312.
Sparke, Michael, printer, 62, 63.
Spectator, quoted, 231.
Spenser, Edmund, 55, 221; *Amoretti*, 146; *Epithalamium*, 72–73; *Ruines of Time*, 173, 192 f.
Spinoza, Baruch, 306.
Spottiswoode, John, Archbishop of St. Andrews, 240.
Steele, Richard, on historians, 231.
Stewart, John, *Abbregement of Roland furious*, 43–44.
Strachey, Lytton, 216.
Stuart, Lady Arabella, 56.
Sully, Maximilien de Béthune, *Memoirs*, 242.
Surrey, Henry Howard, Earl of, 27.
Swaine, Robert, publisher, 63.
Swift, Jonathan, *Gulliver's Travels*, quoted, 232.
Swinburne, Algernon, 167, 325.

Table Talk, 317.
Talfourd, Thomas Noon, 313 f.
Tasso, Torquato, 126, 132, 133.
Taylor, Sir Henry, 321.
Tennyson, Alfred, 310, 320, 321.
Theobald, Lewis, 150, 314.
Theocritus, 113 f.
Thomson, J. A. K., 66 n.
Tibullus, 103, 121, 143.
Tillyard, E. M. W., *Shakespeare's History Plays*, 8.
Tiptree, fat prior of, 16.
Tolstoy, Leo, *Anna Karenina*, 171; on *Othello*, 169, 172.
Torquatus, friend of Horace, 118.
Tottel's Miscellany, 43.
Traversi, D., 81.
Trench, R. C. *Household Book of English Poetry*, 318.
Tresilian, Sir Robert, Chief Justice, 14.
Turner, William, printer, 62.

Tyrconnel, Rory O'Donnell, Earl of, 241.
Tyre, William of, *Godffrey of Bologne*, 33.
Tyrone, Hugh O'Neill, Earl of, 55, 241.

Ulster, 241.

Valerianus, J. Pierius, *Hieroglyphica*, 191.
Valvazone, *La Caccia*, 104.
Varchi, Benedetto, 281.
Virgil, 27 f., 126.
Voltaire, 233–5.

Waith, E. M., 77 n.
Waldegrave, printer in Edinburgh, 224–5.
Walsingham, Edward, 217.
Walton, Izaak, *Life of Donne*, 319, 321.
Walton, John, translator of Boethius, 177.
Warburton, William, emendations of Shakespeare, 151.

Warner, William, *Albion's England*, 10.
Watson, Thomas, 43.
Wentworth, Peter, *A Pithie Exhortation*, 220, 224, 227.
Whetstone, George, 43.
Whitaker, Virgil, 65.
William of Orange, 219.
Willmott, Robert Aris, *Precious Stones, Aids to Reflection*, 317.
Wilson, Arthur, 245.
Wilson, John Dover, 66 n., 327 f.; *What Happens in Hamlet?* 329, 331.
Woodville, Anthony, Baron Scales and 2nd Earl Rivers, 2, 3.
Wordsworth, William, 65; his knowledge of Donne, 310.
Wotton, Sir Henry, 221, 223.

Yeats, William Butler, and Ronsard, 145.

PRINTED IN GREAT BRITAIN
AT THE UNIVERSITY PRESS, OXFORD
BY VIVIAN RIDLER
PRINTER TO THE UNIVERSITY

Histories composed by politicians
pleasing the imagination See p 231